ALL POWER TO THE SOVIETS
Lenin 1914–1917

ALL POWER TO THE SOVIETS
Lenin 1914–1917

BY TONY CLIFF

Chicago

All Power to the Soviets: Lenin 1914–1917
By Tony Cliff

First published 1976 by Pluto Press

Republished 1986 by Bookmarks (London, Chicago, Sydney)

This edition © 2004 by Haymarket Books
P.O. Box 180165, Chicago, IL 60618
www.haymarketbooks.org

This is the second volume of Tony Cliff's biography of Lenin, originally published in three volumes by Pluto Press between 1975 and 1979. Although the volumes follow each other chronologically, each deals with a specific political period in Lenin's life and so may be read independently of the others.

ISBN: 1-931859-10-8

Entered into digital printing October, 2017.

HAYMARKET BOOKS is a project of the Center for Economic Research and Social Change, a nonprofit 501(c)3 organization.

We take inspiration—and our name—from the Haymarket Martyrs, who gave their lives fighting for a better world. Their struggle for the eight-hour day in 1886 gave us May Day, the international workers' holiday, a symbol for workers around the world that ordinary people can organize and struggle for their own liberation.

Write us at P.O. Box 180165, Chicago, IL 60618, or visit www.haymarketbooks.org on the Web.

CONTENTS

FOREWORD

This volume covers the political activities of Lenin between the outbreak of the First World War and the October Revolution. It is in the nature of the subject that by far the greater proportion of the book deals with the period February to October 1917.

Among the many sources on which I have drawn, some deserve special mention because of their general interest and scope. These are N.N. Sukhanov's *The Russian Revolution 1917: A Personal Record*, John Reed's *Ten Days that Shook the World*, and, above all, Leon Trotsky's *History of the Russian Revolution*. Trotsky's monumental work is an outstanding achievement, written by a man of genius who was one of the supreme leaders of the revolution. In the face of this magnificent work, the question that clearly arises is, Why should another book be written dealing with the same period?

Trotsky's book has tremendous strengths, but, in my eyes, a serious defect. To start with the strengths: the revolution is excellently analyzed and described as an event in which the oppressed millions, who for centuries have been kept down, get up off their knees and speak out. The changes in the consciousness of the workers, peasants, and soldiers under the feverish conditions of the struggle are beautifully described.

The one thing noticeably missing is the Bolshevik Party: its rank and file, its cadres, its local committees, its Central Committee. This gap in Trotsky's work must be understood to some extent as a mirror image of the Stalinist distortion of the Bolshevik Party's role in 1917.

In the Stalinist legend the Bolshevik Party, with a few insignificant exceptions, always followed Lenin's will. The party was practically a monolith. But in fact nothing was further from the truth. Again and again Lenin had to fight to win his party members.

Whereas in April his main problem was to overcome the conservatism of the top leadership of the party, in June and at the beginning of July he had to contend with the revolutionary impatience of rank-and-file leaders and members. In September and October he had to fight to spur the leadership on to the great leap of the insurrection: many of the hotheads of April, June, and July—including the Bolshevik Military Organization and the Petersburg Committee of the party—now became overcautious.

Trotsky, who stood outside the Bolshevik camp from its formation in 1903 until after the February Revolution (officially joining the party at the end of July 1917), was naturally anxious to prove that being an "old Bolshevik" did not make everything right. Indeed, the political stance of the Bolshevik leadership before Lenin's return to Russia and the opposition of most prominent party leaders to the insurrection show that Trotsky had a point. However, in stating his case, he undervalued the party as a whole. Throughout his *History* the party is hardly referred to. There is no systematic exposition, for instance, of the different roles of the Vyborg District Committee, the Petersburg Committee, and the Bolshevik Military Organization. As the Bolshevik Party was a mass party with deep roots in the working class, the unevenness within the class, say, between the proletariat of Petrograd and Odessa, naturally had a serious influence on the party's working. This does not come through clearly in Trotsky's book.

To transform words into deeds a centralized party was necessary. But how did the Bolshevik Party really work during the revolution? During the war it was composed of a large number of small groups, some loosely federated, but most of them cut off from each other and from Lenin, who was abroad. These local committees had to develop an independent ability to carry out political action. How were such local groups organized into a coherent fighting party? How did the administration of the party work? What kind of people made up the cadres of the party, what was their social composition, their age, their political experience?

The masses—workers, soldiers, and peasants—appear with all their passion and courage in Trotsky's *History*; but the party, alas, is almost absent. This very much affects Lenin's role in the historical drama. As a result of the events of 1917 and after, Trotsky came to admire Lenin more than any other person of his time. Without any false modesty, he saw Lenin as a teacher and himself as a disciple. In the *History* there are sentences like this: "Besides the factories, barracks, villages, the front and the soviets, the revolution had another laboratory: the brain of Lenin." Lenin, however, could not relate to the masses except through the party.

The role of the party was to raise the level of consciousness and organization of the working class, to explain to the masses their own interests, to give clear political expression to the emotions and thoughts of the masses. If the party was necessary to give the proletariat confidence in its own potentialities, so also was Lenin's role in relation to the party. For Lenin to relate to the masses—for his slogans to find their way to them, and for him to learn from them—there had to exist party cadres. Practically everything Lenin wrote in 1917 was for party members; this is proved by the simple fact that at its height the party press had a circulation only marginally larger than the party membership. Lenin's April Theses were really directed at party members, and his writings on insurrection—practically all of them in a few copies on small sheets of paper—were directed to the party cadres. Lenin's success in arming the party in April and guiding it through all the sudden changes of April, June, July, the Kornilov coup, and finally the insurrection (events with which we deal in this book) was due to the fact that he personified the tradition of Bolshevism, and that he had the confidence of the party cadres as a result of many years of hard revolutionary struggle. Lenin influenced the party, and the party influenced the class and vice versa. The proletariat created the party and the party shaped Lenin.

The present book tries to deal with the interrelations between the working class, the party, and Lenin. It presents a political biography of Lenin, which is meshed in with the political history of the working class. In fact, as the revolution was the zenith of Lenin's, the party's, and the proletariat's activities, the fusion of the three reached its climax at that time. Hence, at that time, one can in no way separate the personal from the general, the biographical from their passion and courage in Trotsky's *History*; but the party, alas, the historical. The year 1917 was the greatest test for Lenin as the leader of the party and the working class.

As usual, I have found myself confronted with the difficult problem of selection and compression of the enormous amount of material available on such a broad subject. This central theme of the dynamic interrelation between the proletariat, the Bolshevik Party, and Lenin has guided the choice of the material for a history of manageable length.

Finally, I must make a couple of technical remarks. The first concerns the name of the capital of Russia. Until the outbreak of the First World War it was called St. Petersburg. Then this German-sounding name was hastily changed to Petrograd. The antiwar position of the Bolsheviks of the city was symbolized by their decision at the time to retain the title of the Petersburg Committee. In this book we use either of the two names—largely according to the context. Usually we call the city Petrograd, but refer to the party committee of the capital as the Petersburg Committee.

Secondly, the dates given in this volume refer to the Julian calendar, which was thirteen days behind the Western Gregorian calendar in the period covered. In a few cases, when referring to events in Western Europe, like Lenin's leaving Switzerland on his way to Russia, we use dates from both calendars.

CHAPTER I

THE WAR

The collapse of the International

On August 1, 1914 (according to the Western calendar), the First World War started. At the time Lenin was living in Poronin, near Krakow, in Polish Austria.

On 7 August the quartermaster of the local *gendarmes* came to our house accompanied by a witness, a local peasant armed with a rifle, to make a search. The officer did not quite know what he was to search for, fumbled in the book-case, found an unloaded Browning pistol, took several notebooks containing statistics on the agrarian problem and asked a few insignificant questions. The witness, in a state of embarrassment, sat on the edge of a chair and looked about in a perplexed manner. The *gendarme* officer poked fun at him and, pointing to a jar of paste, said it was a bomb. Then the officer said that there was a formal complaint against Vladimir Ilyich, and that he really should arrest him, but since he would have to deliver the prisoner tomorrow morning to Novy Targ, the nearest town where military authorities were stationed, it would be just as well for Ilyich to report in the morning in time to board the six o'clock train. The danger of arrest was obvious, and in war time, during the first days of the war, they could easily put him out of the way.[1]

Through the intervention of Social Democratic MPs, Lenin was freed from prison after eleven days. He then got permission to leave Austria for Switzerland. On August 23 he entered Switzerland and settled in Berne.

For Lenin the outbreak of war was not unexpected. What shook him, however, was the support given by the socialist leaders of different countries to their national governments. Above all, he was not prepared for the volte-face of the German Social Democrats; the German party had been regarded as the jewel of the International.

In 1907, at the Congress of the Second International in Stuttgart, a resolution drafted jointly by Luxemburg, Lenin, and Martov had made clear what the attitude of socialists to the future imperialist war should be:

> If a war threatens to break out, it is the duty of the working class and of its parliamentary representatives in the countries involved, supported by the consolidating activity of the International [Socialist] Bureau, to exert every effort to prevent the outbreak of war by means they consider most effective, which naturally vary according to the accentuation of the class struggle and of the general political situation.
>
> Should war break out nonetheless, it is their duty to intervene in favor of its speedy termination and to do all in their power to utilize the economic and political crisis caused by the war to rouse the peoples and thereby to hasten the abolition of capitalist class rule.[2]

Similar resolutions were endorsed by the Copenhagen Congress of the Second International in 1910, and by a special conference convened at Basle in November 1912 to consider the issues raised by the Balkan War.

As late as July 25, 1914, the Executive of the German Social Democratic Party (SPD) issued a clear antiwar manifesto:

> The class-conscious proletariat of Germany, in the name of humanity and civilization, raises a flaming protest against this criminal activity of the warmongers. It insistently demands that the German government exercise its influence on the Austrian government to maintain peace; and, in the event that the shameful war cannot be prevented, that it refrain from belligerent intervention. No drop of blood of a German soldier may be sacrificed to the power lust of the Austrian ruling group [or] to the imperialist profit-interests.[3]

Similar declarations followed daily. Thus on July 30 the SPD's official paper *Vorwärts* declared: "The socialist proletariat refuses all responsibility for the events which are being conjured by a ruling class blinded to the point of madness."[4]

Naturally, when Lenin read in *Vorwärts* the report of the meeting of the Reichstag of August 4, at which the Social Democratic deputies voted for the military budget, he assumed that it was a forgery published by the German general staff to deceive and frighten their enemies. He was not the only person to be deeply shocked by the betrayal of August 4. Thus Trotsky remembers: "The telegram telling of the capitulation of the German Social Democracy shocked me even more than the declaration of war, in spite of the fact that I was far from a naïve idealizing of German socialism."[5] Bukharin wrote about August 4 that it was "the greatest tragedy of our lives."[6] Both Rosa Luxemburg and Klara Zetkin suffered nervous prostration, and were for a time near to suicide.[7]

But Lenin had to come to terms with the truth. "Facts are stubborn things," he often remarked in English. He was quick to reevaluate the situation and develop a clear revolutionary strategy towards the war. In his recollections, the old Bolshevik G.L. Shklovsky could write: "I may testify that the fundamental slogans of Lenin's tactic in the imperialist war had been formulated by him in Austria during the first few days of the war, for he brought them to Berne completely formulated."[8] Throughout the war, Lenin stuck to the policy line that he had developed at this time.

First of all the class nature of the war had to be defined. He wrote:

> The present war is imperialist in character. This war is the outcome of conditions in an epoch in which capitalism has reached the highest stage in its development; in which the greatest significance attaches, not only to the export of commodities, but also to the export of capital; an epoch in which the cartelization of production and the internationalization of economic life have assumed impressive proportions, colonial policies have brought about the almost complete partition of the globe. World capitalism's productive forces have outgrown the limited boundaries of national and state divisions, and the objective conditions are perfectly ripe for socialism to be achieved.

The task of the working class was to fight the imperialist war by using the weapon of the class struggle, culminating in civil war.

> The imperialist war is ushering in the era of the social revolution. All the objective conditions of recent times have put the proletariat's revolutionary mass struggle on the order of the day. It is the duty of socialists, while making use of every means of the working class's legal struggle, to subordinate each and every one of those means to this immediate and most important task, develop the workers' revolutionary consciousness, rally them in the international revolutionary struggle, promote and encourage any revolutionary action, and do everything possible to turn the imperialist war between the peoples into a civil war of the oppressed classes against their oppressors, a war for the expropriation of the class of capitalists, for the conquest of political power by the proletariat, and the realization of socialism.[9]
>
> In all advanced countries the war has placed on the order of the day the slogan of socialist revolution.... The conversion of the present imperialist war into a civil war is the only correct proletarian slogan.[10]

Lenin was not equivocal. To aim at overthrowing one's own ruling class through civil war, one must *welcome* the defeat of one's "own" country.

> A revolution in wartime means civil war; the *conversion* of a war be-
> tween governments into a civil war is, on the one hand, facilitated by
> military reverses ("defeats") of governments; on the other hand, one
> *cannot* actually strive for such a conversion without thereby facilitat-
> ing defeat.[11]

The line of "revolutionary defeatism" is a universal one, applicable to all imperialist countries.

> Present-day socialism will remain true to itself only if it joins neither one
> nor the other imperialist bourgeoisie, only if it says that the two sides
> are "both worse," and if it wishes the defeat of the imperialist bour-
> geoisie in every country. Any other decision will, in reality, be national-
> liberal and have nothing in common with genuine internationalism.[12]

> A revolutionary class cannot but wish for the defeat of its govern-
> ment in a reactionary war, and cannot fail to see that the latter's mili-
> tary reverses must facilitate its overthrow... the socialists of *all* the
> belligerent countries should express their wish that *all* their "own"
> governments should be defeated.[13]

Any retreat from "revolutionary defeatism" might well lead one
to hesitate in carrying through the class struggle, in case this would
weaken national defense.

> In each country, the struggle against a government that is waging an im-
> perialist war should not falter at the possibility of that country's defeat
> as a result of revolutionary propaganda. The defeat of the government's
> army weakens the government, promotes the liberation of the nationali-
> ties it oppresses, and facilitates civil war against the ruling classes....[14]

> To repudiate the defeat slogan means allowing one's revolutionary
> ardor to degenerate into an empty phrase, or sheer hypocrisy.[15]

Against pacifism

As the imperialist war was the product of capitalism, there was in
Lenin's view no way to end wars without overthrowing capitalism.

> As long as the foundations of present, i.e., bourgeois, social relations re-
> main intact, an imperialist war can lead only to an imperialist peace,
> i.e., to greater, more extensive, and more intense oppression of weak na-
> tions and countries by finance capital, which grew to gigantic propor-
> tions not only in the period prior to the war, but also during the war.[16]

Thus Lenin rejected with utter disgust the pacifist program of
Kautsky and his group.

> Any "peace program" will deceive the people and be a piece of

hypocrisy, unless its principal object is to explain to the masses the need for a revolution, and to support, aid, and develop the mass revolutionary struggles breaking out everywhere (ferment among the masses, protests, fraternization in the trenches, strikes, demonstrations, etc.).[17]

Not "peace without annexations," but peace to the cottages, war on the palaces; peace to the proletariat and the working people, war on the bourgeoisie![18]

Socialists cannot, without ceasing to be socialists, be opposed to all war... civil war is just as much a war as any other.... To repudiate civil war, or to forget about it, is to fall into extreme opportunism and renounce the socialist revolution.[19]

An oppressed class which does not strive to learn to use arms, to acquire arms, only deserves to be treated like slaves. We cannot, unless we have become bourgeois pacifists or opportunists, forget that we are living in a class society from which there is no way out, nor can there be, save through the class struggle and the overthrow of the power of the ruling class.... Our slogan must be: arming of the proletariat to defeat, expropriate, and disarm the bourgeoisie.[20]

"Long live the Third International"

Long before the war Lenin had reached the conclusion that in Russia the rift between revolutionaries and reformists in the labor movement could not be healed, that it would be damaging to try to conciliate the two wings of the movement, and that it was necessary to form a separate party of revolutionaries. Now, given the debacle of the international social democratic movement, he was encouraged to generalize these beliefs and to apply them to the world labor movement.

In an article called "The Position and Tasks of the Socialist International," published in *Sotsial-Demokrat*, No. 33, November 1, 1914, he wrote: "The Second International is dead, overcome by opportunism...long live the Third International."[21] It was a tremendous shift for Lenin to free himself so completely from two decades of admiration of the Second International, and above all of the German section.

It is necessary at this point for us to make a detour and deal with Lenin's long-standing illusions about German Social Democracy—the pride of the Second International.

He had to admit that he had been wrong, terribly wrong, in his approbation of Karl Kautsky. For many years, Kautsky had been the only living socialist leader whom Lenin revered. After Marx and Engels, Kautsky was the authority whom Lenin quoted most often in support of the positions he took at various times. The German Social Democratic Party was picked out as an example to be followed.

What Is to Be Done? quotes Kautsky as the main authority for its central theme and praises the German Social Democratic Party as a model for the Russian movement. In December 1906, Lenin wrote: "The vanguard of the Russian working class knows Karl Kautsky for some time now as its writer"; he described Kautsky as "the leader of the German revolutionary Social Democrats."[22] In August 1908, he cited Kautsky as his authority on questions of war and militarism.[23] In 1910, at the time of Rosa Luxemburg's debate with Kautsky on the question of the path to power, Lenin sided with the latter. And as late as February 1914, he invoked Kautsky as a Marxist authority in his dispute with Rosa Luxemburg on the national question.

Even when Lenin had to admit that the German party was not consistently revolutionary, he was very charitable towards it. However, August 4 was no accident, but rather the culmination of a long process of decay of Social Democracy, and above all of its German section. This will be clear if we quote a few examples from the history of the SPD.

In 1904 Karl Liebknecht urged the SPD Congress in Bremen to authorize the development of extensive antimilitarist propaganda among potential recruits. What was the party leaders' reaction? The proposal was rejected as both impractical and unnecessary. The German courts, they said, would never tolerate antimilitarist agitation among youth.[24]

At the Mannheim congress in 1906, Liebknecht again tried to get the party to embark on more determined antimilitarist agitation. He now had an added counter to play: a newly organized Social Democratic youth movement that placed great emphasis on the fight against militarism. Bebel was violent in his opposition to Liebknecht. His unparalleled heat indicated that this was an issue on which he would brook no opposition—and no change.[25]

The Reichstag debates on the military budget in April 1907 gave Bebel his opportunity. The SPD voted against the military budgets only because the financial burden fell upon the people. If the funds were to be provided by direct Reich taxes rather than by indirect taxes, Social Democracy would vote them for the military establishment.

Gustav Noske came to Bebel's aid and expounded the premises

for his position. It was Noske's first major speech in the Reichstag, a fitting start for his later career as political chief of the counter-revolutionary armies in the first stormy year of the Republic. Opposing the persistent representations of the Social Democrats, whom he described as "vagabonds without a fatherland," Noske stated that the party's stand on militarism was "conditioned by our acceptance of the principle of nationality." Advocating the independence of every nation, the Social Democrats would of course fend off attacks on Germany "with as much determination as any gentleman on the right side of the House." They wanted Germany to be "as well armed [wehrhaft] as possible" and for "the whole people [to] have an interest in the military establishment which is necessary to the defense of our fatherland."

The war minister, Count von Einem, was quick to seize upon these protestations of patriotism. He accepted Noske's statement that his party was determined to defend the German Empire against an aggressive war in the same manner and with the same devotion as the other parties. While thus welcoming the Social Democrats into the national camp, von Einem took occasion to point out that the professions of their Reichstag deputies did not coincide with the views of the party agitators. He touched Bebel in a sensitive spot— no doubt unwittingly—by quoting a flaming passage from Liebknecht's newly published *Militarism and Anti-Militarism*, showing how the persistent mishandling of German soldiers in the army could serve as "a splendid means to combat militarism." The minister drew the conclusions for his Social Democratic hearers: the party leaders should liquidate the Social Democratic youth organization whose propaganda was inconsistent with national defense.

Bebel, obviously annoyed and embarrassed at the citations from Liebknecht, declared in answer to von Einem that the party's position was as he had stated it. He added—and it was a bold statement for a Social Democratic leader to make—that comments made or written by persons outside the house "are not and cannot be representative of the party in any way."[26]

In the summer of 1911, an international crisis broke out. On July 1, the cruiser *Panther* was sent to Agadir in Morocco to "protect" German interests. Camille Huysmans, the secretary of the International Socialist Bureau, sent a round robin to all member parties asking for their reaction to the impending crisis. In Germany the correspondence was dealt with by Hermann Molkenbuhr, a senior party official. Molkenbuhr argued in favor of avoiding taking a position.

> If we should prematurely engage ourselves so strongly [as to go on record through an International meeting] and even give precedence to the Morocco question over questions of internal policy, so that an effective electoral slogan could be developed against us, then the consequences will be unforeseeable.... It is a vital interest for us not to permit the internal developments: taxation policy, the privileges of the agrarians...etc., to be pushed into the background. But that could happen if we ourselves were to speak on the Morocco question in every hamlet, and were thus to strengthen the [chauvinistic] counter-tendency.[27]

Molkenbuhr did not even support the idea of a meeting of the International Bureau.

In 1912 the SPD took another step forward. In the Reichstag, the party introduced resolutions to improve premilitary youth training in the public schools, and to procure for the Social Democratic cooperatives a proportion of the supply contracts for the army! The former motion was shelved by the Reichstag, the latter rejected. That Social Democracy should be attempting to obtain its share of war orders, however, was a sign of the times.[28]

Where did Kautsky stand? During this period of the decay of Social Democracy, he did not take a revolutionary position towards imperialism and war, but a pacifist one. He argued that armaments and war were not necessarily the result of capitalism. On the contrary, capitalism might well lead to general peace, as a result of what he called "ultra-imperialism."

> The armaments race had economic causes, but was not, like the quest for markets, an economic necessity. In the case of the growth of monopoly, initial competition between national monopolies yielded to international cartel agreements; similarly in the development of imperialism, the rival nations were already reaching the point where mutual agreement was a necessity for the mitigation of the economic burden of armaments. The imperialist interest of Britain and Germany could, in fact, be better served by an agreement between them in which the other Western European nations would have to join. With the armaments rivalry put aside, "their capitalists could open up the whole area [of the underdeveloped portions of the world], or at least the eastern hemisphere far more energetically...than before." Russia would be contained by this Western alliance for the mutual, rather than competitive, exploitation of the underdeveloped sectors of the globe. Such a scheme might not banish war forever, said Kautsky, but it would at least postpone it. He saw strong support for such a plan already existing in the middle classes, especially in England and France.[29]

All subordinated to parliamentarism

Throughout the decay of German Social Democracy its central theme was the subordination of its politics to the needs of parliamentary elections. Thus in a discussion on Molkenbuhr's letter, Rosa Luxemburg explained why the whole of the SPD leadership, including Bebel, sided with Molkenbuhr.

> The plain truth is that August [Bebel], and still more the others, have pledged themselves to... parliamentarism, and wherever anything happens which transcends the limits of parliamentary action, they are hopeless—no, worse than hopeless, because then they do their utmost to force the movement back into parliamentary channels.[30]

Kautsky did not oppose all extraparliamentary mass action, but he subordinated it to parliamentary activity. Thus he wrote in 1910: "This 'direct action' of the unions can operate effectively only as an auxiliary and reinforcement to, and not as a substitute for, parliamentary action."[31]

Again, in a polemic with Pannekoek in 1912, Kautsky stated that the goal must remain the same as it had always been: the conquest of state power by winning a majority in parliament and by making parliament the controller of the government.[32]

Why Lenin's illusions about Kautsky persisted

With hindsight August 4 appears as an inevitable outcome of the development of German Social Democracy. Why did Lenin not foresee this development?

A number of factors were responsible. First of all, during the years of his exile—until the outbreak of the war—Lenin did not participate in the activities of the socialist movement in the countries where he lived. He was fully occupied in leading the Russian party. Unlike Trotsky, who lacked a party of his own and therefore was able to be active in the Socialist Party of Austria before the war, Lenin was completely absorbed in the activities of the Russian party. His writings were nearly all in the Russian language. The exceptions were a few official documents explaining the position of the Bolsheviks to the higher bodies of the International.

Secondly, in backward Russia, the mass German socialist movement was looked upon as a beacon—as an image of the future of the young and weak Russian labor movement. The SPD was still basking in the glow of its heroic past. During twelve long years from 1878 to 1890 inspired by Friedrich Engels it had had to work illegally under the repressive laws of Bismarck.

Thirdly, on the face of it, the centralism of Lenin was not radically different from that of the German SPD. In his debate about party organization with Rosa Luxemburg, Lenin again and again quoted Kautsky as his authority.

The genesis of the SPD threw a red glow over its present position. The presumed abyss separating it from capitalist society and the state was symbolized by the policeman sitting on the platform of every SPD mass meeting, with the right to stop the proceedings whenever the meeting overstepped what he thought was legitimate. But, however one explains Lenin's attitude before the war to the German Social Democratic Party in general and Karl Kautsky in particular, one must make it clear that he was totally wrong. Lenin was not alone among revolutionaries in this error. The only exceptions were Rosa Luxemburg and Anton Pannekoek, who accurately gauged the opportunism of Kautsky and the SPD.

Now, after the betrayal of August 4, Lenin had no hesitation in declaring the death of the Second International and raising the banner of the new Third International. He clearly linked the demise of the Second International with its opportunistic degeneration. "The collapse of the Second International is the collapse of socialist opportunism. The latter has grown as a product of the preceding 'peaceful' period in the development of the labor movement."[33*]

In "The Position and Tasks of the Socialist International," he wrote:

> The Second International did its share of useful preparatory work in preliminarily organizing the proletarian masses during the long, "peaceful" period of the most brutal capitalist slavery and most rapid capitalist progress in the last third of the nineteenth and the beginning of the twentieth centuries. To the Third International falls the task of organizing the proletarian forces for a revolutionary onslaught against the capitalist governments, for civil war against the bourgeoisie of all countries for the capture of political power, for the triumph of socialism![37]

The Zimmerwald Conference

After months of preparation, on September 5, 1915, a conference of antiwar socialists at last met in the hitherto obscure, tiny village of Zimmerwald in Switzerland. As a result, the name of Zimmerwald was to echo throughout the world. As Trotsky reminisced many years later:

> The delegates, filling four stage-coaches, set off for the mountains. The passers-by looked on curiously at the strange procession. The delegates themselves joked about the fact that half a century after the founding of the First International, it was still possible to seat all the internationalists in four coaches.[38]

Thirty-eight delegates attended, some of whom were observers without votes. From the very beginning of the conference three fairly distinct groups emerged. On the right there were some nineteen or twenty delegates, constituting a majority of the conference, who, although they supported a general demand for peace, opposed any breach with the social patriots or split with the Second International. This group included most of the German delegation, the French, some of the Italians, the Poles, and the Russian Mensheviks. Those who were dissatisfied with this moderate objective and favored a denunciation of civil peace, an organizational break with the social patriots, and a revolutionary class struggle, constituted a left group of eight led by Lenin. To this group belonged Zinoviev, one Lithuanian, the Pole Karl Radek, two Swedish delegates, and Julian Borchard, the delegate of a tiny group, the German International Socialists. Between these two was a smaller center group of five or six, among whom were Trotsky, Grimm, Balabanoff, and Roland-Holst.

The German edition of a pamphlet *Socialism and War* by Lenin and Zinoviev was distributed among the delegates. But the Bolsheviks were unable to persuade the conference to adopt the draft resolution and thesis that Lenin proposed.

A resolution moved by Lenin was overwhelmingly defeated by the conference as childish and dangerous nonsense. Merrheim said that he could not pledge himself to urge the French people to rise up in rebellion against the war; the European situation was not in his view ripe for revolution. Ledebour declared: "Lenin's resolution is unacceptable." "Perhaps," he added, "revolutionary actions might occur, but not because we call for them in a manifesto.... In the belligerent countries people who sign or distribute such a manifesto would at once be liquidated." Ernst Meyer stated that not even a tiny proportion of the German proletariat would be prepared for the kind of action proposed by Lenin's manifesto. An Italian delegate stressed that the task of the conference was to end the world war, not to unleash a civil war.

Lenin's resolution had stipulated, as an essential precondition for the revolutionary mobilization of the proletariat, the splitting of the socialist parties in a ruthless struggle against the majority of the labor leaders, whose minds, it declared, were "twisted by nationalism and eaten up with opportunism" and who "at the moment of world war had delivered the proletariat into the hands of imperialism and abandoned the principles of socialism and therewith the real struggle for the daily needs of the proletariat."

The conference decisively rejected Lenin's efforts to create a breach with the Second International and, found a new organization. Merrheim, for example, declared in the debate: "You, comrade Lenin, are not motivated by the desire for peace, but by the wish to lay down the foundations of a new International; it is this which divides us." In similar vein the official conference report stated: "In no way must the impression be created that this conference aims to provoke a split in or to establish a new International."[39]

The manifesto adopted by the conference was almost identical with Trotsky's draft. There was not a word in it about revolutionary defeatism, or turning the imperialist war into a civil war. Instead it consisted largely of vague liberal and pacifist sentiments:

> [The] struggle is also the struggle for liberty, for brotherhood of nations, for socialism. The task is to take up this fight for peace—for a peace without annexations or war indemnities. Such a peace is only possible when every thought of violating the rights and liberties of the nations is condemned. There must be no enforced incorporation either of wholly or partly occupied countries. No annexations, either open or masked, no forced economic union, made still more intolerable by the suppression of political rights. The right of nations to select their own government must be the immovable fundamental principle of international relations.[40]

The Zimmerwald manifesto naturally did not say a word about the need to create a Third International. Even the question of voting for or against the military budget was evaded: On the categorical demand of the German delegates, the concrete parliamentary measures of class struggle (the refusal of credits, the withdrawal from the ministries, etc.) were not included, though in Trotsky's original draft they had been pronounced imperative for all socialist organizations in time of war.

Towards the end of the conference, Lenin and his friends found it necessary to issue a statement sharply criticizing the Zimmerwald manifesto for its pacifist and vague nature:

> The manifesto adopted by the conference does not give us complete sat-

isfaction. It contains no characterization of either open opportunism or opportunism covered up by radical phrases—that opportunism which is not only the chief culprit of the collapse of the International but which strives to perpetuate that collapse. The manifesto contains no clear characterization of the means of combating the war.

We shall advocate, as we have done heretofore, in the socialist press and at the meetings of the International a decidedly Marxian position in regard to the tasks with which the proletariat has been confronted by the epoch of imperialism.

We vote for the manifesto because we regard it as a call to struggle, and in this struggle we are anxious to march side by side with the other sections of the International.

We request that our present declaration be included in the official report. [Signed] N. Lenin, G. Zinoviev, Radek, Nerman, Höglund, Winter.

Another declaration was signed by Roland-Holst and Trotsky, in addition to the leftists who had introduced the draft resolution. Its text was as follows:

Inasmuch as the adoption of our amendment [to the manifesto] demanding the vote against war credits might endanger to some extent the success of the conference, we withdraw our proposal under protest. We are satisfied with Ledebour's statement in the Commission to the effect that the manifesto contains all that is implied in our proposal.[41]

The Kienthal Conference

The committee elected at Zimmerwald called a second conference, which met from April 24-30, 1916, in the village of Kienthal, near Berne. This time forty-four delegates attended, representing roughly the same groups and parties as were at the first conference.

Again Lenin arrived with a clear-cut program; again he called for revolutionary propaganda and a break with the International. In a memorandum that he submitted to the conference, he declared that socialist antiwar propaganda would be mere shamming unless it simultaneously called on the troops to lay down their arms and preached the need for revolution and the transforming of the imperialist war into civil war for socialism. In his view the conference manifesto should clearly proclaim that the masses were being led astray not only by the capitalists but also by the social chauvinists who mouthed slogans about defending the fatherland in order to further this imperialist war; revolutionary action would be impossible while the war lasted unless socialists were prepared to threaten their own governments with the prospect of defeat—and the defeat of any government in a reactionary war could only serve to hasten

the revolution, which was the sole means of achieving a lasting democratic peace settlement. The struggle against the social chauvinists was vital. It was the duty of socialists to enlighten the masses
on the inevitability of their separation from those who were pursu-
ing bourgeois policies under the banner of socialism.[42]

Again Lenin was in a minority. But this time there were twelve
supporters for his standpoint, as against eight at the first conference.
Moreover, the final resolutions passed at Kienthal were nearer to the
line taken by Lenin and his friends than the Zimmerwald resolution.

There was still a lack of unity, not only between the Zimmerwal-
dian majority and the left minority, but also within the left itself.
Among this group, the questions of self-determination, disarmament,
and arming of the people separated the Dutch, Swedish, Norwegian,
and Polish leftists from the Bolsheviks. Dissensions relating to these
and other controversial matters developed among the Bolsheviks and
involved Lenin in a hot debate with the former *Vpered* group (Lunacharsky, Manuilsky, and others) and with the Bukharin–Piatakov
group, on the national question, the right of self-determination.[*]

Nevertheless, the development of the war and the pressure from
Lenin had made an impression at Zimmerwald. And the Kienthal
manifesto was far sharper than that of Zimmerwald had been seven
months before. The conference eventually agreed to go beyond a
general call for an immediate peace settlement without annexations.
It also demanded that the representatives of the socialist parties
refuse all support for war policies and refuse to grant war credits.[43]

In a special resolution, the conference defined its attitude to the
Second International—the most contentious issue at the meeting.
As Zinoviev rightly stated, it was, in fact, "the most important
point on the agenda, since it was the discussion on this formula
which fundamentally decided the question whether to keep the Second or whether to have a Third International." However, the resolution made no reference to the break with the Second International
that Lenin demanded. It only declared that the Executive Committee of the International, in obstinately refusing to convene a plenary
meeting despite repeated requests from various national sections,
had completely failed in the fulfillment of its duty and had become
an accomplice in the policy of betraying principles, political truce,
and so-called defense of the fatherland. It declared that the parties
that had joined the Zimmerwald movement had the right to demand of their own accord that the Bureau of the Socialist International be convened.[44]

Lenin enters the international arena

Besides Zimmerwald and Kienthal, other conferences attracted the attention and intervention of Lenin. He did not neglect any opportunity to put forward his policy on the war. Thus on March 13-15, 1915, an International Women's Conference met in Berne. Lenin greeted it with a well-prepared program. Representing the Bolsheviks were Krupskaya, Inessa Armand, Zlata Lilina (Zinoviev's wife), E.F. Rozmirovich, and Olga Ravich.

> The prevailing atmosphere of the meeting was one which Lenin denounced as pacifist. The Bolsheviks had at first sought to limit the gathering to a more radical membership, but according to Armand, Zetkin decided to convene "an 'official conference' instead of a conference of the left." The delegates spoke of seeking a "just peace." The Bolsheviks offered a resolution criticizing the socialist parties of the warring powers for having betrayed socialism, calling for an end to civil peace, and demanding a clear break with the Second International. By a vote of twenty-one to six, the meeting rejected the resolution, but in order to win unanimous support for the majority's resolution Zetkin agreed, after consulting Lenin, to publish the Bolshevik resolution in the official report of the conference. The Bolsheviks accordingly declared that while they still disagreed with the majority's resolution, they nevertheless accepted it as a first step in the revolutionary struggle.... Speaking later in Zurich, Armand called the conference "a first step—a portent of greater things" ... Lenin criticized the majority's resolution sharply. "Not a word of censure for the traitors or a single word about opportunism."[45]

On April 17 an International Youth Conference took place. The Bolsheviks were represented by Armand and G.I. Safarov, with Lenin communicating by telephone.

> The political currents of the youth conference resembled those of the women's conference, and when their resolution was defeated by fourteen to four, the Bolshevik delegation staged a walkout. The majority of the conference refused to pass judgment on the Second International. Lenin then received a delegation from the meeting, and another compromise resulted.[46]

For many years Lenin had lived in Switzerland without actively intervening in the local labor movement. Now, with the war, things changed, and he began to participate in the Swiss socialist movement, trying to forge a group of revolutionary internationalists, and to split them off from the Socialist Party. He succeeded in organizing a faction within the Swiss Socialist Party, which eventually became the seedbed of the Communist Party of Switzerland.[47]

Axelrod, the Menshevik leader, could complain with some justification that Lenin was trying to transfer his beloved methods of
factional struggle into the International.[48] As Krupskaya wrote:

> The international range of [Lenin's] activity gave a new tone to his
> work for Russia, it gave it fresh vigor, new color. Had it not been for
> the many years of hard work previously given to building the party,
> to organizing the working class of Russia, Ilyich would not have been
> able so quickly and so firmly to take a correct line with respect to the
> new problems raised by the imperialist war. Had he not been in the
> thick of the international struggle, he would not have been able so
> firmly to lead the Russian proletariat towards the October victory.[49]

> Ilyich ardently devoted himself to the mobilization of the forces
> for the struggle on the international front. "It does not matter that
> we now number only a few individuals," he once remarked, "mil-
> lions will be with us!"[50]

As one historian has rightly said: "Lenin had now established his
position on the left wing of the socialist movement among Russians
as well as internationally."[51] "Of all the émigrés, Lenin stood out as
the one who most successfully exploited his wartime opportunities in
Switzerland. Before 1914 he had had no significant foreign audience;
by 1917 he had a band of followers from a number of countries."[52]

Puny material resources

Throughout the war the Bolshevik organization abroad was
faced with acute financial problems. A hundred francs was regarded as a large sum. Its official journal was appearing once a
month or once in two months, and Lenin was carefully counting
the lines in order not to exceed his budget.

In October 1914, when Lenin decided to restart the journal,
Sotsial-Demokrat, the Bolshevik "treasury" held just 160 Swiss
francs. The Bolsheviks had no printshop of their own, and had to
rely on a Russian printer, Kuzma, an old émigré whose service was
very slow and irregular. He worked only in the evenings. In addition he handled the publications of most of the other Russian émigré groups in Switzerland. At one point, Krupskaya complained,
"The typesetter is nonparty and a positive man. He prints for all
factions in turn."[53] Kuzma was also partial to the bottle, and to
"moods." On February 20, 1915, Lenin wrote to V.A. Karpinsky,
"We are terribly worried at the absence of news and proofs from
you. Has the compositor taken to the bottle again? Or taken on

outside work again?"[54] On August 26 he wrote to Sophia Ravich: "Keep me informed by postcards: 'a bulletin of Kuzmikha's moods and the chances of success.' Both you (and we) are fed up with Kuzma, I understand, but what can we do?"[55] This unreliability of the printer, together with the Central Committee's (CC) continued shortage of funds, made the appearance of *Sotsial-Demokrat* very irregular.

Lenin also tried to publish a regular collection of essays under the title *Sbornik Sotsial-Demokrata*. Only two issues were produced. Copy was prepared for No. 3, but owing to lack of funds, it never appeared.

To add to these problems, Lenin and Krupskaya were harassed by personal financial troubles, especially after the death of Lenin's mother, who had provided him with money over the years. On December 14, 1915, Krupskaya wrote to Lenin's sister, Maria:

> Now I am writing for one special reason. We shall soon be coming to the end of our former means of subsistence and the question of earning money will become a serious one. It is difficult to find anything here. I have been promised a pupil, but that seems to be slow in materializing. I have also been promised some copying but nothing has come of it. I shall try something else, but it is all very problematic. I have to think about a literary income. I don't want that side of our affairs to be Volodya's worry alone. He works a lot as it is. The question of an income troubles him greatly.[56]

In January 1916, Lenin begged a friend to try to find him a cheap room, preferably in a worker's family, and asked about the price of meals in popular canteens.[57] In October he sent an appeal: "As regards myself personally, I will say that I need to earn. Otherwise we shall simply die of hunger, really and truly!! The cost of living is devilishly high, and there is nothing to live on." And he asked repeatedly for editorial and translation work: "If this is not organized I really will not be able to hold out, this is absolutely serious, absolutely, absolutely."[58]

On February 15, 1917—less than a fortnight before the February Revolution—Lenin wrote to Maria complaining bitterly about financial difficulties: "The cost of living makes one despair and I have desperately little capacity for work because of my shattered nerves."[59]

Underlying all these difficulties was the feeling of being completely isolated from Russia. Krupskaya describes how they sat in the libraries more diligently than ever and took walks as usual, but says that all this could not remove the feeling of being cooped up in a democratic cage. Somewhere beyond, a revolutionary struggle was mounting, life was astir, but it was all so far away.[60]

No wonder Lenin's nerves were very much on edge.

> The day after Ilyich's arrival from Zimmerwald we climbed the Rothorn. We climbed with a "glorious appetite," but when we reached the summit, Ilyich suddenly lay down on the ground, in an uncomfortable position almost on the snow, and fell asleep. Clouds gathered, then broke; the view of the Alps from the Rothorn was splendid, and Ilyich slept like the dead. He never stirred and slept over an hour. Apparently Zimmerwald had frayed his nerves a good deal and had taken much strength out of him. It required several days of roaming over the mountains and the atmosphere of Soerenberg before Ilyich was himself again.[61]

Things did not improve as the weeks and months of the war progressed. On the contrary, Lenin's mood became more and more depressed. Thus on January 15, about a month before the February Revolution, Lenin wrote to Inessa Armand: "I am pretty tired. I have got unused to meetings."[62] On February 7 he wrote again: "Yesterday there was a meeting (meetings tire me; nerves no good at all; headaches; left before the end)."[63] However, the harsh experience, personally and politically, was not in vain.

In conclusion

Among the antiwar revolutionaries Lenin stood practically alone in his "extremism," in his advocacy of "revolutionary defeatism." Even Trotsky could write:

> [U]nder no condition can I agree with your opinion, which is emphasized by a resolution, that Russia's defeat would be a "lesser evil." This opinion represents a fundamental connivance with the political methodology of social patriotism, a connivance for which there is no reason or justification and which substitutes an orientation (extremely arbitrary under present conditions) along the line of a "lesser evil" for the revolutionary struggle against war and the conditions which generated this war.[64]

And again:

> If we presuppose a catastrophic Russian defeat, the war *may* bring a quicker outbreak of the revolution, but at the cost of its inner weakness.... The defeat of Russia necessarily presupposes decisive victories by Germany and Austria on the other battlefields ... a Russian revolution, even if temporarily successful, would be an historical miscarriage, needs no further proof.... The Social Democrats could not, and cannot now, combine their aims with any of the historical possi-

bilities of this war, that is, with either the victory of the Triple Alliance or the victory of the Entente.[65]

The superiority of Lenin's position was that by its extremism, by its "bending the stick," by speaking about the defeat of one's own country as the lesser evil, it was better calculated to create a clear division between revolutionaries and social patriots. Lenin's position was direct, his language was simple. What he said could not be misinterpreted. Where he stood nobody could mistake. There was no room for equivocation.

It was with obvious relish that Lenin in August 1915 used a quotation that had impressed him:

> A French philosopher has said: "Dead ideas are those that appear in elegant garments, with no asperity or daring. They are dead because they are put into general circulation and become part of the ordinary intellectual baggage of the great army of philistines. Strong ideas are those that shock and scandalize, evoke indignation, anger, and animosity in some, and enthusiasm in others."[66]

The "exaggerated," one-sided, stick-bending formulation of Lenin's revolutionary defeatism itself aimed to do just this. As he wrote:

> The experience of the war, like the experience of any crisis in history, of any great calamity and any sudden turn in human life, stuns and breaks some people, *but enlightens and tempers others.* Taken by and large, and considering the history of the world as a whole, the number and strength of the second kind of people have—with the exception of individual cases of the decline and fall of one state or another—proved greater than those of the former kind.[67]

The world war, like every profound crisis in society, had its positive side. It put to the test all the various traditions, organizations, and leaderships. It laid bare the rottenness of many who disguised their contradictions during peace time, but could do so no longer. Throughout this very hard time, Lenin and the Bolsheviks were steeled and ready to lead a revolution.

Years later, on September 20, 1919, Lenin could write: "The Bolsheviks have proved to be right; in the autumn of 1914 they declared to the world that the *imperialist war would be transformed into civil war.*"[68]

CHAPTER 2

THE BOLSHEVIK PARTY IN THE
TEST OF THE WAR

Bolshevik leaders and the war

The patriotic wave that engulfed the Russian people at the outbreak of the war did not leave the Bolshevik leaders untouched. As was pointed out quite rightly by Trotsky: "As a general rule, the confusion was most pervasive and lasted longest among the party's higher-ups, who came in direct contact with bourgeois opinion."[1]

When the war issue was discussed in the Duma, both the Menshevik and the Bolshevik deputies refused to meet the government head-on and instead left the session. The result was that the Duma resolution supporting the war effort passed unanimously. The Mensheviks and Bolsheviks then issued a joint declaration that was very equivocal indeed. It is true that it avoided the "false patriotism under which the ruling classes wage their predatory policy," but at the same time it promised that the proletariat would defend the cultural treasures of the people against all attacks, no matter where they came from, whether from within or from without.[2] In the pretence of "defending culture," the Menshevik and Bolshevik deputies were assuming a semipatriotic position.

When Lenin's theses on the war reached Petersburg at the beginning of September 1914, they raised a number of objections among the party leaders, especially to the slogan of "revolutionary defeatism." The Duma fraction tried to tone down the sharpness of Lenin's formulations. It was the same story in Moscow and in the provinces. "The war caught the 'Leninists' unprepared," testifies the Moscow *okhrana* (secret police), "and for a long time ... they could not agree on their attitude toward the war." The Moscow Bolsheviks wrote in code by way of Stockholm for transmission to Lenin that, notwithstanding all respect for him, his advice to "sell the house" (the slogan of defeatism) had not struck a responsive chord.[3]

The old Bolshevik Baevsky noted that the slogan of defeat of one's own government raised objections in Russia and that there was a tendency to eliminate the word "defeat" "as a very odious one."[4] Shliapnikov also recalled that, while the theses on the whole reflected the state of mind of party workers, the question of "defeat" provoked perplexity.[5] *Sotsial-Demokrat* noted that the Bolshevik organization in Moscow adopted the manifesto with the exception of the paragraph dealing with the defeat of one's own country.[6] There is other evidence of reluctance to adopt the defeatist point of view by party workers in Russia and outside, not only at the beginning of the war but right up to the revolution of 1917.[7] Baevsky claimed, however, that it was impossible to speak of "anti-defeatism" during the war as a tendency within the party.[8]

In November, the five Bolshevik deputies to the Duma were arrested. In February 1915, together with another five Bolshevik leaders, they were brought to trial. They, and above all their theoretical mentor, Kamenev, went out of their way to repudiate Lenin's theses. (The only notable exception was the Duma deputy M.K. Muranov.) Kamenev declared that Lenin's theses decidedly contradicted his own views on the current war. He said that Lenin's views were rejected both by the Social Democratic deputies and the central institutions, i.e., the Central Committee, whose spokesman Kamenev claimed to be. Another of the Bolsheviks on trial pointed out that Lenin's theses contradicted the declaration in the name of the Social Democratic fractions that had been read in the Duma on July 27, 1914.[9]

Lenin was more than disappointed. And although he felt somewhat inhibited from too sharp an attack on Kamenev and the others immediately after the trial ended with their exile for life to Siberia, he still made his criticism plain:

> What, then, has the trial of the Russian Social Democratic Labor group proved?
>
> First of all, it has shown that this advance contingent of revolutionary Social Democracy in Russia failed to display sufficient firmness at the trial ... to attempt to prove one's solidarity with the social patriot Mr. Yordansky, as Rosenfeld [Kamenev] did, or one's disagreement with the Central Committee ... is inexcusable from the standpoint of a revolutionary Social Democrat.[10]

Lenin could not ignore the truth, however unpalatable. The party of the revolutionary proletariat was strong enough to openly criticize itself and unequivocally call mistakes and weaknesses by their proper names.[11]

The behavior of the Bolshevik leaders in court, Shliapnikov reported, caused quite serious demoralization in the party ranks:

> The deputies' trial went on in an atmosphere of indecision and wavering. The attitude adopted by the deputies in court was perplexing. One got the impression that the deputies did not comport themselves as would befit the supreme responsible center of the proletariat, but rather as provincial party committees sometimes behave. Many regretted that the comrades' deputies showed so little firmness, but saw the reason for it in the atmosphere of terror.[12]

In his defense, Kamenev cited the formal truth that Lenin's theses on the war, published in the name of the Central Committee, had not received the approval of the committee, as meaning that he did not have the right to publish them.[13]

Other sections of the Bolsheviks were also unhappy about Lenin's line. The Bolshevik colony abroad was very much under the influence of war hysteria. The Committee of Organizations Abroad in Paris, which had served as a center for the Bolshevik groups outside Russia, had disintegrated; two of its members had enlisted in the French army and another had withdrawn, leaving only two active members. In Paris, the Bolshevik group wavered. Although the majority of the group expressed themselves against the war and against volunteering, some of the comrades joined the French army as volunteers.[14] Altogether, out of ninety-four Bolsheviks in France, eleven volunteered for the French army.[15]

The Geneva section of the Bolshevik émigrés also voiced their objections to Lenin's "revolutionary defeatism." A letter to Lenin by Karpinsky criticized the theses as follows: "The text of paragraph 6 should be changed in order not to give rise to a misinterpretation of this passage: that the Russian Social Democrats wish for the victory of the Germans and the defeat of the Russians."[16]

Among the prominent party leaders abroad who took up a defensive position was G.M. Krzhizhanovsky, a close comrade of Lenin's since 1893, who, during the 1905 Revolution, together with Krassin and Bogdanov, had been one of the leaders of the Bolsheviks. Others included CC member I.P. Goldenberg, former Bolshevik Duma deputy G.A. Alexinsky, and Bolshevik writer A.A. Troianovsky.

What was the situation inside Russia? In November 1914, Alexander Shliapnikov traveled to Moscow to find the organization there smashed. Most workers were defensists. Only a few isolated people adhered (not always firmly) to the policy of defeatism. The biggest group of "defeatists" had seven members. They were not yet sure of Lenin's views.[17] Similarly, the Transcaucasian Social Democrats were sharply divided over their position on the war. In October 1914, N.N. Iakovlev arrived in Baku with the text of Lenin's theses, calling for Russia's defeat and the transformation of the world war into a civil war. Although many copies were printed and distributed in both Baku and Tiflis, the organization reached no decision on its attitude to the war.[18]

Even though the Bolshevik organizations in Russia at the beginning of the war were not ready to adopt Lenin's open position of revolutionary defeatism, only an insignificant number of their members were patriots. From the outset the Bolsheviks developed mass propaganda against the war. Numerous antiwar leaflets had already been issued as early as July 1914 by party committees in different parts of Russia.[19]

After a few months of ideological confusion, more and more Bolshevik groups began to take a clear, antiwar, internationalist position. This political awakening followed a revival of the workers' movement in the factories, and was both affected by this movement and influenced it in its turn.

Ebb and flow

The first half of 1914 witnessed a rise in the political strike movement in Russia that approached the level of the 1905 Revolution.

Year	Participants in political strikes	Year	Participants in political strikes
1903	87,000*	1909	8,000
1904	25,000*	1910	4,000
1905	1,843,000	1911	8,000
1906	651,000	1912	550,000
1907	540,000	1913	502,000
1908	93,000	1914 (first half)	1,059,000

* The figures for 1903 and 1904 refer to all strikes, the economic undoubtedly predominating.

On the eve of the war itself, the political strike movement in Petersburg was to culminate in the building of barricades. In protest against brutal police suppression of a demonstration of Putilov workers in support of a strike in the Baku oilfield, a strike, as massive and explosive as any that had erupted in 1905, swept Petersburg. By July 7, 110,000 workers had joined the strike. A couple of days later it had engulfed 200,000 workers. Almost all factories in Petersburg were closed, and many thousands of workers took part in protracted battles with Cossacks and police detachments. Workers' demonstrations, brandishing red flags and singing revolutionary songs, sought to smash their way into the center of the city, but were blocked by Cossacks and mounted police. On July 11, many barricades were built out of telephone and telegraph poles, overturned wagons, and so on. It was not until July 15, four days before the war started, that order was finally restored in the factory district of Petersburg.[21]

Suddenly, with the outbreak of war, the atmosphere changed radically. Patriotic zeal gripped the masses. Buchanan, British ambassador to Petersburg at the time, wrote with enthusiasm in his memoirs of "those wonderful early August days" when "Russia seemed to have been completely transformed."

Trotsky provided an explanation of the change in the psychology of the masses that turned them towards patriotism.

> The people whose lives, day in and day out, pass in a monotony of hopelessness are many; they are the mainstay of modern society. The alarm of mobilization breaks into their lives like a promise; the familiar and long-hated is overthrown, and the new and unusual reigns in its place. Changes still more incredible are in store for them in the future. For better or worse? For the better, of course—what can seem worse ... than "normal" conditions?[22]

To add to the disarray of the labor movement, a mass arrest of Bolsheviks took place in Petersburg: after the July demonstration the government seized about a thousand Bolsheviks and expelled them from the city.[23] At the same time, thousands of the more unruly factory workers were drafted into the army. Roughly 40 percent of the Petersburg proletariat was mobilized (and the gaps in the ranks of the working class were filled by a new influx of inexperienced workers from the countryside).[24]

The first few months of the war were marked by political stupor in the labor movement. On the tenth anniversary of the "Bloody

Sunday" that triggered off the revolution in 1905, only fourteen factories came out on strike, with 2,528 workers. On May Day, only 859 workers came out.[25] The whole first half of 1915 was very quiet indeed. But things changed radically in July. It is true that the number of workers on strike was quite small compared with the last few months before the war—14,490 workers in seventeen factories went on strike for economic reasons; there was not one political strike.[26] However the strikes were extremely bitter. In violent clashes between strikers and police at Kostroma, thirteen workers were killed or wounded; in a similar clash in Ivanovo-Voznesensk there were between twenty and thirty casualties. News of the clashes led to major political strikes in August and September. In August, twenty-seven thousand workers went on strike in Petrograd demanding the withdrawal of Cossack guards from the factories, the release of the five exiled Bolshevik deputies, freedom of the press, etc. Early in September, sixty-four thousand workers came out in Petrograd with political demands. Altogether in 1915, there were 928 strikes, of which 715 were economic, involving 383,587 workers, and 213 were political, involving 155,941 workers.[27]

There was no easing of the struggle in 1916. The commemoration of Bloody Sunday on January 9, 1916, brought fifty-three thousand workers out (85 percent of them in Petrograd). Throughout 1916, and especially in the second half of the year, not only were more and more workers involved in strikes, but the strikes became more and more political in nature. Altogether in 1916, 280,943 workers were involved in political strikes, and 221,136 in economic strikes. A new impetus to the struggle came in January and February 1917. In those two months alone, 256,253 workers were involved in political strikes, and 35,829 in economic strikes, i.e., about 88 percent of all the workers involved were striking for political reasons.[28]

Throughout the war, Petrograd unquestionably held a predominant position in the strike movement.

	Political strikes		Economic strikes		Total	
	Strikes	Workers	Strikes	Workers	Strikes	Workers
Petrograd	256	348,118	242	167,869	498	515,978
Moscow	113	39,279	364	271,295	477	310,574
Russia (total)	463	469,086	1,817	1,056,889	2,280	1,525,975[29]

The figures show that 74 percent of all workers involved in political strikes during the war years were in Petrograd, as against 9 percent in Moscow. (One should remember that there were more industrial workers in Moscow than in Petrograd.)

The record of the Petrograd proletariat is especially impressive if one remembers that about 17 percent of the industrial workers were conscripted into the army and that some 40 percent of the proletariat in the capital were new recruits to the class, i.e., they were relatively inexperienced.[30]

Increasing revolutionary ferment

One very useful source of information about the rising popular movement against the old regime is the minutes of the Council of Ministers. The discussion at these sessions testifies to the tremendous rise in the revolutionary movement among workers in the second half of 1915. Thus at the session held on August 11, 1915, N.B. Shcherbatov spoke about the serious disorders that had taken place in Ivanovo-Voznesensk, where it had been necessary to shoot. The moment was an extraordinarily tense one, as there was no confidence in the garrison. As a result of the shooting, sixteen were killed and more than thirty wounded. The excitement had not died down at all, and he predicted echoes in other factory districts.

Prince E.N. Shakhovskoy, minister of trade and industry, had the most alarming reports from factory inspectors concerning the mood of the workers. Any spark would be sufficient to start a fire. The prime minister (Goremykin) begged the minister of internal affairs (Shcherbatov) to tell them what measures he was taking to check the outrages going on everywhere.

Shcherbatov replied that he was taking all the steps that his duty dictated to him, and that practical possibilities allowed him. He complained that he was expected to fight the growing revolutionary movement without using the troops, because they were regarded as unreliable and might refuse to shoot at the crowd. One could not pacify the whole of Russia with policemen alone, particularly when the ranks of the police were thinning out, not by the day but by the hour, and when the population was being wrought up every day by speeches in the Duma, lies in the newspapers, endless defeats at the front, and rumors about disorders in the rear.[31]

At the session of September 2, 1915 Shakhovskoy said:

Strikes have begun at the Putilov and the metal factories. The super-ficial excuse: the arrest of the elected representatives to the medical insurance cooperatives. The movement immediately took on a sharp character and was complicated by the submission of political demands. One can expect a further growth of the wave of strikes if one does not adopt anticipatory measures right now....

[Minister of War] A.A. Polivanov: If there are not going to be radi-cal changes in the general situation, my thoughts about the future are extremely gloomy ... the unrest at the Putilov factory (which sets the tone for the labor movement) is the beginning of a general strike in protest against the adjournment of the Duma. Everyone is expecting extraordinary events to follow the adjournment.

I.L. Goremykin: All this is only intimidation. Nothing will happen.

Prince N.B. Shcherbatov: The Department of Police does not have, by any means, such soothing information as Your High Excellency. The testimony of all agents is unanimous, to the effect that the labor movement will develop to an extent which will threaten the safety of the state. It is on this basis that the Department of Police demanded that the military authorities make a number of arrests.... As for the reason for the labor disorders—which have gone as far as clashes with the police at the Putilov factory—the demands which are pre-sented are: not to adjourn the Duma; to free the five imprisoned deputies of the left faction; to increase wages by fifteen per cent; and so on. All these, of course, are only excuses to cover up the real aim of the underground leaders of the workers—to take advantage of the misfortunes at the front, and of the internal crisis, to attempt a social revolution and to usurp power.[32]

On September 2, 1915, Shcherbatov described the situation in Moscow in very strong terms.

The workers, and the population as a whole, are gripped by some sort of madness and are like gunpowder. An outburst of disorders is possible at any moment. Yet the authorities in Moscow have virtually no forces. There is one reserve battalion of 800 men, of whom only half are available, as 400 are taken up with guard duty in the Krem-lin and other places. Then there is a squadron of Cossacks and, fi-nally, two militia units stationed in the outskirts. All of these are far from reliable, and it would be difficult to order them against the crowd. There are no troops at all in the rural part of the county. Both the city and the county police are inadequate, numerically, to the de-mands that may be made on them. I must also note the presence, in Moscow, of about 30,000 convalescent soldiers. This is a wild band, not recognizing discipline, making scandals, clashing with the police (recently one of the latter was killed by soldiers), freeing prisoners, and so on. Undoubtedly, if there are disorders, this whole horde will be on the side of the crowd. What would you suggest that the Minis-ter of Internal Affairs do under these circumstances?[33]

The armed forces did not remain unaffected by the popular op-position to the regime. Revolutionary ferment was evident among them as early as 1915. Thus the minister of internal affairs, A. Khvostov, in a letter dated November 15, 1915 to the President of the Council of Ministers, I.L. Goremykin, enclosed information, collected by responsible agents, in connection with the unrest that had recently been observed among the various ship's companies of the Baltic fleet. He felt that it was only natural that revolutionary elements of all shades should exploit the disturbed condition of the Baltic squadron, that they should endeavor to spread discontent among the lower ranks of the army and navy.

Their propaganda was based on the assumption that the war was being waged solely for the benefit of the capitalists, not for the good either of the Russian or of the German people. They sug-gested to the illiterate soldier that no victory, whichever group of powers might win it, could contribute to the welfare of the people, until the socialists of all countries and all classes of society joined in their struggle against the belligerent governments and forced them to surrender; that the only means of achieving this end lay in the speedy termination of the war, regardless of the result; that strenu-ous efforts must be made to impede the production of war materi-als by organizing strikes and popular revolts.[34]

There followed a description of a number of sailors' insurrec-tions on different ships of the Baltic fleet. To quote only one case out of many:

> One cause contributing to this general ferment must be cited: It is the disregard of some of the commanders and senior officers for the men's comfort and well-being. A story is circulated that on one occasion the sailors were served with cabbage soup containing putrid meat riddled with maggots. This provoked much grumbling and criticism. Similar occurrences gave rise to mutinies on the battleship *Imperator Pavel I* and on the cruiser *Rossia*. The sailors, having gathered on the forecas-tle of the latter ship, began to clamor for better food, more humane treatment, and the dismissal of all officers bearing German names. Rear-Admiral Kourosh appeared, revolver in hand, demanding the sur-render of the leaders and the cessation of disorder, threatening in the event of disobedience to shoot every man; but, as on the former occa-sion, the sailors retorted that this was not 1905; that the sailors had learnt wisdom and could not be frightened as before; that, sooner than allow the admiral to shoot them, they would throw him overboard.[35]

The unrest affected not only the fleet, but also the garrison at Kronstadt, where mass action took place following an insurrection on the battleship *Gangut*. As a result, ninety-five men were arrested on board and deported to the town of Reval.

A mixed detachment of cruisers and destroyers were detailed to escort the mutineers. But the crew of the *Ruric* refused to cooperate in conveying their comrades to prison.

According to one description, the disorders on board the *Gangut* caused great excitement among sailors throughout the Baltic fleet and among the coastguards, and led to much discussion on the need to set free the arrested sailors. All the ships passed resolutions to that effect, which were to be officially presented while in winter quarters, and a general strike was to be declared if these demands were refused. If the accused sailors were brought to court and condemned, then the threatened strike was to take place before the winter, and any repressive measures against the crews were to be met by systematic revolt. Similar propaganda was spreading not only among the lower ranks of the fleet, but also among the land forces of the Kronstadt garrisons, who claimed the right to take part in the joint protests against the naval authorities.[36]

At sessions of the Council of Ministers, more and more complaints were heard about the decline in patriotism. Thus on August 4, 1914, the minister of war, A.A. Polivanov, stated: "I rely on impassable spaces, on impenetrable mud, and on the mercy of St. Nicholas, the patron of Holy Russia."[37]

He pointed out that their mobilizations were less successful each time. The police could not manage the mass of draft-dodgers. Men were hiding in the woods and in the grainfields. Another minister, Grigorovich, suggested that the Germans were responsible. Shcherbatov felt that the agitators would exploit the issue to stir up unrest and disturbances. He told the Council of Ministers that the agitation was becoming more anti-militaristic in nature, even openly defeatist. Its direct influence could be seen in mass surrenders.[38]

The Bolshevik organization

On the eve of the outbreak of war, a central role in the organization of the party—especially in Petersburg—was played by the Duma deputies. The Bolshevik Duma deputy from Petersburg, Badaev, wrote: "With the arrest of the [Duma] fraction, the last roots of revolutionary work were torn out, the fundamental and main center of the party in Russia was destroyed."[39]

The significance of the Bolshevik deputies for the workers'

movement was not lost on the government. As Goremykin said at a meeting of the Council of Ministers on August 26, 1915, the problem for the workers' leaders was their lack of organization, which had been smashed by the arrest of the five members of the Duma.[40]

The beginning of the war also saw the breakup of the Petersburg Committee of the party, which was deeply infiltrated by police agents. Its members in July 1914 were V. Schmidt, Fedotov, Antipov, Nikolai Logov, Shurkanov, Ignatev, and Levtsky (the last three were police agents).[41]

The *okhrana* at first confidently believed that the war had destroyed the committee once and for all (although noting that there was evident disaffection among the youth), but they soon noticed that signs of activity were continuing.[42] To begin with, in the second half of 1914, reports indicated that the Petrograd organization had suffered a huge blow. The structure that had been so painstakingly built up had completely collapsed. An *okhrana* report in December 1914 stated that the district organizations were not functioning normally and that underground party work, in the form of factory circles and insignificant professional groups, occurred from time to time only in certain districts, of which the most lively was Vyborg, where the members were particularly advanced and "conscious" metalworkers.[43]

The police raids did not, however, put an end to the Petrograd organization. A few months after each raid smashed the Petersburg Committee, it rose again as from the ashes. As early as the beginning of 1915 a new committee was operating and started to rally party forces, assuming the leadership of the Bolsheviks in Russia as a whole. The various districts made contact with it and other spheres of work began to pick up (for example, the renewal of the paper *Voprosy Strakhovaniya*). An article in *Sotsial-Demokrat*, reporting developments in April 1915, was enthusiastic about the state of affairs, claiming that the committee now covered all the districts of Petersburg with one representative for each two hundred workers: "The workers are very satisfied with the work of the Petersburg Committee. There is a great flow towards the circles, there are not enough leaders, there are links with various cities."[44]

In July 1915, a conference was held in Oranienbaum. There were fifty people present representing all the Social Democratic factions and the Socialist Revolutionaries. Figures cited at this conference claimed that the Bolsheviks had twelve hundred members in Petrograd, the Mensheviks two hundred and the "Unifiers"

(Mezhraiontsy*) sixty to eighty.[45]

By September 1915 more districts were participating. A letter in *Sotsial-Demokrat* reported that the following on the Petersburg Committee were represented: Vyborg district, Narva district, 1st Gorodskoy district, Neva district, Petersburg district, and Vasileostrov district. Moscow district, and the 2nd Gorodskoy district were in the process of organizing themselves. There were also links between the committee and Kolpino, Sestroretsky, and Peterhoff, all some distance from Petrograd itself. Communications with the provinces also seemed good, and it was being asked to supply directives, literature, and information to cities all over European Russia.[46]

The Petersburg Committee was also the ultimate authority over the Bolshevik organizations that were set up in Kronstadt, Helsingfors, and elsewhere, and on the ships of the Baltic fleet. It provided a centralized underground base for all the individual groups to work through and supplied the sailors with literature and facilities for producing their own materials.

The committee sent several of its members to Moscow in the first months of 1915 to help set up a Moscow organization, prepare for a Bolshevik conference, and establish contacts. Leaflets and literature were also being supplied, mainly to Moscow, though it was hoped that they would be carried further afield.

The printing capabilities of the Petersburg Bolsheviks were impressive. Altogether between the end of July 1914 and the February Revolution, they issued more than 160 leaflets with a total circulation of about 500,000—i.e., about five leaflets a month, on average, with more than 16,000 copies in all. This was quite an achievement.[47]

Towards November, the *okhrana* began to retaliate with arrests. However, the party survived them relatively well. In December, more arrests took place. Many committee members were taken and the districts were quite seriously affected, with links breaking down yet again. A base was set up on Vasilevsky Island to try to direct work until a proper center could be reestablished. By the beginning of 1916, signs of recovery were noted by the *okhrana*.[48] The Bolsheviks, however few in number, certainly had the basic organizational talents needed to keep renewing their committees, whatever the odds.

---

* The Mezhraiontsy were a loose group of antiwar socialists including Trotsky, Lunacharsky, Pokrovsky, Ioffe, and other future leaders of the October Revolution, who were neither Bolsheviks nor Mensheviks when the group formed in 1913.

However, on the eve of May Day, 1916, the Petersburg Committee was again smashed by police raids, of which the *okhrana* wrote:

> [T]he work of the Petersburg Committee was temporarily completely brought to a halt, their contacts were lost but this, as on previous occasions, entailed only new attempts to reestablish party work and to create a new leading kollektiv, and also to equip a new press.[49]

In June 1916, a police agent reported that there were two thousand Bolsheviks in Petrograd. The number continued to increase during July and August, with improved organization in factories and better links between them. The *okhrana* saw the Petersburg Committee of the Bolsheviks as "highly serious and dangerous to the peace of society and the order of the state."[50] This fear inspired a series of arrests on the night of July 20, which, once again, did not inflict much long-term damage on the organization.[51]

In October 1916, a detailed letter from the committee to the Central Committee abroad on the state of party work in the capital described how groups were being set up in factories often without any direct help from the Petersburg Committee, and were trying to link up with it. Currently they had links with the following cities: Moscow, Ivanovo-Voznesensk, Kharkov, Ekaterinoslav, Nizhnii Novgorod, Sormovo, Samara, Saratov, Tsaritsyn, Perm, Ekaterinburg, Reval, Narva, Tver, and Tula. From this list it was clear that the committee needed to develop and expand its activity. In addition, soldiers and sailors of the local and Finland garrisons had begun to search them out. There was a possibility of setting up permanent links with the front: a few days earlier a soldier had come from there and asked for literature for his position.[52]

Party membership continued to grow slowly but surely, and by the end of 1916, according to Shliapnikov, there were some three thousand members in Petrograd[53] of which five hundred were in Vyborg, the working-class area in which the strongest Bolshevik organization in the capital was emerging, and which was to retain this position until the February Revolution and after.

By and large, the Petersburg Committee acted as the center of the party. For most of the war period, from November 1914 to the autumn of 1915, and again from the spring of 1916 to the autumn of the same year, the party had no Russian Bureau.[54]

Again and again police raids shattered it. Thus several leading party workers were arrested on December 9, 10, 18, and 19, 1916. Then on January 2, 1917 the entire committee was arrested. The reconstructed committee suffered heavy losses again on February 25, three days before the revolution. Again the Vyborg District Committee was pushed to the fore and assumed the leadership in Petrograd.

The Vyborg District Committee always tended to have greater resources than other district organizations because the factories in Vyborg employed a higher percentage of skilled and therefore better-paid workers. The nearness of the Finnish railway and the outer Petrograd suburbs meant that many people who were not allowed into Petrograd could live there, and that duplicators and other materials could be hidden there. Shliapnikov and the Russian Bureau were based in Vyborg mainly for these reasons.[55]

Despite the weakness of the Petersburg Committee, the Bolshevik position was better than that of the other revolutionary tendencies. According to Shliapnikov, only the Bolsheviks actually had any kind of all-Russian organization. Various estimates of party membership for this period have been made. A 1922 census showed that 10,483 members in 1922 had been members before the February Revolution, with 2,028 in Moscow and 817 in Petrograd. However, this takes no account of the many who died in the 1917 Revolution or the civil war, and a second estimate produced a figure of 23,600.[56]

During the war, large army units were stationed in Petrograd garrisons. The committee was concerned to aim its propaganda at the soldiers, despite the severe punishments for treason that this entailed. To handle this aspect of agitation, a military commission was sporadically organized, attached to the Petersburg Committee. This commission gained in significance as the February Revolution approached and the whole question of arming the workers arose. In spring 1915, the committee's first Military Organization was set up. This established links with certain regiments in the capital, with sailors and troops in Kronstadt, Helsingfors, and Sveaborg, and with troops on the northern front. It was soon destroyed by arrests, however.[57]

The reason for this, it turned out, was that the sensitive job of establishing links with the sailors of the Baltic fleet at the end of 1915 was entrusted to Shurkanov, a police agent.[58] Naturally the *okhrana* was well informed on Bolshevik work in Kronstadt, including details of names and addresses. So, until after the February Revolution, no meeting took place of the Military Organization under the Petersburg Committee.

Throughout the war, as well as police infiltration and raids, the Bolsheviks in Russia suffered from two further recurrent ailments: (1)

lack of intellectuals, and (2) lack of funds. Thus one old Bolshevik described how difficult it was for him to get a leaflet written against the war at the beginning of 1915. In order to write it, he turned to party intellectuals in Moscow, where he worked. He got very little response from them. Many of them supported the war, and a few others were, it seems, too frightened to help. At last he wrote a draft himself, and he and other workers worked very hard on it for a long time, but still some of the phrases did not sound Russian (presumably they were Latvian). So it would probably have read like a German publication. They could not get anyone to edit it for them. None of the intellectuals had a commitment to the contents, which were revolutionary defeatist. Finally the grammatical mistakes had to remain.[59]

A similar complaint came from Saratov. At the end of 1915, nearly every factory in Saratov had a Bolshevik cell of about ten to twenty workers. At first they were happy to be led by the active members, but later they began to demand more competent propagandists. The lack of intellectuals was the ever-present problem.[60]

Again and again Shliapnikov complained bitterly that the intellectuals avoided illegal activity during the war and became involved in the various institutions connected with the war.[61]

Given the great scarcity of intellectuals in the party, the workers' cadres who came to a revolutionary defeatist position on their own, without help from the party intellectuals, and even without contact with Lenin abroad, were naturally quite proud of their achievement. Thus, for instance, a group of Latvians reached the conclusion that the imperialist war should be turned into civil war without seeing Lenin's theses, and without having any theoreticians among their number.[62]

To exacerbate the party's difficulties, the lack of intellectuals was accompanied by severe and frustrating financial problems. Thus we are told by Shliapnikov that when the war broke out, he managed to obtain contacts for supplying literature to Petersburg. However, he was unable to maintain them for lack of money. The Petersburg Committee could not afford the sum of 300–500 rubles a month that was needed.[63] Shliapnikov was very bitter: if he had only had 500 rubles a month, he could have filled Russia with literature.[64]

The bureau could not afford to send anyone to the provinces; they could not keep anyone there for even a month and had to depend on occasional and fortuitous visits.[65] The total income of the Petersburg Committee from May 1 to December 1, 1915 was 2,417.79 rubles[66]—some $435 for seven months!

Reading the memoirs of participants, one is again and again re-minded how far the actual Bolshevik party differed from the image produced by later Stalinist historians and apologetics. It was noth-ing like a centralized, well-administered, united party. In fact, it was composed of a large number of small groups, some loosely federated, but most of them cut off from each other and from Lenin abroad. Each local committee had to develop an independent ability for political action, an ability that was of momentous im-portance during the months of the revolution.

The rising influence of Bolshevism

The Bolsheviks played a crucial role in the mounting working-class activity during the war. Thus a police report of the time as-cribed the change in the mood of the masses to the activities of the "Leninists." It reported that this agitation, which was strongest in the capital, led to the formation of secret cells in the local factories and works, to the holding of meetings and unauthorized gather-ings, and to partial strikes. At the end of August 1915, the workers of the Putilov factory presented the management with a number of economic and political demands. The latter were liberation of the five Bolshevik members of the Duma deported to Siberia in Febru-ary 1915, universal suffrage, freedom of the press, and an exten-sion of the session of the State Duma. According to the report, these demands were backed up by a go-slow strike.[67]

On the anniversary of the 1905 Revolution, on January 9, 1916, as we mentioned earlier, one hundred thousand workers went on strike in Petersburg. The initiative came from the Vyborg district. There were demonstrations in which the soldiers greeted the demon-strators from lorries with shouts of "Hurrah!" But in general the sol-diers were not allowed out of their barracks; the guards there and at the telephone exchanges were reinforced; the soldiers who remained in their barracks told those who went on patrol not to shoot. The demonstrations were repeated the next day, and there was a joint demonstration in the Vyborg district at 6 p.m., with soldiers carrying a red flag. Up to January 9 there had been a total of six hundred ar-rests in all.[68]

In February a new wave of strikes took place in the Putilov works, followed by a three-day lockout. To the workers' demand for a 70 percent wage increase were added political slogans, among them: "Down with the Romanov monarchy," "Down with the war."

A police report blames the "Leninists" for turning the strikers at the Putilov works away from economic demands to political ones.

It is clear that the reasons for the strike were purely economic and that they would probably have remained so, had the revolutionary element not intervened in this case.

The leading "Leninist" group, which calls itself the "Petersburg Committee of the Social Democratic Workers' Party" considers all economic action on the part of the working masses untimely at the present moment and opposes the workers' unorganized attempts to express their discontent with the difficult economic living conditions in individual industrial enterprises. This group remains faithful, however, to the plans and aims of its underground leaders, who are always keen to use large social movements for their purposes. This organization tried to make use of the present strike of the Putilov workers to bring nearer the realization of the ultimate ideals of Social Democracy.[69]

With quite justified pride Lenin and Zinoviev could write in August 1915:

By and large, the working class of Russia has proved immune to chauvinism.

The explanation lies in the revolutionary situation in the country and in the Russian proletariat's general conditions of life.

The years 1912–14 marked the beginning of a great new revolutionary upswing in Russia. We again witnessed a great strike movement, the like of which the world has never known. The number involved in the mass revolutionary strike in 1913 was, at the very lowest estimate, one and a half million, and in 1914 it rose to over two million, approaching the 1905 level. The first barricade battles took place in St. Petersburg, on the eve of the war.

The underground Russian Social Democratic Labour Party has performed its duty to the International. The banner of internationalism has not wavered in its hands.[70]

War industry committees

The Bolsheviks were quite ingenious in carrying out their antiwar political activities. They even made use of legal institutions that they utterly opposed, like the War Industry Committees, to make propaganda and build up their influence and organization.

When the war broke out, the industrialist A.I. Guchkov, member of the Octobrist Party, representing the big bourgeoisie (called "Octobrist" because it based itself on the tsar's edict of October 17, 1905 granting Russia a sham constitution) conceived the idea of creating committees to help promote production, especially of war materials. The aim was to get workers' representatives to collaborate with management. While the Mensheviks were in favor of participation in these committees, the Bolsheviks were against it.

Despite the fear expressed by some ministers that the workers' leaders would use the opportunity to develop agitation with the pretext of elections,[71] full preelection discussions and campaigning were allowed, though there were probably attempts to limit the numbers at any one meeting. All the left-wing tendencies, whatever their policy, took advantage of the legal gatherings of workers in open meetings, which were the first since the beginning of the war and seem to have been well attended.

The Petersburg Bolsheviks made full use of the meetings and discussions to present in a coherent way their reasons for not wishing to participate in the elections or in any activity of the War Industry Committees. Their activity and propaganda on the issue amounted to a significant campaign, with the production of several leaflets, the public appearance of committee members, and an opportunity to get Bolshevik resolutions passed in many factories. There were not many occasions during the war when the Bolsheviks could present themselves so openly—usually their comments were restricted to leaflets thrust into the hands of workers; the War Industry Committee campaign remained a high spot in their activity and one that they regarded as basically successful.

The elections to the War Industry Committees were held in two stages. In the first, every factory with five hundred workers or more elected a delegate for every one thousand employees. In the second, the delegates selected ten men to represent them in the Central War Industry Committees. The Mensheviks supported participation in both stages of the elections. The Bolsheviks favored taking part in the primary elections but boycotting the second stage. Instead of participating in the second stage, they proposed to proclaim their program.

One of the first moves of the Petersburg Committee was to produce a *nakaz,* or set of instructions, for adoption at factory meetings. Delegates to the elections to the committees could then be mandated with this nakaz.[72] This was probably a good tactical move, for it gave Bolshevik orators a focal point around which to work and provided a way of uniting opposition and directing negative criticism. The nakaz was duplicated in the form of a leaflet of substantial length and explained in fairly complex terms what the war was about, who benefited from it, and who suffered, stressing that the working class of any country must always remember that "the enemy of every people was in its own country."[73] The first task in Russia was to establish a democratic republic to sweep away the remains of feudalism and pave the way for socialism. As things were, however, there could be no question of participating in the War Industry Committees. To do so would be no less than a betrayal of the working class.

This nakaz was adopted at the Staryi, Lessner, and Erikson factories, among others.[74] Similar resolutions were passed at Novy Lessner, Putilov, and other factories, again clearly condemning the war as purely in the interests of the capitalists and reminding the workers of the arrest of their representatives in the Duma.[75]

The first meeting of the electors took place on September 27, 1915. It started at noon and went on until after 1 a.m., with no break for a meal, and proved to be a very turbulent meeting, the tension increasing with every speaker.[76] Out of 218 representatives elected from among more than 250,000 workers, 177 were present.[77] There was obviously a good deal of support for the Bolshevik position. Lenin's sister Anna wrote to him a few days later that a solid majority of Bolsheviks were present.[78]

The voting figures demonstrated the support the Bolsheviks had managed to enlist and indicated that their previous campaigning must have been quite thorough. The long Petersburg Committee nakaz was adopted in full as a resolution from the meeting, which then voted 95 to 81 against participation in the War Industry Committees.[79]

In the first round, therefore, the Bolsheviks had successfully turned enough delegates against the War Industry Committees to bring the elections to an end. The fact that the workers' delegates in the capital had rejected the committees was bound to affect elections in other parts of the country. This must have been one of the government's reasons for holding no preelection meetings in Moscow and allowing no time for campaigning. In Moscow the elections were carried out without any speeches being made—the committees could not risk a similar debacle.

In Petersburg, however, the Central War Industry Committee was not ready to accept the first election results as final and decided to hold new elections on November 29. The police were much more active in arresting Bolsheviks. No time was allowed for campaigning. No preelection meetings were held. After the elections, at a meeting with 153 delegates, the Bolsheviks read out their declaration, condemning these second elections as a distortion of the will of the Petersburg workers, and stating once again that the Petersburg proletariat would not participate in any institution aiming to maintain the monarchy with the blood of the workers and peasants. At the end, two-thirds of the delegates left in protest.*

The policy of the Bolsheviks on the War Industry Committees contrasted very sharply with that of the Menshevik leaders. In June 1916, the labor group of the Central War Industries Committee published a statement of its opinions, in which it declared that it was a malignant calumny to accuse the group of secretly harboring defeatist ideas; they would not have entered the War Industry Committees if they had not been partisans of an active war policy. The fact of their taking part in the work of the committees was understood by everyone to mean that the Russian workers had decided to take part in the work of national defense. The labor group in the Moscow committee made a similar statement: "Our country is going through hard times," they wrote,

> ...[F]ifteen of our provinces are occupied by the enemy; millions of old men, women, and children are without a roof over their heads, wandering homeless over the country. Many men have been killed by the enemy and their wives are dying of hunger. In these circumstances the working class has risen to defend its country. To supply the army with all its needs, to organize the civil population, to save the economic forces of the nation from disintegration, a great effort is needed and all the nation's energy must be rallied. Its initiative and capacity for self-help must be given free play."

In conclusion

History conclusively confirmed Lenin's statement of March 1915:

> About forty thousand workers have been buying *Pravda*; far more read it. Even if war, prison, Siberia, and hard labor should destroy five or even ten times as many—this section of the workers *cannot* be annihilated. It is alive. It is imbued with the revolutionary spirit, is anti-chauvinist. It *alone* stands in the midst of the masses, with deep roots in the latter, as the champion of the internationalism of the toilers, the exploited, and the oppressed. It *alone* has held its ground in the general débacle. It alone is leading the semi-proletarian elements *away* from...social chauvinism ... *towards* socialism.[81]

The prominent Petrograd Bolshevik trade unionist Pavel Budaev

---

* *Sotsial-Demokrat* printed some of the resolutions and declarations adopted and gave the nakaz in full in No. 51. If the paper managed to reach other industrial cities these accounts must have been very useful, for workers in the provinces would otherwise know little or nothing of what was happening in the capital. News of the second set of elections did not appear until April 13, 1916 (No. 53), in a letter signed A.B. (Shliapnikov).

described the situation in March 1916 as being at boiling point. Among the printers, nine enterprises were at a standstill because of a strike. Estonian Social Democratic organizations had made contact with organizations in other towns. Leaflets were appearing in Petrograd all the time, and some had been received from Narva.[82]

We can sum up by saying that the war at first set Bolshevism back, but only to accelerate its growth even more powerfully in the ensuing period, and to prepare it for its final victory.

CHAPTER 3

LENIN AND THE
NATIONAL QUESTION

The imperialist war, a war for the division and redivision of the world among the great powers, conferred a central importance on the national question, the question of relations between the oppressed nations and their oppressors. Lenin, the theoretician-practitioner, therefore found it necessary to devote much time and effort to his study of this question.

The national question was of exceptional significance in two countries of prewar Europe—in tsarist Russia, where 57 percent of the population belonged to national minorities, and in the Hapsburg Austrian-Hungarian Empire. The latter had within its borders several large minority groups—Czechs, Poles, Ukrainians, Italians, Serbians, Croatians, Rumanians, besides the dominant Germans and Hungarians. The Austrian socialists were more concerned than socialists elsewhere with discussions of the national question, and to elaborate a program on it. This they started doing after their conference in Bruenn, held in 1899.

In March 1912, Lenin moved to Polish Kracow. This sharpened his sensitivity to the national question. He plunged into a new and extensive study of the problem of nationalities. Another factor also served to increase his interest: the Balkan war and the general intensification of nationalism that presaged the coming world war. Kracow itself was an area where one of the most bitter struggles was waged over the policy regarding the national question, between the Polish Socialist Party of Joseph Pilsudski and the Polish Social Democratic Party of Rosa Luxemburg.

Austrian socialists and the national question

Lenin's move to Austria also shocked him into a clearer realization of the fundamental difference between the accepted policies on the national question of the Austrian socialists and his Russian colleagues. And now, on the eve of the war, the Austrian policy was gaining new adherents in Russia.

Without exception, the delegates to the Bruenn Congress had agreed on the basic principle that the equality of all nationalities within the empire constituted "primarily a cultural demand." The only point on which disagreement existed regarded the ways of satisfying this cultural demand. Two were possible. One consisted in fighting for the *territorial autonomy* of all Austro-Hungarian peoples in cultural and linguistic matters. The other was to seek to establish national-cultural equality and autonomy on a purely *personal, nonterritorial basis.* The former alternative was put forward by the national executive committee of the Austrian Socialist Party. The committee put a resolution to the congress, proposing that the Austrian Empire should be transformed into a democratic federation of nationalities along the following lines: (1) cultural and linguistic autonomy of each nationality within the empire, on a regional basis; (2) federation of all districts of a given nationality into a higher national-cultural body; (3) special laws for the protection of minorities that could not be territorially defined.[1]

The South Slav section of the Social Democratic Party of Austria, on the other hand, proposed that national-cultural autonomy should not be bound by any territorial considerations, but that every citizen should be part of a culturally and linguistically autonomous nation, even if lacking a common territory with fellow nationals.[2] This proposal was intended to forestall any rivalries and hostilities that might arise during an attempt to delimit the various regions, in areas where dozens of different nationalities lived closely together, in small enclaves. After some discussion, however, the congress adopted the resolution of the Central Committee. The latter's rapporteur, Seliger, stated hopefully that the decentralization of Austria would put an end to all national discord within the empire, just as the national-federal organization of the Socialist Party was eliminating all division between workers of different origins.[3]

In reality, the relations between the national sections inside Austrian Social Democracy left much to be desired. Bitter quarrels took place between Czech and German-Austrian workers a few years after the Bruenn Congress.[4] National enmity was also fanned by the reorganization of the Austrian party along national lines.

The ideas of the Austrian socialists on the national question did find a response in Russia, first of all among the Jewish socialists organized in the Bund. The Fourth Congress of the Bund, held in 1901, adopted a general statement in favor of the ideas advanced by the South Slav delegation at Bruenn: "The concept of nationality is also applicable to the Jewish people. Russia...must in the future be transformed into a federation of nationalities, with full national autonomy for each, regardless of the territory which it inhabits."

Carrying this thesis further, the Bund demanded that Russian Social Democracy, with which it was affiliated, recognize the Bund as the organization representing the Jewish proletariat in Russia, and consequently grant it the status of a "federal" unit within the party. This request was turned down at the Second Congress of the Russian Social Democratic Labor Party (1903), and, in protest, the Bund left the congress and the Russian party.[5]

From the Bund, the idea of extraterritorial autonomy spread to the Armenian Dashnaktsutiun, the Belorussian Socialist Hromada, and the Georgian Socialist Federalist Party, Sakartvelo, all of which adopted it as supplementary to territorial national autonomy. In 1907, those minority socialist parties met at a special conference at which the majority of the delegates expressed strong support for the Austrian proposal.[6]

At the August 1912 Menshevik conference held in Vienna, which formed the so-called August Bloc, the national question was discussed. A number of the Russian leaders participated—Martov, Axelrod, Trotsky, and others. But the majority of the delegates came from the ranks of the non-Russian Social Democratic parties: the Jewish Bund, the Latvian Social Democratic Party, the Caucasian parties, and representatives of the Polish Socialist Party and the Lithuanian Social Democratic Party. The conference asserted in its resolution that national-cultural autonomy was not contrary to the party's program. (As a matter of fact, the Menshevik Party incorporated national-cultural autonomy into its program in 1917.)

Until Lenin moved to Austrian Poland in 1912, his polemics on the national question had been almost exclusively with the Bund. Now he had to spread his attack much wider.

Lenin opposes the policy on national-cultural autonomy

The central theme of the Austrian Marxists' position on the national question was adaptation to the status quo: how to solve the national question within the framework of the existing Hapsburg

Empire, rather than how to use the rebellion of the oppressed nations to destroy the empire.

The main Austrian theoretician on the national question was Otto Bauer.

Lenin, like Bauer, came from a multinational empire. However, Lenin did not look for a peaceful and reformist solution to the national problem. The Bolsheviks based their program on the complete destruction of tsarism through a violent revolution. Therefore they refused to regard the national question as something that could be settled by constitutional means. Lenin was conscious of the fact that the nationalist stirrings among the minorities in Russia constituted a very potent revolutionary force, which the socialists should try to harness to their cause.

The doctrine of national cultural autonomy was particularly offensive to Lenin because it implied a *federalist and decentralized* reorganization of the socialist party. Multinational empires should indeed be split apart, he argued, but the proletariat must nevertheless preserve the tightest, most centralized international unity. To smash a centralized tsarist empire, a centralized revolutionary organization was needed.

> It is clear as daylight [Lenin wrote] that the advocacy of such a plan [of "cultural national autonomy"] means, *in fact,* pursuing or supporting the ideas of bourgeois nationalism, chauvinism and clericalism. The interests of democracy in general, and the interests of the working class in particular, demand the very opposite. We must strive to secure the *mixing* of the children of *all* nationalities in *uniform* schools in each locality.... We must most emphatically oppose segregating the schools according to nationality, no matter what form it may take.
>
> It is not our business to segregate the nations in matters of education in any way; on the contrary, we must strive to create the fundamental democratic conditions for the peaceful coexistence of the nations on the basis of equal rights. We must not champion "national culture," but expose the clerical and bourgeois character of this slogan in the name of the international culture of the world working-class movement.
>
> To preach the establishment of special national schools for every "national culture" is reactionary. But under real democracy it is quite possible to ensure instruction in the native language, in native history, and so forth, *without* splitting up the schools according to nationality....
>
> Advocacy of impracticable cultural-national autonomy is an absurdity, which now already is only disuniting the workers ideologically. To advocate the amalgamation of the workers of all nationalities means facilitating the success of proletarian class solidarity, which will guarantee equal rights for, and maximum peaceful coexistence of, all nationalities.[7]

The Austrian Socialist leaders were both destroying the unity of the proletariat and preserving the unity of the Austro-Hungarian Empire because they did not uphold the right of oppressed nations to self-determination.

Lenin, however, had to contend not only with the ideas on the national question of the Austrian leaders who stood on his right, but also with Marxists on the extreme left. First and foremost among these was Rosa Luxemburg.

Rosa Luxemburg's position on the national question

Quite early in her political life, Rosa Luxemburg pointed out that the situation in Europe in general, and in Russia in particular, had changed so much towards the end of the nineteenth century that the attitude of Marx and Engels towards national movements in Europe had become untenable. For them, tsarism was the citadel of reaction, in opposition to which the national movements played a progressive role.

In Western and Central Europe, the period of bourgeois democratic revolutions had passed. The Prussian Junkers had managed to establish their rule so firmly that they no longer needed aid from the tsar. At the same time tsarist rule had ceased to be the impregnable bastion of reaction; deep cracks were beginning to appear in its walls: the mass strikes of workers in Warsaw, Lodz, Petrograd, Moscow, and elsewhere in the Russian Empire; the rebellious awakening of the peasants. In fact, whereas at the time of Marx and Engels the center of revolution was in Western and Central Europe, now, towards the end of the nineteenth century and at the beginning of the twentieth, it had passed east to Russia. Whereas at the time of Marx, tsarism was the main force employed to suppress revolutionary uprisings elsewhere, it now itself needed the help (mainly financial) of the Western capitalist powers. Instead of Russian bullets and rubles traveling westwards, now German, French, British, and Belgian munitions and money flowed in a growing stream to Russia. Rosa Luxemburg pointed out, further, that basic changes had taken place as regards the national aspirations of her motherland, Poland. Whereas at the time of Marx and Engels, the Polish nobles were leaders of the national movement, now, with increasing capitalist developments in the country, they were losing ground socially, and turning to tsarism as an ally in the suppression of progressive movements in Poland. The result was that the Polish nobility had cooled towards aspirations for national independence. The bourgeoisie also became antagonistic to the desire for national independence, as it found the main markets for its industry in Russia: "Poland is bound to Russia with chains of gold," Rosa Luxemburg said. "Not the national state but the state of rapine, corresponds to capitalist development."[8]

The Polish working class, too, according to Rosa Luxemburg, did not support the separation of Poland from Russia, as they saw in Moscow and Petrograd the allies of Warsaw and Lodz. Hence there were no social forces of any weight in Poland interested in fighting for national independence. Only the intelligentsia still cherished the idea, but by themselves they represented a minor influence. Rosa Luxemburg concluded her analysis of the social forces in Poland and their attitude to the national question with the following words: "The recognizable direction of social development has made it clear to me that there is no social class in Poland that has at one and the same time both an interest in and ability to achieve the restoration of Poland."[9]

From this analysis, she came to the conclusion that under capitalism the slogan of national independence had no progressive value and could not be realized by the internal forces of the Polish nation; only the intervention of an imperialist power could bring it into being. Under socialism, argued Rosa Luxemburg, there would be no place for the slogan of national independence, as national oppression would no longer exist, and the international unity of humanity would have been realized. Thus under capitalism, the real independence of Poland could not be realized, and steps in that direction would not have any progressive value, while under socialism, such a slogan would be superfluous. Hence the working class had no need to struggle for the national self-determination of Poland, and this struggle was in fact reactionary. The national slogans of the working class should be limited to the demand for national autonomy in cultural life.

In taking this position, Rosa Luxemburg and her party, the SDKPL, came into bitter conflict with the right-wing members of the Polish Socialist Party (PPS) led by Pilsudski (the future military dictator of Poland). These were nationalists who paid lip service to socialism. Lacking a mass basis for their nationalism, they contrived adventures, plotting with foreign powers even to the extent of relying on a future world war as the midwife of national independence. In Galicia, the stronghold of the right-wing PPS, the Poles, under Austrian rule, received better treatment than those in the Russian Empire, mainly because the rulers of the Hapsburg Empire, a medley of nationalities, had to rely on the Polish ruling class to fortify their imperial rule. The PPS leaders were therefore inclined to prefer the Hapsburg Empire to the Russian, and during the First World War acted as recruiting agents for Vienna and Berlin. Earlier, during the 1905 Revolution, Daszynski, the leader of the PPS in Galicia, had gone so far as to condemn the mass strikes of Polish workers, because, according to him, they tended to identify the struggle of the Polish workers with that of the Russian, and thus to undermine Polish national unity. It is only with a clear view of Rosa Luxemburg's opponents in the Polish labor movement that one can properly understand her position on the Polish national question.

The struggle that she had to wage against the chauvinistic PPS colored her entire attitude to the national question in general. In opposing the nationalism of the PPS she bent so far backwards that she opposed all reference to the right of self-determination in the program of the party. It was for this reason that her party, the SDKPL, split as early as 1903 from the Russian Social Democratic Party.

Bukharin, Piatakov, and Radek

In 1915, the Bolshevik leaders N.I. Bukharin and G.L. Piatakov and the Polish fellow-traveler of the Bolsheviks, Karl Radek, also came out against "the right of nations to self-determination." To quote from the *Theses and Program of the Bukharin-Piatakov Group*, November 1915 (*Theses on the Right of Self-Determination*):

> The slogan of "self-determination of nations" is first of all *Utopian* (it cannot be realized *within the limits* of capitalism) and *harmful* as a slogan which *disseminates illusions*. In this respect it does not differ at all from the slogans of the courts of arbitration, of disarmament, etc., which presuppose the possibility of so-called "peaceful capitalism".... If we advance the slogan of "self-determination" for struggle against "the chauvinism of the working masses," then we act in the same way as when we (like Kautsky) advance the slogan of "disarmament" as a method of struggle against militarism. In both cases the error consists in a one-sided examination of the question, in an omission of the specific gravity of a given "social evil"; in other words, it is a purely rational-Utopian and not revolutionary-dialectical examination of the question....
>
> To struggle against the chauvinism of the working masses of a great power by means of the recognition of the right of nations for self-determination, is equivalent to struggling against this chauvinism by means of the recognition of the right of the oppressed "fatherland" to defend itself.[10]

Lenin was thus forced to fight not only against the right—the

Austrian socialist leaders' policies on the national question—but also against the left, against Rosa Luxemburg and the left communists.

Lenin polemicizes with Luxemburg, Bukharin, Piatakov, and Radek

Lenin spent much of the two years preceding the outbreak of the war engaging in sharp polemics against the followers of Otto Bauer. Thereafter, during the first two years of the war itself, he turned his fire against his Bolshevik colleagues who, following in Rosa Luxemburg's footsteps, opposed the right of self-determination from an ultraleft standpoint.

Lenin agreed with Rosa Luxemburg in her opposition to the PPS, and, like her, argued that the duty of the Polish socialists was not to fight for national independence or secession from Russia, but for the international unity of Polish and Russian workers. However, as a member of an oppressing nation, Lenin rightly was wary in case a nihilistic attitude to the national question should provide grist for the mill of Great Russian chauvinism.

> The Polish Social-Democratic comrades have rendered a great historic service by advancing the slogan of internationalism and declaring that the fraternal union of the proletariat of all countries is of supreme importance to them and that they will never go to war for the liberation of Poland. This is to their credit, and this is why we have always regarded only these Polish Social Democrats as socialists. The others are patriots, Polish Plekhanovs. But this peculiar position, when, in order to safeguard socialism, people were forced to struggle against a rabid and morbid nationalism, has produced a strange state of affairs: comrades come to us saying that we must give up the idea of Poland's freedom, her right to secession.
>
> Why should we Great Russians, who have been oppressing more nations than any other people, deny the right to secession for Poland, Ukraine, or Finland?.... [P]eople don't want to understand that to strengthen internationalism you do not have to repeat the same words. What you have to do is to stress, in Russia, the freedom of secession for oppressed nations, and, in Poland, their freedom to unite. Freedom to unite implies freedom to secede. We Russians must emphasize freedom to secede, while the Poles must emphasize freedom to unite.[11]

The differences between Lenin and Luxemburg on the national question may be summarized as follows: while Rosa Luxemburg, influenced by the struggle against Polish nationalism, inclined towards a nihilistic attitude to the national question, Lenin saw realistically that, the positions of oppressed and oppressor nations being different, their attitude to the same question must be different. Thus, starting from different and opposing situations, they moved in opposite directions but reached the same position on international workers' unity. Secondly, while Rosa Luxemburg disposed of the question of national self-determination as incompatible with the class struggle, Lenin subordinated it to the class struggle (in the same way as he took advantage of all other democratic strivings as weapons in the general revolutionary struggle). Thus, dialectically, Lenin combined the struggle of the oppressed nations with the international unity of the proletariat in the struggle for socialism.

When it came to polemicizing with his own colleagues, Lenin was much less charitable than in his polemics with Luxemburg. After all, she belonged to an oppressed nation. She was a leader of Polish socialists; they were members of a Russian party, a party of the oppressing nation.

In his massive essay "The right of nations to self-determination," written in February–May 1914, Lenin wrote:

> The bourgeois nationalism of *any* oppressed nation has a general democratic content that is directed *against* oppression, and it is this content that we *unconditionally* support.[12]

> To accuse those who support freedom of self-determination, i.e., freedom to secede, of encouraging separatism, is as foolish and hypocritical as accusing those who advocate freedom of divorce of encouraging the destruction of family ties. Just as in bourgeois society the defenders of privilege and corruption, on which bourgeois marriage rests, oppose freedom of divorce, so, in the capitalist state, repudiation of the right to self-determination, i.e., the right of nations to secede, means nothing more than defense of the privileges of the dominant nation and police methods of administration, to the detriment of democratic methods.[13]

> Can a nation be free if it oppresses other nations? It cannot. The interests of the freedom of the Great Russian population require a struggle against such oppression. The long, centuries-old history of the suppression of the movements of the oppressed nations, and the systematic propaganda in favor of such suppression coming from the "upper" classes have created enormous obstacles to the cause of freedom of the Great Russian people itself, in the form of prejudices etc.[14]

These sentiments are reiterated in "The discussion on self-determination summed up," written in July 1916:

> In the internationalist education of the workers of the oppressor countries, emphasis must necessarily be laid on their advocating freedom for the oppressed countries to secede and their fighting for it. Without this

there can be *no* internationalism. It is our right and duty to treat every Social Democrat of an oppressor nation who *fails* to conduct such propaganda as a scoundrel and an imperialist. This is an absolute demand, even where the *chance* of secession being possible and "practicable" before the introduction of socialism is only one in a thousand.[15]

Lenin made it clear that the right of national self-determination was part and parcel of a democratic program, that there could be no socialism without democracy. "No Social Democrat will deny—unless he would profess indifference to questions of political freedom and democracy (in which case he is naturally no longer a Social Democrat)"[16]—the need for oppressing nations to support freedom of secession to oppressed nations. "If we do not want to betray socialism we *must* support *every* revolt against our chief enemy, the bourgeoisie of the big states, provided it is not the revolt of a reactionary class."[17]

It was precisely the struggle against national oppression, and the struggle for free secession, that eliminated the barriers of national antagonism between the workers of different countries and made their close and fraternal cooperation possible. The struggle for the right of secession of oppressed nations was identical in Lenin's mind with the struggle for international proletarian solidarity.

He was well aware of the tremendous revolutionary potential of the rebellion of the oppressed nations.

To imagine that social revolution is *conceivable* without revolts by small nations in the colonies and in Europe, without revolutionary outbursts by a section of the petty bourgeoisie *with all its prejudices,* without a movement of the politically non-conscious proletarian and semi-proletarian masses against oppression by the landowners, the church, and the monarchy, against national oppression, etc.—to imagine all this is to *repudiate social revolution.* So one army lines up in one place and says, "We are for socialism," and another, somewhere else, and says, "We are for imperialism," and that will be a social revolution!.... Whoever expects a "pure" social revolution will *never* live to see it. Such a person pays lip-service to revolution without understanding what revolution is. The socialist revolution in Europe *cannot be* anything other than an outburst of mass struggle on the part of all and sundry oppressed and discontented elements. Inevitably, sections of the petty bourgeoisie and of the backward workers will participate in it—without such participation, *mass* struggle is *impossible,* without it *no* revolution is possible—and just as inevitably will they bring into the movement their prejudices, their reactionary fantasies, their weaknesses and errors. But objectively they will attack *capital,* and the class-conscious vanguard of the revolution, the advanced proletariat, expressing this objective truth of a variegated and discordant, motley and outwardly fragmented, mass struggle, will be able to unite and direct it, capture power.... The dialectics of history are such that small nations, powerless as an *independent* factor in the struggle against imperialism, play a part as one of the ferments, one of the bacilli, which help the *real* anti-imperialist force, the socialist proletariat, to make its appearance on the scene.[18]

The social revolution can come only in the form of an epoch in which are combined civil war by the proletariat against the bourgeoisie in the advanced countries and a *whole series* of democratic and revolutionary movements, including the national liberation movement, in the undeveloped, backward and oppressed nations.[19*]

For many years Lenin argued that the national movement was an untapped source of revolutionary potential to weaken and destroy tsarist autocracy. During the world war, he drew the conclusion that it had enormous power to weaken world imperialism. The development of his attitude to the national question in the years 1912 to 1916 was a bridge between his break with Narodism in his youth[21] and his formation of the Communist International with its anti-imperialist policy after the war.

Given Lenin's belief in the revolutionary potential of the peasantry and the need of the proletariat to win the peasants as its allies, it followed naturally to emphasize the revolutionary potential of the national movements in oppressed nations, where the overwhelming majority of the population were peasants.

His thinking in the early 1890s already contained in embryo the central themes of his further theoretical development: the relentless opposition to the liberal bourgeoisie, the hegemony of the proletariat over the peasantry, and the alliance of the proletariat of the industrial countries with the national liberation movements in the colonies. His position on the national question on the eve of the world war and during it were only a step removed from the development of this position and that of the Comintern at its Second and Third Congresses (1920, 1921). But this reflection takes the story too far ahead.

In recognition of the importance of the national struggle, Lenin even sanctioned the modification of the *Communist Manifesto*'s central exhortation to read "Workers of all countries and all oppressed peoples, unite!"[22]

---

* It seems that many of the leading comrades in Russia did not understand why Lenin was so vehement in his opposition to Bukharin and his associates, as can be seen clearly from what Anna, Lenin's sister, wrote to him about the support she received for her position from Shliapnikov.[20] Both Anna and Shliapnikov insisted that Lenin should build links with Bukharin and Co. around the magazine *Kommunist*, of which they thought very highly.

CHAPTER 4

IMPERIALISM,
THE HIGHEST STAGE OF CAPITALISM

Lenin was convinced that one could not make a correct political appraisal of the war without making clear the essence of imperialism in both its economic and political aspects. A theoretical understanding of imperialism was necessary for consistent political practice during the war. He therefore spent six months of very intensive research (January–June 1916) in writing a short book called *Imperialism: The Highest Stage of Capitalism*. Although it was written with an eye to the tsarist censor, and therefore was phrased with extreme caution, using "that accursed Aesopian language," it did not see the light of day until the middle of 1917—after the February Revolution.

This little book is packed with a vast amount of data. Lenin quotes extensively from bourgeois economists to prove the incontrovertible facts of the nature of modern capitalism. He starts by describing the principal economic features of modern imperialism. In summing up, he lists the following five characteristics of the system:

(1) the concentration of production and capital has developed to such a high stage that it has created monopolies which play a decisive role in economic life; (2) the merging of bank capital with industrial capital, and the creation, on the basis of this "finance capital," of a financial oligarchy; (3) the export of capital as distinguished from the export of commodities acquires exceptional importance; (4) the formation of international monopolist capitalist associations which share the world among themselves; and (5) the territorial division of the whole world among the biggest capitalist powers is completed. Imperialism is capitalism at that stage of development at which the dominance of monopolies and finance capital is established; in which the export of capital has acquired pronounced importance; in which the division of the world among the international trusts has begun, in which the division of all terri-

tories of the globe among the biggest capitalist powers has been completed.[1]

One characteristic feature of capitalism today, Lenin argues, is its parasitism and decay,

> the extraordinary growth of a class, or rather, of a stratum of rentiers, i.e., people who live by "clipping coupons," who take no part in any enterprise whatever, whose profession is idleness. The export of capital, one of the most essential economic bases of imperialism, still more completely isolates the rentiers from production and sets the seal of parasitism on the whole country that lives by exploiting the labor of several overseas countries and colonies.[2]

This sums up the purely economic features of imperialism. Lenin then points out the historical place of this stage of capitalism in relation to capitalism in general, and to the socialism of the future. He writes: "We have seen that in its economic essence imperialism is monopoly capitalism. This in itself determines its place in history, for monopoly that grows out of the soil of free competition, and precisely out of free competition, is the transition from the capitalist system to a higher socio-economic order."[3] Imperialism must be defined as capitalism in transition, or, more precisely, as moribund capitalism.[4]

He goes on to define the relation between imperialism on the one hand and opportunism and social chauvinism in the labor movement on the other.

> Imperialism, which means the partitioning of the world...which means high monopoly profits for a handful of very rich countries, makes it economically possible to bribe the upper strata of the proletariat, and thereby fosters, gives shape to, and strengthens opportunism.[5]

> The receipt of high monopoly profits by the capitalists in one of the numerous branches of industry, in one of the numerous countries, etc., makes it economically possible for them to bribe certain sections of the workers, and for a time a fairly considerable minority of them, and win them to the side of the bourgeoisie of a given industry or given nation against all the others.... And so there is created...[a] bond between imperialism and opportunism.[6]

> This stratum of workers-turned-bourgeois, or the labor aristocracy, who are quite philistine in their mode of life, in the size of their earnings, and in their entire outlook, is the principal prop of the Second International, and in our days, the principal *social* (not military) *prop of the bourgeoisie.* For they are the real *agents of the bourgeoisie in the working-class* movement, the labor lieutenants of the capitalist class, real vehicles of reformism and chauvinism.[7]

The fight against imperialism is a sham and humbug unless it is inseparably bound up with the fight against opportunism.[8]

The last chapter of the book is devoted to a crushing criticism of Kautsky's liberal glossing of modern capitalism—"ultra-imperialism"—the belief that modern capitalism may lead to the world unity of the capitalists and hence to the banishing of wars. Contrary to Kautsky's notion that the international cartels could represent a force for peace, Lenin argues that they are marked by a particular balance of forces between the monopolies; when the balance changes then renewed struggle along national lines must replace the agreements peacefully to divide the world market.[9]

The need to defend Lenin from his admirers

As a result of the Stalinist cult of Lenin, almost canonical authority was invested in this short book, despite the fact that Lenin himself referred to it again and again as a pamphlet, and that its subtitle was "A Popular Outline." He did not claim to have written an original work, but, as he readily acknowledged, was very much in debt to the works of the British Liberal John A. Hobson, author of *Imperialism,* and the Austrian Marxist Rudolf Hilferding, author of *Das Finanzkapital,* subtitled *A Study of the Latest Phase of Capitalist Development.*

To say that Lenin wrote a popular pamphlet does not mean that he did not work hard on it, researching for it very extensively. On the contrary. *The Notebooks on Imperialism* are a massive 739 pages, as against the short pamphlet he produced; he read and annotated 148 books and 232 articles.[10]

The book was brief and the majority of it was devoted to summarizing supporting information. The impact of the facts and figures and condensed theoretical points is very powerful simply because Lenin's aim was very much narrower than that of his Marxist contemporaries who dealt with the same subject—Hilferding, Rosa Luxemburg, Nikolai Bukharin—and whose writings are of much more generalized theoretical interest. To grasp the meaning of Lenin's book, unlike that of, let us say, Rosa Luxemburg's (*The Accumulation of Capital*) or Hilferding's, one does not have to be familiar with Marxist economic writings.

Lenin did not claim to have worked out a complete theory of imperialism in his book. The fact that it did not have the breadth of analysis of Luxemburg's or Hilferding's—the fact, for instance, that the problem of the decline of the rate of profit and the problem of the realization of surplus value, which for Rosa Luxemburg became so central, are not even mentioned in Lenin's booklet—is not accidental.* To the extent that Lenin dealt with the economy, he was much more interested in the *effects* of modern capitalism, and with the practical lessons the workers' movement had to draw from the changes in modern capitalism.

How much Lenin's *Imperialism* owed to the people who had studied modern capitalism a short time before—above all Hobson and Hilferding—is clear from reading the writings of these people. But even more directly than this, Lenin owed a great deal to Bukharin, his young colleague in the leadership of the Bolshevik Party. In his Testament (December 23–24, 1922) Lenin called Bukharin the "biggest theoretician" of the Bolshevik Party. And without doubt Bukharin was the most versatile and well-read economist among the Bolsheviks. In 1915 he wrote a book called *Imperialism and World Economy,* to which Lenin wrote an introduction in December. The manuscript of Bukharin's book was therefore in Lenin's hands before Lenin worked on his *Imperialism.* A comparison of the two books shows that: (1) in terms of the actual description of modern capitalism Lenin is not original at all and borrows practically everything from Bukharin, and (2) the difference between the two books is radical—a difference between a theoretical treatise on imperialism and a political pamphlet on the same subject.

Lenin's book was intended mainly to be an important political tract in a political battle. The tools he mobilized were just sufficient for his purpose, no more and no less. It aimed to make workers clear about the nature of the period in which they lived, and the tasks facing them. Lenin related the economic theories of imperialism to the basic political problems of the epoch, by making the economics a

---

* For a specific criticism of Lenin's theory of imperialism see M. Kidron, "Imperialism, highest stage but one," in *Capitalism and Theory*, London 1974, where it is argued that the concept of finance capital as borrowed from Hilferding describes economic conditions peculiar to Germany where the banks were massively involved in industrial financing and wielded great power over their clients (in Britain, the United States, and France the role of the banks in financing industry was incomparably smaller). Kidron makes a comparison between Lenin's time and our own in regard to the role of capital exports—their direction, etc.

See also T. Cliff, "Economic roots of reformism," in *Socialist Review*, 1965, where Lenin's theory of the labor aristocracy is criticized as not compatible with actual historical data about the wages and conditions of the working class in imperialist countries. We shall return to this problem and elaborate on it in the next volume, when we deal with the Communist International.

guideline for concrete action. The concentration of capital leading to monopolies and the division of the world between the imperialist powers led inevitably to wars. The general imperialist war, by engulfing millions of workers, relentlessly posed the harsh alternatives before the proletariat, not as war and peace, but as imperialist war or civil war against imperialism. Therefore real internationalism was inevitably rooted in revolutionary struggle against imperialism; no internationalism was compatible with reformism. Monopoly capitalism, by harshly exploiting the colonial peoples, and by pulling all nations into the orbit of the world economy, forced the oppressed nation to fight for its national independence, a fight that was becoming crucial to the fate of world imperialism.

To Marxists in the colonial countries—the worst victims of imperialism—Lenin's book has been a powerful weapon of struggle.

CHAPTER 5

CRISIS AND COLLAPSE OF THE TSARIST REGIME

Rulers in disarray

Lenin's prediction that the imperialist war, by exacerbating the internal contradictions of capitalism, would lead to civil war was largely based on the experience of 1904–05. Then the military defeat of tsarism by Japan had led directly to the first Russian revolution. Now the imperialist war was on a much wider scale. The revolutionary repercussions must therefore be greater.

During the war years, the ruling classes in Russia experienced increasing failures of confidence, a decline in morale, and growing splits in their ranks. Leadership crises eroded tsarism and the leading circles of society.

Among the symptoms of a revolutionary situation, Lenin pointed to the following:

> when it is impossible for the ruling classes to maintain their rule without any change; when there is a crisis, in one form or another, among the "upper classes," a crisis in the policy of the ruling class, leading to a fissure through which the discontent and indignation of the oppressed classes burst forth. For a revolution to take place, it is not usually sufficient for the "lower classes not to want" to live in the old way; it is also necessary that "the upper classes should be unable" to live in the old way.[1]

The deeper the general crisis, the more different sections of the ruling class came into conflict with each other. The general hostility of the mass of the people towards the regime led groups within the ruling class to quarrel with each other and with the government, increasing the general hatred felt by the state bureaucracy towards the court coterie. The more isolated the tsar became, the more he sacrificed one minister after another in the hope of avoiding catastrophe.

One historian, Cherniavsky, described the mood among ruling circles during 1915–16 as follows:

> growing awareness of catastrophe; the spread of this awareness, conscious and sometimes unconscious, throughout the government, the educated, and the social elite as a whole; and the resulting paralysis, the inability to decide and to act...overtakes the government.[2]

Commenting on the minutes of the Council of Ministers during August–September 1915, the same historian said: "The...minutes of the Council of Ministers illustrate the psychological precondition of revolution in *the government,* in *the ruling class*—in those who feared and hated revolution, who wished to prevent it in any way possible, and yet did nothing but wait for it."[3] Another historian, V.I. Gessen, could write about the same minutes: "The government had gone on strike. Long ago, while it was officially all-powerful, it had ceased to doubt that the crash would come, sooner or later."[4]

V.I. Gurko, the loyal monarchist deputy minister of the interior, wrote a few years after the revolution: "Every revolution begins at the top: and our government had succeeded in transforming the most loyal elements of the country into critics, if not of the regime, then at any rate of those at its head and of their administrative methods."[5] Cliques around the tsar became of greater and greater significance. The Council of Ministers as a whole declined continually in importance.

One example will show clearly how little the government acted as a *collective,* how little ministers knew about the plans, or the people, formally under their supervision: the case of the military authority's decision to organize a mass evacuation of Kiev in July–August 1915.

One might assume that the war minister or the minister of the interior would have been involved in reaching this decision, or would at least have been consulted about the action. But not so. The minister of war, A.A. Polivanov, said about the evacuation, at a meeting of the Council of Ministers on August 19, 1915:

> The plans and intentions of headquarters are unknown to me, as it is considered unnecessary to keep the Minister of War informed of the course of events. But insofar as it is possible for me to think on military matters, I am convinced that there is no direct danger to Kiev and that...the evacuation [is] to say the least, premature.[6]

The minister of the interior, Prince Shcherbatov, commented:

> In general, what is going on with evacuation is simply unbelievable.

The military authorities have completely lost their heads and all their common sense. Chaos and disorder are created everywhere, as if on purpose. All local life is being turned upside down. It is really, finally, necessary to take some measures to regularize the relations between military and civil authorities. It is impossible, in such an extraordinarily complicated matter as evacuation, which touches all our existence deeply, to concentrate all dispositions in the hands of the military. They're utterly ignorant of the situation in the central provinces, and yet they direct waves of refugees according to their whim.[7]

The minister of foreign affairs, S.D. Sazonov, said:

This whole story outrages me profoundly. The Minister of War expresses the opinion that there is no danger threatening Kiev, while the bewildered gentlemen generals want to evacuate it, to abandon it to Austrian abuse. I can imagine the impression on our allies, when they find out about the abandonment of Kiev, the center of an enormous grain-growing region.[8]

Commenting on August 24 on the same evacuation, A.V. Krivoshein, acting minister of agriculture, said:

Historians will not believe it, that Russia conducted the war blindly and hence came to the edge of ruin—that millions of men were unconsciously sacrificed for the arrogance of some and the criminality of others. What is going on at headquarters is a universal outrage and horror.[9]

The nature of the relations prevailing between the ministers and the head of the government becomes clear from a snippet of conversation at the Council of Ministers' meeting on September 2, 1915, about the dissolution of the Duma:

A.V. Krivoshein: All our discussion today has shown, with great clarity, Ivan Longinovich (Goremykin) [the premier], that the difference between you and the majority of the Council of Ministers, respecting our views of the situation and on the course of policy, has become greater than ever recently. You have reported on this difference to His Majesty the Emperor; but His Majesty deigns to agree with your point of view and not with ours.... Forgive me this one question: How dare you act when [even] the members of the government are convinced of the need for other methods, when the whole government apparatus which is in your hands is in opposition, when both external and internal circumstances are becoming more and more threatening every day?

I.L. Goremykin: I will fulfill my duty to His Majesty the Emperor to the very end, no matter what opposition and lack of sympathy I encounter....

S.D. Sazonov: Tomorrow blood will flow in the streets and Russia will sink into the abyss! Why? For what? It is all so terrible! In any event, I want to declare out loud that, under the present circum-

stances, I do not take on myself the responsibility for your acts....
    I.L. Goremykin: I bear the responsibility for my acts and I am not
asking anyone to share it with me.[10]

No wonder the chronicler of the minutes could write in his introduction to them: "If one is to judge the state of affairs by the
conversations of the Council, then, instead of writing history, one
will soon be hung from a lamppost."[11]
    In desperation, Krivoshein said on August 19, 1915:

The report of the minister of internal affairs [Shcherbatov] has
shaken me deeply.... We must tell His Majesty that the internal situation, as it exists...allows of only two solutions: either a strong military dictatorship, if one can find a suitable person, or reconciliation
with the public. Our Cabinet does not correspond to public hopes
and demands, and it must give way to another in which the country
can believe. To delay, to continue to hold on in the middle and bide
our time is impossible.... I hesitated for a long time before I finally
came to such a conclusion, but right now every day is like a year. The
situation is changing with dizzying speed. From all sides, one is
forced to listen to the grimmest prediction (of what will happen) if no
decisive steps are taken.[12]

Unfortunately this is exactly what the tsar was unable to do: to
establish a "strong military dictatorship" or to liberalize the system
of government. Tsarism became more and more a regime of permanent crisis.
    The importance of the ministers was even further reduced by
the method of their selection; the rule apparently in operation was
a very simple one: the selection of the unfittest. Changes in the
composition of the government were frequent and remarkably
inept. When the war broke out, the prime minister of Russia was
I.L. Goremykin. "Seventy-five years of age, a conservative, and a
life-long bureaucrat, he was, in his own words, 'pulled like a winter
coat out of mothballs,' in January 1914, to lead the government,
and he could as easily have been put back into the trunk."[13]
    This is how Buchanan, the British ambassador, described him:

An amiable old gentleman with pleasant manners, of an indolent
temperament and quite past his work, he had not moved with the
time.... With the consummate skill of the born courtier he had in-
gratiated himself with the Empress, though, except for his ultra-
monarchical views, he had nothing whatever to recommend him.[14]

Goremykin was so old that he repeatedly asked permission to
resign. But the tsar refused. "'The Tsar can't see that the candles

have already been lit around my coffin and that the only thing required to complete the ceremony is myself,' he said mournfully."[15] Being an old-fashioned monarchist, he was too valuable for the tsar to let him go.

In February 1916, however, the tsar at last replaced Goremykin with Stürmer. This is how Buchanan described the new premier:

> With but a second-rate intelligence, without any experience of affairs, a sycophant, bent solely on the advancement of his own interests and extremely ambitious, he owed his new appointment to the fact that he was a friend of Rasputin and that he was backed by the Empress's camarilla.... I may mention, as showing the sort of man that he was, that he chose as his *chef de cabinet* a former agent of the *okhrana* (secret police), Manouiloff by name, who was a few months afterwards arrested and tried for blackmailing a bank.[16]

The French Ambassador was equally uncomplimentary:

> He...is worse than a mediocrity—third-rate intellect, mean spirit, low character, doubtful honesty, no experience, and no idea of state business. The most that can be said for him is that he has a rather pretty talent for cunning and flattery.... His appointment becomes intelligible on the supposition that he has been selected solely as a tool; in other words, actually on account of his insignificance and servility.... [He] has been...warmly recommended to the Emperor by Rasputin.[17]

In November 1916, Stürmer was replaced by Trepov, who in turn was replaced in January by the elderly Prince N.D. Golytsin. Golytsin pleaded in vain with the tsar that he was ill, that in forty-seven years of service he had never dealt with politics (most of his activity during the war had been with the Red Cross) and that "this cup should pass me by."[18] He begged the tsar to choose somebody else. "If someone else had used the language I used to describe myself, I should have been obliged to challenge him to a duel," he said.[19]

Other ministers came and went like passing shadows. The minister of war, Sukhomlinov, was dismissed in June 1915 under very suspicious circumstances. He was accused of massive embezzlement of funds:

> There were rumors of embezzlements in the ministries in charge of providing the various supplies for the army. For a long time the Ministry of the Navy had had a reputation for embezzlement, and when war broke out it was said that this ministry evinced its patriotic feelings by suspending all graft in the making of large contracts. Soon, however, it was reported that graft was again being practiced in the high places of the Ministry of the Navy.[20]

A special commission was appointed
to ascertain who was really responsible for the failure to send supplies to the army. This commission investigated Sukhomlinov's activities and finally demanded that he be indicted before the courts.
Sukhomlinov's trial was accorded so much publicity and discredited
the existing regime to such a degree that it may be fitting to pause
and analyze his personality.[21]

In addition, his assistant, S.N. Miasoedov, was suspected of
being a German spy. He was tried by court-martial, convicted, and
executed.[22] Sukhomlinov was arrested. In his place, Polivanov was
appointed minister of war, but he was dismissed after a few months
and replaced by Shuvaev, whom Buchanan described as "a complete nullity."[23]

When Polivanov was sacked, the tsarina wrote to the tsar: "Oh,
the relief! Now I shall sleep well."[24] Others were appalled. Polivanov was "undoubtedly the ablest military organizer in Russia,
and his dismissal was a disaster," wrote Sir Alfred Knox.[25] One person was even appointed minister of interior because Rasputin, the
"holy man" confidant of the tsarina, liked his voice.

Rasputin once found a court chamberlain named A.N. Khvostov din-
ing at the nightclub Villa Rode. When the gypsy chorus began to
sing, Rasputin was not satisfied; he thought the basses much too
weak. Spotting Khvostov, who was large and stout, he clapped him
on the back and said, "Brother, go and help them sing. You are fat
and can make a lot of noise." Khvostov, tipsy and cheerful, leaped
onto the stage and boomed out a thundering bass. Delighted,
Rasputin clapped and shouted his approval. Not long afterward,
Khvostov unexpectedly became minister of interior. His appointment
provoked Vladimir Purishkevich, a member of the Duma, to declare
in disgust that new ministers now were asked to pass examinations,
not in government, but in gypsy music.[26]

Comic, or macabre?

The minister of the interior who had to face the February Revolution was Aleksander Protopopov. He was a nominee of Rasputin.
"Grigory earnestly begs you to name Protopopov," the tsarina
wrote in September. Two days later she repeated: "Please take Protopopov as minister of interior."[27]

The tsar gave in and telegraphed, "It shall be done." In a letter,
he added, "God grant that Protopopov may turn out to be the man
of whom we are now in need." Overjoyed, the Empress wrote

back, "God bless your new choice of Protopopov. Our Friend says you have done a very wise act in naming him."[28]

It was also Rasputin's idea to give Protopopov responsibility for the most crucial task of organizing food supplies. The tsarina granted him the power of control over food supplies without even bothering to get the tsar's approval. "Forgive me for what I have done—but I had to—our Friend said it was absolutely necessary," she wrote.

> Stürmer sends you by this messenger a new paper to sign giving the whole food supply at once to the minister of interior…. I had to take this step upon myself as Grigory says Protopopov will have all in his hands…and by that will save Russia…. Forgive me, but I had to take this responsibility for your sweet sake.[29]

This stupid man was put in control of the police and the food supply in the crucial winter of 1916–17 because, like the tsar and the tsarina, he was imbued with the medieval spirit of mysticism. Beside his desk he kept an icon that he addressed as a person. "He helps me do everything, everything I do is by His advice," Protopopov explained to Kerensky, indicating the icon.[30]

Buchanan described Protopopov thus: "Mentally deranged, he would, in his audiences with the Empress, repeat warnings and messages which he had received in his imaginary converse with Rasputin's spirit."[31]

In the two and a half years of the war, Russia had four different prime ministers, five ministers of the interior, four ministers of agriculture, and three ministers of war.

Rasputin

The anarchy prevailing at the top of the Russian political establishment enabled a corrupt clique to form around the tsar, at the head of which was none other than Grigory Rasputin, a symbol of the general decadence of society.

> Towards November 1905—that is, at the most critical moment of the first revolution—the Tsar writes in his diary: "We got acquainted with a man of God, Grigory, from the Tobolsk province." That was Rasputin—a Siberian peasant with a bald scar on his head, the result of a beating for horse-stealing. Put forward at an appropriate moment, this "Man of God" soon found official helpers—or rather they found him—and thus was formed a new ruling circle which got a firm hold of the Tsarina, and through her of the Tsar.
> From the winter of 1913–14 it was openly said in Petersburg society

that all high appointments, posts, and contracts depended upon the Rasputin clique.... In epic language the police spies registered from day to day the revels of the Friend. "He returned today 5 o'clock in the morning completely drunk." "On the night of the 25th–26th the actress V. spent the night with Rasputin." "He arrived with Princess D. (the wife of a gentleman of the bedchamber of the Tsar's court) at the Hotel Astoria."... And right beside this: "Came home from Tsarskoe Selo about 11 o'clock in the evening." "Rasputin came home with Princess Sh.—very drunk and together they went out immediately." In the morning or evening of the following day a trip to Tsarskoe Selo. To a sympathetic question from the spy as to why the Elder was thoughtful, the answer came: "Can't decide whether to convoke the Duma or not." And then again: "He came home at 5 in the morning pretty drunk." Thus for months and years the melody was played on three keys: "Pretty drunk," "Very drunk," and "Completely drunk."[32]

In their helplessness before the rising storm, the tsar and the tsarina craved the mystical power of the "Man of God." "Hearken unto Our Friend," the tsarina wrote in June 1915.

Believe him. He has your interest and Russia's at heart. It is not for nothing God sent him to us, only we must pay more attention to what He says. His words are not lightly spoken and the importance of having not only his prayers but his advice is great.... I am haunted by Our Friend's wish and know it will be fatal for us and for the country if not fulfilled. He means what he says when he speaks so seriously.[33]

In September 1916: "I fully trust in Our Friend's wisdom, endowed by God to counsel what is right for you and our country. He sees far ahead and therefore his judgment can be relied upon."[34]

After the tsar's departure to army headquarters in his fictitious capacity as commander in chief, the tsarina openly took charge of the internal affairs of the state, aided and abetted by Rasputin. This suited the fatalistic and weak-willed Nikolai very well.

Rasputin also intervened in military matters. Although her informal mandate from the tsar was to oversee only internal affairs, the tsarina also began to trespass in this field.

Rasputin's inspiration, he told the Empress, had come to him in dreams while he slept: "Now before I forget, I must give you a message from Our Friend prompted by what he saw in the night," she wrote in November 1915.

He begs you to order that one should advance near Riga, says it is necessary, otherwise the Germans will settle down so firmly through all the winter that it will cost endless bloodshed and trouble to make them move...he says this is just now the most essential thing and begs you seriously to order ours to advance, he says we can and we must, and I was to write to you at once.[35]

Rasputin's intervention in military affairs reached its height during the great Russian offensive of 1916. As early as July 25, the tsarina wrote: "Our Friend.... finds better one should not advance too obstinately as the losses will be too great."[36] On August 8: "Our Friend hopes we won't climb over the Carpathians and try to take them, as he repeats the losses will be too great again."[37]

On September 21, the tsar wrote: "I told Alekseev to order Brusilov to stop our hopeless attacks." The tsarina replied happily, "Our Friend says about the new orders you gave to Brusilov: 'Very satisfied with Father's [the tsar's] orders, all will be well.'"[38]

Whom the gods wish to destroy...

Their medieval obscurantism made it impossible for the tsarina and her cabal to grasp the overall significance of the rising waves of revolution. Her arrogance knew no bounds. The people simply needed the whip. Thus on December 14, 1916, less than ten weeks before the monarchy fell, she called on the tsar to arrest all the leading members of the Duma: "Be Peter the Great, Ivan the Terrible, Emperor Paul; smash them all!" In another letter written just five days before the February Revolution, she went even further:

> You have never lost an opportunity to show your love and kindness; now let them feel your fist. They themselves ask for this—so many have recently said to me: "We need the whip." This is strange, but such is the Slavonic nature—the greatest firmness, even cruelty and— warm love. They must learn to fear you; love alone is not enough.[39]

The extent of the tsarina's political perspicacity, and of her understanding of the people, is clear from a letter she wrote to the tsar on February 26, when the capital was in the grip of a general strike:

> This is a hooligan movement, young people run about and shout that there is no bread, simply to create excitement, along with workers who prevent others from working. If the weather were very cold they would all probably stay at home. But all this will pass and become calm, if only the Duma will behave itself.[40]

With the tsarina and her clique conspiring against the Duma, against the ministers, and against the staff generals, it is not surprising that each member of the tsarist administration felt helpless, isolated from everyone, and in conflict with everyone.

Thus at the August 21, 1915, session of the Council of Ministers,

Shcherbatov, minister of internal affairs, said:

> One must submit a written report to His Majesty, and explain that a government which has the confidence neither of the bearer of supreme power, nor of the army, nor of the towns, nor of the *Zemstvos,* nor of the gentry, nor of the merchants, nor of the workers—not only cannot work, it cannot even exist! It is an evident absurdity! We, sitting here, are like Don Quixotes![41]

At the session of August 28, 1915, Krivoshein, the acting minister of agriculture, said:

> Everyone talks about unity and about accord with the nation, and meanwhile the civil and the military authorities cannot agree and have not been able to work together for a whole year. The Council of Ministers discusses, requests, expresses desires, submits wishes, submits demands—and the gentlemen generals spit on all of us and don't wish to do anything.[42]

On August 9, 1915, Sazonov, minister of foreign affairs, announced: "The government hangs in mid-air, having support neither from above nor from below."[43]

The extreme right-wing deputy A.I. Savenko could declare at the session of the Duma on February 29, 1916:

> What a terrible thing it is for the country that, during the time of the greatest trials experienced by our fatherland, the country does not trust the government; no one trusts the government, even the right does not trust the government—in fact the government does not trust itself and is not sure about tomorrow.[44]

The palace revolution that did not take place

As the crisis in the tsarist regime deepened, more and more circles of the ruling class indulged in speculation about the need for a revolution from above…to preempt a revolution from below.

In August 1916, the right-wing Octobrist leader Alexander Guchkov sent a letter to General Alekseev at General Headquarters, copies of which were widely circulated, which read:

> [T]he home front is in a state of complete disintegration…the rot has set in at the roots of state power…the rot on the home front is once more threatening, as it did last year, to drag your gallant armies at the front, your gallant strategy, and the whole country into the hopeless quagmire…one cannot expect communications to function properly under Mr. Trepov; nor good work of our industry when it is entrusted to Prince Shakhovskoy; nor prosperity for our agriculture and a proper management of supplies at the hands of Count Bobrin-

sky. And...this government is headed by Mr Stürmer, who has established (both in the army and among the people at large) a solid reputation of one who—if not an actual traitor is ready to commit treason...you will understand what deadly anxiety for the fate of our motherland has gripped public opinion and popular feeling.

We in the rear are powerless, or almost powerless, to fight this evil. Our methods of struggle are double-edged and can—owing to the excitable state of the popular masses and in particular of the working class—become the first spark of a conflagration, the dimensions of which no one can foresee or localize....

Is there anything you can do? I don't know.[45]

This was practically a call for the general to stage a coup. Guchkov and other members of the ruling class were praying silently that the military would summon up courage to seize power. Alas, General Alekseev refused to take the step.

Three months later, according to Kerensky, the future head of the provisional government, another plot was afoot, for a coup scheduled to take place at the tsar's headquarters on November 15–16. This was a private arrangement between Prince Lvov and General Alekseev. They had made up their minds that the tsarina's hold on the tsar must be broken in order to end the pressure being exerted on him, through her, by the Rasputin clique. At the appointed hour, Alekseev and Lvov hoped to persuade the tsar to send the Empress away to the Crimea or to England.[46]

In January 1917, General Krymov arrived from the front and complained before members of the Duma that the existing state of affairs could not continue any longer.

The feeling in the army is such that all will greet with joy the news of a *coup d'état*. It has to come; it is felt at the front. Should you decide to do this, we will support you. Seemingly, there is no other way out. You, as well as others, have tried everything, but the evil influence of the wife is mightier than the honest words spoken to the Tsar. We cannot afford to lose time.

Shidlovski exclaimed in anger, "We cannot waste pity on him [the tsar], if he ruins Russia." In the noisy argument, the real or imaginary words of General Brusilov were also reported: "If it comes to a choice between the Tsar and Russia, I will take Russia."

Shingarev, a Cadet, said: "The general is right—a *coup d'état* is necessary. But who will dare to initiate it?"

That was just the point. Nobody dared to act. There was endless talk about a coup, but plans did not move an inch forward.

Even close members of the tsar's family were indulging in talk about the urgent need for a coup. Thus M.V. Rodzianko, president of the Duma, recorded:

> The idea that it was necessary to force the Tsar to abdicate seemed to have taken hold of Petrograd at the end of 1916, and the beginning of 1917. A number of people from the higher circles declared that the Duma and its president should undertake this task and save the army and Russia.

Rodzianko goes on to relate some astonishing stories. He describes how one day in January 1917 he was urgently invited to lunch at the Vladimir Palace. After lunch, the Grand Duchess,

> Maria Pavlovna, spoke of the situation in the interior, of the worthless government, of Protopopov, and of the Empress...that it was necessary to change, remove, destroy. I tried to find out what she was driving at and asked what she meant by remove. "Well, I don't know. It is necessary to undertake something. You understand. The Duma should do something.... She should be done away with." "Who?" "The Empress." "Your Highness," said I, "let us forget this conversation."

On January 8, 1917, the tsar's brother, Duke Mikhail Aleksandrovich, came to see Rodzianko. He said:

> I should like to talk to you about what is going on and to consult you as to what should be done. We understand the situation.... Do you think there is going to be a revolution?
>
> Rodzianko: There is still time to save Russia, and even now the reign of your brother could attain unheard of greatness and glory, if the policies of the government were altered. It is necessary to appoint ministers whom the country trusts, who would not hurt the people's feelings. I am sorry to say, however, that this could be done only if the Empress were removed [from political affairs].... She and the Emperor are surrounded by sinister and worthless characters. The Empress is hated and there is a general cry that she should be removed. As long as she is in power we shall drift toward ruin.
>
> Aleksandrovich: Imagine—Buchanan said the same thing to my brother. Our family realizes how harmful the Empress is. She and my brother are surrounded by traitors—all decent people have left them. But what to do?[47]

Exactly. What was to be done? The Duma waited for the generals to act. The generals waited for the Duma. The tsar's own family prayed silently for a coup.

Some foreign diplomats, particularly the British and French ambassadors, were involved in a conspiracy. On December 28, 1916, the French ambassador wrote in his diary:

> Yesterday evening...Prince Gabriel Constantinovich gave a supper

for his mistress, formerly an actress. The guests included the Grand Duke Boris...a few officers and a squad of elegant courtesans. During the evening the only topic was the conspiracy—the regiments of the guard which can be relied on, the most favorable moment for the outbreak, etc. And all this with the servants moving about, harlots looking on and listening, gypsies singing and the whole company bathed in the aroma of Moët and Chandon *brut imperial* which flowed in streams.[48]

The British ambassador remembered:

Revolution was in the air, and the only moot point was whether it would come from above or from below. A Palace revolution was openly spoken of, and at a dinner at the Embassy a Russian friend of mine, who had occupied a high position in the government, declared that it was a mere question whether both the Emperor and Empress or only the latter would be killed. On the other hand, a popular outbreak, provoked by the prevailing food shortage, might occur at any moment.[49]

But all the talk of revolution from above, all the conspiracies, led to nothing. On May 5, 1917, a Cadet, V.A. Maklakov, exclaimed at a private conference of members of the Duma:

[T]here was a moment when it became clear to everybody that under the old regime it was impossible to conclude war, to achieve victory; and for those who believed that a revolution would be ruinous, it was their duty and their task to save Russia from a revolution from below by means of a palace revolution from above. Such was the task which stood before us, but which we did not fulfill. If posterity curses this revolution, then it will also curse those who did not understand the methods which could have forestalled it.[50]

On August 2, 1917, Guchkov sadly echoed Maklakov's sentiments:

The course of action required was a *coup d'état*. The fault, if one can speak of the historical fault of Russian society, lies in the fact that this society, represented by its leading circles, was not sufficiently aware of the need for the coup and did not undertake it, thereby leaving it to blind, spontaneous forces to carry out this painful operation.[51]

Even the very perceptive Lenin was led by the general talk of a coup to believe that leaders of the Russian establishment and the British ambassador were actually organizing one, and that their action contributed to the February Revolution.

The whole course of events in the February–March Revolution clearly shows that the British and French embassies, with their agents and "connections," who had long been making the most desperate

efforts to prevent "separate" agreements and a separate peace between Nicholas II (and last, we hope, and we will endeavor to make
him that) and Wilhelm II, directly organized a plot in conjunction
with the Octobrists and Cadets, in conjunction with a section of the
generals and army and St. Petersburg garrison officers, with the express object of *deposing* Nicholas Romanov.[52]

However, the social crisis that led rich industrialists, generals,
and dukes to talk about a coup also paralyzed them. In 1908
Rodzianko had declared his admiration for the Young Turks (the
group of army officers who had seized power). But he and his
Russian friends could not imitate them. There was no revolutionary proletariat behind them, pushing forward.

The lack of determination to carry out a palace revolution led
to its replacement by a caricature—the assassination of Rasputin,
on December 16–17, 1916, by Prince Felix Usupov, heir to the
largest fortune in Russia, Grand Duke Dmitri Pavlovich, and the
extreme right-wing monarchist Duma deputy, Purishkevich. They
saw in this murder the last available means of saving the monarchy.

The impact of Rasputin's death was just the opposite of what its
perpetrators hoped for. It did not blunt the crisis, but sharpened it.
People in every walk of life talked about the murder and could see
that even the Grand Dukes had no recourse against the tsarist
clique except by poison and the revolver. Violence against the
monarchy was inevitable. tsarism survived the murder of Rasputin
by only ten weeks.

CHAPTER 6

FROM THE FEBRUARY REVOLUTION TO DUAL POWER

The February Revolution

In 1917, on the traditional day for commemorating Bloody Sunday (January 9), workers from 114 enterprises, some 137,500 in all, came out on strike. This was not an exceptional event. However, in the last week of February a new, much wider and deeper strike movement developed. It resulted from a lockout at the Putilov works, and from the dwindling bread supply.

On February 18, workers in one section of the Putilov works put forward a claim for a 50 percent wage increase. When the management refused to concede their demand they began a sit-down strike. On February 21, they were sacked. The strike spread to other sections, and on February 22, the management announced the closure of the whole plant for an indefinite period. This meant that thirty thousand well-organized workers were on the streets. The lockout at Putilov made a substantial contribution to the rapid spread of the strike movement.

As for the bread supply—in Petrograd in mid-February, only ten days' supply of flour remained. The regional military commander, General S.S. Khabalov decided, along with municipal authorities, to set up a rationing system. The people learned of it, and the following morning, February 16, there were long queues in front of the bakers' shops and outside all the food stores. The stores, emptied within a few hours, closed their shutters. Crowds gathered and windows were broken. During the following days, such incidents recurred again and again.

February 23 was International Women's Day. After speeches in the factories, crowds of women poured into the streets, clamoring for bread. Here and there red flags appeared with the slogan,

"Down with the autocracy."

A secret *okhrana* report vividly described the events of February 23 and 24:

> On February 23 at 9 a.m., the workers of the plants and factories of the Vyborg district went on strike in protest against the shortage of black bread in bakeries and groceries; the strike spread to some plants located in the Petrograd, Rozhdestvenskii, and Liteinyi districts, and in the course of the day 50 industrial enterprises ceased working, with 87,534 men going on strike.
>
> At about 1 p.m., the workmen of the Vyborg district, walking out in crowds into the streets and shouting "Give us bread," started at the same time to become disorderly in various places, taking with them on the way their comrades who were at work, and stopping tramcars; the demonstrators took away from the tram drivers the keys to the electric motors, which forced 15 tramway trains to quit the lines and retire to the Petrograd tramway yard.
>
> The strikers, who were resolutely chased by police and troops summoned [for this purpose], were dispersed in one place but quickly gathered in other places, showing themselves to be exceptionally stubborn; in the Vyborg district order was restored only toward 7 p.m.[1]

The next day, the workers' movement had not abated. Thus a memorandum from the *okhrana* compiled later in the evening of February 24 stated:

> The strike of the workers which took place yesterday in connection with the shortage of bread continued today; in the course of the day 131 enterprises with 158,583 workers shut down.
>
> After arriving in the morning at their plants, the workers of the enterprises which had decided to go on strike departed after short discussions, partly to their homes and partly to the streets, where they perpetrated disorders....
>
> In this way the crowd quickly increased to two to three thousand men. At the corner of the Bolshoi Prospect and Grebetskaia Street the demonstrators were met by a detail of police, which, being small in number, was unable to stop the movement and had to let them go on. On the Kamennoostrovskii Prospect the crowd was dispersed by Cossacks and mounted police.
>
> The demonstrators included a large number of students....
>
> At about 9 a.m., after arriving at work, 3,500 workers of the "Aivaz" plant gathered on the premises of the automobile section and organized a meeting at which speakers who had arrived from the outside expressed their discontent with the government and called the workers to unite and to make an energetic demonstration demanding from the Duma the elimination of the present government; at the same time they emphasized that if they acted, they would be supported not only by workmen but also by various employees, by those of the railways, of the tramways, of the telegraph and of the

post office. The demands should be accompanied by demonstrations, but no destruction should be perpetrated. They should proceed on the streets in separate groups, not in crowds, and they should try to reach the Duma by 3 p.m. In conclusion, a resolution demanding the removal of the government was adopted. A crowd of about 3,000 workmen moving along the Nevskii Prospect stopped at house no. 80 and listened to a speaker who called for the overthrow of the existing regime and proposed that they gather next day, 25 February, at 12 noon near the Kazan Cathedral.

In the communication of the police sergeant, on the basis of which the above event is reported, it was added: "The Cossacks, who stood close to the crowd, did not disperse it." There are other communications regarding the "inactivity" of Cossacks and soldiers.[2]

The next day, on February 25, the *okhrana* report expressed even greater alarm, pointing out that troops, and even Cossacks, were not ready to suppress the workers.

On 25 February a crowd of about 6,000 workmen proceeding from the Bolshoi Samsonievskii Prospect along Botkinskaia Street toward Nizhnii Novgorod Street was met by Cossacks and a detail of police; present on horseback was Shalfeev, Chief of Police of the 5th District. The crowd dragged him down from the horse and began to beat him with sticks and an iron hook used to switch railway points; policemen fired into the crowd (evidently the Cossacks were inactive) and the shots were returned from the crowd. The Chief of Police was seriously wounded and was taken to a military hospital.

The crowd is still on the spot. Details are being ascertained...

On...25 February, the report of the superintendence of the Vasilevskii district's 1st precinct to the Commander of the Finland Guard regiment's reserve battalion—a copy of which was delivered to the *okhrana*—also speaks of the inactivity of the Cossacks. The report advised of the disorders which occurred on the 25th on Vasilevskii Island, disorders which were suppressed by the police and the soldiers of the Finland regiment, while "the platoon of the 1st Don Cossack regiment, which arrived at the spot, did not take any measures for the restoration of order...."

If resolute measures are not taken to quell the disorders, barricades might be erected on Monday.

It should be noted that, among the military units summoned for the purpose of suppressing the disorders, one may observe [cases of] fraternization with the demonstrators, and some units even manifest approval, encouraging the mob by saying "press harder." If the moment were to be lost and the leadership taken by the upper layer of the revolutionary underground, events would assume very wide proportions.[3]

On February 26, for the first time, there appears in an *okhrana* report a direct description of a soldier's mutiny:

Police Sergeant Kharitonov reported that at 6 p.m. the 4th company of the Pavlovsk Guard regiment, in an outburst of indignation against their [regimental] training detachment, which had been detailed to the Nevskii Prospect, and which had fired at the crowd after leaving its barracks which are located in the riding school of the court stables, proceeded toward the Nevskii Prospect under the command of a noncommissioned officer with the intention of removing [the details of the training detachment] from their posts; however, on its way, in the vicinity of the Church of Christ the Savior, the 4th company met a mounted patrol of 10 policemen; the soldiers abused the policemen, calling them "pharaohs," and firing several volleys at them, killing one policeman and one horse, and wounding one policeman and one horse. Then the soldiers (of the 4th company) returned to the barracks, where they staged a mutiny. Colonel Eksten came to put it down and was wounded by one of the soldiers; his hand was cut off; later a detachment of the Preobrazhenskii Guard regiment was summoned; it disarmed and surrounded the mutineers.

On February 26, General Khabalov received a peremptory telegram from the tsar, worded as follows: "I command you to suppress from tomorrow all disorders on the streets of the capital, which are impermissible at a time when the fatherland is carrying on a difficult war with Germany."

The tsar's order caused a sharp change in the tactics of the military authorities in Petrograd. Hitherto the use of firearms had been avoided. Now Khabalov gave his subordinate officers instructions to fire on crowds that refused to disperse after warning. The regime took a gamble. If the troops obeyed, the revolutionary movement would be crushed. But what if they did not?

To increase their show of resolute action, the police arrested about a hundred people on the night of February 26, including five members of the Petersburg Committee of the Bolshevik Party. On the surface, the course of events on that day, which was a Sunday, represented a victory for the government. There was firing on the crowds in four separate places in the central part of the city; and on Znamenskaia Square, a detachment of the Volinskii regiment used machine guns as well as rifles, with the result that about forty people were killed and a similar number wounded. Towards the evening there was an outburst of rebellion in one company of the Pavlov regiment; but it was put down with the aid of other troops, and the ringleaders imprisoned in the fortress of Peter and Paul.[4]

The next day, however, the mutiny in the army spread. This mutiny, that was to transform the prolonged street demonstrations into a victorious revolution, started in the very unit that had inflicted the heaviest losses on the demonstrating workers the day before—the Volinskii regiment. During the night the soldiers discussed their impressions of the day's shootings, and agreed that they would no longer fire on the crowd. When Captain Lashkevich appeared in the barracks of the detachment on the morning of February 27, he was greeted with shouts of "We will not shoot."

An *okhrana* report tells the story:

> At 9 a.m. Police Sergeant Liubitskii reported that the training detachments of the Volinskii regiment have revolted at no. 13/15 of the Vilna Alley, and Captain Lashkevich, who was in charge of the cadres, was killed by a rifle shot; later the Litovskii regiment revolted; it is stationed in the barracks at Kirochnaia Street, where it started to plunder the arsenal, removing cartridges and rifles in automobiles; the part of the Preobrazhenskii regiment which is stationed in these barracks joined them.
>
> Police Sergeant Liubitskii reported that at 12 noon in the Preobrazhenskii regiment (Kirochnaia Street no. 37) the soldiers killed Colonel Bogdanovich, commander of the regiment, because he had refused to distribute cartridges and weapons; groups of these soldiers scattered in the directions of the Nevskii Prospect, the Duma, and the Vyborg district, where the arsenals of this regiment are located; they sent soldiers by horse and by car to all the other military units for the purpose [of inciting to] mutiny other units as well. Shooting has started. The crowds on Gospitalnaia, Paradnaia, and other streets are very large.[5]

According to N.N. Sukhanov, an honest eyewitness and excellent chronicler of the revolution, some twenty-five thousand soldiers had left their barracks to mingle with the crowd while the rest of the garrison—altogether 160,000 strong—were not prepared to actually suppress the workers.[6] According to another source, as many as 70,000 soldiers joined the 385,000 workers on strike on February 27.[7]

February 28 brought the final collapse of the tsarist forces: the last remaining "loyal" troops surrendered; the fortress of Peter and Paul capitulated without firing a single shot; and the tsar's ministers were either arrested or else surrendered to the new authorities.

A spontaneous revolution

The revolution was completely spontaneous and unplanned. As Trotsky correctly states: "[N]o one, positively no one—we can assert this categorically upon the basis of all the data—then thought that February 23 was to mark the beginning of a decisive drive against absolutism."[8]

Sukhanov observes: *"Not one party was preparing for the great uphaeval"*[9]

Similarly a former director of the *okhrana* stated that the revolution was "a purely spontaneous phenomenon, and not at all the fruit of party agitation."[10]

The worker leader, Kaiurov, of the Vyborg District Committee of the Bolsheviks, who took a very active part in the February Revolution, testified that on February 23 "no one thought of such an imminent possibility of revolution." When on February 22 some women workers met to discuss the organization of International Women's Day the next day, Kaiurov advised them to refrain from hasty action.

> But to my surprise and indignation, on 23 February, at an emergency conference of five persons in the corridor of the Erikson works, we learned from comrade Nikifor Ilyin of the strike in some textile factories and of the arrival of a number of delegates from the women workers, who announced that they were supporting the metal workers.
>
> I was extremely indignant about the behavior of the strikers, both because they had blatantly ignored the decision of the District Committee of the party, and also because they had gone on strike after I had appealed to them only the night before to keep cool and disciplined.
>
> With reluctance, [writes Kaiurov] the Bolsheviks agreed to this [spreading of the strike] and they were followed by other workers—Mensheviks and Social Revolutionaries. But once there is a mass strike, one must call everybody into the streets and take the lead.[11]

It was not until February 25 that the Bolsheviks came out with their first leaflet calling for a general strike—*after* 200,000 workers had already downed tools!

The same day, Shliapnikov, the leading Bolshevik in Petrograd, refused to supply arms to the insistent workers: "I decisively refused to search for arms at all, and demanded that the soldiers should be drawn into the uprising, so as to get arms for all the workers. This was more difficult than to get a few dozen revolvers; but in this was the whole program of action."[12] Was Shliapnikov far-seeing, or afraid of taking responsibility?

To return again to Kaiurov: he could write, long after the events, "Absolutely no guiding initiative from the party centers was felt.... The Petersburg Committee had been arrested, and the representative of the Central Committee, Comrade Shliapnikov, was unable to give any directives for the coming day."

Sunday, February 26, was relatively quiet. The factories were closed, so that the strength of the masses could not be gauged. The workers could not assemble in the factories as they had done on the preceding days, and that hindered the demonstration. Quite naturally, rank-and-file leaders like Kaiurov could not assess the mood of the people. And so on the evening of the same Sunday he came to the conclusion that "the revolution is petering out. The demonstrators are disarmed. No one can do anything to the government now that it has taken decisive action."

Corroboration of the spontaneous nature of the February Revolution comes from another source—the *okhrana*. On February 26, one of its agents, whose pseudonym was "Limonin," an agent inside the Bolshevik Party, reported:

> The movement which has started has flared up without any party preparing it and without any preliminary discussion of a plan of action. The revolutionary circles began to react only toward the end of the second day when the desire to develop the success of the movement to the widest limits possible became noticeable.... The general attitude of the non-party masses is as follows: the movement started spontaneously, without any preparation, exclusively on the basis of the food crisis.[13]

One must hasten to say that the revolution's spontaneity does not mean that its participants and rank-and-file leaders lacked political ideas. Trotsky asked the question: Who led the February Revolution? And he gave the following accurate reply:

> We can then answer definitely enough: Conscious and tempered workers educated for the most part by the party of Lenin. But we must here immediately add: This leadership proved sufficient to guarantee the victory of the insurrection, but it was not adequate to transfer immediately into the hands of the proletarian vanguard the leadership of the revolution.[14]

The bourgeoisie is afraid to take power

Throughout its history the Russian bourgeoisie proved to be cowardly and counterrevolutionary. Sazonov, the tsarist foreign minister, assessed it accurately when he said, at a session of the Council of Ministers on August 26, 1915, "Miliukov [the Cadet leader] is the greatest bourgeois, and he fears a social revolution more than anything else. And, in general, the majority of the Cadets are trembling for their fortunes."[15]

Even during the days of February 25–27, while tsarism was under the severest popular attack, the bourgeoisie still tried to avoid the revolution and to come to terms with the monarchy.

Sukhanov wrote:

> As far as the leading circles were concerned, all their thoughts and efforts boiled down, not to shaping the revolution, or joining it and trying to make themselves the crest of the wave, but exclusively to avoiding it. Attempts were being made at deals with Tsarism; the political game was in full swing. All this was not only independent of the popular movement but at its expense and obviously aimed at its destruction.
>
> At this moment the position of the bourgeoisie was quite clear: it was a position on the one hand of keeping their distance from the revolution and betraying it to Tsarism, and on the other of exploiting it for their own manoeuvres.[16]

However, this position could no longer be maintained when it became clear on February 27 and 28 that the revolution was victorious. Now the capitalists tried to loot the revolution they had not supported.

> As a matter of fact, at that moment [writes Sukhanov] Miliukov, and in his person the whole of propertied Russia, was confronted by a genuinely tragic problem...as long as Tsarism was not conclusively done for, it was necessary to cling to it, *support* it, and construct any domestic or foreign program of national liberalism on the *basis* of it. This was understood by every bourgeois element with any experience at all.
>
> But what was to be done when Tsarism had *almost* fallen beneath the blows of the popular movement but its final fate was not known? Obviously, the natural solution was to maintain neutrality until the last minute and not burn one's boats. But in practice it was clear that there had to be definite limits to neutrality, beyond which neutrality itself would burn the boats on one side and perhaps on both. Here one must be specially clear-sighted, supple, and agile.
>
> But the real tragedy began later. What was to be done after the popular revolution had wiped Tsarism off the face of the earth? To take the power out of the hands of Tsarism was natural. To make an alliance with Tsarism to smash the revolution, if it tried to sweep away both the bourgeoisie and Tsarism in the same breath, was even more natural and absolutely inevitable. But what if, on the one hand, Tsarism was hopeless, and on the other the *possibility of standing at the head of the revolution was not excluded? What if some prospect of "using" it developed?* What was to be done then? Take the power out of the hands of the revolution and the democracy after they had become masters of the situation?[17]

On February 27, Rodzianko, a big landlord and thorough monarchist, went to the tsar to seek a compromise: with a new tsar, perhaps the Tsarevich Aleksei with his uncle Michael as regent, or if need be Michael himself as tsar. But this came to nothing. Nikolai abdicated and offered the crown to his brother, but the latter was not ready to take it without guarantees for his safety, which could not be given at such a time. So the monarchy was ended.

> I don't know whom Rodzianko consulted in the name of the Duma and the propertied classes [writes Sukhanov], but in any case it had become clear in those hours that the tactic of vanquishing the revolution through a united front with the forces of Tsarism had perhaps already become rather riskier than the tactic of vanquishing the democratic movement by trying to exploit the revolution and keep it in check by leading it.[18]

> Our bourgeoisie…betrayed the people not the day after the overturn but even before the overturn took place: it hadn't started a revolution with the intention of turning against the people at an opportune moment, but had been dragged by the hair into the movement when the people's revolution had already developed to its full extent. This bourgeoisie of ours left no room for doubt as to its goals.[19]

Unfortunately for the bourgeoisie, before the tsar had even abdicated a new institution was born—the Soviet of Petrograd. In the space of a few days there was no town in Russia that did not have a soviet. By March 22, seventy-seven soviets were in touch with the Petrograd Soviet (not counting the soldier soviets and the factory soviets).[20]

The soviet has the power

On Friday evening, February 24, elections to a Soviet of Workers' Deputies were already being held in the factories of Petrograd. Thus the soviet was born even before the final victory of the February Revolution.

By February 28, Sukhanov writes,

> the real power, was in its [the soviet's] hands, insofar as there was any authority at all at that time. And this was obvious to every man in the street.
> *Formally* the power belonged to the Duma Committee…. But theirs was only a paper, or if you like a "moral" power…in these crucial hours of convulsion it was absolutely unable to *govern*.

The only organization that could restore "order and normal life in the city" was the soviet,

> which was beginning to acquire control over the masses of the workers and soldiers. It was clear to everyone that all effective workers' organizations were at the disposal of the Soviet, and that it was for it to set in motion the immobilized tramways, factories, and newspapers, and

even to restore order and safeguard the inhabitants from violence.[21]

A month later, at the end of March, things were no different.

The popularity and authority of the Soviet went on growing like a snowball amongst the urban and rural masses...not only in these masses but also in political circles and state institutions—there was taking root an awareness of the Soviet's real power and potentialities, and of the helplessness of the government and its agencies.
   The official government machine, in one part after another, began idling more and more. Independently of what either side desired, the official mechanism was being supplanted by the Soviet.[22]

The soviet was to remain the greatest power in the land until the end of the February regime.

But the bourgeoisie should have power...

For the Menshevik leaders it was axiomatic that power should be in the hands of the bourgeoisie, as, according to their "Marxism" this was preordained by the immutable laws of history.

Even Sukhanov, who was on the extreme left, internationalist wing of Menshevism, was a complete slave to this assumption. Thus, before the February Revolution it was clear to him that:

The government that was to take the place of Tsarism must be exclusively bourgeois.... The entire available state machinery, the army of bureaucrats, the *Zemstvos* and municipalities, which had had the cooperation of all the forces of the democracy, could obey Miliukov, but not Chkheidze. There was, however, and could be, no other machinery.[23]

If anyone dared to lift a finger against the bourgeoisie, it would be pushed into a counterrevolutionary stance, which would result in the defeat of the revolution.

The whole of the bourgeoisie as one man would have thrown all the strength it had in the scales on the side of Tsarism and formed with it a strong and united front—against the revolution. It would have roused up against the revolution the entire middle class and the press.... In these circumstances a socialist seizure of power would mean the inevitable and immediate failure of the revolution.[24]

To add to the impossibility of overthrowing the bourgeoisie came the war. Only the bourgeoisie could deal with foreign policy. It was, Sukhanov says,

out of the question to add an immediate radical change in foreign policy, with all its unforeseeable consequences, to all the difficulties of a revolution.... It seemed to me absolutely indispensable to lay the problems of foreign policy temporarily on the shoulders of the bourgeoisie, in order to create the possibility of a struggle for the most rapid and painless liquidation of the war under a bourgeois government that was carrying on the military policy of the autocracy.... It was clear then *a priori* that if a bourgeois government and the adherence of the bourgeoisie to the revolution were to be counted on, it was temporarily necessary to *shelve the slogans against the war*.... In general the solution of the problem of power seemed to me self-evident.... Power must go to the bourgeoisie.[25]

The leaders of the soviet beg the bourgeoisie to take power

The soviet had all the power in its hands, but was bound by its leaders' policy to transfer it to the liberal bourgeoisie. Tsereteli, the strongman of the Mensheviks in the soviet, explained the "necessity of a compromise with the bourgeoisie. There can be no other road for the revolution. It's true that we have all the power, and that the government would go if we lifted a finger, but that would mean disaster for the revolution."[26] And so the soviet leaders begged the liberal leaders to take power. They threatened them with dire consequences if they did not. They promised to stop the excesses of the masses, and to place self-imposed restrictions on the soviet itself.

Sukhanov explains:

We must be wary of confronting them [the capitalists] with any demands which might make them consider the experiment not worthwhile and turn to other methods of consolidating their class rule.

We must make every effort not to "disrupt the combination," and therefore limit ourselves to a minimal, really indispensable program on just what concrete conditions should the power be entrusted to Miliukov's government?

In essence I thought there was just one such condition: the assurance of *complete political freedom in the country, an absolute freedom of organization and agitation.*[27]

The soviet had the power to rule but was ready to give it up, if only the capitalists would give their word not to lock the soviet up and gag it. Its leaders begged, cajoled, threatened.... They did everything they could to make the bourgeoisie take power.

Sukhanov "threatened" Miliukov, the leader of the bourgeoisie, on February 27:

At this moment, a few rooms away, the Soviet of Workers' Deputies is assembling. The success of the popular uprising means that within a few hours all the effective real power in the state, or at least in Petersburg, if not the government itself, will be in its hands. With the capitulation of Tsarism it is the Soviet that will be master of the situation. At the same time popular demands in such circumstances will inevitably be expanded to the most extreme limits. The movement does not have to be driven along by anyone just now—it is already running downhill too fast without that. But confining it within definite bounds would require enormous efforts. Besides, any attempt to keep the popular demands within set limits would be quite risky; it might discredit the controlling groups of the democracy in the eyes of the masses. The movement might turn into an uncontrollable explosion of elemental forces.[28]

A couple of days later, as a member of a delegation from the executive of the soviet, Sukhanov told the provisional government: "The Soviet...would leave the formation of a provisional government to the bourgeois groups, on the view that this followed from the existing general situation and suited the interests of the revolution."[29]

What was the provisional government's reaction?

Miliukov had taken very accurate bearings. He understood that without an accord with the Soviet no government could either arise or remain in existence. He understood that it was entirely within the power of the Ex. Com. [of the soviet] to give authority to a bourgeois regime or withhold it. He saw where the real strength lay, he saw in whose hands were the means of assuring to the new government both the indispensable conditions for work and its very existence.... As for the "minimal" nature of our demands and the general attitude taken by the...Ex. Com., Miliukov had not expected such "moderation" and "good sense." He was agreeably surprised by our general attitude towards the question of power and felt the greatest satisfaction at the...solution of the problem of war and peace as it affected the formation of the government. He didn't even think of concealing his satisfaction and pleasant surprise.

And Miliukov said, "Yes, I was thinking as I listened to you how far our working-class movement has advanced since 1905."[30]

The bourgeoisie takes power from the revolution that it detests

V.B. Stankevich, who moved in bourgeois circles, describes the mood of those circles after the revolution:

Officially they celebrated, eulogized the revolution, cried "Hurray!" to the fighters for freedom, adorned themselves with red ribbons, and marched under red banners.... Everyone said, We, our revolution, our victory, and our freedom. But in their hearts, in their tête-à-têtes they were horrified, trembled, felt themselves prisoners of a hostile elemental force that was traveling an unknown road. Unforgettable is the figure of Rodzianko, that portly lord and imposing personage, when, preserving a majestic dignity but with an expression of deep suffering despair frozen on his pale face, he made his way through a crowd of disheveled soldiers in the corridor of the Tauride Palace. [*] Officially it was recorded: The soldiers have come to support the Duma in its struggle with the government. But actually the Duma had been abolished from the very first day. And the same expression was on the faces of all the members of the Provisional Committee of the Duma and those circles which surrounded it. They say that the representatives of the progressive bloc in their own homes wept with impotent despair.[31]

The testimony of V.V. Shulgin, a member of the Fourth Duma and supporter of the provisional government, is even more revealing. In his memoirs he writes:

This constant outpouring of humanity brought in sight new faces but, no matter how many there were, they all had a kind of stupid, animal, even devilish appearance. God, how ugly it looked! So ugly that I gritted my teeth. I felt pained and helpless and bitterly enraged.

Machine guns! That's what I wanted. I felt that only the tongues of machine guns could talk to the mob, and that only machine guns and lead could drive back into his lair the frightful beast. This beast was no other than His Majesty the Russian people. That which we feared, tried to avoid at all costs, was before us. The revolution had begun.

If we only had machine guns. But we could not have any. Our great stupidity and irreparable mistake was that we had not prepared any real force. If we had had even a single regiment on whom to depend, a single general with determination, the situation might have been different. But we had neither the one nor the other...and what's more we could not have either. At this time Petrograd had no dependable troops left or perhaps it had not had any as yet.... Officers! We will talk about them later. At this time, no one even thought of looking to "officers" companies' for support.[32]

There was no love lost between the provisional government and the soviet; it was purely a marriage of convenience. Detesting the soviet from which it received state power, the provisional government nevertheless ground its teeth and accepted its support.

This may have seemed to it a sorry turn of events [wrote Sukhanov], nevertheless it was the lesser evil and the only way out for the bourgeoisie. It was vital to acquire all the attributes of power—even at the

---

[*] Where both the Duma's Provisional Committee—and later the provisional government—and the Soviet of Workers' and Soldiers' Deputies held their meetings.

price of a compromise, even at a very high price. For this there was only one real means.

This was—a formal marriage to the petty-bourgeois Soviet majority. Love was absent—but there was clear and obvious calculation. In itself the Soviet was not, of course, desirable; but it was a question of the *dowry*. And as a dowry the Soviet would bring the army, the real power, immediate confidence and support, and all the technical means of administration.[33]

Why did the soviet leaders deliver power to the provisional government?

How can one explain the fact that a victorious revolution, which made the workers and soldiers the masters of the situation, did not overthrow the bourgeois order? Why did the leaders of the Soviet deliver power to the liberal bourgeoisie?

To refer only to the ideology of Menshevism, which saw the revolution as a bourgeois revolution, would not be enough. Neither could the paradox be explained by the fact that the Socialist Revolutionaries (and with them the Mensheviks) spoke about "revolutionary democracy"—as being neither bourgeois nor socialist—thus emptying the political regime of social content. Why did these ideas prevail? The answer lies in the preponderance at the beginning of the revolution of the petty-bourgeois masses—peasants in the main—led by intellectuals, and the immaturity of the revolution.

The basis of representation in the soviet gave the advantage to the soldiers—the peasants in uniform. There was one delegate from each company of soldiers, as against one delegate for each thousand workers. Originally the companies in question had been those of the swollen reserve regiments, each with a thousand or more soldiers, but soon every company, regardless of size, was sending one delegate to the soviet. As a result the 150,000 troops in the garrison had double the representation of the 450,000 workers in the city.[34] The soldiers therefore had four to five times more representatives than the workers in proportion to their numbers; there were two thousand soldiers and eight hundred workers in the soviet.[35]

Among the workers, again, those from smaller plants were very much better represented than those from larger ones. The large factories, with 87 percent of the workers of Petrograd, had 484 delegates to the soviet, while the others, with 13 percent of the workers, had 422 delegates.[36*]

And who represented the soldiers? Mainly petty-bourgeois intellectuals. This is how Sukhanov describes the soldiers' representatives in the soviet immediately after the February Revolution:

> Most of these soldiers' and officers' delegates made a right-democratic, or purely philistine, or simply Cadet-minded mass. In part they were people of the liberal professions and of liberal views who had hastily fastened on some kind of socialist label, indispensable in the Soviet democratic organizations; but in part they were really soldiers put forward by soldiers' organizations in accordance with the prevailing war-mongering moods. Most of them clustered around the SR core.[38]

The SR (Socialist Revolutionary) Party, by far the largest in the soviet, attracted masses of petty-bourgeois and even bourgeois elements.

> They were the petty-bourgeois democracy—peasants, shopkeepers, cooperators, minor officials, the third estate, the great mass of the indigent intelligentsia.... This, the largest party, had attracted into itself both some of the temperamental upper bourgeoisie and some of the effusively liberal landowners, and in the footsteps of the highly popular new War Minister, Kerensky, solid masses of military people—regular officers and even generals—had begun to enter the party. Two and a half months before, presumably, not one of the latter would have hesitated to shoot or hand over to the executioner any passer-by he even suspected of being an SR.[39]

Dual power

However, a regime based on dual power is bound to be very unstable. Inherent in it is the likelihood of civil war between the two state powers. How can one contain both in the midst of a rising revolutionary crisis? To this, the left Menshevik Sukhanov tried to give a theoretical answer.

> One must imagine all the complexity of the position of a victorious and profoundly democratic revolution which had made the proletariat the actual masters of the situation, while at the same time leaving untouched both the foundations of the bourgeois order and even the formal authority of the old ruling classes; one must understand all the complexity and contradictoriness of this position created by the revolution in order to appreciate how difficult, crucial, and tick-

---

* The same underrepresentation of the large factories and overrepresentation of the small ones occurred in the soviets of other cities. Thus in Moscow the twenty giant enterprises (like Guzhon, Dynamo, etc.) with seventy-two thousand workers, were represented in the soviet by sixty delegates, while the small enterprises (less than four hundred workers each) also with seventy-two thousand workers, had more than one hundred delegates.[37]

lish the labor problem was at this period, and what experience, firmness, tact, and skill it required, between the hammer and the anvil,
between the protesting rebellious workers and the employers, end-
lessly threatening strikes and lockouts.[40]

There could be only one answer to the problem raised by dual
sovereignty, if it were to be preserved: one power—the soviet—
would have to subordinate itself to the other—the provisional government. And this was exactly what the Menshevik and SR leaders
strove to do.

> There were widespread demands for peace, land, and bread amongst
> the masses. The government could not and would not grant them.
> And in this class struggle the Soviet was on the side of the govern-
> ment. It passed off the government's sabotage as the realization of the
> program, while it exhorted the masses to tranquility and loyalty.
> *That is, the Soviet was fighting against the people and the revolution
> and for the policy of the bourgeois government.*[41]

The capitalists knew they were impotent. "The provisional government has no real power at its disposal," Guchkov, the minister
of war, wrote to General Alekseev, on March 9,

> and its decrees are carried out only to the extent this is permitted by
> the Soviet of Workers' and Soldiers' Deputies. The Soviet controls the
> most important elements of real power, such as the army, the rail-
> ways, the post and telegraphs. It is possible to say flatly that the pro-
> visional government exists only as long as is allowed by the Soviet of
> Workers' and Soldiers' Deputies. In particular, it is now possible to
> give only those orders which do not radically conflict with the orders
> of the above-mentioned Soviet.[42]

The soviet "was obliged to apply all its energies to hand over to
the government the totality of its power and lay it at its feet. This
was the Soviet 'line.'"[43]

And what was the banner under which the army of the petty-
bourgeoisie marched behind the bourgeoisie? The answer: democracy. The Menshevik and Socialist Revolutionary leaders in Russia
in 1917 only confirmed what Engels had written in a letter to Bebel
on December 11, 1884, about the role of "pure democracy":

> [W]hen the moment of revolution comes, of its acquiring a temporary
> importance as the most radical *bourgeois* party...and as the final
> sheet-anchor of the whole bourgeois and even feudal regime...the
> whole reactionary mass falls in behind it and strengthens it; every-
> thing which used to be reactionary behaves as democratic. In any case
> our sole adversary on the day of the crisis and on the day after the cri-
> sis will be the *whole collective reaction which will group itself around*

pure democracy, and this, I think, should not be lost sight of.[44]

Lenin explains

Lenin, unlike Sukhanov and other Mensheviks, did not fall for a futile explanation of the fate of the revolution in terms of some suprahistorical schema, that the revolution was bourgeois because of immutable laws that made it so. For Lenin the key was action. In a pamphlet written at the beginning of April, called *The Tasks of the Proletariat in Our Revolution,* he explained that the compromisers controlled the soviet as a result of: (1) the immaturity of the revolution, and (2) the weight of the petty-bourgeois mass.

> [The revolution] *drew* unprecedentedly vast numbers of ordinary citizens *into the movement*...millions and tens of millions of people, who had been politically dormant for ten years and politically crushed by the terrible oppression of Tsarism and by inhuman toil for the landowners and capitalists, *have awakened and taken eagerly* to politics. And who are these millions and tens of millions? For the most part small proprietors, petty-bourgeois, people standing midway between the capitalists and the wage workers. Russia is the most petty-bourgeois of all European countries.
>
> A gigantic petty-bourgeois wave has swept over everything and overwhelmed the class-conscious proletariat, not only by force of numbers but also ideologically; that is, it has infected and imbued very wide circles of workers with the petty-bourgeois political outlook.[45]

The petty-bourgeoisie tended to trust the capitalists:

> An attitude of unreasoning trust in the capitalists—the worst foes of peace and socialism—characterizes the politics of the *popular masses* in Russia at the present moment; this is the fruit that has *grown* with revolutionary rapidity on the social and economic soil of the most petty-bourgeois of all European countries. This is the *class* basis for the "agreement" between the provisional government and the Soviet of Workers' and Soldiers' Deputies.[46]

As a result of the influence of the petty-bourgeoisie, power was given to the bourgeoisie.

> The highly important feature of the Russian revolution is the fact that the Petrograd Soviet of Soldiers' and Workers' Deputies, which ...enjoys the confidence of most of the local Soviets, is *voluntarily* transferring state power to the bourgeoisie and *its* provisional government, is voluntarily *ceding* supremacy to the latter, having entered into an agreement to support it.[47]

The result was dual power.

> This dual power is evident in the existence of *two governments:* one is the main, the real, the actual government of the bourgeoisie, the "Provisional Government" of Lvov and Co., which holds in its hands all the organs of power; the other is a supplementary and parallel government, a "controlling" government in the shape of the Petrograd Soviet of Workers' and Soldiers' Deputies, which holds no organs of state power, but directly rests on the support of an obvious and indisputable majority of the people, on the armed workers and soldiers.[47]

But it could not last long.

> The dual power merely expresses a *transitional* phase in the revolution's development, when it has gone farther than the ordinary bourgeois-democratic revolution, *but has not yet reached a "pure"* dictatorship of the proletariat and the peasantry.[48]

The February Revolution failed to overthrow capitalism not because of some suprahistorical law of Menshevik "Marxism," but because of the immaturity of the revolution, i.e., the lack of class consciousness and organization of the proletariat. As Lenin put it in his *April Theses* [see chapter 7]

> The specific feature of the present situation in Russia is that the country is *passing* from the first stage of the revolution—which, owing to the insufficient class consciousness and organization of the proletariat, is in the hands of the bourgeoisie—to its second stage, which must place power in the hands of the proletariat and the poorest sections of the peasants.[49]

The February Revolution led to the establishment of the provisional government headed by Prince Lvov and consisting mainly of Cadets and Octobrists. Its most important personalities were Miliukov (Foreign Affairs) and Guchkov (War). Kerensky, as minister of justice, was the only "socialist" in it. It had the support of the compromisist leaders of the soviet—the Socialist Revolutionaries, whose main leader was V. Chernov, and the Mensheviks, whose main leader at the time was N.S. Chkheidze.

CHAPTER 7

LENIN REARMS THE PARTY

The Bolshevik Party after the February Revolution

Although the revolution was led by class-conscious workers who were mostly Bolsheviks, it was not led by the Bolshevik Party. Furthermore, the number of class-conscious workers active in the revolution could be counted in thousands, or tens of thousands, while the number who were aroused by the revolution was measured in millions. No wonder the leadership of the rank-and-file Bolsheviks in the February Revolution, although able to achieve the victory of the insurrection, could not secure political power for the working class or the Bolshevik Party.

The Putilov works with their forty thousand workers contained only 150 Bolsheviks by February 1917; in the working-class and factory district of Vyborg, there were no more than about five hundred Bolsheviks.[1] Out of fifteen hundred to sixteen hundred delegates in the Petrograd Soviet in February, only about forty were Bolsheviks.[2]

The proportion of Bolsheviks in the Petrograd Soviet was even smaller than their actual proportion among the people, because the Mensheviks and SRs rushed to take seats in the soviet while many Bolsheviks were still participating in the street battles. I. Zalezhkii observed at the March 4 meeting of the Petersburg Committee of the Bolsheviks

> that the seizure of seats in the Petrograd Soviet of Workers' and Soldiers' Deputies by the Liquidators [Mensheviks and SRs—TC] took place because at the time when the Bolsheviks were working illegally, the Liquidators were acting freely. In the first days of the February revolution the Bolsheviks were with the masses on the streets, and the Liquidators rushed straight to the Duma.[3]

The Bolsheviks were politically in complete disarray at the time. They hardly constituted a distinct grouping in the soviet. Sukhanov described the situation at the time thus:

> The fractions themselves had not yet taken shape in the Soviet. References to party adherence were very rare. Opinions overlapped and... were very feebly differentiated.
>   Also, from the fraction point of view the deputies did not sit in any kind of order. In those days there was no tendency to split up into fractions and the deputies sat as chance directed.[4]

Sukhanov asserts that at a session of the Executive Committee of the soviet on March 1, when the question at issue was that of handing over power to the bourgeoisie, not one voice was raised in opposition, despite the fact that eleven of the thirty-nine members of the Executive Committee were Bolsheviks, and that the three members of the Russian Bureau of the Central Committee were present (A.G. Shliapnikov, V.M. Molotov, and P.A. Zalutsky).[5] At the session of the soviet as a whole on March 2 only fifteen out of the forty Bolsheviks present voted against the transfer of power to the provisional government—i.e., to the bourgeoisie.[6]

On March 3, the Petersburg Committee of the Bolshevik Party passed a resolution that it would "not oppose the power of the provisional government *insofar as* its activities correspond to the interests of the proletariat and of the broad democratic masses of the people."[7] The formula "insofar as" (*postolku, poskolku*) appeared in the resolution of the Executive Committee of the Petrograd Soviet on relations with the provisional government, and became a way of referring to this particular policy of supporting the government.

Again, when some Bolsheviks in the Petrograd Soviet moved a resolution calling for the soviet to form a government, they received only nineteen votes, with many party members opposing the motion.[8]

No doubt the fact that the Mensheviks and SRs had an overwhelming majority in the soviet influenced the attitudes of the Bolsheviks. As Shliapnikov put it: "Evidently the victory of the Menshevik Social Democrats and the Socialist Revolutionaries at the last plenum [of the soviet on March 2] on the question of power, came as a psychological shock to the Petersburg Committee moving it to the right."[9]

The Vyborg Committee's position

It must, however, be made clear that there was resistance to the opportunist line of both the Petersburg Committee and the right wing of the Bolshevik group in the soviet. The resolution of the Petersburg Committee supporting the provisional government *"postolku, poskolku"* was resisted in the committee itself, with three members from the Vyborg Committee voting against it—K.I. Shutko, M.I. Kalinin, and N.G. Tolmachev.[10]

The Vyborg District Committee, which had the best organized district of Petrograd in its working-class area in the northwest of the city, took a militant left-wing line throughout. In fact, it played a central role in the February Revolution. Not only was it closely involved in the action in one of the two main working-class areas of the city (the other being the Narva district in the southwest), but on February 26, it took command of the entire Petrograd Bolshevik organization after the arrest of most of the members of the Petersburg Committee.

Vyborg was the district where the key modern engineering works in Petrograd were located. A measure of Bolshevik influence there was that throughout the period between February and October, the Bolsheviks had a majority in the Vyborg District Soviet. In Kronstadt, which had always been thought to be a bulwark of Bolshevism, there were only eleven deputies out of about three hundred at the beginning of the period, and even by October, only 136, or less than half the soviet. In fact the Vyborg District Committee had a decisive influence on revolutionary Kronstadt and Helsingfors, the bastions of Bolshevism in the period leading up to October.

The Vyborg District Committee was also well organized, and had participated fully in the greatest event of the century, the victorious February Revolution. It had every reason to feel self-reliant and confident.

On February 27, during the revolution itself, it issued a leaflet calling for the election of a soviet, and the revolutionary overthrow of the autocracy and transfer of power to the soviet.[11] Resolutions urging the transfer of power to the soviets were passed almost unanimously at factory meetings. A general meeting of the Vyborg Bolsheviks on March 1 adopted a resolution calling for the soviets to seize power immediately and abolish the Duma's Provisional Committee.[12]

On March 5, O.G. Lifshits, from Vyborg, moved the following draft resolution at a meeting of the Petersburg Committee of the

Bolshevik Party:

> 1. The task of the moment is the founding of a provisional revolutionary government, growing out of the unification of local Soviets of Workers, Peasants, and Soldiers' Deputies in the whole of Russia.
> 2. To prepare for the full seizure of central power it is necessary to: (a) strengthen the power of the Soviets of Workers and Soldiers' Deputies; (b) proceed locally to the partial seizure of power by overthrowing the organs of the old power and replacing them by Soviets of Workers, Peasants, and Soldiers' Deputies, the tasks of which are the arming of the people, the organization of the army on democratic principles, the confiscation of the land, and the carrying out of all the other demands of the minimum program....
>
> The power of the provisional government which was founded by the Provisional Committee of the State Duma, will be recognized and supported only until the formation of a revolutionary government from the Soviets of Workers, Peasants, and Soldiers' Deputies and only in so far as its actions are consistent with the interests of the proletariat and the broad democratic masses.[13]

Shutko, the Petersburg Committee member from Vyborg, was the only one to vote for this resolution; Lifshits's vote was consultative.

The formulation of the Vyborg District Committee position had much in common with Lenin's "Letters from Afar" (March 7–26) and his *April Theses* (of April 4). It spoke about the need to transfer power to the soviets, as Lenin did. But unlike Lenin, the Vyborg comrades limited the scope of the new government to a minimum program: they did not go beyond the old Bolshevik formula of democratic dictatorship of the proletariat and peasantry, i.e., beyond the boundaries of the bourgeois revolution.

The Petersburg Committee

The conflict between the Vyborg District Committee and the Petersburg Committee reflected radical differences in attitudes to the workers' strike movement of the time.

The battle for the eight-hour day went on throughout practically the whole of March.[*] On March 5, the Petrograd Soviet adopted by 1,170 votes to 30 a resolution calling on all workers to return to work. The Vyborg District Committee of the Bolsheviks declared this resolution null and void as long as the workers had not achieved the eight-hour day, a pay raise, etc. The committee organized a demonstration against the soviet decision, stating:

> The Vyborg District Committee RSDLP(b), having discussed the

question of returning to work, considers that the Petersburg Committee ought to organize an all-city demonstration, since it considers that in the moment that it is living through, the proletariat ought to undertake a yet stronger struggle for the basic slogans: a democratic republic, the eight-hour working day, confiscation of all the land, and also the moment demands from us a definite answer on the question of the war. We consider that this slogan on ending the war ought to be put forward on this demonstration.[14]

However, the Petersburg Committee refused to support the resolution. The Vyborg comrades were enraged. A delegate from Vyborg stated at the March 7 session of the Petersburg Committee: "The Vyborg District expresses dissatisfaction with the Petersburg Committee's tardiness in bringing its decisions to the attention of the factories. This is why they decided to carry out the eight-hour working day independently in their own district."

In addition, the following resolution from Vyborg was moved (and noted):

The Vyborg District Committee RSDLP(b), having discussed the decision of the Petrograd Soviet of Workers' and Soldiers' Deputies on returning to work, considers this decision premature, in view of the fact that there was no decision about conditions of work.

There were a number of reasons why the Petersburg Committee stood so far to the right of the Vyborg District Committee. First, it was further from the grass roots and less integrated with the proletarian masses. Secondly, as has been pointed out by one historian, the majority of the Petersburg Committee did not participate in the February Revolution, and a number of its members had been away from the field of battle (in prison) for a long time before.[15]

The left of the Petersburg Committee, who voted against conditional support for the provisional government (*postolku, poskolku*), was made up of the three delegates from Vyborg named above.

The Russian Bureau of the Central Committee

A third position, between those of the Petersburg Committee and the Vyborg District Committee, was taken by the Russian Bureau of the Central Committee. This bureau had three members: Shliapnikov, Molotov, and Zalutsky. The main body of the Central Committee elected in 1912 was in exile, either abroad or in Siberia. The Russian Bureau represented the exiled committee on the spot. All three members had escaped arrest during the war and all three were active during the February Revolution.

On February 27, the bureau issued a manifesto "to all citizens of Russia." The manifesto called for the establishment of a provisional revolutionary government:

> The task of the working class and the revolutionary army is to create a revolutionary provisional government which will lead the new regime, the new republican regime.... Workers of all factories and plants, as well as the insurgent troops, must elect without delay their representatives to the provisional revolutionary government, which must be established by the revolutionary insurgent people and their armies.

The task of this government should be the implementation of the minimum program and the preparation of the constituent assembly:

> The provisional revolutionary government must decree provisional laws which will safeguard the freedom and rights of the people, confiscate church and crown lands and turn them over to the people, institute the eight-hour day, and convoke the constituent assembly on the basis of direct, equal and secret universal suffrage.[16]

The aims of the Russian Bureau and the Vyborg District Committee were the same. The difference was in the emphasis placed by the latter on creating the provisional government from below through the formation of soviets.

The Russian Bureau was concerned that the Vyborg District Committee's line might lead to a premature uprising, and on March 3 it ordered the withdrawal of the leaflet that was circulating in Vyborg calling for the overthrow of the provisional government.[17]

In the first half of March, the bureau co-opted a number of new members. The new enlarged bureau was, it seems, somewhat to the left of the original one. On March 9, however, it adopted a resolution on the provisional government that was still considerably to the right of the Vyborg District Committee. Although it was more critical of the government than previously, and its statement included a number of revolutionary elements, it referred to the soviet as "the embryo of the revolutionary power," while at the same time contradicting itself by speaking about the need for a division of labor between the soviets and the provisional government:

> At the present moment these Soviets should exercise the most decisive control over all the actions of the provisional government and its agents both in the center and in the provinces; and they should themselves assume a number of functions of state and of an economic character arising from the complete disorganization of economic life in the country and from the urgent necessity to apply the most resolute mea-

sures for safeguarding the famine-stricken population whom war has ruined. Therefore the task of the day is: The consolidation of all forces around the Soviet of Workers' and Soldiers' Deputies as the embryo of revolutionary power, alone capable both of repelling the attempts on the part of the Tsarist and bourgeois counter-revolution as well as of realizing the demands of revolutionary democracy and of explaining the true class nature of the present government.

The most urgent and important task of the Soviets, the fulfillment of which will alone guarantee the victory over all the forces of counter-revolution and the further development and deepening of the revolution, is, in the opinion of the party, the universal arming of the people, and, in particular, the immediate creation of Workers' Red Guards throughout the entire land.[18]

This Russian Bureau resolution put forward the soviets as the bearers of the new power.

Thus, despite all the vacillations and vagueness, both the Vyborg District Committee and the Russian Bureau were moving toward a position close to Lenin's *before* he returned to Russia, although very different from his position regarding the bourgeois democratic limits of the revolution.

On the question of the war, the Petersburg Committee was to the right of the bureau. At best, the views of the majority of the Petersburg Committee were muddled. The minutes of the committee of March 7 record:

Com. Fedorov, G.F., whilst being in principle for the ending of the war, considers it impossible categorically to demand its ending, since if the front is weakened there is a risk of losing those freedoms which we have already succeeded in securing. The danger of a German regime being established is a considerably greater danger than the reestablishment of the prerevolutionary government.

Com. Avilov, B.V., formulated the view of the Petersburg Committee in the following manner: (1) the war is imperialist; (2) the ending of the war should be the result of the agreed actions of the international proletariat; (3) an immediate end to the war under present conditions, i.e., the continued power of the German imperialist government and the presence of danger from the counter-revolution in Russia, is inadmissible; on the contrary, we must declare that until these dangers are removed our front must be defended against German attack.[19]

Kamenev, Stalin, and Muranov

The disarray in the Bolshevik ranks was increased by the return of Kamenev, Stalin, and Muranov from Siberia. On March 12, they arrived in the capital and immediately took over the editing of

Pravda, which had begun publication a week earlier. The comrades accepted this takeover as natural, for after all, two of these men (Kamenev and Stalin) were the only members of the Central Committee in Russia at the time, and the third (Muranov) was a former Duma deputy. The change in the editorial board of *Pravda* led the paper to swing sharply to the right. As Sukhanov put it, "In a flash it *(Pravda)* became unrecognizable."[20]

The new editors announced that the Bolsheviks would decisively support the provisional government "insofar as it struggles against reaction or counter-revolution"—forgetting that the only important agent of counterrevolution at the time was this same provisional government. The new editors expressed themselves no less categorically on the war. Thus Kamenev took a position almost indistinguishable from that of the social chauvinists:

> The war goes on. The great Russian revolution did not interrupt it. And no one entertains the hope that it will end tomorrow, or the day after. The soldiers, the peasants, and the workers of Russia who went to war at the call of the deposed Tsar, and who shed their blood under his banners, have liberated themselves, and the Tsarist banners have been replaced by the red banners of the revolution. But the war will go on, because the German army has not followed the example of the Russian army and is still obeying its Emperor, who avidly seeks his prey on the battlefields of death.
>
> When an army stands against an army, the most absurd policy would be to propose that one of them lay down its arms and go home. This policy would not be a policy of peace but a policy of slavery, a policy which the free people would reject with indignation. No, the free people will stand firmly at their posts, will reply bullet for bullet and shell for shell. This is unavoidable.
>
> The revolutionary soldiers and officers who have overthrown the yoke of Tsarism will not quit their trenches so as to clear the place for the German or Austrian soldiers or officers, who as yet have not had the courage to overthrow the yoke of their own government. We cannot permit any disorganization of the military forces of the revolution! War must be ended in an organized way, by a pact among the peoples which have liberated themselves, and not by subordination to the will of the neighboring conqueror and imperialist.[21]

15 March, the day of the appearance of the first number of the "reformed *Pravda,*" [writes Shliapnikov] was a day of triumph for the "defensists." The whole of the Tauride Palace, from the members of the Committee of the Duma to the Executive Committee, the very heart of revolutionary democracy, was brimful of one piece of news—the victory of the moderate and reasonable Bolsheviks over the extremists. In the Executive Committee itself, we were met with venomous smiles. It was the first and only time that *Pravda* won the praise of "defensists"

of the worst type. In the factories, this number of *Pravda* produced stupefaction among the adherents of our party and its sympathizers, and the spiteful satisfaction of our enemies. In the Petrograd Committee, at the Bureau of the Central Committee and on the staff of *Pravda*, many questions were received. What was happening? Why had our paper left the Bolshevik policy to follow that of the "defensists"? But the Petrograd Committee was taken unawares, as was the whole organization, by the *coup d'état*, and was profoundly displeased, accusing the Bureau of the Central Committee. Indignation in the workers' suburbs was very strong, and when the proletarians learnt that three former editors of *Pravda*, just come from Siberia, had taken possession of the paper, they demanded their expulsion from the party.[22]

Pravda was soon compelled to print a sharp protest from the Vyborg District Committee:

> If the paper does not want to lose the confidence of the workers, it must and will bring the light of revolutionary consciousness, no matter how painful it may be to the bourgeois owls [emphasis in original].[23]

While the Vyborg District Committee was protesting against the line of *Pravda*, the Petersburg Committee fell more and more under its influence. Thus on March 18, Kamenev proposed that it should change its "insofar as" policy towards the provisional government to actual support; against some opposition the committee adopted Kamenev's proposal.[24]

Despite the Vyborg District's protests and those of many workers, until Lenin's return to Russia, *Pravda's* general political line continued to accommodate the provisional government and the defensists, and to be conciliatory towards the government and the war.

All over the country...

It has to be made clear that *Pravda's* line—that the revolution was a bourgeois democratic revolution, that the provisional government needed to be supported *postolku, poskolku,* and concessions made to "defensism"—was followed by local Bolshevik leaders all over Russia. It is unlikely that this was simply a result of the influence of *Pravda*.

The Kharkov Bolshevik paper *Sotsial-Demokrat* wrote on March 19:

> Until German democracy takes power into its hands our army must stand up like a wall of steel, armed from head to foot against Prussian militarism, for the victory of Prussian militarism is the death of our freedom.[25]

The Moscow Bolshevik daily *Sotsial-Demokrat* of March 20 stated: "Until peace has been achieved—we do not throw away our arms."[26]

The formula of support for the provisional government was reported again and again, for instance, *Krasnoiarskürabochii*, the Bolshevik paper of Krasnoiarsk, on March 15,[27] and the Moscow *Sotsial-Demokrat* on March 9[28] and in April.[29] The Kharkov Bolshevik paper went so far as to demand from the provisional government that it should carry out the minimum program of the party![30]

In Baku, the enthusiasm of the Bolshevik leaders was such that they joined the local provisional government.[31]

The All-Russian Bolshevik Conference

The Bolshevik leaders Kamenev and Stalin formulated their right-wing position even more clearly at the All-Russian Conference of the Bolshevik Party held on March 28.[32]

In his report "On the Attitude to the Provisional Government," Stalin stated:

> The power has been divided between two organs, of which neither one possesses full power. There is and there ought to be friction and struggle between them. The roles have been divided. The Soviet of Workers' and Soldiers' Deputies has in fact taken the initiative in effecting revolutionary transformations. The Soviet of Workers' and Soldiers' Deputies is the revolutionary leader of the insurrectionary people; an organ of control over the provisional government. On the other hand, the provisional government has in fact taken the role of fortifier of the conquests of the revolutionary people. The Soviet of Workers' and Soldiers' Deputies mobilizes the forces and exercizes control, while the provisional government...takes the role of the fortifier of those conquests by the people.... Such a situation has disadvantageous, but also advantageous sides.

Here Stalin overlooks *class* distinctions and speaks simply about the division of labor between the provisional government and the soviets. The workers and soldiers advance the revolution and the bourgeois government fortifies the conquests of the revolution!

> Insofar as the provisional government fortifies the steps of the revolution, to that extent we must support it; but insofar as it is counterrevolutionary, support to the provisional government is not permissible.

Stalin then declared his support for the resolution of the Krasnoiarsk Soviet of Workers' and Soldiers' Deputies, which stated:

The submission of the provisional government to the basic demands of the revolution can be secured only by the unrelaxing pressure of the proletariat, the peasantry and the revolutionary army, who must with unremitting energy maintain their organization around the Soviets of Workers' and Soldiers' Deputies born out of the revolution, in order to transform the latter into the terrible force of the revolutionary people ...to support the provisional government in its activities only insofar as it follows a course of satisfying the demands of the working class and the revolutionary peasantry in the revolution that is taking place.

In the discussion on the war, which did not produce any resolution from the conference, the right Bolsheviks' attack was even more open and objectionable. Thus Vasiliev, the delegate from Saratov, moved a resolution stating:

Revolutionary democratic Russia does not seek an inch of foreign soil, or a penny of foreign property. But not an inch of our own soil or a penny of our own property can be taken away from us...so long as peace is not concluded we must stand fully armed; and in guarding the interests of new democratic Russia we must increase tenfold our efforts, for we are now defending our budding liberties. The revolutionary army must be powerful and unconquerable. It must be provided by the workers and by the provisional government with everything necessary to strengthen its forces. Discipline in the ranks, being the necessary condition of an army's strength, must be sustained not out of fear but out of free will, and based upon mutual confidence between the democratic officer staff and the revolutionary soldiers.

There were a number of protests against the Stalin-Kamenev line at the conference. Thus Skrypnik declared:

The government is not fortifying, but checking the cause of the revolution.
　　There can be no more talk of supporting the government. There is a conspiracy of the provisional government against the people and the revolution, and it is necessary to prepare for a struggle against it.

Nogin said: "It is clear that we ought not now to talk about support but about *resistance.*" But, on the whole, Stalin and Kamenev undoubtedly had the majority of the conference with them.

The conference then discussed the question of uniting the Bolsheviks and Mensheviks into one party, as suggested by Tsereteli. Stalin was wholly in favor of the proposal. "We ought to go. It is necessary to define our proposals as to the terms of unification. Unification is possible along the lines of Zimmerwald-Kienthal."

Molotov spoke in opposition, but Stalin stuck to his guns:

There is no use running ahead and anticipating disagreements. There is no party life without disagreements. We shall live down trivial dis-agreements within the party. But there is one question—it is impossi-ble to unite what cannot be united. We will have a single party with those who agree on Zimmerwald and Kienthal, i.e., those who are against revolutionary defensism.[33]

Unity on the basis of the vague pacifist resolutions of Zimmer-wald and Kienthal, resolutions that Lenin had voted against! Unity with Tsereteli, the man who moved the Menshevik–Socialist Revo-lutionary coalition to the right, and who three months later ar-rested and disarmed the Bolsheviks!

Writing years after these events, Trotsky stated quite accurately: "A reading of the reports…frequently produces a feeling of amaze-ment: is it possible that a party represented by these delegates will after seven months seize the power with an iron hand?"[34]

In anticipation

Long before the February 1917 Revolution Lenin had warned against the danger of defensism raising its ugly head once the tsar was removed—of his regime being replaced not by proletarian rule, but by a bourgeois democratic government. In an article called "So-cial Chauvinist Policy Behind the Cover of Internationalist Phrases" (published in *Sotsial-Demokrat*, No. 49, December 21, 1915), he ar-gued against Martov's statement: "It is self-evident that if the present crisis should lead to the victory of a democratic revolution, to a re-public, then the character of the war would radically change."

Lenin hammered the point hard:

All this is a shameless lie. Martov could not but have known that a democratic revolution and a republic mean a bourgeois-democratic revolution and a bourgeois-democratic republic. The character of this war between the bourgeois *and imperialist* great powers would not change *a jot* were the military-autocratic and feudal imperialism to be swept away in one of these countries. That is because, in such con-ditions, a purely bourgeois imperialism would not vanish, but would only *gain strength*.[35]

A few weeks earlier, Lenin had argued that it was not "admissible for Social Democrats to join a provisional revolutionary government …with revolutionary chauvinists."

By revolutionary chauvinists we mean those who want a victory over Tsarism so as to achieve victory over Germany, plunder other coun-tries, consolidate Great Russian rule over the other peoples of Russia, etc. Revolutionary chauvinism is based on the class position of the petty bourgeoisie. The latter always vacillates between the bourgeoisie and the proletariat. At present it is vacillating between chauvinism (which prevents it from being consistently revolutionary, even in the meaning of a democratic revolution), and proletarian internationalism. At the moment the Trudoviks, the Socialist Revolutionaries, *Nasha Zarya*, Chkheidze's Duma group, the Organizing Committee, Mr. Plekhanov, and the like are the political spokesmen for this petty bourgeoisie in Russia.

If the revolutionary chauvinists won in Russia, we would be opposed to a defence of *their* "fatherland" in the present war. Our slogan is: against the chauvinists, even if they are revolutionary and republican—*against* them, and *for* an alliance of the international proletariat for the socialist revolution.[36]

And with insight and impressive foresight, Lenin wrote:

A new political division has arisen in Russia on the basis of new, higher, more developed and more complex international relations. This new division is between the chauvinist revolutionaries, who desire revolution so as to defeat Germany, and the proletarian internationalist revolutionaries, who desire a revolution in Russia *for the sake of* the proletarian revolution in the West, and simultaneously with that revolution. This new division is, in essence, one between the urban and the rural petty bourgeoisie in Russia, and the socialist proletariat.[37]

He foresaw the danger of an alliance of petty bourgeois democratic defensists with the liberal bourgeoisie.

Equally clear is the liberal bourgeoisie's stand—exploit the defeat and the mounting revolution in order to wrest concessions from a frightened monarchy and compel it to share power with the bourgeoisie. Just as clear, too, is the stand of the revolutionary proletariat, which is striving to consummate the revolution by exploiting the vacillation and embarrassment of the government and the bourgeoisie. The petty bourgeoisie, however, i.e., the vast mass of the barely awakening population of Russia, is groping blindly in the wake of the bourgeoisie, a captive to nationalist prejudices, on the one hand, prodded into the revolution by the unparalleled horror and misery of war, the high cost of living, impoverishment, ruin, and starvation, but on the other hand, glancing *backward* at every step towards the idea of defence of the fatherland, towards the idea of Russia's state integrity, or towards the idea of small-peasant prosperity, to be achieved through a victory over Tsarism and over Germany, but without a victory over capitalism.[38]

Consequently, in the present war, the Russian proletariat could "defend the fatherland" and consider "the character of the war radically changed," only and exclusively *if* the revolution were to put the party of the proletariat in power, and were to permit only that party to guide the entire force of a revolutionary upheaval and the entire machinery of state towards an instant and direct conclusion of an alliance with the socialist proletariat of Germany and Europe.[39]

On the basis of this internationalist stand, Lenin now, after the February Revolution, developed a whole new revolutionary strategy and tactics, the first product of which were his "Letters from Afar."

Lenin's "Letters from Afar"

While the Bolshevik leadership in Russia was in a state of disunity, with the top leaders veering towards defensism, towards supporting the provisional government, and towards unity with the Mensheviks, Lenin was fuming at being "accursed afar." Before coming back to Russia he was already very worried, as a result of the scanty information filtering through to him, about the Bolshevik leadership's position. A letter of March 30 to J.S. Hanecki, a member of the Bureau Abroad of the Central Committee of the Bolsheviks, is filled with alarm:

> Our party would disgrace itself forever, commit political suicide, if it tolerated such a deception…I personally will not hesitate for a second to declare, and to declare in print, that I shall prefer even an immediate split with anyone in our party, whoever it may be, to making concessions to the social-patriotism of Kerensky and Co. or the social pacifism and Kautskianism of Chkheidze and Co.[40]

After this seemingly impersonal threat, Lenin makes it clear that he has certain individuals in mind as the main culprits: "Kamenev must realize that he bears a *world*-historic responsibility."[41]

However Lenin did not limit himself to cursing the opportunism of Kamenev and his associates. He quickly got to work to draw up a political strategy for the party and the proletariat. Between March 7 and March 26 he wrote five "Letters from Afar" (the fifth was unfinished). Only the first was published by *Pravda*. In this he wrote:

> Side by side with this government—which as regards the *present* war is but the agent of the billion-dollar "firm" "England and France"— there has arisen the chief, unofficial, as yet undeveloped and comparatively weak *workers' government*, which expresses the interests of the proletariat and of the entire poor section of the urban and rural population. This is the *Soviet of Workers' Deputies* in Petrograd…. The Soviet of Workers' Deputies is an organization of the workers, the embryo of a workers' government, the representative of the interests of the entire mass of the *poor* section of the population, i.e., of nine-tenths of the population, which is striving for *peace, bread,* and *freedom….* He who says that the workers must *support* the new gov-

ernment in the interests of the struggle against Tsarist reaction...is a traitor to the workers, a traitor to the cause of the proletariat, to the cause of peace and freedom.... For the only *guarantee* of freedom and of the complete destruction of Tsarism lies in *arming the proletariat*, in strengthening, extending, and developing the role, significance, and power of the Soviet of Workers' Deputies.[42]

Lenin's statements were produced as if from a machine gun!

The "task of the day" at *this* moment must be: Workers, *you have performed miracles of proletarian heroism, the heroism of the people, in the civil war against Tsarism. You must perform miracles of organization, organization of the proletariat and of the whole people, to prepare the way for your victory in the second stage of the revolution.*[43]

Who were the allies of the proletariat in the revolution?

It has *two* allies; first, the broad mass of the semi-proletarian and partly also of the small-peasant population, who number scores of millions and constitute the overwhelming majority of the population of Russia.... Second, the ally of the Russian proletariat is the proletariat of all the belligerent countries in general.[44]

He continued,

With these two allies, the proletariat, *utilizing the peculiarities of the* present transition situation, can and will proceed, first to the achievement of a democratic republic and complete victory of the peasantry over the landlords, instead of the Guchkov–Miliukov semi-monarchy, and then to *socialism,* which alone can give the war-weary people *peace, bread, and freedom.*[45]

In the second "Letter from Afar," Lenin put forward clearly the need for a second revolution and the need to establish a workers' government: "Only a proletarian republic, backed by the rural workers and the poorest section of the peasants and town dwellers, can secure peace, provide bread, order, and freedom."[46]

The third letter goes further in elaborating the task and the structure of the future workers' state:

We need a state. But *not the kind* of state the bourgeoisie has created everywhere, from constitutional monarchies to the most democratic republics....

We need a state, but *not* the kind the bourgeoisie needs, with organs of government in the shape of a police force, an army, and a bureaucracy (officialdom) separate from and opposed to the people. All bourgeois revolutionaries merely perfected *this* state machine, merely transferred *it* from the hands of one party to those of another.

The proletariat, on the other hand, if it wants to uphold the gains of the present revolution and proceed further, to win peace, bread and freedom, must "smash," to use Marx's expression, this "ready-made" state machine and substitute a new one for it by *merging* the police force, the army, and the bureaucracy with the *entire armed people*. Following the path indicated by the experience of the Paris Commune of 1871 and the Russian revolution of 1905, the proletariat must organize and arm *all* the poor, exploited sections of the population in order that they *themselves* should take the organs of state power directly into their own hands, in order that *they themselves should constitute* these organs of state power.[47]

Again Lenin comes to the key problem of the revolution: organization.

Comrade workers! You performed miracles of proletarian heroism yesterday in overthrowing the Tsarist monarchy. In the more or less near future (perhaps even now, as these lines are being written) you will again have to perform the same miracles of heroism to overthrow the rule of the landlords and capitalists, who are waging the imperialist war. You will not achieve *durable victory* in this next "real" revolution if you do not perform *miracles of proletarian organization!*[48]

The fourth letter deals with the question "How to achieve peace?"

The Tsarist government began and waged the present war as an *imperialist*, predatory war to rob and strangle weak nations. The government of the Guchkovs and Miliukovs, which is a landlord and capitalist government, is forced to continue, and wants to continue, *this very same kind* of war. To urge that government to conclude a democratic peace is like preaching virtue to brothel keepers.[49]

He argued,

If political power in Russia were in the hands of the *Soviets* of Workers, Soldiers, and Peasants' Deputies, these Soviets, and the *All-Russia Soviet* elected by them, could, and no doubt would, agree to carry out the peace program which our party (The Russian Social Democratic Labour Party) outlined as early as October 13, 1915.

This program would probably be the following:

1. The All-Russia Soviet of Workers', Soldiers', and Peasants' Deputies (or the St. Petersburg Soviet temporarily acting for it) would forthwith declare that it is *not* bound by *any* treaties concluded *either* by the Tsarist monarchy *or* by the bourgeois governments.

2. It would forthwith publish *all* these treaties in order to hold up to public shame the predatory aims of the Tsarist monarchy and of *all* the bourgeois governments without exception.

3. It would forthwith publicly call upon *all* the belligerent powers to conclude an *immediate armistice*.

4. It would immediately bring to the knowledge of all the people our, the workers' and peasants' *peace terms*: liberation of *all* colonies;

liberation of *all* dependent, oppressed, and unequal nations.

5. It would declare that it expects nothing good from the bourgeois governments and calls upon the workers of all countries to overthrow them and to transfer all political power to Soviets of Workers' Deputies.

6. It would declare that the *capitalist gentry themselves* can repay the billions of debts contracted by the bourgeois governments to wage this criminal, predatory war, and that the workers and peasants *refuse to recognize* these debts.[5]

The fifth "Letter from Afar" sums up the previous letters regarding the tasks facing the Russian proletariat, and adds the following points:

> The proletariat can and must, in alliance with the *poorest* section of the peasantry, take further steps towards *control* of production and distribution of the basic products, towards the introduction of "universal labour service," etc.... In their entirety and in their development these steps will mark the *transition to socialism,* which cannot be achieved in Russia directly, at one stroke, without transitional measures, but is quite achievable and urgently necessary as a result of such transitional measures.... In this connection, the task of immediately organizing special Soviets of Workers' Deputies in the *rural districts,* i.e., Soviets of agricultural *wage*-workers *separate* from the Soviets of the other peasants' deputies, comes to the forefront with extreme urgency.[51]

What magnificent clarity—and this was written thousands of miles from the arena of struggle, and on the basis of very scanty information!

No wonder the editors of *Pravda* did not enthuse about the "Letters from Afar." They published only the first of the five, with about one-fifth of it cut out. Among crucial phrases censored was Lenin's accusation that those who advocated that the workers should support the new government in the interests of the struggle against tsarist reaction were traitors to the workers, to the cause of the proletariat, and to the cause of freedom. He might have applied this to Kamenev, Stalin, and Muranov.

Lenin returns to Russia

It took Lenin five weeks from the victory of the February Revolution to manage to reach Russia. "From the moment news of the February revolution came, Ilyich burned with eagerness to go to Russia," Krupskaya remembers.

> England and France would not for the world have allowed the Bolsheviks to pass through to Russia. This was clear to Ilyich—"We

fear," he wrote to Kollontai—"we will not succeed in leaving this cursed Switzerland very soon." And taking this into consideration, he, in his letters of 16–17 March, made arrangements with Kollontai how best to reestablish contacts with Petrograd.

As there was no legal way it was necessary to travel illegally. But how? From the moment the news of the revolution came, Ilyich did not sleep, and at night all sorts of incredible plans were made. We could travel by airplane. But such things could be thought of only in the semi-delirium of the night. One had only to formulate it vocally to realize the utter impracticability of such a plan. A passport of a foreigner from a neutral country would have had to be obtained, a Swedish passport would be best as a Swede arouses less suspicion. A Swedish passport could have been obtained through the aid of the Swedish comrades, but there was the further obstacle of our not knowing the Swedish language. Perhaps only a little Swedish would do. But it would be so easy to give one's self away. "You will fall asleep and see Mensheviks in your dreams and you will start swearing, and shout, scoundrels, scoundrels and give the whole conspiracy away," I said to him teasingly.[52]

Then Martov came up with an excellent idea for getting to Russia. He proposed a plan to obtain permits for emigrants to pass through Germany in exchange for German and Austrian prisoners of war interned in Russia. But no one wanted to go in that way, except Lenin, who grasped at the plan.

The political risk involved in being aided by Germany was very great indeed. There was a serious danger of being accused of collaboration with the enemy. It needed enormous daring and willpower to take advantage of a "sealed train," but Lenin did not lack these.

On March 17, he declared that the "only hope to get out of here is in an exchange of Swiss émigrés for German internees." On March 18, he announced his own readiness to act, and invited any of his followers who wished to return to contact him,[53] declaring, "We must go at any cost, even through hell."[54]

In Russia, the foreign minister, Miliukov, announced that any Russian citizen traveling through Germany would be subject to legal action.[55] But nothing could deter Lenin from taking the only way open to him to get to revolutionary Russia. On March 27, a group of thirty-two Bolsheviks risked the route through Germany in a "sealed train."

More than a month later, Martov took his courage into his hands and followed suit. On May 5, he and a number of other Mensheviks, together with Natanson, the SR leader, Lunacharsky, Balabanova, and Manuilsky, followed in Lenin's footsteps. Altogether there were 257 passengers on this journey, including 58 Mensheviks, 48

Bundists, 34 Socialist Revolutionaries, 25 Anarcho-Communists, 18
Bolsheviks, and 22 without party affiliation. On June 7, a third sealed
train left Switzerland for Russia with 206 passengers, including 29
Mensheviks, 25 Bundists, 27 Socialist Revolutionaries, 26 Anarcho-
Communists, 22 Bolsheviks, 19 unaffiliated, and 39 non-émigrés.[56]

Lenin dared. He dared to use the conflict between the German
high command and the Anglo-French-Russian alliance in order to
further the interests of the revolution. Ludendorff hoped that the
revolution in Russia would lead to the disintegration of the Russian
army, and thus help the military plans of hard-pressed Germany.
Lenin took advantage of Ludendorff's plans to further his own.

The historical agent who intervened to cross Lenin's plans with
those of the German high command was the ex-revolutionary Parvus.
This Russian-born member of the German Social Democratic Party,
who had been active in the 1905 Revolution but then turned to making money on a large scale through military commercial enterprises,
was now the unofficial adviser to the German Foreign Office on Russian internal affairs. So, under his influence, a few days after the February Revolution, Brockdorff-Rantzau, German ambassador in
Copenhagen and a confidant of Parvus, wrote to the Foreign Office,
"Germany must create in Russia as much chaos as possible." Overt
intervention in the course of the revolution must be avoided, but

> [w]e should…in my opinion, stake everything on deepening the an-
> tagonisms between the moderate and the extreme parties in secret:
> for we have the greatest interest in the latter winning the upper hand,
> because then the transformation becomes inevitable and will assume
> forms which must shake the existence of the Russian empire.

Favoring the extreme element, Brockdorff-Rantzau emphasizes,
is in the German interest, "because through it more thorough work
will be undertaken and a quicker conclusion brought about." In
about three months, "it can be counted on in all probability, that
the disintegration will be far enough advanced to guarantee the collapse of the Russian power through a military intervention on our
part."[57]

These views coincided with those of General Ludendorff.

> Militarily [General Ludendorff judges a few weeks after the revolution
> in Russia] the Russian revolution can only be characterized as an advan-
> tage for us. Through its effects the war situation has developed so fortu-
> nately for us that we no longer need to reckon with a Russian offensive
> and can already now pull forces out…. If the situation in the East is
> eased still more, then we can disengage still more forces there…. With

this addition we will even up the relation of forces in the West in our favor. So we can await the coming situation with greater confidence.[58]

The German authorities were remarkably short-sighted. As one historian describes the situation:

One instinctively puts the question in this context, whether the German agencies responsible were not aware that working with Bolshevism in a way was playing with fire. Did the belief really hold sway that imperial Germany could come to terms with the Russian social revolution without itself one day being seized by it?

The German files contain no statements about such deliberations on the part of the responsible government agencies. Also they hardly gave rise to the supposition that they are more thoroughly occupied with the theory and practice of Bolshevism there or have even grasped the true nature of Lenin and his ideas.

The main aspects of German politics result far more from the wrong calculation, from the limitations of the moment: first the war must be won or at least the peace in the East established; what comes *afterwards* is not now at issue. The Bolsheviks are possibly in a position quickly to bring about a separate German Russian peace and so to effectively frustrate the plans for detente in the East.[59]

Lloyd George summed up this superficial way of thinking in the following words:

It is difficult to take long views in war. Victory is the only horizon. It is a lesson to the statesmanship which takes shortsighted views of situations and seizes the chance of a temporary advantage without courting the certainty of future calamity.[60]

Two opposing historical plans crossed each other's paths, Lenin's and Ludendorff's. There is no doubt who was the more far-sighted of the two—or who gained the advantage. On October 25, the Bolsheviks seized power. A year later, under the influence of the Russian Revolution, the German masses overthrew Ludendorff.

In using the sealed train, with all the political risks involved—the danger of being called a German agent, an accusation that played a significant role in the events of the Russian Revolution—Lenin showed both his farsightedness and his political courage.

At the Finland station

A number of Lenin's followers went to meet him in Finland. "We had hardly got into the car and sat down," writes Raskolnikov, a young naval officer and a Bolshevik, "when Vladimir Ilyich flung at Kamenev: 'What is that you have written in *Pravda*?

We saw several numbers and really swore at you.'"[61]

The Petersburg Committee mobilized several thousand workers and soldiers to welcome Lenin at the Finland railway station in the Vyborg district. The description of the official meeting, which took place in the so-called "Tsar's room" of the Finland station, constitutes a very lively page in Sukhanov's memoirs:

Behind Shliapnikov, at the head of a small cluster of people behind whom the door slammed again at once, Lenin came, or rather ran, into the room. He wore a round cap, his face looked frozen, and there was a magnificent bouquet in his hands. Running to the middle of the room, he stopped in front of Chkheidze as though colliding with a completely unexpected obstacle. And Chkheidze, still glum, pronounced the following "speech of welcome" with not only the spirit and wording but also the tone of a sermon:

"Comrade Lenin, in the name of the Petersburg Soviet and of the whole revolution we welcome you to Russia.... But—we think that the principal task of the revolutionary democracy is now the defense of the revolution from any encroachments either from within or from without. We consider that what this goal requires is not disunity, but the closing of the democratic ranks. We hope you will pursue these goals together with us."

Chkheidze stopped speaking. I was dumbfounded with surprise: really, what attitude could be taken to this "welcome" and to that delicious "But—?"

But Lenin plainly knew exactly how to behave. He stood there as though nothing taking place had the slightest connection with him—looking about him, examining the persons round him and even the ceiling of the imperial waiting-room, adjusting his bouquet (rather out of tune with his whole appearance), and then, turning away from the Ex. Com. delegation altogether, he made this reply:

"Dear comrades, soldiers, sailors, and workers! I am happy to greet in your persons the victorious Russian revolution, and greet you as the vanguard of the worldwide proletarian army.... The piratical imperialist war is the beginning of civil war throughout Europe.... The hour is not far distant when at the call of our comrade, Karl Liebknecht, the peoples will turn their arms against their own capitalist exploiters.... The worldwide socialist revolution has already dawned.... Germany is seething.... Any day now the whole of European capitalism may crash. The Russian revolution accomplished by you has prepared the way and opened a new epoch. Long live the worldwide socialist revolution!"

Appealing from Chkheidze to the workers and soldiers, from the provisional government to Liebknecht, from the defense of the fatherland to international revolution—this is how Lenin indicated the tasks of the proletariat.

It was very interesting! Suddenly, before the eyes of all of us, completely swallowed up by the routine drudgery of the revolution, there was presented a bright, blinding, exotic beacon, obliterating everything we "lived by." Lenin's voice, heard straight from the train, was a "voice from outside." There had broken in upon us in the revolution a note that was not, to be sure, a contradiction, but that was novel, harsh, and somewhat deafening.... To another *Marseillaise*, and to the shouts of the throng of thousands, among the red-and-gold banners illuminated by the searchlight, Lenin went out by the main entrance and was about to get into a closed car, but the crowd absolutely refused to allow this. Lenin clambered on to the bonnet of the car and had to make a speech.

"...any part in shameful imperialist slaughter...lies and frauds... capitalist pirates..." was what I could hear, squeezed in the doorway and vainly trying to get out on to the square to hear the first speech "to the people" of this new star of the first magnitude on our revolutionary horizon.[62]

At a meeting later in the evening, Lenin elaborated on the same theme. It shook not only the Mensheviks but even loyal Bolsheviks. As Sukhanov describes it:

I shall never forget that thunder-like speech, which startled and amazed not only me, a heretic who had accidentally dropped in, but all the true believers. I am certain that no one had expected anything of the sort. It seemed as though all the elements had risen from their abodes, and the spirit of universal destruction, knowing neither barriers nor doubts, neither human difficulties nor human calculations, was hovering around Kshesinskaia's reception room above the heads of the bewitched disciples.[63]

Lenin said that the Soviet Manifesto bragged to Europe about the successes it had achieved:

It spoke of the "revolutionary force of democracy," of total political liberty. But what kind of force was this, when the imperialist bourgeoisie was at the head of the country? What kind of political liberty, when the secret diplomatic documents were not published, and we couldn't publish them? What kind of freedom of speech, when all the printing facilities were in the hands of the bourgeoisie and guarded by a bourgeois government!

"When I was on the way here with my comrades, I thought we should be taken from the station straight to the Peter-Paul. As we see, we turned out to be far from that. But let us not lose hope that we may still not escape it."

The "revolutionary-defensist" Soviet led by opportunists and social-patriots could only be an instrument of the bourgeoisie.

"We don't need a parliamentary republic, we don't need bourgeois democracy, we don't need any government except the Soviets of Workers', Soldiers', and Farm-labourers' Deputies!"[64]

Next day at a joint meeting of Bolsheviks, Mensheviks, and independents, Lenin's stand was given a shocked reception. The

Menshevik Bogdanov reacted in the following way:

> "This is the raving of a madman! It's indecent to applaud this clap-trap!" he cried out, livid with rage and contempt, turning to the audi-ence. "You ought to be ashamed of yourselves! Marxists!"[65]

I.P. Goldenberg, a former member of the Bolshevik Central Com-mittee, and soon to join the Mensheviks, declared: "Lenin has now made himself a candidate for one European throne that has been va-cant for thirty years—the throne of Bakunin! Lenin's new words echo something old—the superannuated truths of primitive anarchism."[66]

Lenin was in no doubt of his isolation among the Bolshevik leaders.

> At the beginning of his speech Lenin had definitely said and even em-phasized that he was speaking for himself personally, without having consulted his party.
>
> The Bolshevik sect was still in a state of bafflement and perplexity. And the support Lenin found may underline more clearly than any-thing else his complete intellectual isolation, not only among Social Democrats in general but also among his own disciples. Lenin was supported by no one but Kollontai (a recent Menshevik), who re-jected any alliance with those who could not and would not accom-plish a social revolution! Her support called forth nothing but mockery, laughter, and hubbub.[67]

Next day, on April 4, Lenin presented to the party conference a short written summary of his views, which under the name of the *April Theses* turned out to be one of the most decisive documents of the revolution. Three days later these *Theses* were published in *Pravda*.

> 1. In our attitude towards the war, which under the new government of Lvov and Co. unquestionably remains on Russia's part a predatory imperialist war owing to the capitalist nature of that government, not the slightest concession to "revolutionary defensism" is permissible....
>
> 2. The specific feature of the present situation in Russia is that the country is *passing* from the first stage of the revolution—which, owing to the insufficient class-consciousness and organization of the proletariat, placed power in the hands of the bourgeoisie—to its *sec-ond* stage, which must place power in the hands of the proletariat and the poorest sections of the peasants....
>
> 3. No support for the provisional government; the utter falsity of all its promises should be made clear, particularly of those relating to the renunciation of annexations. Exposure in place of the impermissi-ble, illusion-breeding "demand" that *this* government, a government of capitalists, should cease to be an imperialist government....
>
> 4. The masses must be made to see that the Soviets of Workers'

Deputies are the *only possible* form of revolutionary government, and that therefore our task is, as long as *this* government yields to the influence of the bourgeoisie, to present a patient, systematic, and persistent *explanation* of the errors of their tactics, an explanation especially adapted to the practical needs of the masses.

As long as we are in the minority we carry on the work of criticism and exposing errors and at the same time we preach the necessity of transferring the entire state power to the Soviets of Workers' Deputies, so that the people may overcome their mistakes by experience.

5. Not a parliamentary republic—to return to a parliamentary republic from the Soviets of Workers' Deputies would be a retrograde step—but a republic of Soviets of Workers, Agricultural Labourers', and Peasants' Deputies throughout the country, from top to bottom.

Abolition of the police, the army and the bureaucracy.

The salaries of all officials, all of whom are elective and displaceable at any time, not to exceed the average wage of a competent worker.

6. The weight of emphasis in the agrarian program to be shifted to the Soviets of Agricultural Labourers' Deputies.

Confiscation of all landed estates.

Nationalization of *all* lands in the country, the land to be disposed of by the local Soviets of Agricultural Labourers' and Peasants' Deputies. The organization of separate Soviets of Deputies of Poor Peasants. The setting up of a model farm on each of the large estates (ranging in size from 100 to 300 *desiatins*, according to local and other conditions, and to the decisions of the local bodies) under the control of the Soviets of Agricultural Labourers' Deputies and for the public account.

7. The immediate amalgamation of all banks in the country into a single national bank, and the institution of control over it by the Soviet of Workers' Deputies.

8. It is not our *immediate* task to "introduce" socialism, but only to bring social production and the distribution of products at once under the *control* of the Soviets of Workers' Deputies.

9. Party tasks:

(a) Immediate convocation of a party congress;

(b) Alteration of the party program, mainly:

  (i) on the question of imperialism and the imperialist war;

  (ii) on our attitude towards the state and *our* demand for a "commune state";

  (iii) amendment of our out-of-date minimum program.

(c) Change of the party's name.

10. A new International.[68]

The *Theses* [Sukhanov remembers] were published in Lenin's name alone; not one Bolshevik organization, or group, or even individual had joined him. And the editors of *Pravda* for their part thought it necessary to emphasize Lenin's isolation and their independence of him. "As for Lenin's general schema," wrote *Pravda*, "it seems to us unacceptable, in so far as it proceeds from the assumption that the bourgeois democratic revolution is finished and counts on the immediate conversion of that revolution into a socialist revolution."[69]

A complete break with "democratic dictatorship"

Lenin's "Letters from Afar" and his *April Theses* marked a complete break with the position he himself had held for many years, defining the Russian revolution as a bourgeois democratic revolution led by the democratic dictatorship of the proletariat and peasantry.

Since 1905, the Bolshevik Party had waged a struggle against tsarism under the slogan of "the democratic dictatorship of the proletariat and peasantry." The Bolsheviks argued that the coming revolution would be a *bourgeois* democratic revolution. By this was meant a revolution resulting from a conflict between the productive forces of capitalism, on the one hand, and tsarism, landlordism, and other relics of feudalism on the other. The task of this dictatorship would not be to create a socialist society, or even the forms transitional to such a society, but to get rid of the dead wood of medievalism.

Lenin did not change this opinion until after the revolution of February 1917. In *The War and Russian Social Democracy* (September 1914), for example, he was still writing that the Russian revolution must limit itself to "the three fundamental conditions for consistent democratic reform, viz., a democratic republic (with complete equality and self-determination for all nations), confiscation of the landed estates, and an eight-hour working day."[70]

It is clear, moreover, from all Lenin's writings up to 1917, that he expected a substantial interval to elapse between the coming bourgeois revolution and the proletarian, socialist revolution.

However, as explained elsewhere,[71] Lenin poses two different answers to the question: What happens after the victory of the revolution? The first, to be found in his writings between 1905 and 1907, is that there will be a period of capitalist development. The second can be summed up as: Let us take power, and then we shall see:

> From the democratic revolution we shall at once and precisely in accordance with the measure of our strength, the strength of the class-conscious and organized proletariat, begin to pass to the socialist revolution. We stand for uninterrupted revolution. We shall not stop half-way.[72]

Now came the February Revolution, and the different ingredients of Lenin's schemas were combined together.

The workers and the soldiers were the bosses. They had the

power. To that extent it could be said that the democratic dictatorship of the workers and peasants had been achieved. But at the same time the government was in the hands of the bourgeoisie; the nationalization of the land and the right of self-determination, elements central to the program of the democratic dictatorship, had not been achieved. Life proved much more complicated than Lenin's schemas of 1905 onwards.

In "Letters on Tactics," written between April 8 and April 13, Lenin explained:

> Marxism requires of us a strictly exact and objectively verifiable analysis of the relations of classes and of the concrete features peculiar to each historical situation. We Bolsheviks have always tried to meet this requirement, which is absolutely essential for giving a scientific foundation to policy.
>
> "Our theory is not a dogma, but a guide to action," Marx and Engels always said, rightly ridiculing the mere memorizing and repetition of "formulas," that at best are capable only of marking out *general* tasks, which are necessarily modifiable by the *concrete* economic and political conditions of each particular *period* of the historical process.[73]

He continued,

> Before the February–March Revolution of 1917, state power in Russia was in the hands of one old class, namely the feudal landed nobility, headed by Nicholas Romanov.
>
> After the revolution the power is in the hands of a *different* class, a new class, namely, the *bourgeoisie*.
>
> The passing of state power from one *class* to another is the first, the principal, the basic sign of a *revolution*, both in the strictly scientific and in the practical political meaning of that term.
>
> To this extent, the bourgeois, or the bourgeois-democratic, revolution in Russia is *completed*.
>
> But at this point we hear a clamour of protest from people who readily call themselves "old Bolsheviks." Didn't we always maintain, they say, that the bourgeois-democratic revolution is completed only by the "revolutionary-democratic dictatorship of the proletariat and the peasantry?" Is the agrarian revolution, which is also a bourgeois-democratic revolution, completed? Is it not a fact, on the contrary, that it has *not even* started?
>
> My answer is: The Bolshevik slogans and ideas *on the whole* have been confirmed by history; but *concretely* things have worked out *differently*; they are more original, more peculiar, more variegated than anyone could have expected.
>
> To ignore or overlook this fact would mean taking after those "old Bolsheviks" who more than once already have played so regrettable a role in the history of our party by reiterating formulas senselessly *learned by rote* instead of *studying* the specific features of the new

and living reality....

"The revolutionary-democratic dictatorship of the proletariat and the peasantry" has *already* become a reality in the Russian revolution.... "The Soviet of Workers' and Soldiers' Deputies"—there you have the "revolutionary-democratic dictatorship of the proletariat and the peasantry" already accomplished in reality.

The person who *now* speaks only of a "revolutionary-democratic dictatorship of the proletariat and the peasantry" is behind the times, consequently, he has in effect *gone over* to the petty bourgeoisie against the proletarian class struggle; that person should be consigned to the archive of Bolshevik pre-revolutionary antiques (it may be called the archive of "old Bolsheviks")....

Theory, my friend, is grey, but green is the eternal tree of life.... According to the old way of thinking the rule of the bourgeoisie could and should be *followed* by the rule of the proletariat and the peasantry, by their dictatorship. In real life, however, things have *already* turned out *differently*; there has been an extremely original, novel, and unprecedented *interlacing of the one with the other*. We have side by side, existing together, simultaneously, *both* the rule of the bourgeoisie (the government of Lvov and Guchkov) and a revolutionary-democratic dictatorship of the proletariat and the peasantry, which is *voluntarily* ceding power to the bourgeoisie, voluntarily making itself an appendage of the bourgeoisie.[74]

The backruptcy of the "old Bolshevik" formula of "democratic dictatorship" was epitomized in the existence of dual power, as Lenin states in an article of that title:

Nobody previously thought, or could have thought, of a dual power.

What is this dual power? Alongside the provisional government, the government of the *bourgeoisie, another government* has arisen, so far weak and incipient, but undoubtedly a government that actually exists and is growing—the Soviets of Workers' and Soldiers' Deputies.

What is the class composition of this other government? It consists of the proletariat and the peasants (in soldiers' uniforms). What is the political nature of this government? It is a revolutionary dictatorship, i.e., a power directly based on revolutionary seizure, on the direct initiative of the people from below, and *not on a law* enacted by a centralized state power.[75]

How far the "old Bolshevik" formula had become a reactionary one Lenin pointed out clearly when he polemicized against Kamenev. Kamenev had written:

As for Comrade Lenin's general scheme, it appears to us unacceptable, inasmuch as it proceeds from the assumption that the bourgeois-democratic revolution is *completed*, and builds on the immediate transformation of this revolution into a socialist revolution.

Lenin rejoined:

> There are two big mistakes here.
> First. The question of "completion" of the bourgeois-democratic revolution is *stated* wrongly. The question is put in an abstract, simple, so to speak one-color, way, which does not correspond to the objective reality. To put the question *this way*, to ask *now* "whether the bourgeois-democratic revolution is completed" and say *no more*, is to prevent oneself from seeing the exceedingly complex reality, which is at least two-colored. This is in theory. In practice, it means surrendering helplessly to *petty-bourgeois revolutionism.*
> Indeed, reality shows us *both* the passing of power into the hands of the bourgeoisie (a "completed" bourgeois-democratic revolution of the usual type) and, side by side with the real government, the existence of a parallel government which represents the "revolutionary-democratic dictatorship of the proletariat and the peasantry." This "second-government" has *itself* ceded power to the bourgeoisie, has chained *itself* to the bourgeois government.

He summed up:

> Is this reality covered by comrade Kamenev's old Bolshevik formula, which says that "the bourgeois-democratic revolution is not completed?"
> It is not. The formula is obsolete. It is no good at all. It is dead. And it is no use trying to revive it.[76]

As a matter of fact the concept of "democratic dictatorship of proletariat and peasantry" was found to be a far less clear guide than Trotsky's formula of the permanent revolution. The latter made it clear that the revolution would not confine itself to bourgeois democratic tasks but must immediately proceed to carry out proletarian socialist measures.

> In the event of a decisive victory of the revolution, power will pass into the hands of that class which plays a leading role in the struggle—in other words, into the hands of the proletariat.
> *The proletariat in power will stand before the peasant as the class which has emancipated it....* The political domination of the proletariat is incompatible with its economic enslavement. No matter under what political flag the proletariat has come to power, it is obliged to take the path of socialist policy. It would be the greatest Utopianism to think that the proletariat, having been raised to political domination by the internal mechanism of a bourgeois revolution can, even if it so desires, limit its mission to the creation of republican-democratic conditions for the social domination of the bourgeoisie.... The barrier between the "minimum" and the "maximum" program disappears immediately [when] the proletariat comes to power.[77]

Lenin had repeatedly to learn from experience, to overcome his own ideas of yesterday; he had to learn from the masses. But, as had happened many times before when history made sharp turns, the old Bolsheviks were not able to make the quick adjustment needed. The party leaders in Russia still believed after February that the task was to establish a democratic dictatorship of the proletariat and the peasantry. Lenin had to repeat again and again: "We must abandon old Bolshevism."

The Bolshevik leaders oppose the *April Theses*

The reaction to the *April Theses* at the April 6 session of the Central Committee was very unfavorable:

Kamenev: In the *Theses* there is no concrete instruction...the revolution is bourgeois and not social...imperialism does lead to socialism, but so long as nothing happens in the West too much burden is imposed on the shoulders of Russia....

Goloshchekin: What is needed is a platform; the *Theses* do not supply this.

Shliapnikov: The *Theses* have two parts. The first part—attitude to the war—completely acceptable. The second part does not give practical slogans....

Zinoviev: Perplexing...

Stalin: ... A schema but no facts, hence unsatisfactory.[78]

Even Zinoviev did not side with Lenin, although he had been abroad with Lenin for years and for a number of years shared with him the editorship of the central organ of the Bolsheviks, *Sotsial-Demokrat.*

Kamenev, a Bolshevik almost from the birth of Bolshevism, as Sukhanov stated, had "always stood on its right, conciliationist, passive wing."

As a political figure, Kamenev was undoubtedly an exceptional, though not an independent, force. Lacking either sharp corners, great intellectual striking power, or original language, he was not fitted to be a leader; by himself he had nowhere to lead the masses. Left alone he would not fail to be assimilated by someone. It was always necessary to take him in tow, and if he sometimes balked it was never very violently.... At the beginning of the revolution he jibbed against Lenin, jibbed at the October Revolution, jibbed at the general havoc and terror after the revolution, jibbed on supply questions in the second year of the Bolshevik regime. But—he always surrendered on all points. Not having much faith in himself, he recently (in the autumn of 1918) said to me, in order to justify himself in his own eyes: "As for myself, I am more and more convinced that Lenin never makes a mistake. In the last analysis he is always right. How often has it seemed that he was slipping up—either in his prognosis or in his political line! But in the last analysis his prognosis and his line were always justified."[79]

Stalin, lacking wide theoretical horizons, adapted himself to the prevailing conservative mood among the leading "old Bolsheviks." His main characteristic was his lack of imagination. As Sukhanov writes about him: "Stalin...during his modest activity in the Ex. Com. produced—and not only on me—the impression of a grey blur, looming up now and then dimly and not leaving any trace. There is really nothing more to be said about him."[80]

Being among the top leadership of the Bolshevik Party did not guarantee that one was free of conservatism, or routinism. V.N. Zalezhsky, a member of the Petrograd Committee, recalled: "Lenin's theses produced the impression of an exploding bomb." Zalezhsky confirms Lenin's complete isolation after that warm and impressive welcome. "On that day [April 4] Comrade Lenin could not find open sympathizers even in our own ranks."[81]

> "Many of the comrades pointed out," Tsikhon recalled, "that Lenin has lost contact with Russia, did not take into consideration present conditions, and so forth." The provincial Bolshevik Lebedev tells how in the beginning the Bolsheviks condemned Lenin's agitation, "which seemed Utopian and which was explained by his prolonged lack of contact with Russian life."[82]

On April 8, the Petersburg Committee rejected Lenin's *April Theses* by a vote of thirteen to two with one abstention.[83]

The enemies of Bolshevism are full of glee

The opponents of Bolshevism came to the conclusion that Lenin was finished—so mad did his ideas sound, and so isolated was he among his party comrades. Thus Sukhanov remembers:

> Skobolev and I strolled about the room, Miliukov came up to us. The conversation turned upon Lenin. Skobolev told Miliukov about his "lunatic ideas," appraising him as a completely lost man standing outside the movement. I agreed in general with this estimate of Lenin's ideas and said that in his present guise he was so unacceptable to everyone that now he was not at all dangerous for our interlocutor, Miliukov. However, the future of Lenin seemed different to me: I was convinced that after he had escaped from his foreign academic atmosphere and come into an atmosphere of real struggle and wide practical activity, he would acclimatize himself quickly, settle

down, stand on firm ground and throw overboard the bulk of his anarchist "ravings." What life failed to accomplish with him, the solid pressure of his party comrades would help with.[84]

Victor Chernov, the leader of the Socialist Revolutionaries and later a minister in the provisional government, had this to say:

> Let us…not be unduly frightened by Lenin's political excesses, just because their derivation and character are too clear. The extent of their influence, and consequently also their dangers, will be extremely limited and "localized."[85]

Lenin wins the party

In spite of this inauspicious beginning, Lenin was able to win a large proportion of the party to his stand in an astonishingly short time.

The initial victory came at the First Petrograd City Conference (April 14–22). The going was by no means easy. One delegate after another stated his disagreement with Lenin's *Theses.*

Shutko declared: "Democratic dictatorship of the proletariat, this is fundamental for us. If one wants to support realistically our revolution, it is necessary to organize this democracy."

Bagdatev, the left extremist secretary of the Bolshevik Committee of the Putilov Works, asked: "Assuming that the Soviets of Workers' and Soldiers' Deputies took power—what would they do? Social revolution? Obviously not. Obviously we can realize only our minimum program. However even this cannot be achieved without the socialist revolution in Western Europe."

Petrikovskii accused Lenin of Blanquism.

Kalinin said: "I belong to the old Bolsheviks, Leninists, and I consider that old Leninism has not by any means proved good-for-nothing in the present peculiar moment, and I'm astonished at the declaration of comrade Lenin that the old Bolsheviks have become an obstacle at the present moment."

Almost the only delegate who spoke in support of Lenin was Ludmilla Stal. She said:

> All the comrades before the arrival of Lenin were wandering in the dark. We knew only the formulas of 1905. Seeing the independent creative work of the people, we could not teach them. I turn now to the comrades of the Vyborg district and propose that they learn the full importance of the moment. Our comrades were only able to see as far as preparing for the constituent assembly by parliamentary

means, and took no account of the possibility of going further. In accepting the slogans of Lenin, we are now doing what life itself suggests to us. We need not fear the Commune and say that we have already a workers' government; the Paris Commune was not only a workers,' but also a petty-bourgeois government.[86]

From Stal's words it is evident that the Vyborg Bolsheviks feared that Lenin's policy of using soviet power to move towards socialism would cut the cities off from the peasants and that 1917 would merely repeat the events of the Paris Commune of 1871. However, their opposition was not stubborn, as they had much in common with Lenin in their approach to the events of the day.

In spite of the apparent lack of support for Lenin at the Petrograd City Conference, practically all the vocal delegates speaking against him, Lenin's resolution on the attitude to be taken to the provisional government won handsomely: thirty-three for, six against, and two abstentions.[87] Following the conference, in early May, a new Executive Committee of the Petersburg Committee was elected; the only "old" members it contained were those who had opposed the right-wing majority in March.[88]

Another step towards winning the party was the Seventh All-Russian Conference of the party held on April 24–29. There was still vocal opposition to the *April Theses*. Kamenev said:

Lenin is wrong when he says that the bourgeois democratic revolution is finished.... The classical relics of feudalism, the landed estates, are not liquidated.... The state is not transformed into a democratic society.... It is too early to say that bourgeois democracy has exhausted all its possibilities.[89]

Rykov argued:

Where will arise the sun of the socialist revolution? I think that under the present conditions, with our standard of living, the initiation of the socialist revolution does not belong to us. We have not the strength, the objective conditions, for this.

Gigantic revolutionary tasks face us, but the fulfilment of these tasks does not carry us beyond the framework of the bourgeois revolution.[90]

And Bagdatev could say:

Kamenev's report on the whole anticipated my position. I also find that the bourgeois democratic revolution has not ended and Kamenev's resolution is acceptable for me.... I think that Comrade Lenin had too early rejected the point of view of old Bolshevism.

At the same time he showed his radicalism by stating:

[E]verywhere and always every day, we have to show the masses that until power has been transferred into the hands of the Soviets of Workers' and Soldiers' Deputies, there is no hope for an early end of the war and no possibility for the realization of their program.[91]

What muddled thinking!

After a long discussion Lenin won decisively. A small right-wing group still spoke in favor of "watchful control" over the provisional government, but the overwhelming majority sided with his call for a struggle for all power to the soviets. An overwhelming majority of the delegates also sided with him on the question of the war. The conference declared that the war continued to be an imperialist war, and hence the proletariat had to oppose it completely. It condemned "revolutionary defensism" and insisted that the war should end with a democratic peace after power had been transferred to the proletariat. Finally, the conference advocated mass fraternization at the front as a means of stimulating revolution abroad.[92] This resolution was passed *nem. con.*, with seven abstentions.[93]

Yet Lenin did not have his way on all the issues before the conference. A resolution "On the current moment" was won by only a small margin: seventy-one for, thirty-nine against, eight abstentions.[94] A resolution against the coalition government was passed *nem. con.* with two abstentions.[95] At the very end of the conference, Zinoviev proposed a resolution: "To take part in the international conference of Zimmerwaldists designated for May 18" (in Stockholm). The report says: "Adopted by all votes against one."[96] That one was Lenin.

There was a further indication of the fact that Lenin's victory was not complete. The right wing of the party managed to elect four of its number (Kamenev, Nogin, Miliutin, and Fedorov) to the new nine-member Central Committee. The other members were Lenin, Sverdlov, Smilga, Zinoviev, and Stalin, who by now had veered towards Lenin. The number of votes received by the right-wingers for the Central Committee was quite impressive. The figures were: Lenin, 104; Zinoviev, 101; Stalin, 97; Kamenev, 95; Miliutin, 82; Nogin, 76; Sverdlov, 71; Smilga, 53; Fedorov, 48.[97]

An interesting incident occurred during the elections. There was some opposition to the election of Kamenev. One delegate argued that his behavior in court at the beginning of the war, when he had tried to ingratiate himself and had given evidence while other Bolshevik defendants refused, and his article in *Pravda* of March 15 made him unsuitable to be on the Central Committee. Although

Lenin had previously attacked Kamenev on just these two issues, he now came to his defense.[98] He knew the importance of the cadres. Kamenev, who had been in the party throughout its existence, was of too much value to be pushed aside. Possibly Lenin's bad judgement of character played a role here: a few months later, on the eve of the October Revolution, he was to demand Kamenev's expulsion from the party. Personal grudges were never an element in Lenin's political relations, with friend or foe.

"Old Bolshevism"— an impediment

So long as Lenin was not at the helm of the party, its course was erratic. Stalin, on issuing a collection of articles of his in 1924, had to admit:

> These articles reflect certain waverings of the majority of our party on the questions of peace and the power of the Soviets which occurred, as is known, in March and April 1917.... It is not surprising that Bolsheviks, scattered by Tsarism in prisons and places of exile, and just able to come together from different ends of Russia in order to work out a new platform, could not immediately understand the new situation. It is not surprising that the party, in search of a new orientation, then stopped halfway in the questions of peace and Soviet power. The famous *April Theses* of Lenin were needed before the party could come out on the new road with one leap.... I shared this mistaken position with the majority of the party and renounced it fully in the middle of April, associating myself with the *April Theses* of Lenin.[99]

Lenin, the father of Bolshevism, the man who had shaped the slogan of "the democratic dictatorship of the proletariat and peasantry," and who provided its theoretical support, was the best equipped in April 1917 to overcome its limitations. This slogan restricted the revolution to bourgeois democratic ends. Now, after February, it became an obstacle to any struggle for workers' power that had to go beyond capitalism; to establish workers' control in industry and above all to put an end to the imperialist war. Now history relentlessly posed the alternative: either the revolution would be bourgeois democratic or it should culminate in the dictatorship of the proletariat.

Tradition plays a great role in the revolutionary movement— both positively and negatively. Tradition is necessary to the revolutionary class, as a rich arsenal from which weapons can be borrowed. However, it can be an inhibiting factor: the wrong weapons can be chosen!

How to explain the amazing speed with which Lenin won his victory within the party? How did he manage in less than a month to achieve such substantial success in rearming the party?

It is true that the Bolshevik Party, with years and years of struggle behind it, had selected and steeled its members. But in the process of training, as we have seen throughout the history of Bolshevism, a certain conservatism arose, especially among the committeemen. At practically all sharp turning points, Lenin had to rely on the lower strata of the party machine against the higher, or on the rank and file against the machine as a whole. The proletarian mass often sensed sooner than the leaders the real objective situation and the needs of the class. It was part of Lenin's greatness that he shared this sense, and found the courage to tell the truth, however unpopular; telling the truth is at the heart of revolutionary politics.

If the Bolshevik Party had been made up of docile rank-and-file members led by an omniscient leader, the whole episode of the rearming of the party in April could not have arisen. As we have seen, before Lenin reached Russia, in Petrograd and above all in the Vyborg District, party members came out with the radical policy of opposition to the war, demanding the overthrow of the provisional government, and the establishment of soviet power. However, Lenin's role was crucial, because he did not simply reflect these radical views but overcame the conservative elements enshrined in them—the concept of "democratic dictatorship" of which he himself was the author. Even the best of the Vyborg comrades needed the *April Theses* to overcome the contradictory and equivocal position they held. A revolution, above all, cannot for long suffer inconsistency and equivocation.

Lenin's decisive role

"How would the revolution have developed if Lenin had not reached Russia in April 1917?" Trotsky asks, and answers:

> If our exposition demonstrates and proves anything at all, we hope it proves that Lenin was not a demiurge of the revolutionary process, that he merely entered into a chain of objective historic forces. But he was a great link in that chain....
>
> ...Is it possible...to say confidently that the party without him would have found its road? We would by no means make bold to say that. The factor of time is decisive here, and it is difficult in retrospect to tell time historically. Dialectic materialism at any rate has nothing in common with fatalism. Without Lenin the crisis, which the oppor-

tunist leadership was inevitably bound to produce, would have assumed an extraordinarily sharp and protracted character. The conditions of war and revolution, however, would not allow the party a long period for fulfilling its mission. Thus it is by no means excluded that a disoriented and split party might have let slip the revolutionary opportunity for many years.[100]

Sukhanov explains how Lenin managed to turn the party rudder as follows:

> In practice Lenin had been historically the exclusive, sole, and unchallenged head of the party for many years, since the day of its emergence. The Bolshevik Party was the work of his hands, and his alone. The very thought of going against Lenin was frightening and odious, and required from the Bolshevik mass what it was incapable of giving.
>
> Lenin the genius was an historic figure—this is one side of the matter. The other is that, except Lenin, there was nothing and no one in the party. The few massive generals without Lenin were *nothing*, like the few immense planets without the sun (for the moment I leave aside Trotsky, who at that time was still outside the ranks of the order).[101]

It is true that Lenin had remarkable authority among party members, which had been won over many years of struggle. But this authority and Lenin's success in rearming the party in April are explained not by the backwardness of the Bolsheviks, as claimed by Sukhanov, their enemy, but on the contrary by their strength. Throughout its existence, the dynamism of Bolshevism was leading towards the proletarian revolution. One must take into account the dynamic forces that Lenin was relying on and shaping: the proletariat's fight against tsarism and against its accomplices, the liberal bourgeoisie; the proletariat's struggle as the spearhead of the peasantry; the proletariat leading an armed insurrection; the Marxist party fighting for the conquest of power, and so on. In this algebra of revolution, the real value of the unknown or doubtful element in Lenin's equation—how far the revolution would go beyond the minimum program—would be decided largely by the development of the struggle itself.

No one but Lenin could have rearmed the party ideologically in the short time the revolution allowed. Referring to the rearming of the Bolshevik Party in April Trotsky wrote:

> Had I not been present in 1917 in Petersburg, the October revolution would still have taken place—on the condition that Lenin was present and in command. If neither Lenin nor I had been present in Petersburg, there would have been no October revolution: the leadership of the Bolshevik Party would have prevented it from occurring—of this I

have not the slightest doubt! If Lenin had not been in Petersburg, I doubt whether I could have managed to conquer the resistance of the Bolshevik leaders.... But I repeat, granted the presence of Lenin the October revolution would have been victorious anyway.[102]

Even Trotsky, the most talented leader, second only to Lenin in authority in the party during the October Revolution and the civil war that followed it, could not have substituted for him. He lacked the authority granted by years of common struggle and membership of the party. After Trotsky returned to Russia in May, Lenin again and again tried to persuade his colleagues to grant Trotsky, the brilliant writer, a prominent role in the direction of the Bolshevik press, but to no avail. As late as August 4, the Central Committee elected a chief editorial board for the Bolshevik newspapers made up of Stalin, Sokolnikov, and Miliutin. A proposal that Trotsky should join the board when released from prison was defeated by a vote of eleven to ten.[103*]

August 4! This was after Trotsky had announced his solidarity with the Bolshevik Party during the July Days, and as a result was in Kresty prison! This was a couple of days after the Sixth Congress had elected him to the Central Committee of the party with a handsome vote; the four who received the highest votes were Lenin, 133 (out of a possible 134); Zinoviev, 132; Trotsky, 131; Kamenev 131.[105] It indicates the extent of the prejudices among the top party leaders against the "new boy." They still considered Trotsky as an outsider. Indeed, it was some time before Trotsky regarded himself as a Bolshevik. "I cannot describe myself as a Bolshevik. It is undesirable to stick to old labels," he declared at the very first joint discussion between the Bolsheviks and his group.[106**]

Trotsky was a brilliant general without an army to speak of,

---

* In fact, on September 6, on his first appearance at the Central Committee two days after his release from prison, Trotsky was appointed unopposed as one of the party's chief editors.[104]

** Trotsky was a leader of a small group, the Mezhraiontsy, of some four thousand members. They did not aim to form a party, but to unite the Bolsheviks with the international wings of the Mensheviks. A note in the first edition of Lenin's *Collected Works*[107] characterized the Mezhraiontsy as follows: "On the war question, the Mezhraiontsy held an internationalist position and in their tactics they were close to the Bolsheviks." Their influence was confined to a few working-class districts in Petrograd. Among the leaders of the Mezhraiontsy were a number of people destined to play a central role in the October Revolution and the Soviet regime following it: Trotsky, Lunacharsky, Ioffe, Uritsky, Iurenev, Riazanov, Karakhan, Manuilsky, and others.

while Lenin was the recognized leader of a great party. As an individual Trotsky would make his words heard, but only a massive and well-disciplined party could transform words into deeds. Lenin and Lenin alone was able to rearm the great party of Bolshevism.

The statement "No Lenin, no October" looks like a negation of Marxism, of the materialist interpretation of history. And to the "Marxist" school of Karl Kautsky, Otto Bauer, and their like, who castrated Marxism, turning it into a fatalistic scholarly commentary on events, it seems so. However, the heart of Marxism is that people make history, people are the active subject of social change. And as the working class is not homogeneous, it is up to the advanced section of the class to coalesce in a revolutionary party. Without such a party, there can be no victory of the revolution. Of course the party has to be rooted in the class, has to be taught by the experience of the class, and has to lead the class. Unevenness also exists inside the party, between different comrades with different levels of experience, talent, and so on. In the struggle, the development and selection of cadres for leadership takes place.

Revolutions tend towards centralism because their aim is the taking of state power, and the state is highly centralized. Hence at the moment of the revolution, more than ever before, a decisive role is played by the leadership in the central direction of the revolutionary forces. The initiative of the revolutionary centralist leadership does not negate democracy; on the contrary, it is its dynamic realization. The great revolutionary leader is great because he expresses the needs of the millions, because the slogans he puts forward, the tactics and strategy he uses, fit the needs of the time.

Lenin emerged from the party crisis in April with enormous moral authority; he had the courage to defy the prevailing mood in the party, and, with extraordinary powers of persuasion, to sway his comrades.

Above all, in April, Lenin demonstrated his amazing revolutionary imagination when, in the midst of the general euphoria, he stated that he was looking forward to "a break-up and a revolution a thousand times more powerful than that of February."[108]

CHAPTER 8

LENIN, THE PARTY, AND THE PROLETARIAT

"Patiently explain"

Once Lenin had won the Bolshevik Party to his *April Theses*, he set out to analyze how the party could win the majority of the proletariat, the poor, and the soldiers to its side, so as to be able to carry the proletarian revolution to a victorious conclusion. He did this in a pamphlet he wrote at the beginning of April, entitled *The Tasks of the Proletariat in Our Revolution*.

The pamphlet was typed in several copies and handed out to party members before and during the April Conference of the Bolsheviks (April 24–29). It appeared in print for the first time in September. It makes it clear that while the program of the party must define the basic relations between the proletariat and other classes, party tactics must dictate the concrete and temporary class relations. The state of mind of the masses must influence the immediate tactics at any moment of time.

The main practical work must be propaganda among the masses.

Only by overcoming [the] unreasoning trust (and we can and should overcome it only ideologically, by comradely persuasion, by pointing to the *lessons of experience*) can we set ourselves free from the prevailing *orgy of revolutionary phrase-mongering* and really stimulate the consciousness both of the proletariat and of the mass in general, as well as their bold and determined initiative *in the localities*—the independent realization, development, and consolidation of liberties, democracy, and the principle of people's ownership of all the land.

The bourgeoisie and landlords were at that moment keeping the people in subjection, Lenin argued, not by violent oppression but by

deception, flattery, fine phrases, promises by the millions, petty sops, and concessions of the unessential while retaining the essential.

> The peculiar feature of the present situation in Russia is the transition at a dizzy speed from…violent oppression of the people to *flattering* and deceiving the people by promises.

The greater deception was associated with the war effort —with so-called revolutionary defensism.

> The bourgeoisie deceives the people by working on their noble pride in the revolution and by pretending that the *social and political* character of the war, as far as Russia is concerned, underwent a change because of this stage of the revolution, because of the substitution of the near-republic of Guchkov and Miliukov for the Tsarist monarchy.

There were no shortcuts by which to overcome revolutionary defensism.

> What is required of us is the *ability* to explain to the masses that the social and political character of the war is determined not by the "good will" of individuals or groups, or even of nations, but by the position of the *class* which conducts the war, by the class *policy* of which the war is a continuation, by the *ties* of capital, which is the dominant economic force in modern society, by the *imperialist character* of modern capitalism, by Russia's dependence in finance, banking, and diplomacy upon Britain, France, and so on. To explain this skilfully in a way the people would understand *is not easy*; none of us would be able to do it at once without committing errors.[1]

In arguing against revolutionary defensism one must be very sensitive to the real psychological motives that stir the masses.

> The slogan "Down with the War!" is, of course, correct. But it fails to take into account the specific nature of the tasks of the present moment and the necessity of *approaching* the broad mass of the people *in a different way*. It reminds me of the slogan "Down with the Tsar!" with which the inexperienced agitator of the "good old days" went simply and directly to the countryside—and got a beating for his pains. The mass believers in revolutionary defensism are *honest*, not in the personal, but in the class sense, i.e., they belong to *classes* (workers and the peasant poor) which in *actual fact* have nothing to gain from annexations and the subjugation of other peoples. This is nothing like the bourgeois and the "intellectual" fraternity, who know very well that you *cannot* renounce annexations without renouncing the rule of capital, and who unscrupulously deceive the people with fine phrases, with unlimited promises, and endless assurances.
>   The rank-and-file believer in defensism regards the matter in the simple way of the men in the street: "I don't want annexations, but the Germans are 'going for' *me*, therefore I'm defending a just cause and not any kind of imperialist interests at all." To a man like this it must be explained again and again that it is not a question of his personal wishes, but of mass, *class*, political relations and conditions, of

the connection between the war and the interests of capital and the international network of banks, and so forth. Only such a struggle against defensism will be serious and will promise success—perhaps not a very rapid success, but one that will be real and enduring.[2]

What sensitivity Lenin showed towards the real feelings of the masses, even when they followed the reactionary policies of defensism!

Being adaptable does not mean being unprincipled. On the contrary, one must on no account make any concessions to the moods of the masses. "The slightest concession to revolutionary defensism is a *betrayal of socialism*, a complete renunciation of *internationalism*, no matter by what phrases and 'practical' considerations it may be justified."[3]

One form of concession to revolutionary defensism is that of demanding of the provisional government that it should carry out a peace policy:

> To go on demanding that it should proclaim the will of the peoples of Russia for peace, that it should renounce annexations, and so on and so forth, is in practice merely to deceive the people, to inspire them with false hopes and so retard the clarification of their minds. It is indirectly to reconcile them to the continuation of a war the true social character of which is determined not by pious wishes, but by the class character of the government that wages the war, by the connection between the class represented by this government and the imperialist finance capital of Russia, Britain, France, etc., by *the real and actual policy* which that class is pursuing.[4]

In fighting against revolutionary defensism one must give a clear answer to the question: How can the war be ended?

> *It is impossible* to slip out of the imperialist war and achieve a democratic, non-coercive peace without overthrowing the power of capital and transferring state power to *another* class, the proletariat.
>
> The Russian revolution of February–March 1917 was the beginning of the transformation of the imperialist war into a civil war. This revolution took the *first* step towards ending the war; but it requires a *second* step, namely, the transfer of state power to the proletariat, to make the end of the war a *certainty*. This will be the beginning of a "break-through" on a world-wide scale, a break-through in the front of capitalist interests; and only by breaking through *this* front *can* the proletariat save mankind from the horrors of war and endow it with the blessings of peace.[5]
>
> There is no possibility of this war ending in a democratic, non-coercive peace or of the people being relieved of the burden of *billions* paid in interest to the capitalists, who have made fortunes out of the

war, except through a revolution of the proletariat.

> The most varied reforms can and must be demanded of the bour-
> geois governments, but one cannot, without sinking to Manilovism and
> reformism, demand that people and classes entangled by the thousands
> of threads of imperialist capital should *tear* those threads. And unless
> they are torn, all talk of a war against war is idle and deceitful prattle.[6]

The Russian proletariat has an especially great responsibility in
the fight against the imperialist war.

> Much is given to the Russian proletariat; nowhere in the world has the
> working class yet succeeded in developing so much revolutionary en-
> ergy as in Russia. But to whom much is given, of him much is re-
> quired.... No other country in the world is as free as Russia is *now*. Let
> us make use of this freedom, not to advocate support for the bour-
> geoisie, or bourgeois "revolutionary defensism," but in a bold, honest,
> proletarian, Liebknecht way *to found the Third International....*[7]

> There is one, and only one, kind of real internationalism, and that
> is—working wholeheartedly for the development of the revolution-
> ary movement and the revolutionary struggle in *one's own* country,
> and supporting (by propaganda, sympathy, and material aid) *this
> struggle*, this, *and only this*, line in *every* country without exception.[8]

The spur and the rein

It is easy to talk about the need to "patiently explain," but how
could one do this and yet avoid spreading passivity among the
masses? How could the party both restrain the mass movement from
premature assault on the provisional government without weakening
it, and at the same time spur the movement on? After all, strength is
accumulated in struggle, and not in a passive evasion of it.

Political upheavals have never happened without "excesses."
Long ago, Chernyshevsky, whom Lenin so admired, put it: "The
pathway of history does not resemble the pavements of the Nevskii
Prospect: it cuts now across dusty, dirty fields, now across swamps,
now across wilds."

How can one lead a mass movement with all its excesses, without
falling into adventurism on the one hand, or overcautiousness on the
other? These were central problems that Lenin faced again and again
between the February Revolution and the October insurrection.

Then again, how can one deal with the question of whether the
active minority should be encouraged to go ahead and by its struggle inspire and encourage the majority, or whether this would put it
in danger of isolation?

Again and again, when Lenin talked about the fighting masses that the party had to lead, he stated that this did not necessarily mean the majority of the working class. A revolutionary party had to be based in the working class, but not necessarily in the whole class. For a long time it might be established only among a minority of the class—its vanguard. As he wrote on August 22, 1907:

> Not to support a movement of the avowedly revolutionary minority—means, in effect, rejecting all revolutionary methods of struggle. For it is absolutely indisputable that those who participated in the revolutionary movement throughout 1905 were the *avowedly revolutionary minority*: it was because the masses who were fighting were in a minority—they were nonetheless masses for being in a minority—that they did not achieve full success in their struggle. But all the successes which the emancipation movement in Russia did achieve, all the gains it did make, were *wholly* and *without exception* the result of this struggle of the masses alone, who were in a minority.[9]

If majorities are won *in struggle*, how can one avoid falling into the trap of passive adaptation to present moods of the majority, while not giving way to adventurism? If the party encourages the active minority, how can it avoid the danger of tying its hands by minor gains, of being led astray and forgetting to fight for total victory? How can one be firm in keeping the ultimate goal clearly in sight, while adapting oneself to the immediately achievable?

Then again how can the party fight for the overthrow of the regime without being trapped in skirmishes that may turn into a generalized battle? In 1906, Lenin wrote: "Do you think that a serious test of the regime is possible in a broad, heterogeneous, complex, popular movement without a preliminary series of local strikes; that a general uprising is possible without a series of sporadic, minor, non-general uprisings?"[10] In the electric atmosphere of 1917, Lenin's ability to relate the smaller struggles to the overall one were to be put to the severest test.

The unevenness in the development of different sections of the working class in different places is such that while encouraging the advanced centers, one must keep in mind the total picture, so as to prevent the advanced centers from becoming completely isolated from the rest of the country.

Kronstadt

Let us take the case of Kronstadt. On this island, the people, above all the sailors, were very impatient indeed, and became far more radical than the rest of the country in the first few weeks after the February Revolution. On April 18, when the news spread that Foreign Minister Miliukov had sent a note to the Allies supporting "war till victory," the Kronstadt Soviet, which rejected a Bolshevik resolution condemning the government, found itself quite isolated in the town. Large crowds gathered outside the Bolshevik headquarters, at mass meetings in factories and barracks, and passed a Bolshevik resolution that called for "the overthrow of the provisional government and the transfer of all power to the Soviets."[11] One of the large street meetings, numbering some twenty thousand people, was addressed by a Bolshevik member of the Soviet Executive Committee, S.C. Roshal, who called for the overthrow of the government.[12] The Executive Committee of the Soviet of Kronstadt then expelled Roshal for indiscipline. Immediately the Bolsheviks began a campaign for the reelection of the soviet, a campaign which proved to be extremely successful. Elections were held, and the Bolsheviks, who had been the smallest party in the soviet, became the largest.

Unfortunately the Kronstadt Bolsheviks' campaign for the overthrow of the provisional government was contrary to the policy of the Central Committee, and was condemned in a Central Committee resolution on April 22.[13] This resolution was not aimed only at the Kronstadt Committee. The Helsingfors Committee and even some Petrograd Bolsheviks had also put forward the same slogan.

However, the Kronstadt Committee of the Bolsheviks rejected the Central Committee reprimand. On May 5, the new Kronstadt Soviet assembled. On May 13, the new Executive Committee of the Soviet decided to formalize the fact that the soviet was the sole power on the island and issued a draft resolution to this effect. On May 16, the Kronstadt Soviet decided that it would break off all relations with the provisional government and would recognize only the Petrograd Soviet.[14] On May 18, a member of the Central Committee came to Kronstadt demanding to know what was going on. Raskolnikov and Roshal were summoned to Petrograd where they were reprimanded by Lenin.[15]

The events in Kronstadt threatened the Bolshevik Party's whole strategy of "patiently explaining." The Kronstadt Soviet continued to refuse to back down, despite a demand on May 26 from the Executive of the Petrograd Soviet that they do so.[16] It looked as if the provisional government might risk an armed intervention against Kronstadt and the suppression of the Bolshevik Party. The Central Committee of the party felt the situation to be extremely dangerous. On May 27, however, Trotsky managed to persuade the Kronstadt Soviet to accept a compromise offered by the Petrograd Soviet, which allowed it to retreat without losing too much face.

The firebrands of Kronstadt had to be restrained in order to keep the general revolutionary front united.

Unevenness between different places

Again and again Lenin had to intervene to restrain the hotheads of Petrograd, Kronstadt, and Helsingfors—during the April Days, the June Days, and the July Days.

It was a problem to know how to act as the fireman without dampening enthusiasm, without pushing the workers towards despondency; how to prevent a rash move while encouraging the workers to active struggle, and how to do so when differences in levels of consciousness between sections of the proletariat and between centers were very great.

The unevenness between different places did not disappear with the march of the revolution. A sample of replies from local party committees in twenty-five towns during the Sixth Congress shows that the percentage of organized Bolsheviks among the factory workers in the towns varied from 1 percent to 12 percent—the average for the twenty-five towns being 5.4 percent.[17]

Again, variations in the political level between different localities are shown very clearly from an analysis of elections to town Dumas in the summer of 1917. Thus the Bolshevik share of the seats was

Municipalities	Percent
Over 100,000 people (27 towns)	12.00
50,000–100,000 people (35 towns)	8.23
Under 50,000 people (68 towns)	1.41[18]

In Petrograd and Moscow, the share of the Bolsheviks was considerably larger:

Dumas	Percent
Petrograd District (May 27–29)	20.4
Moscow City (June 25)	11.5
Petrograd City (August 20)	33.4
Moscow District (September 24)	50.9

Formally, of course, the two million people in Petrograd, constituting nearly 1.5 percent of the total population of Russia, should have neither more nor less importance than any other two million people. However, the revolution does not stick to the rules of formal democracy. All revolutions are highly centralistic. In the English Revolution of the seventeenth century, the French of the eighteenth, and the Russian of the twentieth, the role of the capital city was decisive. As we have seen, the vanguard of the Russian proletariat, even before the war, was in Petrograd. St Petersburg played a dominant role in the development of the Bolshevik Party and the proletariat in the years 1912–14. In organizational terms, the Bolsheviks in St. Petersburg were far ahead of their comrades elsewhere. The specific weight of the Petrograd proletariat was accentuated in 1917, both absolutely and relatively, compared with the rest of the country.[19]

It would be stupidly formalistic to assume that every thousand Bolsheviks had equal weight, wherever they lived, worked, and struggled. Compare the Bolshevik membership of Vyborg District with, let us say, that of the Ukrainian cities Kiev, Odessa, Nikolaev, and Ekaterinoslav[20]:

	Beginning of March	April Conference	Sixth Congress	October–November
Vyborg	500	3,290	6,632	6,985
Kiev	200	1,900	4,000	5,000
Odessa			1,600–1,700	4,000
Nikolaev	400	1,500	3,500	4,000
Ekaterinoslav		400 (9 Sept.)	900	1,600
4 Ukrainian cities together	600	3,800	10,100–10,200	14,600

The Vyborg Bolsheviks, fewer in number than those of the four Ukrainian towns, were in fact far more important historically.

The Bolsheviks quite rightly put their emphasis on the key areas of the industrial centers and the garrison towns—Petrograd, Finland, the fleet, the northern armies, the Moscow industrial area, and the Urals.

The class and the party

The sailors of Kronstadt, the soldiers of Minsk, the workers of Petrograd, Moscow, and Saratov, the peasants ransacking the landlords' mansions all over Russia were in thousands upon thousands of different groups. Even if they were pushing in the same direction, they still had very different levels of consciousness. If it had not been for this unevenness in consciousness there would not have been a need for a revolutionary party.

The party exists in order to hasten the elimination of this unevenness by raising consciousness to the highest possible level. The party aims to spread the actions of the masses, to unite the actions of the masses from one end of the country to the other, to coordinate the different efforts, to select the most favorable moments for action, to be the proletariat's general staff. But, unfortunately, if unevenness in the class makes the party necessary, the same unevenness affects the party, making the question of its guidance very complicated indeed.

As the Bolshevik Party was a mass party with deep roots in the working class, naturally the unevenness in the class must have had a decisive influence on local party organization.

With the Petrograd workers impatient for a showdown with the provisional government, it is no wonder that, as we shall see later, in April, June, and July, the leading local Bolsheviks were "ultra-left," far to the left of the Central Committee, and straining at the leash. At the same time party leaders elsewhere, practically throughout the provinces, were dragging behind the Central Committee and belonged overwhelmingly to the right wing of the party.

How could both the militant Vyborg and Narva district organizations of the party and the extreme right-wing organizations of Kiev and Odessa be kept in tandem?

While the Vyborg comrades were striving as early as February for the overthrow of the provisional government, the Bolsheviks in many cities were refusing even to split from the Mensheviks. In many workers' centers, such as Ekaterinburg, Ferm, Tula, Orel, Baku, Kolomna, Yaroslav, Kiev, and Voronezh, the Bolsheviks did not break away from the Mensheviks until the end of May.[21]

In Minsk, Tiflis, Nizhni-Novgorod, Omsk, Tomsk, Odessa, Nikolaev, Zlatoust, Kostroma, Sevastopol, and Vitebsk, the Bolsheviks split from the Mensheviks only in June.[22] In many other centers they did so only in August or September.[23] three hundred fifty-one party organizations remained joint Bolshevik-Menshevik organizations, in many cases until as late as September.[24] In fact, in some centers, the Bolsheviks separated from the Mensheviks only after the October Revolution.

On the whole, the further from Petrograd, the stronger the conciliatory tendencies prevailing among the Bolsheviks. They persisted longest in the Ukraine, Siberia, and Central Asia. Of fifteen city committees in Siberia, eight did not split from the Mensheviks until after the Sixth Party Congress (July26–August 3), and five until October or even later.

Unevenness between party organizations existed not only between different cities, but even within one and the same city, between different factories. Thus in Petrograd the number of Bolsheviks in different factories was

Putilov (March 2)	100
Aivaz (September)	14
Metallist (July)	200–300
Skorokhod (September)	550[25]

The party explosion

To add to the difficulties, what Lenin had to rely on was not a smooth-running party organization with a large cadre of well established local leaders, but one that was in a tremendous turmoil of growth.

To get an idea of this growth, let us look at the changes in the membership of the party in a number of centers over the weeks and months following the February Revolution.

	Beginning of March	Seventh Conference April 24–29	Sixth Congress (July 26– August 3)
Petrograd	2000	16,000	36,000
Moscow	600	7,000	15,000
Ivanovo-Vosnesensk	10	3,564	5,440
Ekaterinoslav	400	1,500	3,500
Lugan	100	1,500	2,596
Kharkov	105	1,200	–
Kiev	200	1,900	4,000
Saratov	60	1,600	3,000
Ekaterinburg	40	1,700	2,800[26]

How could one expect stable leadership in Ivanovo-Voznesensk, where membership grew from 10 to 5,440 over five months; in Ekaterinburg, where membership grew from 40 to 2,800; or in

Saratov, where it grew from 60 to 3,000?

The administrative weakness of the party center

And what was the central party apparatus that had to deal with this exploding party membership, with the numerous city committees scattered over enormous distances, with very few local cadres, many still hesitant even about breaking organizationally with the Mensheviks?

A group of five or six women party workers made up the secretariat.[27] Their offices were two rooms plus a toilet in Ksheshinskaia Palace, the headquarters of the Bolsheviks in Petrograd. One room served as an office, the other as a reception room. The toilet was a storeroom for the party records. After the July Days the secretariat moved to the apartment of one of its senior members, Elana Stasova, and a short time later to a boys' school.[28]

Heading the secretariat between April and October was Iakov Mikhailovich Sverdlov, a man of amazing energy and organizational ability, a Bolshevik since the beginning of Bolshevism, who had experienced many years of imprisonment and exile in Siberia.

> Sverdlov was so small and so frail [Trotsky writes] that one would have thought he was ill; yet there was something in him which gave the impression of authority and quiet strength. He presided over the discussion without raising his voice, without interrupting the speakers; he worked evenly and smoothly like a well-oiled engine. The secret of his success lay not in his talent for conducting the debate, but in the fact that he was extremely well acquainted with those present in the hall and also that he knew exactly what he was trying to achieve. Before each conference he would meet every delegate individually, would question him and sometimes also brief him. Even before he opened the conference, he already had a more or less clear general idea of what turn the discussion would take. But even without the preliminary conversations he knew better than anybody else in what way this or that party worker would react to every particular problem. The number of our comrades with whose political personalities Sverdlov was well acquainted was quite considerable, if one applies the standards of that time. He was a born organizer and planner. He saw every political problem first of all in the light of its intrinsic meaning for the party organization: he saw immediately how particular people and particular groups would react to it and how the alignments inside the organization would shape themselves and what consequently the relationship between the party and the masses outside the organization would be. Almost automatically, he was translating algebraic formulae into arithmetical realities. He was able to check the worth of important political

slogans against revolutionary actuality.[29]

Sverdlov fitted the "no red-tape, no bureaucracy" method of work of the Central Committee.

> The Central Committee, having barely emerged from its underground existence, was still in organization and methods far from the all-powerful, all-embracing chancellery of recent years. The main part of the equipment of the Central Committee was carried by Sverdlov in his side-pocket.[30]

The financial resources of the center were extremely small. The income of the Russian Bureau between December 2, 1916, and February 1, 1917, amounted to 1,117 rubles, 50 kopeks.[31] When the February Revolution broke out, the Russian Bureau had in hand oniy 100 rubles.[32] At that time, a ruble was equivalent to two shillings. Taking into account the rate of inflation since then one can assume that a ruble of 1917 would have the purchasing power of a pound sterling today. So we must imagine that the Bolshevik headquarters in 1917 had the equivalent of £100 (approximately $180 in current U.S. dollars.)

In the months that followed, the party center continued to be in very great straits. The secretariat was responsible for collecting the contributions from the provinces. In the secretariat correspondence,[33] not much appears on this topic until the late summer or early autumn, but by that time serious attention was devoted to collecting 10 percent of each local organization's regular income, and 40 percent of special collections; however, there is repeated evidence that the center obtained very little money from the local committees. Thus on September 27, Stasova, in the name of the secretariat, wrote a letter to 333 local committees complaining that only 24 of them had paid the 10 percent dues owed to the center. And the amounts paid since the April Conference were puny. Thus the Reval Committee paid 1,068 rubles for July and August; the Moscow Committee 574.56 for May, June, and July; the Tiflis Committee 50, etc. Altogether only 3,643.7 rubles were paid by all the local committees: "As you see comrades, the amount is so small that one may think that the Russian Social Democratic Workers' Party has only hundreds of members."[34]

As against subscriptions, the funds raised by general collections among workers and soldiers were far more substantial. Thus, for instance, on April 13, *Pravda* made an appeal for funds to equip a printshop for itself. By April 22, 75,334.45 rubles had been collected,[35] and by the time of the Sixth Congress, workers and soldiers had donated 140,000 rubles towards the party printing press.[36] The standard donation for workers was one day's wages. In addition workers collected money to pay for the supply of party literature to the troops. Thus on May 19, the workers in the Novyi Lessner factory in Petrograd collected 33,781 rubles just for this purpose alone.[37] On May 27, 4,545.11 rubles were donated for the same purpose by the Provodnik factory in Moscow.[38]

These collections explain how the secretariat was able to hand out considerable amounts to different party bodies and papers. Thus between May 30 and June 7, *Bakinski Rabochii* got 2,116 rubles; between June 27 and September 18, 2,700 rubles were given to the Minsk and North Western Committee of the party; on May 17, *Okopnoi Pravda* (the army paper) received 1,000 rubles; on September 6 the Ekaterinburg Committee received 600; on May 30, the Polish paper of the Petrograd Committee, *Tribuna*, received 1,500 rubles.[39] But the Bolshevik Party was still in financial straits throughout 1917.

Twenty days before the October Revolution, the minutes of the Central Committee record:

> 1. Sverdlov reports on the request which has come from the Petrograd Area Committee to be given a subsidy on the scale of 2,500–3,000 rubles needed to start work in the province.
>
> After a discussion, Sverdlov's proposal to give 1,000 rubles, indicating that it is hoped that it will be returned, is adopted.
>
> 2. Sverdlov reports that a regional bureau of our party's Military Organization has been formed on the southwest front and that the bureau requests that several thousands be given to publish a front newspaper.
>
> It is decided to give between 2,000 and 3,000 rubles.[40]

A thousand rubles for the Petrograd organization!

Not only was the party secretariat poor in financial resources; its human resources were also so limited as to restrict even correspondence with the local committees. Between March and October, the secretariat sent about 1,740 letters to local organizations, of which about 1,000 went out between March and August (an average of 165 per month), and 740 in September and October (370 per month). Since the number of city committees on the eve of the October Revolution was 288,[41] these figures are not very impressive—there was less than one letter per city committee per month!

In addition a number of telegrams were sent by the secretariat: in March to 34 organizations; April, 12; May, 14; June, 46; July,

28; August, 7; September, 66; October, 75.[42] The Secretariat inter-
viewed a number of visitors from local organizations: in April (excluding delegates to the Seventh Congress), 17; in May, 130
(including many Bolsheviks returning from emigration and now directed to the localities); in June and July, 30; in August, 86; in September, 37, in October, more than 100.[43]

The most common complaint in letters from local committees
to the secretariat was that no speakers and lecturers were supplied.[44] The scarcity of experienced cadres is reflected in the complaint from Helsingfors that in a party with 4,500 to 4,600
members there were only three experienced people: one managed
the paper, the other was an agitator, and the third a lecturer.[45]

It was very common for provincial committees to complain
about neglect by the Central Committee, charging it with being no
more than the "Petrograd Committee," on account of its apparent
unconcern for the remainder of Russia. During the Sixth Congress,
the complaints rained down thick and fast. Thus, for instance, P.N.
Milonov (from Samara): "The Central Committee as the leading
organ of the whole party should direct the activities of the various
local organizations, which await its directives. But the CC, the so
to say leading organ of the whole party, took into account only the
conditions in Petrograd."[46]

V.P. Nogin, the CC member from Moscow: "We must admit
that in the activities of all party organizations and the CC in particular, there were many mistakes and blunders. We must admit first
of all, what stares us in the face, that the CC spends most of its
time on work in Petrograd,"[47]

B.Z. Shumiatskii, the delegate from Central Siberia: "It seems to
us that the CC acts as a subsidiary department of the Petrograd organization."[48]

I.T. Smilga stated that complaints were increasingly being heard
that *Pravda* was not a national paper but only a Petrograd paper.[49]

In reply Sverdlov rebuked the delegates for this attitude, declaring that the complaining comrades, when asked to explain themselves, usually replied that neither Lenin nor Zinoviev had come to
speak in their town or village. Such answers, he concluded, betrayed a lack of understanding of the vast demands made upon the
Central Committee.[50]

Stalin referred to complaints that "the Central Committee had
not formed contacts in the provinces and that its activities had been
confined chiefly to Petrograd." And he said:

The reproach of isolation from the provinces is not without foundation. But it was utterly impossible to cover the entire provinces. The reproach that the Central Committee virtually became a Petrograd Committee is to some extent justified. This is a fact. But it is here, in Petrograd, that the policy of Russia is being hammered out. It is here that the directing forces of the revolution are located.

The apparatus of the Central Committee…is, of course, a weak apparatus. To demand, therefore, that the Central Committee take no steps without first consulting the provinces is tantamount to demanding that the Central Committee should not march ahead of events but trail behind them. But then it would not be a Central Committee.[51]

The minutes of the Central Committee on the whole confirm the charge brought by the provincial Bolsheviks. They deal with hardly any locality other than Petrograd. Even when they do, they provide indirect confirmation of the accusation of neglect of the provinces. Thus the minutes of August 31 state:

[I]t was pointed out that the work of the CC must be widened to cover the whole of Russia because up to now the CC's work, for purely technical reasons, has been concentrated chiefly in Petersburg. To further this policy, a group of travelling agents must be formed and this is especially necessary in order to organize the northwest and southern regions and the Volga area where solidarity is weak.[52]

The editors of the minutes (published in 1958) added: "No materials have been found on the group of travelling CC agents."[53] The lack of any *actual* centrally integrated party organization shows itself clearly in the preparations for the October insurrection.

Many local committees were not adequately informed about the impending insurrection in Petrograd and as a consequence were ill prepared to take similar action themselves. Even in the central industrial region, which was in fairly close contact with the Moscow Regional Bureau, the machinery creaked badly. On 15–16 October, a member of the bureau addressed a congress of soviets at Ivanovo, urged the need to "adopt a course for a rising," and secured an appropriate resolution; yet a local committee man, F. Samoilov, relates that he and his colleagues were waiting daily for directives from the center. At nearby Kineshma, the Bolshevik chairman of the Soviet brought back the news of the revolutionary plan early in October and a revkom (revolutionary committee) was elected; "but it must be said that this troika did not do much in practice" and its attention was monopolized by more peaceful activities. A committeeman in Voronezh complains, "we received absolutely no information from our party centers…[and] were left completely in the dark," whereas the local Socialist Revolutionaries were well informed of events in the capital. Equally outspoken is Antonov of Saratov: "Our party committee, which was closely follow-

ing the approaching dénouement, impatiently awaited the guiding instructions promised by the Central Committee. Alas! None came." It
was the same plaintive cry at Kazan: "We received no instructions of
any kind [and] were left to our own devices...."

Of course, a good deal of improvisation was only to be expected, and
information will have been frequently transmitted informally through
nonparty channels. Yet the prevailing impression given by the sources is
that the provinces were expected to fend for themselves, and that "organized preparations" for the rising, where they were made, took a sur-
prisingly casual form. In most cases the impulse to action was given by
the news that the Bolsheviks had struck in the two capital cities.[54]

To weaken even further the actual administrative centralization
of the party, there was substantial resistance in the localities to the
idea of forming regional organizations. In the southwest, in April, a
regional committee was created embracing seven provinces, with
the radical revolutionary Evgeniia Bosh as secretary. However, it
was opposed by the Kiev Party Committee members Iurii and
Leonid Piatakov, both on the right wing of Bolshevism. The
Kievans were supported by the committees of three other major
Ukrainian cities: Odessa, Nikolaev, and Ekaterinoslav.

In the lower Volga area no regional committee could be created,
owing to the rivalry between the Saratov Committee, led by V.P.
Antonov Saratovski, and the Samara Committee led by Kuibishev. In
Moscow, the conflict was between the City Committee led by the
right-wing Bolsheviks Nogin and Rykov, on the one hand, and the
group of left Bolsheviks—Bukharin, Ossinsky, Vladimir Smirnov, and
Lomo—on the other hand, who controlled the Regional Bureau.[55]

What an incredible gulf between Lenin's concept of a centralized party and the actual situation among the Bolsheviks in 1917!

In fact, as a result of comparing the minutes of the Central
Committee with those of the Petersburg Committee, and also reading the correspondence of the secretariat and memoirs of Bolshevik
activists from different localities, one reaches an inescapable conclusion: the party organization was administratively far more effi-
cient at the lower levels than at the top.

The informality of the Central Committee

Given the Stalinist myths about Bolshevism, one would imagine
the workings of the Central Committee to have been bound by red
tape and bureaucracy. But there was nothing of the sort.

First of all, *attendance* at Central Committee meetings shows how far this body was from bureaucratic formalism. The Sixth Congress elected twenty-one members to the Central Committee. However, the numbers of members present at various sessions when records were kept ranged between six and sixteen, with an average of ten per session.[56] At the October 10 session which took the historic decision about the insurrection only eleven members were present![57]

The Central Committee again and again reached decisions that its members forgot all about immediately afterwards. To give one or two examples: The minutes of the Central Committee session of October 10 state

> Comrade Dzerzhinsky suggests that a Political Bureau be created from members of the CC to provide political leadership in the days ahead.
> After an exchange of views, the suggestion is approved. A Political Bureau of 7 people is created…: Lenin, Zinoviev, Kamenev, Trotsky, Stalin, Sokolnikov, Bubnov.[58]

However, this Political Bureau, whose task was to guide the insurrection, did not meet once. The comrades forgot about the resolution!

Then again, the minutes of October 16 state:

> The CC organizes a Military Revolutionary Center consisting of the following: Sverdlov, Stalin, Bubnov, Uritsky, and Dzerzhinsky. This center is included in the Soviet Revolutionary Committee.[59]

Again, this "center" never met.

> Sverdlov…worked before and after the resolution of 16 October in close contact with the Chairman of the Military Revolutionary Committee. Three other members of the "center," Uritsky, Dzerzhinsky, and Bubnov, were drawn into work for the Military Revolutionary Committee, each of them individually, as late as 24 October as if the resolution of 16 October had never been passed. As for Stalin…he stubbornly kept from joining either the Executive Committee of the Petrograd Soviet or the Military Revolutionary Committee, and did not appear at any of its sessions.[60]

The center is not once mentioned in the CC minutes after October 16.

In reporting on party membership, Sverdlov also showed a great lack of concern about pedantic exactness. Thus at the October 16 session he reported that membership had reached "no fewer than 400,000."[61] This figure must have been a huge exaggeration, since Sverdlov claimed only 240,000 members in August 1917,[62] and in the spring of 1918 he reported to the Seventh Party Congress that membership had increased to 300,000.[63]

As a matter of fact, this lack of formalism was absolutely vital for the effective working of the party as a revolutionary body.

> An overformal party structure inevitably clashes with two basic features of the revolutionary movement: (1) the unevenness in consciousness, militancy, and dedication of different parts of the revolutionary organization; and (2) the fact that members who play a positive vanguard role at a certain stage of the struggle fall behind at another.[64]

Above all, the state of the Bolshevik Party in 1917 demonstrated that a revolutionary party is not born ready-made for revolution. It does not arise like Minerva from the head of Zeus. It is moulded, transformed in the process of the revolutionary struggle, and above all in the revolution itself. For, as Marx said in his "Thesis on Feuerbach:" "The materialist doctrine concerning the changing of circumstances and education forgets that circumstances are changed by men and that the educator must himself be educated." It is true that the situation among the Bolsheviks in 1917 was far removed from Lenin's concept of a centralized party. However, the party did exist. It had twenty-four thousand members in February 1917. The ideas of Bolshevism were not disembodied ideas, but were represented in thousands upon thousands of proletarian cadres who had been forged during years of struggle. Only because of this was it possible for Bolshevism to translate words into deeds in time and to lead a successful revolution.

The cadres of Bolshevism

To quote something that I wrote elsewhere:

> The fact that, despite all the factors encouraging instability, the party survived with all the vigor it did, was due to its deep roots in the class, to its being a real mass workers' party. Of course all magnitudes are relative. A 1922 Bolshevik Party census covering 22 *guberniias* and *oblasts* showed that 1,085 members had joined the party before 1905.[65]
>
> A rough estimate puts the number at about double for areas excluded from the census. Allowing for the fact that a large number of party members must have lost their lives during the revolution and the civil war, we see a considerable continuity of membership between 1905 and 1922. These were the cadres who gave the party its stability. For a party working under illegal conditions, in a country where the industrial proletariat numbered only some two and a half million, a cadre organization of several thousands surviving for many

years is a remarkable achievement.[66]

The official estimate of the membership of the party in January 1917, before its emergence into the open and the return of exiled members, is 23,600.[67] This was a broad enough base for further expansion during the months of the revolution: from 79,204 at the end of April to 240,000 at the end of July.

The party was very proletarian in composition. Over the years the number of working people present at party congresses rose steadily, as can be seen from the following table:

Social Composition of Congress Delegates[68]

Congress	Workers	Peasants	White-collar and other	Unknown
II (1903)	3 (5.9%)	0	40(78.4%)	8(15.7%)
III(1905)	1 (3.3%)	0	28(93.4%)	1 (3.3%)
IV(1906)	36(24.8%)	1(0.8%)	108(74.4%)	0
V (1907)	116(34.5%)	2(0.6%)	218(64.9%)	0
VI(1917)	70(40.9%)	0	101(59.1%)	0

Workers made up a very large proportion of party members. In January 1917 the social composition of the party was

	Workers	Peasants	White-collar	Other	Total
Number	14,200	1,800	6,100	1,500	23,600
Percentage	60.2	7.6	25.8	6.4	100[69]

No figures are available for changes in the composition of the party after the February Revolution, but there is no doubt that an overwhelming majority of the people who joined the party in this period were workers and soldiers. Figures published for individual regions show that it was almost entirely proletarian in composition. Thus in Reval on August 13, there were 3,182 members, of whom 2,926 were workers, 209 military, and 47 intellectuals.[70]

Replies to questionnaires addressed to delegates to the Sixth Congress answered the question about the role of intellectuals, teachers, and students in local party work with monotonous similarity. Kronstadt: "[L]ocal students and teachers do not undertake

local work"; Finland: "Intellectuals (besides officers)—none";
Moscow: "New forces of intelligentsia—practically absent";
Ivanovo-Voronezh: "No local intelligentsia"; Kuznetsov: "No intel-
lectuals"; Riga: "Practically no intellectuals," and so on and so on.[71]
As Trotsky summed it up:

> The intelligentsia hardly came into the Bolshevik Party at all. A
> broad layer of so-called "old Bolsheviks," from among the students
> who had associated themselves with the revolution of 1905, had
> since turned into extraordinarily successful engineers, physicians,
> government officials, and they now unceremoniously showed the
> party the hostile aspect of their backs.* Even in Petrograd there was
> felt at every step a lack of journalists, speakers, agitators; and the
> provinces were wholly deprived of what few they had had. "There
> are no leaders; there are no politically literate people who can explain
> to the masses what the Bolsheviks want!"—this cry came from hun-
> dreds of remote corners, and especially from the front.[72]

Lenin was delighted that his party was made up largely of
young people—they were the ones with energy and real revolutionary spirit.[74] On February 27 he wrote to Inessa Armand:
"The young are the only people worth working on!"[75] In 1917
the party members were younger than ever. At the Sixth Congress
the ages of the delegates were

Age	Delegates
18–19	5
20–24	25
25–29	49
30–34	49
35–39	30
40–44	11
45–47	2

The average age was 29. The minimum age was 18 and the
maximum 47.[76]
On the whole the delegates had been members of the Bolshevik
Party for quite a long time:

---

* The tiny influence the Bolsheviks had among students at the time is clear when
one looks, for instance, at the Student Congress of Voronezh *guberniia* (June
14–17): of 250 delegates only 16 were Bolshevik.[73]

Years	Delegates	Years	Delegates
Less than 1	4	Less than 9	5
" 2	2	" 10	8
" 3	8	" 11	15
" 4	14	" 12	24
" 5	15	" 13	19
" 6	6	" 14	16
" 7	4	" 15	4
" 8	4		

The average length of membership was eight years, three months.[77]

How had these delegates been hardened in the struggle? The questionnaire already referred to showed their legal status at the time of the February Revolution:

Free	79	
In prison	2	0
In exile	4	1
Hard labor	2	
In emigration	1	3
On the run	3	
On military service	12	

Each delegate had been arrested an average of three or four times; had been in prison for an average of eighteen months; in exile eight months; deported for five months; sentenced to hard labor for three months.[78]

During the long and testing years of the 1905 Revolution and the years of illegality, prison, and exile that followed, the cadres lived with the masses and were part of them. The sharing of long, hard battles created strong party discipline and deep party loyalty, which explains why, despite all the trials of the months February–October 1917—the abrupt changes in party tactics, the errors committed by many party leaders and members—the number of people who left the party was minimal. The Bolshevik Party was a revolutionary party through and through.

It was the mass proletarian character of the Bolshevik Party, its youth, and its steeling over the years that made it the spearhead that could lead revolution to victory.

The central role of the press

The fact that the center supplied the local committees with very few speakers and lecturers and that there was very little systematic communication at all between them did not mean to say that the local committees were left to work out their policies and tactics as well as they could on their own. On the contrary, a central role in guiding the local committees was played by the party press.

At the beginning of July, forty-one newspapers and journals were published by the Bolshevik Party, twenty-seven in Russian and the remainder in the languages of various minorities (five Latvian, two Lithuanian, two Armenian, two Estonian, one Polish, one Georgian, one Azerbaidzhan). Of these seventeen were daily papers (fourteen in the Russian language), eight appeared three times a week, five twice weekly, seven weekly, three fortnightly, and one monthly. The total number of copies printed was about 320,000 a day. More than half were printed in Petrograd (*Pravda*, 90,000 daily; *Soldatskaia pravda*, 50,000).[79]

As the total circulation of the Bolshevik press was only about a third larger than the membership of the party, it is clear, firstly, that the main function of the papers was to organize and direct the party members, and secondly, that the periphery of the party was largely attracted to it and incorporated into it through the press.

The fact that the circulation was not much greater than the membership cannot be explained by illiteracy among the Russian industrial proletariat: the overwhelming majority were literate. Among industrial workers (in 1918), the rate of literacy was 80.3 percent for men and 48.2 percent for women, while among the population as a whole between the ages of sixteen and fifty (in 1920) the rate of literacy was men 53.73 percent, women 36 percent.[80]

It is interesting to compare the circulation of the Bolshevik press under conditions of freedom and legality with its circulation before the war—under the harshest conditions of persecution. At the beginning of July 1917, as we said, *Pravda*'s circulation was ninty thousand daily; in January–February 1914, the average circulation was some twenty-five thousand.[81] Thus the circulation rose three and a half times, while Bolshevik membership in Petrograd had increased more than tenfold.

The press also played a central role in directing party committees and party members. It seems there was not a party city committee that did not receive a bundle of copies of *Pravda*: Minsk, 600 copies daily; Lugansk, 200; Odessa, 200; and so on.[82]

The Bolshevik Party forged for the victory of the revolution

The ideas of revolutionary socialism were not disembodied ideas, but were represented in a fine body of men and women, trained and tested over many years of struggle so as to be able to show both revolutionary relentlessness and the utmost tactical flexibility. With complete justification, Lenin could write a few years after October:

Bolshevism...went through fifteen years of practical history (1903–17) unequalled anywhere in the world in its wealth of experience. During those fifteen years, no other country knew anything even approximating to that revolutionary experience, that rapid and varied succession of different forms of the movement—legal and illegal, peaceful and stormy, underground and open, local circles and mass movements, and parliamentary and terrorist forms. In no other country has there been concentrated, in so brief a period, such a wealth of forms, shades, and methods of struggle of *all* classes of modern society, a struggle which, owing to the backwardness of the country and the severity of the Tsarist yoke, matured with exceptional rapidity, and assimilated most eagerly and successfully the appropriate "last word" of American and European political experience.[83]

The party was highly disciplined. This discipline was not an accidental, mechanical, or artificial product of some regulation or other, but the result of struggle:

Only the history of Bolshevism during the *entire* period of its existence can satisfactorily explain why it has been able to build up and maintain, under most difficult conditions, the iron discipline needed for the victory of the proletariat.

The first questions to arise are: how is the discipline of the proletariat's revolutionary party maintained? How is it tested? How is it reinforced? First, by the class-consciousness of the proletarian vanguard and by its devotion to the revolution, by its tenacity, self-sacrifice, and heroism. Second, by its ability to link up, maintain the closest contact, and—if you wish—merge, in certain measure, with the broadest masses of the working people—primarily with the proletariat, *but also with the non-proletarian* masses of working people. Third, by the correctness of the political leadership exercized by this vanguard, by the correctness of its political strategy and tactics, provided the broad masses have seen, *from their own experience,* that they are correct. Without these conditions, discipline in a revolutionary party really capable of being the party of the advanced class, whose mission it is to overthrow the bourgeoisie and transform the whole of society, cannot be achieved. Without these conditions, all attempts to establish discipline inevitably fall flat and end up in phrase mongering and clowning. On the other hand, these conditions cannot emerge at once.

They are created only by prolonged and hard-won experience.[84]

The Bolshevik Party was a magnificent school of tactics and strategy. As I have written elsewhere:

> A clear scientific understanding of the *general* contours of historical development of the class struggle is essential for a revolutionary leader. He will not be able to keep his bearings and his confidence through the twists and turns of the struggle unless he has a general knowledge of economics and politics. Therefore Lenin repeated many times that strategy and tactics must be based "on an exact appraisal of the objective situation," while at the same time being "shaped after analyzing class relations *in their entirety.*" In other words they must be based on a clear, confident, theoretical analysis—on science.[85]
>
> It is, in fact [Lenin wrote], one of the functions of a party organization and of party leaders worthy of the name, to acquire, through the prolonged, persistent, variegated, and comprehensive efforts of all thinking representatives of a given class, the knowledge, experience, and—in addition to knowledge and experience—the political flair necessary for the speedy and correct solution of complex political problems.[86]

And there is no situation more complex or that changes more quickly than that of revolution, as the days between February and October 1917 amply demonstrate.

At such a time, the need for rapid and sharp tactical changes is absolutely vital.

> Capitalism would not be capitalism if the proletariat *pur sang* were not surrounded by a large number of exceedingly motley types intermediate between the proletarian and the semi-proletarian (who earns his livelihood in part by the sale of his labor-power), between the semi-proletarian and the small peasant (and petty artisan, handicraft worker, and small master in general), between the small peasant and the middle peasant, and so on, and if the proletariat itself were not divided into more developed and less developed strata, if it were not divided according to territorial origins, trade, sometimes according to religion, and so on. From all this follows the necessity, the absolute necessity, for the Communist Party, the vanguard of the proletariat, its class-conscious section, to resort to changes of tack, to conciliation and compromises with the various groups of proletarians, with the various parties of the workers and small masters. It is entirely a matter of *knowing how* to apply these tactics in order to *raise*—not lower—the *general* level of proletarian class-consciousness, revolutionary spirit, and ability to fight and win.[87]

A revolutionary leadership needs not only an understanding of the struggle as a whole, but the capacity to put forward the right slogans at every turning point. These do not derive simply from the party program, but must fit the circumstances, above all the moods and feelings of the masses, so that they can be used to lead the workers forward. Slogans must be appropriate not only to the general direction of the revolutionary movement, but also to the level of consciousness of the masses. Only through the *application* of the general line of the party does its real value become manifest.[88]

Revolutionary leaders can fall into the trap of limiting their horizon to that of the advanced elements of the class. Again and again that was what happened to the Bolshevik leadership of Petrograd and the Military Organization of the party (in the April Days, the June Days, and the July Days). Such a mistake is very dangerous. One "must *soberly* follow the *actual* state of the class-consciousness and preparedness of the entire class (not only of its communist vanguard) and of all the *working people* (not only of their advanced elements)."[89] "A vanguard performs its task as vanguard only when it is able to avoid being isolated from the mass of the people it leads and is able really to lead the whole mass forward."[90]

If the party must avoid the danger of adventurism, it must also steer clear of the trap of "tailism"—of waiting for majority support before it acts.

The proletarian revolution is impossible without the sympathy and support of the overwhelming majority of the working people for their vanguard—the proletariat. But this sympathy and this support are not forthcoming immediately and are not decided by elections. They are won in the course of long, arduous, and stern class struggle. The class struggle waged by the proletariat for the sympathy and support of the majority of the working people does not end with the conquest of political power by the proletariat. *After* the conquest of power this struggle *continues*, but in *other* forms.[91]

What the party needs for victory is support on the decisive front:

Capitals, or, in general, big commercial and industrial centers (here in Russia the two coincided, but they do not everywhere coincide), to a considerable degree decide the political fate of a nation, provided, of course, the centers are supported by sufficient local, rural forces, even if that support does not come immediately.[92]

In October the Bolsheviks were able to take power, although they had the support of only a minority of the population, because they had

(1) an overwhelming majority among the proletariat; (2) almost half of the armed forces; (3) an overwhelming superiority of forces at the decisive moment at the decisive points, namely: in Petrograd and Moscow and on the war fronts near the center.[93]

It is not enough to be a revolutionary and an adherent of socialism or a communist in general. You must be able at each particular moment to find the particular link in the chain which you must grasp with all your might in order to hold the whole chain and to prepare firmly for the transition to the next link.[94]

To achieve such a victory the party had to hold on to the "key links" in the chain of events:

What was the central event in 1917? Withdrawal from the war. The entire nation demanded this, and it overshadowed everything. Revolutionary Russia accomplished this withdrawal from the war.... No matter how many outrageous and absurd things we may have done in other spheres, the fact that we realized what the main task was proved that everything was right.[95]

One should not, of course, assume that the Bolshevik Party did not commit mistakes, grave ones, and many of them. Of course not. But it rectified them both quickly and sincerely. This was characteristic of Bolshevism throughout its history and above all during the revolutionary months of 1917.

A political party's attitude towards its own mistakes is one of the most important and surest ways of judging how earnest the party is and how it fulfils *in practice* its obligations towards its class and the *working people*. Frankly acknowledging a mistake, ascertaining the reasons for it, analyzing the conditions that have led up to it, and thrashing out the means of its rectification—that is the hallmark of a serious party; that is how it should perform its duties, and how it should educate and train its class and then the masses.*[96]

Above all, Bolshevism knew how to learn from the experience of the masses in the struggle.

History as a whole [Lenin wrote], and the history of revolutions in particular, is always richer in content, more varied, more multiform, more lively and ingenious than is imagined by even the best parties, the most class-conscious vanguards of the most advanced classes. This can readily be understood, because even the finest of vanguards express the class-consciousness, will, passion, and imagination of tens of thousands, whereas at moments of great upsurge and the exertion of all human capacities, revolutions are made by the class-consciousness, will, passion, and imagination of tens of millions, spurred on by a most acute struggle of classes. Two very important

---

* The lack of pomposity in Lenin's attitude towards his own mistakes is shown by his remark to Karl Radek when he found him one day reading a collection of his articles written in the year 1903. Lenin laughed heartily. "It is very interesting to read what fools we were then."[97]

practical conclusions follow from this: first, that in order to accomplish its task the revolutionary class must be able to master *all* forms or aspects of social activity without exception...second, that the revolutionary class must be prepared for the most rapid and brusque replacement of one form by another.[98]

Lenin in the preparations for October

Relations similar to those between the party and the proletariat existed between Lenin and the party. If the party was necessary to give the proletariat consciousness and confidence in its own potentialities, Lenin's role in relation to the party was equally essential.

The rank-and-file revolutionary sees only a tiny part of the battlefield. The party leader has to grasp the totality of the situation. This task is very difficult indeed, because of the swiftness of changes and the enormous unevenness between different sections of the proletariat, the soldiers, and the peasantry; given a party organization that is both trying to influence the different sections of the population and at the same time being very much influenced by them; and with the problems created by the severe scarcity of party resources.

In the months from April to October, Lenin demonstrated his strategic and tactical genius. These months demanded the most difficult adjustments in party tactics, as the consciousness of the masses changed more rapidly than ever before, in a very complicated fashion that was full of contradictions. While adapting himself to the immediate situation, Lenin relentlessly subordinated everything to the final aim—the seizure of power by the proletariat. The combination of principled intransigence with tactical adaptation achieved its finest form.

Throughout all the zigzags in tactics, Lenin's leitmotif was constant: to raise the level of consciousness and organization of the working class, to explain to the masses their own interests, to give clear political expression to the feelings and thoughts of the people. He knew how to express the program of the revolution in a few clear and simple slogans that fitted the dynamic of the struggle and meshed in with the experience and needs of the masses.

Lenin did not "talk down" to the workers as an expert in strategy and tactics, but learned his lessons alongside the advanced workers, shoulder to shoulder with them on the basis of the experience of the mass struggle. The proletariat made the party and made Lenin. And Lenin helped to shape the party and the proletariat.

By drawing ever broader masses of workers, soldiers, and peasants into the struggle under the banner of the revolution, by increasing the scope of the party's influence, by raising the level of self-activity and consciousness of the masses, by constant self-education of the proletariat, the party, and the leadership, Bolshevism led the people to victory in October.

CHAPTER 9

LENIN LOWERS THE TEMPERATURE

At the beginning of April, Lenin was engaged in rearming the party ideologically—in convincing it that the February Revolution was only the first stage of the revolution, that it had to be followed by the proletariat taking state power into its hands. Again and again he repeated that "the workers and the poor peasants...[are] a thousand times more leftward than the Chernovs and Tseretelis, and a hundred times more leftward than we are."[1]

Now, during the April Days, as later in the June and July Days, his tactics were those of a firefighter—cooling the enthusiasm of party members, including many of its rank-and-file leaders, for a direct assault on state power; dissuading them from joining the most resolute section of the workers and soldiers who were striving for precisely that—for an immediate overthrow of the provisional government, without taking into account whether the majority of the working class had reached the same position. Lenin was very conscious of the danger of the proletarian vanguard running too far ahead and becoming cut off from the rest of the working class, thus providing a path for the victory of reaction.

The job of fireman was a very difficult one. Many years later, in a speech dealing with the July Days, Krupskaya said:

> You know, when it is necessary to agitate in favor of action, that's easy.... But when people want to act and it is necessary to say "No comrades, the barricades must come down...you'll have to wait with your uprising," that is very difficult. And for the Bolsheviks it was very hard to do this.[2]

The April Days

Lenin's first test in this role of fireman came during the April Days. The events were provoked by Miliukov, minister of foreign affairs in the provisional government. On March 23, he put his program before the press: seizure of Constantinople, seizure of Armenia, division of Austria and Turkey, seizure of northern Persia.[3] The popular reaction was so hostile that Kerensky hastened to announce: "Miliukov's program is merely his personal opinion." Tsereteli demanded that the government should make it clear that for Russia the war was exclusively one of defense. The Cadet minister gave way, and on March 27 the government announced

> that the aim of free Russia is not domination over other nations, or seizure of their national possessions, or forcible occupation of foreign territories, but the establishment of a stable peace on the basis of the self-determination of peoples. The Russian people does not intend to increase its world power at the expense of other nations.

But the provisional government would be "fully observing at the same time all obligations assumed towards our allies."[4]

On April 18, on which day May Day was traditionally celebrated, Miliukov sent a note to Russia's allies. It urged that the peace-loving phrases of the government should not give anyone "any reason to think that the revolution which has taken place will lead to the weakening of Russia's role in the common struggle of the Allies. 'Quite the contrary, the general aspiration of the whole people to bring the World War to a decisive victory has only been strengthened.'"[5] This declaration was greeted with widespread protests. Even the Menshevik *Rabochaia Gazeta* was enraged.

> On April 18, on the day when the Russian democracy proclaimed the international brotherhood of peoples and called upon the world democracy to unite in a struggle for peace, on that very day it received a stab in the back from the provisional government....
>
> This is truly a step of madness, and immediate firm actions on the part of the Soviet of Workers' and Soldiers' Deputies are needed to avert its terrible consequences.[6]

Chkheidze complained bitterly: "Miliukov is the evil genius of the revolution."

Hardly had the text of the note become known when there was a storm of popular indignation. On April 20, mass demonstrations took place. The demonstrators moved towards the Mariinsky Palace, where the provisional government was sitting, bearing banners with such slogans as, "Down with the provisional government," "Down with Miliukov," "Down with the imperialist policy," "Miliukov, Guchkov, resign!"

The immediate summons to the demonstration was issued not

by a party, but by an individual, so the story goes—one F.F. Linde, "scholar, mathematician, philosopher," a nonparty man. He was an anarchist, but at the same time a defensist. He feared that Miliukov's note could weaken the army by stirring it up. There was only one way to prevent such a disaster. The soviet should take over the foreign affairs of the revolution. This was his aim in calling the demonstration.[7] (Linde was later killed on the southwestern front by his own soldiers while serving as a commissar and attempting to lead them into battle.[8])

> "Taking counsel with no one," says his biographer, "he acted at once, went straight to the Finland regiment, assembled its committee and proposed that they march immediately as a whole regiment to the Mariinsky Palace.... Linde's proposal was accepted, and at three o'clock in the afternoon a significant demonstration of the Finlanders was marching through the streets of Petrograd with challenging placards." After the Finland regiment came the soldiers of the 180th Reserve, the Moscow regiment, the Pavlovsky, the Keksgolmsky, the sailors of the 2nd Baltic fleet—25,000 or 30,000 men in all, and all armed. The commotion spread to the workers' district; work stopped, and whole factories came out into the streets after the soldiers.[9]

However, the story is not as simple as that. The demonstration was not the handiwork of a single individual. A number of Bolshevik activists did take an active part in the development of the demonstrations on April 20 and during the following few days. On April 21 the demonstrators were out in full force again, and as working-class columns came up against bourgeois processions along the Nevskii Prospect, and were greeted with banners proclaiming support for Miliukov and the provisional government, blood was shed in the streets of the capital for the first time since the tsar's fall.

What was the role of Bolshevik Party leaders in the April Days?

The central leadership was not involved in the April movement until it was well under way. On the morning of April 20, an emergency meeting of the Central Committee adopted a resolution written by Lenin, which condemned Miliukov's note and suggested that only by transferring power to the soviet was the achievement of immediate peace possible. However, the resolution did not call on workers and soldiers to go out into the streets.[10]

Rank-and-file Bolshevik Party members, however, from factory and garrison regiments, did help to bring about the street demonstrations in the first place. On April 20, when the roused masses were gathered at the Mariinsky Palace, some district delegates at

the afternoon session of the First Bolshevik Petrograd City Conference appealed for the immediate overthrow of the provisional government and V.I. Nevsky, of the Bolshevik Military Organization,
spoke in favor of mobilizing troops, evidently for the seizure of
power by the soviet.

> Ludmilla Stal, a long-time Bolshevik and member of the Petersburg
> Committee, tried to dampen this hotheadedness with the admonition
> that delegates "should not be further left than Lenin himself," and the
> conference delegates ultimately voted to call the workers and soldiers
> to "organized expressions of their solidarity with the resolution of the
> Central Committee," i.e., its cautious first resolution condemning the
> Miliukov note and suggesting the transfer of power to the Soviet.
>   At a meeting of the Executive Commission of the Bolshevik Peters-
> burg Committee late the same evening, however, the question of
> overthrowing the provisional government was reconsidered and evi-
> dently attracted increased support.[11]

> The only leader of this movement identified in official Soviet ac-
> counts is S. Ia. Bogdatev, an outspoken Petersburg Committee mem-
> ber from the Putilov factory and candidate for the Bolshevik Central
> Committee at the Seventh All-Russian Bolshevik Party Conference.
> Bogdatev is credited with having prepared a leaflet over the signature
> of the Petersburg Committee appealing for the immediate overthrow
> of the provisional government; this was widely circulated on 21 April
> and was primarily responsible for the sudden appearance among
> demonstrators of "Down with the provisional government"
> banners.[12]

Among the most impatient of the Bolsheviks were those of
Kronstadt and Helsingfors. A number of Kronstadt sailors came
to Petrograd under the leadership of the young Bolshevik officer
Raskolnikov, with the aim of overthrowing the provisional government. The Helsingfors Soviet, then under Bolshevik domination, promised "at any moment to support with armed force
demands for the overthrow of the provisional government."

Lenin uses the hoses

In a speech to the Petrograd City Conference on April 14, Lenin
emphasized that peaceful, patient persuasion was the only legitimate way for Bolsheviks to fight for proletarian power.

> The government must be overthrown, but not everybody under-
> stands this correctly. So long as the provisional government has the
> backing of the Soviet of Workers' Deputies, you cannot "simply"
> overthrow it. The only way it can and must be overthrown is by win-

ning over the majority of the Soviets.[13]

Now, during and after the April Days, Lenin was even sharper in opposing "ultraleft" impatience in the party ranks. He voiced his disagreement with the unauthorized activities of the Petersburg Committee and other Bolshevik hot heads in a resolution of the Central Committee adopted on the morning of April 22:

> The slogan "Down with the provisional government" is an incorrect one at the present moment, because, in the absence of a solid (i.e., a class-conscious and organized) majority of the people on the side of the revolutionary proletariat, such a slogan is either an empty phrase, or objectively, amounts to attempts of an adventurist character.
>
> We shall favor the transfer of power to the proletarians and semi-proletarians only when the Soviets of Workers' and Soldiers' Deputies adopt our policy and are willing to take the power into their own hands.

April 20 and 21 showed the organizational weakness of the party, the lack of discipline in its ranks. "The organization of our party, the consolidation of the proletarian forces, clearly proved inadequate at the time of the crisis."

> The slogans of the moment are: (1) To *explain* the proletarian line and the proletarian way of ending the war; (2) To *criticize* the petty-bourgeois policy of placing trust in the government of the capitalists and compromising with it; (3) To carry on propaganda and agitation from group to group *in every regiment*, in *every* factory, and, particularly, among the most backward masses, such as domestic servants, unskilled laborers, etc., since it was their backing in the first place that the bourgeoisie tried to gain during the crisis; (4) To *organize, organize,* and once more *organize* the proletariat, in every factory, in every district, and in every city quarter.[14]

At the Seventh All-Russian Bolshevik Party Conference on April 24, Lenin made it clear that the task of marshaling the masses for the overthrow of the provisional government now appeared to him as more complex than it had in the days immediately following his return to Russia:

> The government would like to see us make the first imprudent move towards revolutionary action, as this would be to its advantage.... We cannot say that the majority is with us; what we need in the present situation is caution, caution, caution. To base proletarian tactics on subjective desires means to condemn it to failure.
>
> In what did our adventurism consist? It was the attempt to resort to forcible measures. We did not know to what extent the masses had swung to our side during that anxious moment. If it had been a

strong swing things would have been different. We advanced the slogan for peaceful demonstrations, but several comrades from the Petrograd Committee issued a different slogan. We cancelled it, but were too late to prevent the masses from following the slogan of the Petrograd Committee. We say that the slogan "Down with the provisional government" is an adventurist slogan, that the government cannot be overthrown now. That is why we have advanced the slogan for peaceful demonstrations. All we wanted was a peaceful reconnoitring of the enemy's forces; we did not want to give battle. But the Petrograd Committee turned a trifle more to the left, which in this case is certainly a very grave crime. Our organizational apparatus proved weak—our decisions are not being carried out by everyone. Together with the correct slogan "Long live the Soviet of Workers' and Soldiers' Deputies!" stood the incorrect slogan "Down with the provisional government." At the time of action, to go a "trifle more to the left" was wrong. We regard this as a very serious crime, as disorganization. Had we deliberately allowed such an act, we would not have remained in the Central Committee for one moment. It happened because of the weakness of our organizational apparatus. Yes, there were shortcomings in our organization.[15]

In an article published in *Pravda* on April 25, Lenin openly admitted the party mistakes.[16]

As always, he insisted that the revolutionary party must be able to learn from its own mistakes, to be severely self-critical. In all his criticism of other Bolsheviks he never forgot that the party leader could not shirk responsibility for *all* party members.

A political leader is responsible not only for the quality of his leadership but also for the acts of those he leads. He may now and again be unaware of what they are about, he may often wish they had not done something, but the responsibility still falls on him.[17]

This is central to democratic centralism.

Lenin did not hesitate to support the Executive Committee of the Petrograd Soviet in banning demonstrations on April 21. Thus the resolution of the Central Committee of April 22, which he drafted, said:

The resolution of the Petrograd Soviet of April 21 banning all street meetings and demonstrations for two days must be unconditionally obeyed by every member of our party. The Central Committee already distributed yesterday morning, and is today publishing in *Pravda*, a resolution which states that "at such a moment any thought of civil war would be senseless and preposterous," that all demonstrations must be peaceful ones, and that the responsibility for violence will fall on the provisional government and its supporters. Our party therefore considers that the above-mentioned resolution of the Soviet of Workers' and Soldiers' Deputies as a whole (and especially the part banning armed demonstrations and shooting in the air) is entirely correct and must be *unconditionally obeyed.*[18]

There is no doubt at all that at the time the Bolsheviks were in a minority even among the workers of Petrograd. Sukhanov estimates that at the beginning of May the Bolsheviks had a third of the Petrograd proletariat behind them.[19] In some districts, however, they had a majority. In the soviets of Vyborg and Narva districts and Vasiliev Island, the Bolsheviks were in the majority towards the end of April.

Things were much worse elsewhere. Even as late as the end of June, the Bolsheviks received only 11.66 percent of the votes in the elections to the City Council in Moscow.[20] Only in purely industrial centers like Orekhovo-Zuevo, Ivanovo-Voznesensk, Lugansk, and Tsaritsyn, or in military outposts like Reval and Narva, did the Bolsheviks win such elections.[21] At the All-Russian Congress of Soviets, which met on June 3, there were 105 Bolsheviks out of a total of 777 delegates.

In organizational terms, the Bolsheviks still suffered from a lack of clear demarcation from other parties. At the same time, the masses were swayed by the most contradictory ideas, and their thinking was extremely confused, as one or two examples will illustrate.

A meeting of the Kishenev garrison on May 7 passed a resolution supporting the Soviet of Workers' and Peasants' Deputies, calling for the conclusion of peace without annexations and contributions on the basis of the right of nations for self-determination and the transfer of land to the peasants without compensation. At the same time, the meeting declared its support for the provisional government.[22]

Again, the Soviet of Workers' and Soldiers' Deputies of Sudogda (in Vladimirskaia *guberniia)* declared on May 25 that the war was in the interests of the capitalists, and at the same time declared its support and trust in the socialists who joined the provisional government.[23]

As Lenin summed up the contradictions in the consciousness of the masses at the time in an article called "A Disorderly Revolution" *(Pravda,* June 25): "The masses are still looking for the 'easiest' way out [of the crisis]—through the bloc of the Cadets with the bloc of Socialist Revolutionaries and the Mensheviks."[24]

The first coalition government

The crisis of the April Days forced the bourgeoisie to look for a wider base for itself, and the Menshevik and SR leaders found themselves impelled to give their support. The idea of a coalition government was very popular indeed. As Trotsky put it,

> The masses, in so far as they were not yet for the Bolsheviks, stood solid for the entrance of socialists into the government. If it is a good thing to have Kerensky as a Minister, then so much the better six Kerenskys. The masses did not know that this was called coalition with the bourgeoisie, and that the bourgeoisie wanted to use these socialists as a cover for their activities against the people. A coalition looked different from the barracks and from the Mariinsky Palace. The masses wanted to use the socialists to crowd out the bourgeoisie from the government. Thus two forces tending in opposite directions united for a moment in one. In Petrograd, a series of military units, among them an armored car division friendly to the Bolsheviks, declared in favor of coalition government. The provinces voted for the coalition by an overwhelming majority.[25]

The leaders of the Mensheviks and SRs saw in the coalition government a way of checking Bolshevism. Thus the SR paper, *Volia Naroda,* on April 29 wrote:

> The socialist parties are forced now to choose openly and definitely between joining the provisional government —that is, [rendering] energetic support to the state revolutionary government—and frankly declining—that is, rendering indirect support to Leninism, which disintegrates the country by preparations for civil war and defeat at the front.
>
> There is no doubt that the overwhelming majority of Russian socialists will be able to undertake the responsibility for the future of Russia, will save the country from internal breakdown and from a disgraceful defeat.[26]

On May 1, the Executive Committee of the Petrograd Soviet decided, by a majority of forty-four to nineteen with two abstentions, in favor of the entry of Mensheviks and SRs into a coalition government. The nineteen who voted against were twelve Bolsheviks, three Menshevik-Internationalists, and four SRs.[27]

When the coalition was established, the Menshevik paper, *Rabochaia Gazeta,* welcomed it with enthusiasm: "[T]he provisional government cut itself off completely from imperialist influences. And it quite definitely enters upon the road for the most rapid achievement of universal peace through international means."[28]

Alas, in fact, the establishment of the coalition was merely the springboard for a military offensive.

The offensive

Increasing pressure was being exerted on Russia by the allies to launch a military offensive. Government circles were not unfavorable to the idea. They hoped that such an offensive would take the heat out of the revolution. As the French minister of war, Painlevé, put it: "The German-Russian fraternization had caused such ravages that to leave the Russian army inactive would mean to risk its rapid disintegration."

Under the banner of the coalition, the enthusiasm of the defensist leaders in the soviet knew no bounds. Thus, on May 6, *Izvestiia,* the daily paper of the Executive Committee of the soviet, could write:

> We know that heavy trials await us on the road to this peace. We know that while the peoples have not as yet awakened and have not risen against their enslavers, our soldiers will have to conduct the hated war with all their energy and courage. But they can now conduct it in the firm belief that their heroic efforts will not be used for evil [ends]. Whether they will be defending themselves at a fortified position, or whether they will be conducting an attack dictated by strategical or tactical considerations, the soldier may now believe that all these military operations are equally serving one and the same goal—the defense of the revolution from destruction and the earliest possible conclusion of universal peace. From now on, they can and must accomplish their military feats in the firm belief that they are acting for a national cause, for the cause of the workers of the whole world.[29]

After a few weeks of preparation, the government decided to launch the offensive. On June 16, Kerensky, Minister of War and the Navy, issued an order to the troops:

> *Warriors, our country is in danger!* Liberty and revolution are threatened. The time has come for the army to do its duty. Your Supreme Commander [General Brusilov], beloved through victory, is convinced that each day of delay merely helps the enemy, and that only by an immediate and determined blow can we disrupt his plans. Therefore, in full realization of my great responsibility to the country, and in the name of its free people and its provisional government, I call upon the armies, strengthened by the vigor and spirit of the revolution, to take the offensive.[30]

The demonstration that did not take place: Lenin wavers

Between the middle of May and the middle of June, increasing government agitation for the offensive, added to the threat of transfer of army units from Petrograd to the front, infuriated the troops in the capital. At a meeting of the Petrograd Military Organization of the Bolshevik Party on May 23, it was reported that the Pavlovsky, Izmailovsky, Grenadier, and First Reserve Infantry regiments, among others, "were ready to go out on their own if a positive decision were not adopted at the center."[31] A number of soldiers spoke in support of a demonstration against the provisional government, and nobody opposed the idea.

On June 6, N.I. Podvoisky and V.I. Nevsky, leaders of the Bolshevik Military Organization, brought up the question of the demonstration at a joint meeting of the Central Committee, the Military Organization, and the Executive Committee of the Petersburg Committee.[32] Lenin came out strongly in support of the demonstration. Kamenev opposed it. Fedorov, a party moderate, cautioned that the demonstration should be unarmed, to which Nevsky replied that such a demonstration would be "amateurish" if arms were not carried; Cherepanov, of the Military Organization, ended this exchange with the comment, "The soldiers will not demonstrate without arms. The question is settled."[33]

Kamenev was supported by Zinoviev and Nogin in his opposition to the demonstration. It is interesting that Krupskaya, who rarely opposed her husband, expressed apprehension in regard to the proposed demonstration. "It won't be peaceful, and so perhaps it should not be started."[34]

On the same day, the Petersburg Committee also discussed the question of the demonstration.[35] The overwhelming majority of the committee was enthusiastic about it. Only one speaker, V.B. Vinokurov, supported Kamenev, Zinoviev, and Nogin in their stand.

A final incident that spurred the masses on to the demonstration was, on the face of it, a minor one—the threatened eviction on June 7 of the anarchists from their headquarters in Durnovo Villa, previously the property of the tsarist minister of the interior, in the heart of the Vyborg factory district.

P.N. Pereverzev, minister of justice, issued an order, giving the anarchists twenty-four hours to vacate their headquarters. The anarchists refused to comply, and appealed to the Vyborg factory workers and soldiers to support them. The next day thousands of workers came out on strike, closing twenty-eight factories, and several armed demonstrations took place in the district.

On June 8, a joint meeting of the Central Committee, the Petersburg Committee, and the Military Organization, attended by responsible trade-union and factory representatives, decided on an immediate demonstration by workers and soldiers.[36] Soon after this meeting, the Central Committee, with the added votes of three representatives of the Executive of the Petersburg Committee, resolved to organize a mass demonstration to be held at 2 p.m. on Saturday, June 10.[37] A leaflet issued in the name of the Central Committee, the Petersburg Committee, the Military Organization, the Editorial Board of *Pravda,* etc., called for a demonstration. Among the slogans suggested were:

> Down with the Tsarist Duma!
> Down with the State Council!
> Down with the ten capitalist ministers!
> All power to the All-Russian Soviet of Workers', Soldiers', and Peasants' Deputies!
> Re-examine the "Declaration of the rights of the soldier!"
> Abolish the "orders" against soldiers and sailors!
> Down with anarchy in industry and the lockout capitalists!
> Hail the control and organization of industry!
> Time to end the war! Let the Soviet of Deputies declare just conditions of peace!
> Neither separate peace with Wilhelm, nor secret treaties with the French and English capitalists!
> Bread! Peace! Liberty![38]

On hearing of the Bolshevik plan for a demonstration, the Executive Committee of the soviet immediately issued a call prohibiting it.

> *There must not be a single company, a single regiment, a single group of workers on the street.*
> *[There must not be] a single demonstration today.*
> *A great struggle still lies ahead of us.*[39]

To add to this pressure on the Bolshevik leadership to call off the demonstration, news came next day of the angry opposition of the Bolshevik delegates to the All-Russian Congress of Soviets, who had not been kept informed of their own Central Committee's plans.[40] The delegates from the provinces were far to the right of the Petrograd Bolsheviks and were furious about the planned delegation.

> One of the members of the Bolshevik delegation, Kuzmin, voiced his personal bitterness at the congress session on June 9: "Comrades, as sad as it may be, I must state: most of us, the Bolshevik representatives here, representatives of three million workers and soldiers, as it turns out, did not even know that all this was being organized. Here I, a representative, only now found out that such a demonstration was being organized."[41]

But the Bolshevik leadership stuck to its guns. On the night of June 9, a meeting attended by six members of the Central Committee (Lenin, Nogin, Kamenev, Smilga, Zinoviev, and either Sverdlov or Stalin), six members of the Petersburg Committee, and two members of the Military Organization, decided by fourteen votes to two to go ahead with the demonstration.[42]

Semashko, leader of the powerful First Machine Gun regiment, and Rakhia, one of the more extreme Petersburg Committee members, argued that the demonstration, being armed, should be prepared, if necessary, "to sieze the railroad stations, arsenals, banks, post office, and telegraph."[43] However, this plan was not supported by Lenin or the rest of the Bolshevik leadership.

At 2 a.m. on June 10, Lenin, Zinoviev, Kamenev, Sverdlov, and Nogin met with representatives of the Bolshevik Soviet delegation at the All-Russian Congress. The latter appealed for the cancellation of the demonstration. On this occasion, no representatives of the Petersburg Committee or the Military Organization were present. The pressure was such that the Central Committee members retreated: Zinoviev, Kamenev, and Nogin voted for canceling the demonstration, and Lenin and Sverdlov abstained.[44] So, hurriedly, the CC issued a cancellation.[45]

In a number of factories, Bolsheviks adopted resolutions censuring the Central Committee. The retreat met with very widespread resentment in the party ranks.

> In his memoirs I.P. Flerovsky, a prominent Kronstadt Bolshevik, remembers that at Kronstadt news of the cancellation was greeted with disbelief and fury and that the hours immediately after word of the cancellation was received "were among the most unpleasant" of his life. At the Sixth Congress he reported that "inhuman measures" were necessary to prevent the sailors from responding to Anarchist-Communist appeals (as well as those of some undisciplined Bolsheviks) and immediately rushing to Petrograd.[46]

M. Ia. Latsis noted in his diary and reported to the Petersburg Committee that there were cases of rank-and-file Bolsheviks tearing up their party membership cards in disgust.[47]

The Petersburg Committee members were mostly furious about the leadership's retreat. On June 11, an emergency meeting of the Petersburg Committee was called in order to hear an explanation from the Central Committee.[48]

Lenin started his speech by acknowledging that the dissatisfaction of many of the members of the Petersburg Committee was fully justified. He explained, however, that

> the Central Committee had no alternative for two reasons: first, we were formally banned from holding the demonstration by the semi-organ of power; secondly, the motive for the ban was stated as follows: "We know that concealed forces of the counter-revolution want to take advantage of your demonstration." In support of this motive, we were given names, such as that of a general, whom they promised to arrest within three days, and others. And they declared that a demonstration of the Black Hundreds[*] had been arranged for 10 June with the intention of breaking into our demonstration and turning it into a skirmish.
>
> Even in ordinary warfare, it sometimes happens that a planned offensive has to be cancelled for strategic reasons. This is all the more likely to occur in class warfare, depending on the vacillation of the middle, petty-bourgeois groups. We must be able to take account of the situation and be bold in adopting decisions.[49]

For the future, Lenin stated,

> The proletariat must reply by showing the maximum calmness, caution, restraint, and organization, and must remember that peaceful processions are a thing of the past.
>
> We must give them no pretext for attack. Let them attack, and the workers will realize that it is an attack on the very existence of the proletariat. But reality is on our side, and it is a moot point whether their attack will succeed—at the front there are the troops, among whom discontent is very strong, and in the rear there is the high cost of living, economic dislocation, and so on. The Central Committee does not want to force your decision. Your right, the right to protest against the actions of the Central Committee, is a legitimate one, and your decision must be a free one.[50]

Volodarsky, in the name of the Executive of the Petersburg Committee, was most harsh in his censure.

> The Central Committee acted hastily and thoughtlessly, but the question is when? At the time when it decided to demonstrate or when it cancelled the demonstration? What should we do?.... We must answer three questions: (1) Was it necessary to cancel our demonstration? (2) Is a situation which permits the vacillations of one man to change all decisions permissible in our party? (3) What are our next steps going to be?[51]

Tomsky, also a member of the Executive of the Petersburg Committee, added his criticism:

> No matter how we disguise our retreat with the words that we are wise men, that we acted wisely, the fact of our retreat remains. Our congress delegation, which through our own fault was uninformed

---

[*]An ultra-reactionary organization created under the patronage of the tsarist police.

about our grandiose demonstration, influenced the mood of the Central Committee. Is it permissible for the delegation to pressure the party Central Committee?

In closing, Tomsky summed up his feelings regarding the conduct of the Central Committee, emphasizing the damage that had been done to its prestige.

Nobody will deny, [he asserted] that the Central Committee committed a political mistake—it was guilty of intolerable wavering. It is not important that there is widespread distrust of the Central Committee; what is important is that the faith in the [Central Committee] leadership of those of us who are [Petersburg Committee] executives has been undermined.[52]

I.K. Naumov, secretary of the Bolshevik delegation in the Petrograd Soviet, criticized the party for poor planning, but pointed out that the cancellation had favorable aspects. He suggested that the damage done to faith in the party leadership was not altogether a bad thing: "Let it be completely undermined," said Naumov, "it is necessary to trust only in oneself and the masses."[53]

The Menshevik and SR leaders intervene

At the same session of the Congress of Soviets that condemned the Bolsheviks, the Menshevik Bogdanov, in the name of the Presidium, moved that an official demonstration should be organized on the coming Sunday, June 18. The Menshevik and SR leaders thought that the Bolsheviks were in retreat, and that they would be able to show them who had the support of the masses. Thus Tsereteli triumphantly addressed the Bolsheviks, especially Kamenev, in an indignantly didactic speech:

Here we have before us now an open and honest review of the forces of the revolution. Tomorrow there will be demonstrating not separate groups but all the working class of the capital, not against the will of the Soviet, but at its invitation. Now we shall all see which the majority follows, you or us. This isn't a matter of underhand plots but a duel in the open arena. Tomorrow we shall see.

The slogans of the demonstration were chosen by the Menshevik and SR leaders so as to be as popular as possible: "Universal peace," "Immediate convocation of a constituent assembly," "Democratic republic."[54] Not a word about the coalition or the offensive. Lenin asked in *Pravda*: "And what has become of 'complete confidence in the provisional government, gentlemen'.... Why does your tongue stick in your throat?" The compromisers did not dare to call on the masses to express support for the government of which they themselves were members.

On June 13 the Petersburg Committee held an emergency meeting. In the name of the Central Committee, Zinoviev explained to the meeting that the proposed demonstration would provide "a political means for applying pressure on the government." "We must create a demonstration within a demonstration." Party members as well as trade unions, factories, and military units should be urged to march under the June 10 slogans, plus some new ones. A number of people present were cool towards the demonstration. After all, they had burned their fingers a few days earlier.[55]

When it came to it, the demonstration on June 18 was massive. About 400,000 people participated: "[I]t was on a magnificent scale. All workers and soldiers in Petersburg took part," Sukhanov writes.

> But what was the political character of the demonstration?
> "Bolsheviks again," I remarked, looking at the slogans, "and there behind them is another Bolshevik column."
> "Apparently the next one too," I went on calculating, watching the banners advancing towards me and the endless rows going away towards Michael Castle a long way down the Sadovoy.
> "All power to the Soviets!" "Down with the ten capitalist ministers!" "Peace for the hovels, war for the palaces!"
> In this sturdy and weighty way worker-peasant Petersburg, the vanguard of the Russian and the world revolution, expressed its will. The situation was absolutely unambiguous. Here and there the chain of Bolshevik flags and columns was interrupted by specifically SR and official Soviet slogans. But they were submerged in the mass; they seemed to be exceptions, intentionally confirming the rule. Again and again, like the unchanging summons of the very depths of the revolutionary capital, like fate itself, like the fatal Birnam wood—there advanced towards us: "All power to the Soviets!" "Down with the ten capitalist ministers!"
> I remembered the purblind Tsereteli's fervor of the night before. Here was the duel in the open arena! Here was the honest legal review of forces in an official Soviet demonstration![56]

"Judging by the placards and slogans of the demonstrators," wrote Gorky's paper, "the Sunday demonstration revealed the complete triumph of Bolshevism among the Petersburg proletariat."[57]

On the same day, mass demonstrations took place all over Russia: in Moscow, Kiev, Minsk, Reval, Riga, Kharkov, Helsingfors, and many other towns.[58] On the following day Lenin wrote:

> The demonstration of 18 June was a demonstration of the strength

and policy of the revolutionary proletariat, which is showing the direction for the revolution and indicating the way out of the impasse. This is the tremendous historical significance of last Sunday's demonstration, and its essential difference from the demonstrations during the funeral of the victims of the revolution and on May Day. Then it was a universal *tribute* to the revolution's first victory and to its heroes. The people looked back over the first stage of the road to freedom, which they had passed very rapidly and very successfully. May Day was a *holiday* of hopes and aspirations linked with the history of the world labor movement and with its ideal of peace and socialism.

Neither of the two demonstrations was intended to point the *direction* for the revolution's further development, nor could it do so. Neither demonstration put before the people, or raised in the name of the people, specific, definite, and urgent questions as to how and in what direction the revolution should proceed.

In this sense, 18 June was the first political demonstration of *action*, an explanation of how the various classes act, how they want to and will act, in order to further the revolution—an explanation not given in a book or newspaper, but on the streets, not through leaders, but through the people.[59]

This demonstration said everything that could be said without an uprising. The job of the Bolsheviks was still to go on patiently explaining. On June 22, the Bolshevik press appealed to the garrison: "Do not trust any summons to action in the street." And Lenin continued to insist on the need to avoid adventurism, to continue to organize and organize, educate and educate.

> The socialist proletariat and our party must be as cool and collected as possible, must show the greatest staunchness and vigilance. Let the future Cavaignacs* begin first. Our party conference has already given warning of their arrival. The workers of Petrograd will give them no opportunity to disclaim responsibility. They will bide their time, gathering their forces and preparing for resistance *when* those gentlemen decide to turn from words to action.[60]

---

* General Cavaignac saved the bourgeoisie from the workers in Paris in June 1848.

CHAPTER 10

LENIN AND THE SOLDIERS' MUTINIES

Soldiers rebel

The central burning issue, more urgent than any other in the Russian Revolution, was the question of the war. By 1917 the suffering of the soldiers had reached its limit. Of the 15.5 million men who had been called up, it is estimated that 7.2 to 8.5 million had been killed or wounded, or were missing. The peasant uprisings provoked and were provoked by soldiers' mutinies. By the time the peasants were burning manor houses, and sometimes killing their masters, the soldiers had reached the point of lynching unpopular officers and deserting en masse from the front. Furthermore, the soldier—who was a peasant in uniform—on quitting the front or the rear garrison and returning to the village, played a central role in spreading revolutionary ideas in the countryside.

> Those cases in which soldiers took the lead in peasant disorders constituted in March, according to Vermenichev's calculations, 1 percent, in April 8 percent, in September 12 percent, and in October 17 percent. These figures cannot pretend to be accurate, but they show the general tendency unmistakably.[1]

The disintegration of the Russian army proceeded rapidly. It was an inevitable product of the revolution.

"Surely, the fact is evident," wrote Engels to Marx on September 26, 1851, "that a disorganized army and a complete breakdown of discipline has been the condition as well as the result of every victorious revolution."[2]

The soldier in the tsarist army was deprived of the most elementary human rights. He was forbidden to smoke in the street, to ride inside tramcars, or to frequent clubs, public dances, restaurants, eating places, and other establishments where drinks were sold. He was prohibited from attending public lectures and theatrical performances, or receiving books or newspapers without the permission of his commanding officer.[3] After the February Revolution, the peasant-soldier was no longer prepared to be used as cannon fodder in a war led by landlord-generals.

The provisional government tried its best to prevent the disintegration of the army. On February 28, Miliukov declared to a group of soldiers that they must all be "organized, united, and subordinated to one authority."[4]

> [I]n trying to restore the bonds between the officers and the soldiers, [the provisional government] wanted those bonds to be just what they had been under Tsarism. It had every reason for hoping that the officers' corps, in joining the revolution and placing itself at the disposition of the Duma, would be making itself a faithful servant of the bourgeoisie.[5]

In the months preceding the revolution, discipline in the tsarist army was already disintegrating. The February Revolution accelerated the process. After all, it took place not only without the officers, but against them. "From the morning of February 28," says the Cadet Nabokov, then wearing an officer's uniform, "it was dangerous to go out because they had the gun to rip off the officers' epaulettes."[6]

Many of the officers rushed to pin on red ribbons a couple of days after the revolution. But could the soldiers trust them? V.B. Stankevich, political commissar of the provisional government for the northern front, in his memoirs, makes it quite clear what the actual feelings were between officers and soldiers in the early days after the February Revolution.

> It was the fact that the soldiers, breaking discipline, left the barracks not merely without their officers but even despite their officers, and in many cases against their officers, even killing some of them who tried to fulfill their duty. And now by universal, popular, official acclaim, obligatory for the officers themselves, the soldiers were supposed to have realized by this a great deed of emancipation. If this was indeed a heroic exploit, and if the officers themselves now proclaimed it, then why had they not themselves led the soldiers out onto the streets—for you see that would have been easier and less dangerous for them than for the soldiers. Now after the victory is won, they adhere to the heroic feat. But is that sincere and for how long? You see during the first moments they were upset, they hid themselves, they changed into civilian clothes.... Even though next

day all the officers returned. Even though some of the officers came running back and joined us five minutes after the soldiers went out, all the same it was the soldiers who led the officers in this, and not the officers the soldiers. And those five minutes opened an impassable abyss cutting off the troops from all the profoundest and most fundamental assumptions of the old army.[7]

Many officers were very slow to adapt themselves. They hoped for a restoration of the old regime. Thus the Duma deputy, N.O. Yanushkevich, on visiting troops about a fortnight after the revolution, reported:

[T]here are those among the higher officers who behave tactlessly. Everywhere we had to hear the complaint that the red bow, when it is worn, is torn away. We were also told that the portraits [of the tsar] are not being removed; the soldiers enter and see that the Emperor's portrait is on the wall; it arouses their indignation.

At certain places we received definite information that there were threats of execution by firing squad in the event of the portrait being removed. This tactlessness has created a dreadful atmosphere.[8]

Officers resented the provisional government's order that they should be more polite towards their subordinates.

At several meetings, we talked with officers. Some of them understand their task, but others do not wish to realize that the old life has been destroyed, that they must change themselves. They consider that they have been very badly treated; they are indignant at the orders including Guchkov's regarding politeness; they say that it will ruin the morale of the army…. The soldiers accuse their commanders of everything, and it took much effort to explain to them that it was the fault of the old regime, that their immediate superiors had nothing to do with it.[*9]

The soldiers could not forget that one of the disciplinary measures used by the officers under the tsar had been flogging. Above all, they knew that while they were peasants and workers, the officers were landlords' sons or members of bourgeois families.

The provisional government and the compromisers in the soviet hoped against hope that exhortation, if repeated sufficiently often, would create trust between soldiers and officers. On March 9 the minister of war, Guchkov, and the chief of staff, General Alekseev, issued a manifesto to the soldiers and citizens, stating:

---

[*]General Alekseev, the chief of staff, used to refer in private to the Soviets of Soldiers' *(soldatskikh)* Deputies as the Soviets of Dogs' *(sobachikh)* Deputies.[10]

The restoration of good and friendly relations between officers and soldiers, and a strengthening of discipline, are among the major cares of the provisional government....

The provisional government declares that the army has the obligation to obey the orders of its military commanders, and believes that the soldiers will understand it and will form a close circle around their officers, seeing in them the leaders who have always led them to victory. Only by obeying their officers may the soldiers break the resistance of the enemy and deny him victory over free Russia. Soldiers, you are called to complete the great historical task of our fatherland. Follow your officers and remember that without respect for the person and the honor of your officer, there can be no unity, there can be no victory.[11]

Order No. 1—The soviet compromises

In the heat of the February Revolution, when soldiers went about tearing off officers' epaulettes, the idea of electing all officers became popular. The first leaflet calling for this change was issued on the morning of March 1 by the Mezhraiontsy, and read:

Elect your own platoon commanders, company commanders, and regiment commanders, elect company committees for taking charge of food supplies. All the officers must be under the control of these company committees. Accept only those officers whom you know to be friends of the people.... Soldiers! Now that you have revolted and won, former enemies will come to you along with your friends—officers who call themselves your friends. Soldiers! The tail of a fox is more to be feared than the tooth of a wolf.[12]

The SR and Menshevik leaders in the soviet were so infuriated by this leaflet that they issued a general denunciation of it in their daily, *Izvestiia,* on March 3.[13] However, the revolutionary mood among the troops was such that the compromisers did not feel it was possible simply to preserve the old disciplinary setup. The result was a compromise, Order No. 1, issued by the Petrograd Soviet on March 1:

...In all companies, battalions, regiments, parks, batteries, squadrons, in the special services of the various military administrations, and on the vessels of the navy, committees from the elected representatives of the lower ranks of the above-mentioned military units shall be chosen immediately.

...In all its political actions, the military branch is subordinated to the Soviet of Workers' and Soldiers' Deputies and to its own committees.

...The orders of the Military Commission of the State Duma shall be executed only in such cases as do not conflict with the orders and resolutions of the Soviet of Workers' and Soldiers' Deputies.

...All kinds of arms, such as rifles, machine guns, armored automobiles, and others, must be kept at the disposal and under the control of the company and battalion committees, and in no case should they be turned over to officers, even at their demand.

...In the ranks and during their performance of the duties of the service, soldiers must observe the strictest military discipline, but outside the service and the ranks, in their political, general civic, and private life, soldiers cannot in any way be deprived of those rights that all citizens enjoy. In particular, standing at attention and compulsory saluting, when not on duty, is abolished.... Also, the addressing of the officers with the titles "Your excellency," "Your honor," etc., is abolished, and these titles are replaced by the address of "Mister general," "Mister colonel," etc. Rudeness toward soldiers of any rank, and especially, addressing them as "thou" (*ty*) is prohibited, and soldiers are required to bring to the attention of the company committees every infraction of this rule, as well as all misunderstandings occurring between officers and privates.

The present order is to be read to all companies, battalions, regiments, ships' crews, batteries, and other combatant and non-combatant commands.[14]

This order set up a system of dual power inside the army. It was quite rightly described by Trotsky as "the single worthy document of the February revolution,"[15] and by Sukhanov as "practically the sole independently creative political act of the Soviet Plenum throughout the revolution."[16]

Order No. 1 was drawn up hastily as a response to the specific situation in Petrograd and its authors hoped that it would apply only in the capital. Unfortunately,

it was printed in large numbers and distributed along the entire front in a matter of days.... There was not a single sector of the 2,000-mile front which remained unaffected by its influence, although the northern sectors were more heavily inundated than the rest. Officers noticed immediately how enthusiastically their men followed its prescriptions: soldiers ceased saluting and standing at attention, addressed them as "Mister lieutenant" and insisted on the formal "*vy*" Within a matter of days officers were faced with committees which presented demands, requested explanations, countermanded orders, and instituted controls over arms and ammunition. Not infrequently officers were requested to recognize the committee structure by issuing special orders. All attempts by officers to explain that the order was unofficial, and in any event applied only to Petrograd, were in vain.[17]

As dual power was very unstable, pressure was exerted against Order No. 1, from both the right and from the left, from the moment it was published.

Order No. 2

As soon as the Petrograd Soviet had issued Order No. 1, its leaders became afraid of their own handiwork. The executive was no doubt encouraged in this attitude by Kerensky, who detested the order, as Sukhanov remembers:

> Kerensky came flying in like a hurricane, completely beside himself and out of breath with rage and despair. Pounding on the table he not only accused the authors and publishers of this leaflet of provocation, but called it the work of the Tsarist secret police. He threatened the culprits with all sorts of punishments.[18]

To pacify Kerensky, and even more important, the generals and the capitalists, the Menshevik and Socialist Revolutionaries in the soviet issued Order No. 2; this limited the application of Order No. 1 to the Petrograd military district, and emphasized that even in Petrograd the Army Committees *should not* intervene in military affairs.

> Order No. 1 of the Soviet of Workers' Deputies proposed to all companies, battalions, and other military units to elect committees (company, battalion, etc.), appropriate to each particular unit, but that order did not provide that these committees should elect the officers of each unit…. The soldiers are bound to submit to all orders of the military authorities that have reference to the military service.[19]

As a symbol of the need to check the soldiers' appetite for freedom came a new order by the minister of war, about the rights of soldiers to free transport, free attendance at theaters, concerts, etc. When the soldiers had asserted these rights after the February Revolution, they had taken it for granted that freedom meant "free of charge." Now on March 22, Guchkov issued Order No. 114, which made it clear that soldiers were free to go to theaters, use public transport, etc., but that they were not exempt from payment![20]

"Declaration of Soldiers' Rights"

Dual power, as a regime operating in a crisis, led to repeated formulations and reformulations of the rights and duties of soldiers. Thus on May 11, Kerensky, who had replaced Guchkov as minister of war issued a new decree, Order No. 8, "Declaration of Soldiers' Rights," which spelled out the rights of the commanders:

> …[U]nder combat circumstances, the commander has the right on his own responsibility to take all measures, down to applying armed force inclusive, against his subordinates who fail to carry out his or-

ders. These measures are not considered to be disciplinary penalties....

The right of appointment to duties and of temporary suspension of officers of all grades from duties in instances provided by law *belongs exclusively to commanders*. Likewise they alone have the right to give orders with regard to combat activity and the preparation for battle of a unit, its training, its special duties, duties in the [departments] of inspection and supply.[21]

This declaration irritated even the moderate left. The All-Russian Congress of Soviets, dominated by SRs and Mensheviks, criticized it for undermining soldiers' rights.

In the field of civil rights in general, the right of every serviceman to participate in, and to organize, any kind of meeting must be proclaimed.... The restriction on the freedom of speech to "the time when off duty" must be abolished.

The right of the commander to use force of arms against insubordinates (Article 14) must be excluded from the declaration.

In revoking Article 18 or Order No. 8, it must be declared that the soldiers' organs of self-government shall have the right to challenge or recommend [appointment] of persons in command, as well as the right to participate in army administration on a basis prescribed explicitly in regulations.[22]

The Bolsheviks, were, of course, even more critical than the SRs and the Mensheviks in the Congress of Soviets.

The army disintegrates

The class struggle between peasants and landlords was reflected in the army in increasing insubordination by soldiers towards officers. The drive for expropriation of land was feeding the soldiers' rebellious spirit; even more was the desire for peace, in a situation where the officers were ordering the soldiers to go on fighting the bloody and useless war.

The disintegration of the army accelerated. By October 1917, some two million soldiers had deserted—mostly between February and October.[23] Two hundred thousand had been rounded up, but when they were returned to the front they only increased the speed with which the army was collapsing.

On March 18, General Lukomskii, director of military operations, drew up a report following a conference in Stavka, which stated:

The state of the army. The army is undergoing [a period of] sickness. It will take probably two or three months to readjust the relations between officers and men.

At the present time one observes low spirits among the officer personnel, unrest among the troops, and a great number of desertions.

The fighting capacity of the army is lowered and at the present time it is difficult to anticipate an improvement.[24]

On May 27, the provisional government ordered four regiments—the 45th, 46th, 47th, and 52nd—to be disbanded for insubordination.[25]

A few excerpts follow which have been picked at random from reports to army headquarters:

> A telegram from the Rumanian front of 9 June, among other things, states: "X division—The spirit of the troops has improved, but, according to the words of the division commander, 'as before, however, there is no absolute certainty that an order to attack would be obeyed....'"
>
> The 5th Army has communicated...some following details of the conditions under which the regrouping for the operation takes place: in X corps, the order was not carried out; in X division, which had refused to extend its front to the left, individual companies of X regiment set out for the positions, while 1,067 men refused to go; in X regiment, one battalion refused to move. In the rest of the regiments, the situation is as tense, and disorders can be expected when their turn for relief arrives.... In X regiment, the order has not been carried out by five companies. In X corps, X division broke away from its staff and artillery, gathered around X regiment, elected, according to the X Division Commander's report, its own revolutionary staff, and is sending out agents into other units for propaganda.... In some regiments of the 36th division, they declare that they have no authorities but Lenin.
>
> Telegram received on 7 July from the Rumanian front, signed by Regimental Commander Reko, that on 4 July the 8th Company of the regiment refused to go out to positions for the offensive, and only after lengthy exhortations and admonitions did the regiments set out on the night of the 6th in the strength of eight companies with an insufficient number of riflemen.

The commander of the 11th Army, in a report to Stavka on July 12, said:

> It is even hard to conjecture where the enemy might be stopped. The entire commanding and officer personnel is powerless to do anything short of self-sacrifice.... The tragedy of the high command lies in the fact that instead of sending the loyal detachments against the enemy it has to direct them to suppress the mutinying companies and whole divisions in the rear and to stop marauding and pillaging. The need of depending on numbers of loyal troops and companies to restore order leads to dissent within the army, which in turn results in its further demoralization.[26]

At a second conference at Stavka on July 16, General Denikin described the situation on the western front:

It was "in a state of complete disintegration."

The men were obedient up to a point—while our line of action was passive—but as soon as the men were required to be aggressive, the full extent of disintegration came to light.

In the course of between two and three weeks, we succeeded, by the extraordinary work of the commanding personnel, in deploying the 10th Army, but under what conditions: 48 battalions refused to go into combat. One of the three shock corps was deployed, it took two to three weeks to deploy another one, while the third was not deployed at all. Insubordination, robbery, and looting swept through the units, and distilleries were ravaged. Certain units, like the 703rd Suramskii regiment, for example, disintegrated....

I moved the 20th Corps to replace the right flank corps, because I considered it to be the best one. However, as soon as it received an order to advance, one of its divisions marched 30 *versts* in the very first night, but then returned to its original position. Another division refused to advance altogether. After lengthy negotiations it was finally deployed.[27]

At the same conference General Alekseev said: "We have no army, either on the front or in the rear...all that remains is human dust."[28]

The army generals try to reimpose discipline

The generals realized that unless iron discipline was imposed in the army everything would be lost. The call for the reimposition of strict discipline became more and more strident. Thus on July 11 the supreme commander, General Brusilov, wrote to the minister of war, Kerensky:

Time does not wait. It is necessary to restore immediately iron discipline in all its plenitude and the death penalty for traitors. If we do not do it at once, without delay, then the army will perish, Russia will perish.[29]

On the same day, the government decided to restore the death penalty at the front—reverting to the situation before March 12, when it had been abolished. But this did not satisfy the generals. On July 16, General Denikin told a conference in the presence of Kerensky: "The death penalty [should] be introduced not only in the theater of war but also in the rear where replacements are stationed."[30] General Lukomskii remarked that the death penalty should apply to "civilians who are corrupting the army."[31]

But not all the generals were as convinced of the effectiveness of the death penalty in restoring discipline. Thus General Klembovskii remarked:

> What can help? The death penalty? But is it really possible to execute entire divisions? Prosecution? Then half the army would turn out to be in Siberia. You will not frighten the soldier by penal servitude. "Penal servitude? So what? After five years I will come back," they say, "and at least I will be uninjured."[32]

The reintroduction of the death sentence met with bitter opposition, even from the compromising left. Thus on August 19, Iakovlev, on behalf of the SR group in the Petrograd Soviet, moved a resolution demanding the abrogation of the death penalty, arguing that "the death penalty, introduced by the new regime under the pretext of combatting crime, is beginning to take form with ever greater clarity as a means of frightening the soldiers with a view to subjugating them to the officers."[33]

Although the SRs and the Mensheviks in the government had been responsible for its reintroduction, only four members of the soviet (including Tsereteli) voted against this resolution.

At the same time, the generals were increasing their pressure from the right against the situation of dual power in the army and the multiplicity of authorities tearing it apart. Thus General Denikin stated at the Stavka conference:

> In touring the front, the Supreme Commander received the impression that the soldiers were good, [but] that the commanders were frightened and had permitted their authority to slip out of their hands. This is not quite correct. Authority did not slip out of the hands of the commanders, it was torn out of their hands.... Another cause for disintegration in the army is the commissars.... There cannot be dual authority in the army. The army must have one head and one authority....
>
> Thus, this institution cannot be tolerated in the army.
>
> A further cause for disintegration in the army is the committees....
>
> The committees are removing commanders. Thus, they removed the commanders of the corps, the Chief of Staff of the corps, and the commander of the 1st Siberian division of the 1st Siberian corps. I did not give permission for this removal, but the commander of the corps came to me crying and sobbing and I had to let him leave.
>
> I have statistical data at my disposal; there were 50 cases of commanders being removed from the front.[34]
>
> The officers' corps is in a terrible position....
>
> Yes, they are martyrs.... They are abused...they are beaten. Yes, they are beaten. Hiding in their tents, they sob, but they will not tell about this. They are being killed.[35]
>
> Detachment and regiment committees enter into discussions of vir-

tually every question.... The committees bring multiple authority into the army, and discredit, rather than strengthen, the authority of the commanders.[36]

In order to regenerate the army [General Denikin went on to say], it is necessary that...politics be completely excluded from the army; the declaration be abolished; commissars and committees be abolished; authority be restored to the commanders; discipline be introduced.... The death penalty be introduced not only in the theater of war but also in the rear where replacements are stationed. Revolutionary courts must be established for the reserve regiments as well.[37]

All the generals present at the conference agreed with Denikin. But the question was: how to go about abolishing the committees and the commissars? Kerensky came to the rescue with the advice to do it gradually and by stealth.

If we were to adopt the maximal program of General Denikin...we must expect tremendous disorders. Personally, I have nothing against...recalling the commissars, and closing down the committees. But I am convinced that on the very next day, a state of complete anarchy would start spreading over Russia and the commanding personnel would start being butchered. Such sharp transitions must not occur.[38]

Kerensky received support from the Cadet foreign affairs minister, Tereshchenko.

One must become reconciled to the commissars, albeit reluctantly for they cannot be abolished at the present time.

Only a month ago, it seemed impossible to introduce the death penalty. Now it is accepted unanimously by the government, and its introduction did not give rise to difficulties, and the people accepted it with calm.

However, the death penalty cannot now be introduced in the rear. The masses must be made aware of the necessity of the measure as soon as possible.

To abolish the committees, as everyone is suggesting, cannot be done now. This must be approached gradually.[39]

The compromising leaders of the soviet, afraid of their own shadows, unable to trust the generals, and frightened of the "dark masses" were not prepared to allow abolition of the committees and commissars. On July 18, the Central Executive Committee of the Soviet of Workers' and Soldiers' Deputies and the Executive Committee of the Soviet of Peasants' Deputies issued a statement that

no encroachment on the rights and freedom of action of these organs [the committees] must be permitted, especially with regard to army organizations, since their work represents an absolute condition for the restoration of discipline and the combat efficiency of the army.[40]

Lenin lances the ulcer

Lenin's thoughts and feelings coincided completely with those of the soldiers. On the question of soldier/officer relations, he completely rejected not only the Alekseevs and Denikins, but also the Tseretelis and Chkheidzes, who wanted to compromise between the two camps.

Lenin asked the question: "Should officers be elected by the soldiers?" And he answered unequivocally: "Not only must they be elected, but every step of every officer and general must be supervised by persons especially elected for the purpose by the soldiers."

Then he asked: "Is it desirable for the soldiers, on their own decision, to displace their superiors?" And answered: "It is desirable and essential in every way. The soldiers will obey and *respect* only elected authority."[41]

The soldiers' efforts to achieve peace received Lenin's complete and unreserved support. For him, the struggle for peace meant that the soldiers did not have to wait to act, but should do so straightaway, by fraternizing with the German soldiers. Again and again, Lenin refers to this fraternization as a central weapon in achieving peace.

> By starting to fraternize, the Russian and German soldiers, the proletarians and peasants of both countries dressed in soldiers' uniforms, have proved to the whole world that intuitively the classes oppressed by the capitalists have discovered the right road to the cessation of the butchery of peoples.[42]

Fraternization, he wrote, was an instinctive expression of the wish of the soldiers for peace.

> The class-conscious workers, followed by the mass of semi-proletarians and poor peasants guided by the true instinct of oppressed classes, regard fraternization with profound sympathy. Clearly, fraternization is a path to peace. Clearly, this path does not run through the capitalist governments, through an alliance with them, but runs *against* them. Clearly, this path tends to develop, strengthen, and consolidate fraternal confidence between the workers of different countries. Clearly, this path is *beginning to wreck* the hateful discipline of the barrack prisons, the discipline of blind obedience of the soldier to "his" officers and generals, to his capitalists (for most of the officers and generals either belong to the capitalist class or protect its interests). Clearly, fraternization is the revolutionary initiative of the *masses,* it is the awakening of the conscience, the mind, the courage of the oppressed classes; in other words, it is a rung in the ladder leading up to the socialist proletarian revolution.[43]

This movement must go beyond the instinctive level; must be translated into a clear political program:

> ...[I]s instinct alone sufficient? You would not get far if you relied on instinct alone. This instinct must be transformed into political awareness.
>
> In our "Appeal to the Soldiers of All the Belligerent Countries," we explain into what this fraternization should develop—into the passing of political power to the Soviets of Workers' and Soldiers' Deputies.[44]

Bolshevik influence in the armed forces increases

Desertion from the army grew and grew. In one month alone, June, 30,507 soldiers deserted (8,540 from the western front; 13,755 from the southwestern front; 3,790 from the Rumanian front).[45]

By October, as already mentioned, there were two million army deserters dispersed all over the country. The Russian soldier, one historian wrote, demobilized or deserting,

> went home—and shattered the matrix. He established his authority in the village, and wrenched it out of the age-old ruts, imparting to it a leftward twist which served the Soviet power well for years to come.... When the SRs lost the soldiers they lost the peasants too, and so the revolutions.[46]

Soldiers were moving towards Bolshevism because of their increasing anger against the war. One expression of this anger was an article in the Moscow *Soldat-Grazhdanin* (*Citizen-Soldier*) of May 25:

> "Until the end," croaks the crow, picking the human bones on the battlefield. What does he care about the old mother who awaits the return of her son or the octogenarian who with trembling hand leads the plow?
>
> "War to the end," cries the student to thousands of people on the public square and assures them that our hardships are due to the Germans. During this time, his father, who has sold oats at sixteen rubles a pud, sits in a noisy cabaret where he maintains the same ideas.
>
> "To the end," clamor the agents of the allied government while touring the battlefields strewn with the bodies of the proletarians. Can the soldier in the trenches cry "War to the end"? No. He says something else:
>
> Until the end of the war, we'll be without food.
>
> Until the end of the war, Russia won't be free.
>
> Comrades, let him who cries "War to the end" be sent to the front lines. Then we'll see what he says.[47]

Many soldiers were spontaneously reaching a position on the war similar to that of the Bolshevik Party, if not more extreme. As Sukhanov recounts:

As early as 21 September, at a Petersburg Soviet session an officer who had been at the front made a speech saying:

"The soldiers in the trenches don't want either freedom or land now. They want only one thing now—the end of the war. Whatever you may say here, the soldiers are not going to fight any more...." This caused a sensation even in the Bolshevik Soviet. Exclamations were heard: "Even the Bolsheviks don't say that!" But the officer, no Bolshevik, calmly waited, conscious of duty done. "We don't know and we don't care what the Bolsheviks say. I'm reporting what I know and what the soldiers have sent me to tell you."[48]

In organizational terms, the strength of the Bolshevik Party in the army to start with—at the time of the February Revolution—was infinitesimal. In Petrograd, two months after the revolution, there were only 500 members of the Bolshevik Military Organization in a garrison of some 160,000. However, numbers grew quite quickly in the following weeks and months. There were 1,800 at the end of July, and 5,800 by the end of October. In Moscow, the number of organized Bolsheviks in the local garrison grew from 200 in April to 2,000 at the end of July, and to 5,000 in November. The total number of Bolsheviks in the army at the time of the February Revolution was a couple of thousand. By the time of the April Conference, it had risen to 6,000, and on June 16 it was 26,000. After that, soldiers in practically all corps, divisions, batteries, and other units began to join the party. On October 5, on the northwestern front alone, there were 48,994 party members and 7,452 candidates. On October 15, on the northern front there were 13,000 party members. At the party conference of the southwestern front in September, 7,000 members were represented. In November, there were more than 6,500 members in the 9th Army alone. In the 12th Army, there were 1,700 Bolsheviks at the beginning of July; 3,897 at the end of July; and 5,000 on December 23.[49]

The influence of the Bolsheviks in the army was disproportionately large. Thus Stankevich writes in his memoirs:

Practically every division had its Bolshevik, with a name better known than the name of the Division Commander.... Since it was clear that without removing them it would be impossible to deal with the dissolution of the army, we gradually got rid of one celebrity after another.[50]

The fear aroused among the generals—by a single Bolshevik—is graphically shown in the case of one Bolshevik soldier, Dmitri Petrovich Mikhailov, who put the highest generals in the land into a lengthy correspondence about him.

To General V.I. Gurko:

An agitator from the Petrograd Soviet, Dmitri Petrovich Mikhailov, armed with authorization dated 25 April, No. 126, has visited our division. Among other things, he urges fraternization with the Germans and only today has organized fraternizations in the 220th regiment. They have spread to the 218th. The officers' arguments have been unavailing. Does Mikhailov really have such authority to act thus? Forwarded to headquarters.

—General Cheglov

In view of the formal disapproval by the Petrograd Soviet of all fraternization at the front, affirmed by the appeal of 30 April, Mikhailov must realize that he is contravening said declaration.... It would be advisable to persuade the "Front Committee' to arrest Mikhailov pending clarification by the Soviet.

—General Gurko

Following your telegram of 2 May. Due to impossibility of acting by force, have been unable to arrest Mikhailov. In the 55th Division, he is agitating against the officers, wants them replaced by elected officers.

It has already been done in some regiments.

Something must absolutely be done to cause the Petrograd Soviet to recall Mikhailov by telegram to end this disintegration which is beginning in this army corps.

—Chief of Staff for Alexeev[51]

In their fear of Bolshevism, the authorities tried to obstruct the distribution of the Bolshevik papers. Thus the Executive Committee of the Tiflis Soviet confiscated forty thousand copies of *Pravda,* which Georgian workers were preparing to dispatch to the Caucasian front.[52] Soldiers were complaining bitterly that they paid subscriptions for *Pravda* but could only get the Cadet *Rech* and the Menshevik *Den.*[53] The circulation of the Bolshevik papers in the army was extremely small: *Soldatskaia Pravda* at the beginning of July was distributing fifty thousand copies.[54] The numbers in the armed forces were some nine million!

Nevertheless things were moving ahead fast, because, as Lenin put it: "Revolution enlightens all classes with a rapidity and thoroughness unknown in normal, peaceful times."[55] The land program and the peace program of Bolshevism were linked inseparably with the soldiers' rebellion against their officers, against the old tsarist discipline.

The provisional government, with the generals, was trying to reestablish discipline in the war-weary and revolutionary army, in which soldiers refused to obey officers and listened only to their own elected committees. The Menshevik and SR leaders had pledged themselves to help the government in this task, yet they called on their soldiers to defend Order No. 1 against the tsarist officers.*

The government wanted to protect the gentry's property while the peasants, including those in uniform, were clamoring for the large estates to be shared out. The Menshevik and SR leaders tried to postpone the solution of this burning question until the convention of the constituent assembly, which was indefinitely postponed.

It was inevitable that this structure, built on equivocation and delusion, should topple onto the heads of those who had erected it. The mass of the soldiers did just that. Lenin was their voice and inspiration.

---

* General Brusilov, looking back over the stormy events of 1917, uttered a well justified criticism when he wrote: "The position of the Bolsheviks I understood, because they preached: 'Down with the war and immediate peace at any price,' but I couldn't understand at all the tactics of the Socialist Revolutionaries and the Mensheviks, who first broke up the army, as if to avoid counter-revolution,

CHAPTER 11

THE PEASANTRY IN THE REVOLUTION

The revolution engulfs the villages

The rebellious towns, together with the mutinous soldiers, brought about the awakening of the countryside. In the first few weeks after the February Revolution, the countryside remained almost completely quiet, but this could not continue for long.

In many cases the landlords, frightened of the specter of revolution, did not undertake the spring sowing. All over Russia, anxious about the future, they hastened to sell their property—either to rich peasants or to foreigners. The mass of the peasantry saw this and became agitated. The first demand that spread extensively was for a stop to all land sales. Sukhanov tells how one of the peasant delegates, with tears in his eyes, pleaded with the ministers to promulgate a law prohibiting the land from being sold.

> He was impatiently interrupted by the pale and agitated Kerensky. "Yes, yes, that will be done. The provisional government is already taking steps. Tell them there is nothing to worry about. The government and myself will do our duty."
>
> One of the deputation, however, obviously mistrusting the minister's assurance, tried to put in the remark that the law had been promised long since but that nothing was happening. The others were obviously in sympathy. Kerensky was furious and began a thorough tongue-lashing, practically stamping his foot:
>
> "I said it would be done, that means it will! And—there is no need to look at me so suspiciously!"
>
> I give this verbatim—Kerensky was right, the little peasants were looking *suspiciously* at the famous people's minister.[1]

They became more and more impatient. "Well, nothing has changed yet," peasants from a village near Riazan wrote, "and the revolution is already six weeks old."[2]

At the second session of the Central Land Committee at the beginning of July, the representative of Nizhni-Novgorod province reported that there was only one topic of conversation among the peasants. "We are tired of waiting, we have waited three hundred years, and now that we have conquered power, we do not want to wait any more."[3]

The conservative paper *Russkaia Volia* of May 4 described the mood among delegates to the All-Russian Peasant Congress thus:

> The delegates' main grievance, voiced on behalf of the peasants, is that while all classes are already reaping the fruits of the revolution the peasants alone are still waiting for their share. The peasants alone are told to wait until the constituent assembly meets and settles the land question.
>
> "We don't agree," they say. "We're not going to wait, just as others have not waited. We want the land now, at once."[4]

The peasants did not limit themselves to thinking and talking, but started to act. From the end of March, news came trickling in of peasant encroachment on landlords' property.

The *muzhiks* started by appropriating vacant lands. Then they seized the haystacks, which they themselves had made. Then they seized equipment belonging to the landlord. Heading the movement were areas where semi-serf methods of exploitation had particularly deep roots and the poverty of the peasantry was greatest.

Statistics compiled by the provisional government Central Land Committee give a concrete picture of the agrarian movement in various *guberniias* of European Russia. They are divided into six groups according to the number of peasant uprisings. The first and lowest group, with ten or fewer incidents, includes the *guberniias* of Olonets, Vologda, Iaroslavl, Viatka and Ural oblast, Estland, Kovno, Grodno, and Kavkaz. The second group, with eleven to twenty-five uprisings, includes the *guberniias* of Moscow, Vladimir, Kostroma, Perm, Astrakhan, the Cossack Don oblast, and Tauride. The third group, with twenty-six to fifty uprisings, is made up of the *guberniias* of Lifland, Petrograd, Novgorod, Tver, Kaluga, Nizhni-Novgorod, Ufa, Kharkov, Ekaterinoslavl, Bessarabia, Podolia, Volynia, and Vilna. The fourth, with from fifty to seventy-five cases, embraces the *guberniias* of Vitebsk, Smolensk, Orlov, Poltava, Kiev, Kherson, Saratov, and Orenburg. The fifth, with seventy-six to one hundred cases, contains the *guberniias* of Minsk, Tula, Kursk, Voronezh, Tambov, Penza, and Simbirsk. Finally, the sixth and highest group, with 101 or more cases, includes the *guberniias* of Pskov,

Mogilev, Riazan, Kazan, and Samara.[5]

The number of offenses committed by the peasantry increased sharply, as can be seen from the following table[6]:

	March	*April*	*May*	*June*	*July*	*Aug.*	*Sept.*
Land seizures	2	51	59	136	236	180	103
Trees felled and lumber theft	12	18	19	71	112	69	96
Equipment theft	?	10	7	71	92	32	27
TOTAL	17	204	259	577	1,122	665	628

The number of manor houses destroyed also rose abruptly[7]:

March	12
April	21
May	25
June	22
July	27
August	35
September	106
October	274

In the months leading up to October, the peasants' illegal actions became more and more violent. The number of raids on landed estates went up by 30 percent from August to September, and by a further 43 percent in October.

Of the 624 districts constituting old Russia, 482 witnessed violent attacks on landlords in August; in September, the proportion was even higher. Moreover, not only the number, but also the intensity of these disturbances was constantly increasing—October saw half as many acts of violence again as the whole period of February to September.

In late summer and autumn, manor after manor went up in flames. The right-wing paper *Novoe Vremia* had the following story to tell on October 3:

> Not a day goes by that news does not appear in the press about the atrocious pogroms which take place in the village. In the spirit of anarchy, the propaganda-inspired masses are not satisfied to seize the lands of the private owners. They also remove the workers from properties, fell forests, and destroy crops.
> The nonresistance of the provisional government, which limits it-

self in the struggle with anarchy to mere appeals, which naturally no one takes seriously, has resulted in veritable pogroms by the population in its effort to seize land. Estates of private owners are destroyed by arson and in other ways. Livestock and equipment are seized. Various agricultural enterprises are put out of use completely. The owners and their employees, in so far as they succeed in saving themselves from attacks or actual murder, flee to the cities, leaving their estates to the mercy of fate.[8]

Another paper, *Vlast Naroda,* wrote on the same day:

The waves of pogroms rise ever higher. They threaten to flood all of Russia, to sweep away all that still remains in the chaos of the breakdown of the Russian state, to turn the great Russian revolution into a disorderly, bloody scuffle.... Rural Russia is enveloped in a glow of fire from *pomeshchiki* [landlords'] estates. Model agricultural holdings are being destroyed. The productive forces of the country are dying.... Without waiting for the constituent assembly, the peasants seize land, violate the sovereign rights of all the people, destroy the national wealth.[9]

The government procrastinates

Shortly after coming to power, on March 19, the provisional government declared that agrarian reform was a cherished and urgent objective. At the same time it announced:

The land question cannot be resolved by means of any [arbitrary] seizures. Violence and robbery are the worst and most dangerous expedients in the realm of economic relations.... The land question must be resolved by means of law, passed by the representatives of the people.

Proper consideration and passage of a land law is impossible without serious preparatory work: the collection of materials, the registration of land reserves, [the determination of] the distribution of landed property, and the conditions and forms of land utilization, and so forth....

On the basis of the above considerations, the provisional government has resolved:

1. To recognize the urgency of the preparation and elaboration of materials on the land question.

2. To entrust this [task] to the Ministry of Agriculture.

3. To form a Land Committee in the Ministry of Agriculture for the purpose indicated.

4. To direct the Minister of Agriculture to submit to the government at the earliest moment a plan for the establishment of such a committee together with an estimate of the funds necessary for its work.[10]

So, instead of action by the masses, there was to be a collection of information by government bureaucrats!

A month after this declaration, on April 21, the government issued an appeal concerning the land question:

> The most important question for our country—the land question—can be properly and finally resolved only by the constituent assembly, elected by universal, equal, direct, and secret...suffrage. But in order to make such a resolution possible it is necessary to gather information from all regions on the land needs of the population and to prepare a new law on land organization for the constituent assembly....
>
> A great disaster threatens our native land should the local population take upon itself the reorganization of the land system without waiting for the decision of the constituent assembly. Such arbitrary actions carry the threat of general ruin.[11]

One historian writes:

> If the peasants were going to wait for the orderly processes of the constituent assembly instead of taking matters into their own hands, they demanded at least some measures in the interim that would better their lot and ease the burden of war, the full weight of which had fallen upon their shoulders. They also wanted to be very sure that the land fund would not be drawn down in the meantime by legitimate or fictitious deals between estate owners and small or foreign buyers who would be in a better position to claim exemption from confiscatory legislation.[12]

The minister of agriculture, Victor Chernov, leader of the SRs, was anxious to do just this—to prohibit the sale of land before the convocation of the constituent assembly. But attempts to preserve the status quo in respect to landownership by withdrawing the commodity from the market proved very difficult. Here the minister had arrayed against him the entire business community, which held that a ban on land deals would depreciate land values, which in turn would impair the credit structure of banks and endanger the savings of small investors. Needless to say, the Cadets offered strenuous resistance to the proposed measure.[13] The prime minister, Prince Lvov, himself a landowner of Tula province, also opposed Chernov. Confronted by this degree of opposition, Chernov could not get his projected law through the cabinet.

He also wanted to put all land under the administration of land committees until the constituent assembly should declare its final fate. Given that there had been so much trouble over a measure that Chernov termed the most rudimentary of all needing legislation, it is not surprising that this more far-reaching plan was not even considered by the first coalition ministry.

When, at the end of August, Chernov was forced out of the gov-

ernment by the right, his successor as minister of agriculture, the SR
S.L. Maslov, produced a watered-down draft law. Instead of placing
all land without exception under the land committees, as the SR Congress of May 1917 had demanded, Maslov's draft suggested bringing
only the land rented to peasants, cultivated with their equipment or
left idle, into the scope of the projected legislation. In general, that
part of privately owned land that was farmed with the owner's equipment was not to be affected. While state and appanage lands were to
go into the fund subject to the land committees, allotment lands were
not, and the exemption list was swelled by properties used for spe-
cialized farming (viniculture, horticulture, and so forth), and also, apparently, by ecclesiastical properties, unless these were considered as
falling within the category of state properties. Maslov's law was to
leave rich peasants (*kulaks*) untouched; under the party program,
their surplus land was to go into the common fund.[14]

Even the land the peasant was to get he would not get for nothing. "Rent," said clause 33 of the bill, "shall be paid to the committees which shall hand over the remainder [after various
payments to the Treasury, etc.] to the rightful owners."

Maslov's land bill came before the cabinet in mid-October. The
fall of the government prevented it from becoming the law of the
land.

SRs and Mensheviks to the rescue

The agrarian policy of the provisional government received con-
tinual support from the SR and Menshevik leaders of the soviet.
For instance, on March 26, an editorial in *Izvestiia,* the daily newspaper of the executive of the soviet, stated:

> Not only the interests of the peasantry, but the interests also of the en-
> tire Russian democracy demand that the gentry's estates be confiscated
> and transferred to the democratic state.... A month ago the demand
> "All land—to the people!" seemed [like] a distant dream.
>
> But a few months will pass and this dream, too, will become a reality.
> The people will receive all the land.
>
> But this should be accomplished in such a way that the transfer-
> ence of land to the people will take place in a completely orderly
> manner, so that the interests of free Russia will not suffer.[15]

Similarly, the SR paper, *Dyelo Naroda,* stated in an editorial on
March 16:

> With the penetration into the village of the first news of the revolu-

tion, agrarian disorders occurred in some places. At the *oblast* congress of the Socialist Revolutionary Party, it was reported that in some villages peasants began to seize landowners' lands, to attack agronomists who, complying with the orders of the old government, were requisitioning grain and hay, etc.

The regional conference of the SR Party, having discussed the situation that has arisen, sharply condemned such attempts and declared that "confiscation of cultivated…privately owned lands may be conducted only by legislative means through the constituent assembly which will grant land and freedom to the people." The same resolution was passed also by the conference of peasant representatives in the Moscow Council of Workers' Deputies. That resolution proclaimed: "No pogroms or arbitrary seizures of land will be tolerated."

Need we add that the decision of the party should be just this and no other?

The editorial ended with the following words:

Guard the sacredness and success of the revolution! Do not turn the great work into a reign of arbitrary rule and violence! Do not confuse the socialization of land with its arbitrary seizure for personal gain! Do not tolerate any pogroms!

Fight against them! Organize and be prepared for the elections to the constituent assembly which must give the people both land and freedom!!![16]

Wait, wait…that was all the government and compromisers had to say to the peasants.

The peasants refuse to wait for the constituent assembly

Chernov writes:

What were they waiting for? They were told: for the constituent assembly. Unfortunately, this assembly was postponed with depressing regularity. No better means for sickening the peasant of the constituent assembly could have been invented.

And so the idea that there was no need to wait for the constituent assembly and that the land must be seized at once found ready soil. At the second session of the Chief Land Committee, a Smolensk representative reported the talk of the peasants in Sychevsky district: "They say of the constituent assembly: Well, Nicholas was overthrown without the constituent assembly; why can't the gentry be driven from the face of the earth without it?" The Bolsheviks, who were on the job, nudged them: They can be. You have only to set up a workers' and peasants' dictatorship and settle all problems "in two shakes of a lamb's tail," with a mere flourish of the pen at the foot of revolutionary decrees.[17]

So punitive forces are used...

The government resorted increasingly to the use of troops to suppress agrarian riots. On April 8, it was reported:

> The query of the general staff reported by the Assistant Minister of the Interior D.M. Shchepkin with regard to whether it is necessary to give the commanders of the troops of the districts the right to send military detachments when demanded, for participating in the suppression of agrarian disorders.
>
> Resolved:
>
> 1. To let the Ministry of the Interior inform the guberniia commissars by circular that it is their responsibility together with that of the local public committees to suppress immediately with the use of all legal means any kind of attempt in the sphere of agrarian relations against the person or property of citizens if such attempts have taken place.
>
> 2. To let the Ministry of the Interior inform the general staff that necessary instructions with regard to the question raised by the staff have been forwarded to the *guberniia* commissars who will be responsible in case it is necessary to enter into direct contact with the military authorities concerned.[18]

Then on July 31, the commander in chief, General Kornilov, issued an order covering "the whole theater of war":

> I forbid.
>
> ...The hindrance of harvesting by agricultural machines.
>
> ...The seizure by violence, in an unlawful way, of livestock or material inventory.
>
> ...The unlawful removal from field work on estates owned by the state or by private individuals, or on other [land] holdings, of the prisoners of war or any permanent or migrant laborers [working] thereon; I order the return of the unlawfully removed prisoners of war.
>
> ...The forcing of permanent or migrant laborers to raise the labor prices agreed upon beforehand.
>
> ...The seizure by force of sown or harvested grain, fodder, grass, and hay.
>
> ...The hindrance of harvesting in any way.
>
> ...The hindrance of the cultivation and saving of winter crop fields.[19]

On September 8 Kerensky, as supreme commander, an office that he had assumed following the Kornilov affair,* reissued and confirmed this order. But, perhaps significantly, he did so without specific reference to its application only in the theater of war.[20]

During the months March–June, 17 cases of the use of armed

---

* August 27–30. See Chapter 16.

force against peasants were counted; in July–August there were 39 cases; in September–October, 105 cases.[21]

On October 10, the minister of the interior, Nikitin, urged government commissars in provinces and towns to "rally the healthy elements of the population for struggle with increasing anarchy, which is steadily leading the country to destruction," and to "fill up the police with selected reliable people."[22]

On October 21, just four days before the provisional government was overthrown, Nikitin again urged government commissars

> to make every effort to combat anarchy, using cavalry detachments where these were necessary. But the provisional government no longer had enough reliable troops to save its capital, much less to restore order all over the vast Russian countryside.

Many years later, Chernov regretted the day troops were used to suppress agrarian disorders:

> That was stark madness. There was no better means of demoralizing the army than to send it, with its 90 percent of peasants, to crush the movement of millions of its brethren.
>
> In Samara province the soldiers' wives raised rebellion: "Let us go and mow the grass of the gentry; why are our husbands suffering for the third year?" The gentry brought a detachment of soldiers from Hvalynsk. But when the soldiers, who were the peasants themselves, saw the *muzhiks* mowing the rich grass, they tried their hand at mowing; they were tired of their rifles. The peasants fed the soldiers, talked to them, and then set to work all the harder.
>
> In Tambov province, a military detachment came at the summons of Prince Vyazensky. It was greeted by a roar from the crowds: "What are you doing, coming to defend the prince, coming to beat your own fathers? Throw the devils into the river!" The commander took into his head to fire into the air. He was struck by a stone and ordered the troops to disperse the mob, but the soldiers did not stir. The officer spurred his horse and escaped from the enraged peasants by fording the river. His detachment scattered and let the crowd surround the prince, whom they arrested and sent to the front as a "slacker." At a nearby station, he was lynched by a detachment of Siberian shock troops on their way to the front.
>
> In Slavuta, Izyaslavsky district, Volhynia province, a detachment of fifty Cossacks was sent to the Sangushko estate to pacify the peasants. A detachment of infantry from the front was also quartered nearby. The Cossacks went out to reconnoiter in the woods. The soldiers then "set out with the peasants. First, they burst into the prince's palace. The prince tried to flee. The soldiers quickly scattered to search for him. They overtook him near a steep bridge and tossed him on their bayonets. The soldiers and peasants, without wasting time, carried three iron chests from the mansion, with several million

rubles in gold, silver, and paper money, distributed the money to the poor, and then burned the chambers of the prince. The peasants went boldly out to divide the land, afraid of no one."

Grey-uniformed peasants, aroused by the revolution in the city, were sent against the village, which would not and could not go on indefinitely under the Tsarist agrarian laws, once Tsarism had fallen. A more suicidal policy could not have been invented.[23]

The SRs split

From May 6 to the end of August, Chernov, founder, top leader, and theoretician of the Socialist Revolutionary Party, was minister of agriculture. He bore the primary responsibility for the state's agrarian policy during the heyday of the provisional government. At his side, as deputy ministers, were the SRs N.I. Rakitnikov and P.A. Vikhliaev. Below the ministry, there was a hierarchy of land committees set up under the law of April 24, with *volost* or cantonal committees at the bottom of the structure and the Central Land Committee in Petrograd at the top.

> The land committees ran the gamut of political coloration from a rosewater tint of intellectualism to the deeper red hue of direct action, the rule being that the closer to the base of the structure the weaker the role of the intellectuals and the greater the degree of radicalism. At all levels the SRs predominated, but they were not all the same kind of SRs, the dirt-soil peasants on the popularly elected *volost* committees having quite a different outlook from the theoretical revolutionists or technicians on the higher organs, where many of the members sat by appointment. The primary consideration with the former was to get the land before it eluded their grasp, as in 1905, and with the latter, to bridge over class differences while the war continued.[24]

By June the leadership of the movement to improve the status of the peasantry had passed into the hands of local land committees. In the absence of laws from the center, the committees went in for self-action: they lowered the payments on rented land, forbade landowners to increase the exploitation of forests while they still had them, took over untilled fields for assignment to peasants, and in general did things that the peasants demanded and the landowners resented.[25]

Early in the autumn, mass agrarian disorders broke out in Tambov province, a black earth region in the heart of SR country. The party chieftains of Petrograd were still determined to oppose the disorders, but not so the local SRs.

And so the whole Tambov organization, together with the Soviet hierarchy, stepped out of line with the party center, and with the all-Russian Executive Committee, and proposed that the provincial authorities put into effect the agrarian program without waiting for legislation on the national scale, which was never enacted. This was a revolutionary step in defiance of constituted authority, and if it opened up a novel solution of the existing deadlock by combining coalition in the capital with revolutionary action in the provinces, it also marked the crumbling of the main part of the party organization.[26]

Throughout 1917, a growing cleavage divided the SR Party between the left—those elements ready to go to the limit with the *muzhiks* against the landlords—and the right-wing leadership.

In March and April, the left SRs had acquired control of the peasant movement in certain provinces of Russia and the Ukraine, in Kazan and Ufa, in Kharkov and Kherson, and here and there were other islands of strength.[27] In the capital itself, Petrograd, from the beginning of the revolution, the local organization of the SRs was working-class in composition, left in politics, and aligned against the central leadership. In Kronstadt, the whole SR organization belonged to the left.

At the first All-Russian Conference of Soviets (March 29–April 3) a group of left SRs had already rebelled openly against the party leadership and supported the Bolshevik minority. With time the split in the party became wider and wider. The Kornilov coup gave further encouragement to the left SRs to assert their independence. In the October insurrection, they sided with the Bolsheviks, and collaborated with them in the government born out of the revolution.

Lenin keeps abreast of the peasant revolution

Lenin thrashed the agrarian question out so thoroughly during the 1905 Revolution that, by the time of the second revolution, his and the Bolsheviks' ideas on the subject were very well defined.

First of all, the key to the agrarian revolution was the democratic mass organization of the rural population. In his article "Socialism and the Peasantry," written in September 1905, Lenin had said:

There is only one way to make the agrarian reform, which is unavoidable in present-day Russia, play a revolutionary-democratic role: it must be effected on the revolutionary initiative of the peasants themselves, despite the landlords and the bureaucracy, and despite the state, i.e., it must be effected by revolutionary means.... And this is the road we indicate when we make our prime demand the establishment of revolutionary peasant committees.[28]

Now, at the beginning of April 1917, he wrote:

> For the organization of the peasants, carried out from below without the officials and without the "control and supervision" of the landowners and their hangers-on, is the only reliable pledge of success for the revolution, for freedom.[29]

He reiterated the point in his "Report on the Agrarian Question to the April Conference of the Party":

> [T]o us, the thing that matters is revolutionary initiative, and the law must be the result of it. *If you wait until the law is written, and yourselves do not develop revolutionary initiative, you will have neither the law nor the land.*[30]

The peasants should not fall for the compromising argument:

> As to the land, wait until the constituent assembly. As to the constituent assembly, wait until the end of the war. As to the end of the war, wait until complete victory. That is what it comes to. The capitalists and landowners, having a majority in the government, are plainly mocking at the peasants.[31]

> To counteract the bourgeois-liberal or purely bureaucratic sermons preached by many Socialist Revolutionaries and Soviets of Workers' and Soldiers' Deputies, who advise the peasants not to seize the landed estates and not to start the agrarian reform pending the convocation of the constituent assembly, the party of the proletariat must urge the peasants to carry out the agrarian reform at once on their own, and to confiscate the landed estates immediately, upon the decisions of the peasants' deputies in the localities.[32]

He proposes an independent organization of agricultural workers

Throughout the development of the agrarian policy of Bolshevism there were two central points in Lenin's thinking: (1) the working class must lead the peasantry; (2) the workers must be organized separately from the peasants. Thus in 1906 he wrote:

> [S]upporting the revolutionary peasant, the proletariat must not for a moment forget about its own class independence and its own special class aims. The peasant movement is the movement of another class. It is not a proletarian struggle, but a struggle waged by small proprietors. It is not a struggle against the foundation of capitalism, but a struggle to cleanse them of all survivals of serfdom.[33]

> We stand by the peasant movement to the end; but we have to remember that it is the movement of another class, *not the one* which

can and will bring about the socialist revolution.[34]

In 1917, he pursued the point further:

> [I]t is necessary to organize separately the proletarian elements (agricultural laborers, day-laborers, etc.) *within* the general peasant Soviets, or (sometimes *and)* set up separate Soviets of Agricultural Laborers' Deputies.[35]

In a speech to the First Congress of Peasant Deputies, on May 22, he said in the name of the Bolsheviks:

> We should like, and we advise it, to have in each peasant committee, in each *volost, uyezd,* and *guberniia,* a separate group of agricultural laborers and poor peasants who will have to ask themselves: "If the land becomes the property of the whole people tomorrow—and it certainly will, because the people want it to—then where do we come in? Where shall we, who have no animals or implements, get them from? How are we to farm the land? How must we protect our interests? How are we to make sure that the land, which will belong to the whole people, which will really be the property of the nation, should not fall *only* into the hands of *proprietors?* If it falls into the hands of those who own enough animals and implements, shall we gain anything by it? Is that what we made this great revolution for? Is that what we wanted?".... There is only one way to escape the yoke of capitalism and ensure that the people's land goes to the *working people,* and that is by organizing the agricultural laborers, who will be guided by their experience, their observations, and their distrust of what the village sharks tell them even though these sharks wear red rosettes in their buttonholes and call themselves "revolutionary democrats."
>
> The poor peasants can only be taught by independent organization in the localities, they can only learn from their own experience. That experience will not be easy, we cannot and do not promise them a land flowing with milk and honey. The landowners will be thrown out because the people wish it, but *capitalism* will remain. It is much more difficult to do away with capitalism, and the road to its overthrow is a different one. It is the road of independent, separate organization of the agricultural laborers and the poor peasants. And that is what our party proposes in the first instance.[36]

In a couple of articles entitled "The Need for an Agricultural Laborers' Union in Russia," written specially for the All-Russian Trade Union Conference of June 21–28, Lenin said:

> All classes in Russia are organizing. Only the class which is the most exploited and the poorest of all, the most disunited and downtrodden—the class of Russia's agricultural wage-laborers—seems to have been forgotten....
>
> It is the indisputable and paramount duty of the vanguard of Russia's proletariat, the industrial workers' trade unions, to come to the

aid of their brothers, the rural workers.

The industrial workers should "not confine themselves to narrow craft interests and forget their weaker brethren." Lenin went on to outline some necessary practical steps:

> All organized workers should give one day's wages to promote and strengthen the unity of town and country wage-workers.... Let this fund be drawn on to cover the expenses of putting out a series of the most popular leaflets, of publishing a rural workers' newspaper—at least a weekly to begin with—and of sending at least a few agitators and organizers to the countryside to *immediately set up* unions of agricultural laborers in the various localities.
>
> A most determined war must be declared on the preconceived notion that the coming abolition of private landownership can "give land" to every farmhand and day-laborer and undermine the very foundations of wage-labor in agriculture. This is a preconceived notion and, moreover, an extremely harmful one....You cannot eat land. You cannot farm without livestock, implements, seed, a reserve of produce, or money. To rely on "promises" from anyone—that the wage-workers in the countryside will be "helped" to acquire livestock, implements, etc.—would be the worst kind of error, unpardonable naivety....
>
> That is why it must be made the immediate task of the rural workers' trade union not only to fight for better conditions for the workers in general, but in particular to *defend their interests as a class* during the coming great land reform.[37]

Organize the large farms

Lenin made it clear that the organization of agricultural workers in trade unions, or even soviets, was not enough to overcome the exploitation in the countryside. Thus he wrote in April 1917:

> We cannot conceal from the peasants, least of all from the rural proletarians and semi-proletarians, that small-scale farming under commodity economy and capitalism *cannot* rid humanity of mass poverty, that it is necessary to *think* about going over to large-scale farming conducted on public lines and to *tackle this job at once* by teaching the masses, and in turn *learning from the masses,* the practical expedient measures for bringing about such a transition.[38]

In a speech to the Congress of Peasants' Deputies, already quoted above, Lenin stated:

> [O]ur party recommends...that every big economy, for example, every big landed estate, of which there are 30,000 in Russia, should be organized as soon as possible into a model farm for the *common* cultivation of the land jointly by agricultural laborers and scientifi-

cally trained agronomists, using the animals, implements, etc., of the landowners for that purpose. Without this *common* cultivation under the direction of the Soviets of Agricultural Laborers, the land will not go entirely to the *working people*. To be sure, joint cultivation is a difficult business and it would be madness of course for anybody to imagine that joint cultivation of the land can be decreed from above and imposed on people, because the centuries-old habit of farming on one's own cannot suddenly disappear, and because money will be needed for it and adaptation to the new mode of life.[39]

Lenin steals the SR program

Lenin did not hesitate to adopt the program that emerged from the mass peasant movement, and that was by and large identical with the program of the SR Party.

On August 19, 1917, the *Izvestiia* of the All-Russian Congress of Peasants' Deputies published an article entitled "Model Mandate Compiled on the Basis of 242 Mandates Submitted by Local Deputies to the First All-Russian Congress of Peasants' Deputies Held in Petrograd, 1917." The crucial points of the mandate were

abolition of private ownership of all types of land, including the peasants' lands, without compensation; transfer of lands on which high-standard scientific farming is practised to the state or the communes; confiscation of all livestock and implements on the confiscated lands (peasants with little land are excluded) and their transfer to the state or the communes; a ban on wage-labor; equalized distribution of land among the working people, with periodical redistributions, and so on. In the transition period, pending the convocation of the constituent assembly, the peasants demand the *immediate* enactment of laws prohibiting the purchase and sale of land, abolition of laws concerning separation from the commune, farmsteads, etc., laws protecting forests, fisheries, etc., abolishing long-term and revising short-term leases, and so on.[40]

Lenin, who was in hiding in Finland and was now convinced that the moment for the seizure of power was near, thought that the model decree was central to the success of the revolution.

The Socialist-Revolutionaries are deceiving themselves and the peasants precisely by assuming and spreading the idea that these reforms, or similar reforms, are possible without overthrowing capitalist rule, without all state power being transferred to the proletariat, without the peasant poor supporting the most resolute, revolutionary measures of a proletarian state power against the capitalists.[41]

The 242 demands, he argued, could be realized only when a

ruthless war was declared on capitalism under the leadership of the proletariat. Thus he took over *in toto* the declared agrarian program of the SRs, but added to it the vital twist that it could be achieved only as part of a proletarian revolution against capitalism.

The demands were destined to be incorporated in the decree on land of the Bolshevik government issued on October 26. When this was submitted to the All-Russian Congress of Soviets, and protests were heard that it was the work of the SRs, Lenin replied:

> Voices are being raised here that the decree itself and the mandate were drawn up by the Socialist Revolutionaries. What of it? Does it matter who drew them up? As a democratic government, we cannot ignore the decision of the masses of the people, even though we may disagree with it. In the fire of experience, applying the decree in practice, and carrying it out locally, the peasants will themselves realize where the truth lies. And even if the peasants continue to follow the Socialist Revolutionaries, even if they give this party a majority in the constituent assembly we shall still say—what of it? Experience is the best teacher and it will show who is right. Let the peasants solve this problem from one end and we shall solve it from the other. Experience will oblige us to draw together in the general stream of revolutionary creative work, in the elaboration of new state forms. We must be guided by experience; we must allow complete freedom to the creative faculties of the masses.[42]

How pathetic was Chernov's complaint: "Lenin copies out our resolutions, and publishes them in the form of 'Decrees.'"[43] Lenin's justification was very simple: the needs of the revolution were the supreme law. He wrote:

> We Bolsheviks were opposed to this law. Yet we signed it, because we did not want to oppose the will of the majority of peasants. The majority will is binding on us always, and to oppose the majority will is to betray the revolution.
> We did not want to impose on the peasants the idea that the equal division of the land was useless, an idea which was alien to them. Far better, we thought, if, by their own experience and suffering, the peasants themselves come to realize that equal division is nonsense. Only then could we ask them how they would escape the ruin and *kulak* domination that follow from the division of the land.[44]

When a German delegate at the Second Congress of the Comintern in 1920 accused the soviet government of a "direct relapse into long outworn petty-bourgeois ways of thought" and "a sacrifice of the interests of the proletariat in favor of the peasantry," Lenin tartly replied that "otherwise the small peasant will not notice the difference between the former government and the dictatorship of the Soviets," and that "if the proletarian state power does not act in this way, it will not be able to maintain itself."[45]

It was a paradox of history that, under a government in which a number of SRs participated, the peasants had to take the road of revolution in order to carry out the SR program, supported and led by the Bolsheviks, who fought the SRs for many years.

Organizationally the Bolsheviks were extremely weak in the countryside. There were only a handful of party members living in the villages. Nevertheless, the willingness of Lenin and the Bolsheviks to *listen* to the peasants gave them an impact greatly disproportionate to their organizational strength.

Lenin knew how to learn from the *muzhik,* and the latter appreciated it. Consider his appearance before the peasant congress on May 20. It seemed, says Sukhanov, as though Lenin had blundered into a pit of crocodiles. However, "The little muzhiks listened attentively and probably not without sympathy. But they dared not show it."[46]

The same thing was repeated in the soldiers' section, which was extremely hostile to the Bolsheviks. Sukhanov relates:

> I sat down in about the seventh row, in the heart of the soldier audience. The soldiers were listening with the greatest interest as Lenin berated the coalition's agrarian policy and proposed that they should settle the matter on their own authority, without any constituent assembly. But the speaker was soon interrupted by the chair: his time was up. Some arguing began about whether to allow Lenin to continue his speech. The Presidium evidently didn't want to, but the assembly had nothing against it. Lenin, bored, was standing on the platform wiping his bald spot with a handkerchief; recognizing me from a distance he nodded to me gaily. I heard comments around me: "Talks sense, hey?" one soldier said to the other.
> By a majority vote the assembly ordered that Lenin be allowed to finish speaking. The ice was broken: Lenin and his principles had begun penetrating even the nucleus of the Praetorians.[47]

In the Congress of Peasants' Soviets, Lenin got only 20 votes, against the 810 received by Chernov, and Kerensky's 804. But the latter became more and more open enemies of the peasant revolutionary movement, while Lenin was completely in tune with it.

Lenin's identification with the oppressed

There was nothing more foreign to Lenin than the aristocratic attitude of Liberal-Mensheviks towards the "dark" *muzhik.* One has only to compare Lenin's position with, let us say, that of the left Menshevik Sukhanov. Sukhanov's writing is full of disdain for the crudity of the peasantry.

> Out of the trenches and obscure holes and corners had crept utterly crude and ignorant people whose devotion to the revolution was spite and despair, while their "socialism" was hunger and an unendurable longing for rest. Not bad material for experiments but—those experiments would be risky.[48]

How horrible the peasant in uniform looks:

> right there, over the very cradle, at the very helm of the revolution there stood the peasantry, in all its terrible mass, and holding a rifle into the bargain. It was declaring: "I am the lord not only of the country, not only of the Russian state, but of the revolution, which could not have been accomplished without me"....The army's direct participation in the revolution was no more than a form of peasant interference in the revolutionary process. From my point of view, that of a marxist and internationalist, it was profoundly harmful.[49]

In Sukhanov's eyes, Lenin's support of the peasants was a capitulation to anarchism.

> Lenin, by "giving the peasants the land at once" and preaching seizure, was in fact subscribing to anarchist tactics and an SR program. Both one and the other were pleasing and understandable to the peasant, who was far from being a fanatical upholder of marxism. But both one and the other had been railed at night and day by the marxist Lenin for at least fifteen years. Now this was flung aside. To please the peasants and be understood by them Lenin became both an anarchist and an SR.[50]

On the contrary, as early as 1905, Lenin had understood how to learn from the *muzhik* and to perceive the heartbeat of the revolutionary democrat even behind the peasants' monarchist exterior.[51]

He felt with the peasants who were rising from the depths, who, after centuries of oppression and darkness, were aroused for the first time by the thunder of revolution to assert themselves as human beings. He quoted with approval a letter from a peasant to the Moscow Bolshevik daily, *Sotsial-Demokrat*: "'[W]e must,' says the letter, 'press the bourgeoisie harder to make them burst at the seams.... But things will turn out badly if we don't press the bourgeoisie hard enough.'"[52]

Clouds on the horizon

However, there were dark clouds on the horizon. The Bolsheviks failed completely in their efforts to organize the agricultural workers into trade unions. Soviets of agricultural workers became important only in a very few localities, mainly in the Baltic provinces. To run ahead of our story, the estates—even those worked as large-scale units—were mostly broken up and not preserved as model farms, as Lenin wanted. In the summer and autumn of 1918, the Bolsheviks made a brief concerted effort to organize the rural poor in separate bodies—in Committees of Poor Peasants. The committees survived for only a few months before the Bolsheviks had to disband them.

Rosa Luxemburg argued prophetically, shortly after the October Revolution, that a socialist land policy must aim to encourage the socialization of agricultural production:

> [O]nly the nationalization of the large landed estates, as the technically most advanced and most concentrated means and methods of agrarian production, can serve as the point of departure for the socialist mode of production on the land. Of course, it is not necessary to take away from the small peasant his parcel of land, and we can with confidence leave him to be won over voluntarily by the superior advantages of social production and to be persuaded of the advantages first of union in cooperatives and then finally of inclusion in the general socialized economy as a whole. Still, every socialist economic reform on the land must obviously begin with large and medium land ownership. Here the property right must first of all be turned over to the nation, or to the state, which, with a socialist government, amounts to the same thing; for it is this alone which affords the possibility of organizing agricultural production in accord with the requirements of interrelated, large-scale social production.

The Bolsheviks did the opposite: they gave the land to the individualistic peasants:

> Formerly there was only a small caste of noble and capitalist landed proprietors and a small minority of rich village bourgeoisie to oppose a socialist reform on the land. And their expropriation by a revolutionary mass movement of the people is mere child's play. But now, after the "seizure," as an opponent of any attempt at socialization of agrarian production, there is an enormous, newly developed and powerful mass of owning peasants who will defend their newly won property with tooth and nail against every socialist attack.[53]

This isolation of a small working class in a sea of antagonistic, backward, petty-capitalist peasants, proved to be crucially important in Stalin's rise to power. Rosa Luxemburg's estimate of the Bolshevik land policy shows true insight into the situation in the

Russian Revolution, and points out the dangers frequently inherent in their policies. But the situation did not give the Bolsheviks any choice about the revolutionary land policy they implemented: acceding to the democratic, spontaneous wish of the peasants to distribute the land expropriated from the landlords.

The fact that the agricultural workers did not act *independently* from the property-owning peasants testified to the backwardness of capitalism in Russia. The fact that at the same time the agrarian revolution was so strong and drew in all layers of the peasantry showed how far capitalist development *had* taken place, and had come into conflict with the old forms of landed property.

The prospective conflict between the mass of the Russian property-owning peasantry and the small proletariat, Lenin knew, could lead to great difficulties in the future. However, he believed that it could be overcome by the international spread of the proletarian revolution.

CHAPTER 12

LENIN AND WORKERS' CONTROL

Just as Lenin gave a lead to the peasants and soldiers by calling on them to act, to act immediately, and to be self-reliant, so he was able to relate even more directly and intimately to the industrial workers in their struggle. Whereas the peasants were striving for land and peace, and the soldiers for peace and land, the proletariat was striving for workers' control in industry and peace.

The complete collapse of discipline in the factories was both a condition and a result of the revolutionary situation. So the workers' struggle to defend their wages and conditions inevitably escalated to the throwing out of hated factory owners and foremen, and the forcible keeping open of plants that the owners wished to close. Their struggle for workers' control locked in with the victorious October Revolution.

The rise of factory committees

During the February Revolution and the following few days, a feverish organization of factory committees took place all over Petrograd. Throughout the city, in diverse ways and under a variety of names, committees of workers were quickly set up. At the Thornton textile mills, a strike committee served as the nucleus of the factory committee elected on February 26, 1917, a day before the Petrograd Soviet was formed; the workers of the Treugolnik rubber factory and of the Petrograd pipe factory chose their committees while meeting to elect delegates to the soviet; in other enterprises the delegates to the city or district soviets also served as factory-committee members, together with additional representatives from the various shops; in the vast Putilov metalworks, the Peterhoff District Soviet acted as factory committee until one could be organized.

The enthusiastic organization of factory committees spread quickly from the capital to the provinces. As early as February 28, a Moscow textile mill held simultaneous elections for a workers' committee and for delegates to the Moscow Soviet, and during the next three days other committees were formed in the largest plants. By the end of March, factory committees had taken root in virtually every sizeable enterprise in Moscow and its suburbs. It was not very long before they existed in every industrial center of European Russia, from Minsk to Baku, from Kiev to Ekaterinburg, appearing first in the larger establishments, then, within a very short time, taking root in all but the very smallest.[1]

The first battle in which the factory committees were involved was the achievement of the eight-hour day. Of a hundred motions at factory workers' meetings for the period March 3–28, 51 percent demanded an eight-hour day.[2]

On March 5, the Petrograd Soviet adopted a resolution by 1,170 to 30 calling on all workers to return to work.[3] The workers reacted in their own way. In Vyborg, they prepared a demonstration against the soviet decision. They decided that it was null and void as long as their demands for an eight-hour day, a pay raise, etc., had not been met. Strikes continued to paralyze about ten firms. On March 8, the Menshevik *Rabochaia Gazeta* appealed to the strikers, claiming that they were discrediting the soviet by not obeying it. On March 10, the Menshevik newspaper recalled the lessons of 1905: not to rush things, to get well organized before making any demands. On March 14, the Soviet Propaganda Commission launched a new appeal in *Izvestiia*, aimed this time at the streetcar workers and the transportation industry. "Don't wait till Monday to go back to work," implored the soviet. It promised to intervene if the heads of firms made no concessions. On March 21, in the workers' section of the soviet, the Menshevik Bogdanov noted that the return to work was going badly and that it would probably continue to do so if working conditions did not improve. The soviet then undertook to negotiate with management in the capital. Casting caution to the wind, the latter accepted the eight-hour day, and the formation of factory committees and grievance committees. Identical agreements were reached at Saratov and in other provincial cities.[4]

However, the workers were not limiting their demands to the eight-hour day, higher wages, or better working conditions. On March 4, the workers of the Skorokhod shoe factory in Petrograd also demanded the recognition of their factory committee and the right to control the hiring and firing of labor. In the Petrograd radio-telegraph factory, a workers' committee was organized expressly to "work out rules and norms of the internal life of the factory," while other factory committees were elected mainly to adjust work rules or to supervise the activities of the administration. In short, the workers' demands for better conditions of labor were accompanied by an equally pressing claim to a role in directing the operation of their enterprises.[5]

An incipient form of workers' control arose overnight among the committees of strong factories, first of all in the state-owned armament plants.

> It was in precisely these factories that the "workers' council" experience after February was fullest. Supervisors, foremen, and floor managers were largely elected by the workers. This was partly due to the fact that the former management had seen itself as agents of the Tsarist government and therefore went to ground in February, but it was also partly because the highly skilled ordnance workers thought they could manage capitalist production, at shop-floor level at least, better than their bosses.[6]

The metal industry of Petrograd, devoted almost exclusively to the war effort, employed nearly 60 percent of the workers in the capital. The largest of its factories was operated by the Artillery and Naval Departments, and contained about a quarter of the Petrograd proletariat. Early in March, a group of fifteen workers' representatives from factories of the Artillery and Navy Departments recognized the need for cooperation among the factory committees of all state establishments, and called for the introduction of workers' control over production.[7] This meeting was the prelude to a conference on March 13, which included factory-committee representatives of the twelve largest metalworks under the Artillery Department, employing approximately one hundred thousand workers. The delegates to this earliest factory-committee conference—the forerunner of a series of citywide conferences in 1917—demanded official recognition by the government of the workers' committees and the eight-hour day, and called for workers' control over the activities of management.[8]

At a conference of state factories on April 2, a resolution was passed to give the factory committees a voice in the hiring of management personnel and the right to examine the accounts and correspondence of the enterprises. To counteract the movement for workers' control, the provisional government issued a decree on

April 23 establishing factory committees. The aim of the decree was to divert workers into regular, safe channels of collaboration with management, in the solution of the economic problems facing the country during the war. The function of the factory committees was defined thus:

> (a) representation of the workers to the administration of the enterprise on questions concerning relations between the employers and workers, as, for example, on salaries, working hours, rules of internal organization, etc.; (b) settlement of questions concerning internal relations among the workers of the enterprise; (c) representation of the workers in their relations with government and public institutions; (d) cultural and educational activity among the workers of the enterprise and other measures designed to improve their existence....
> Meetings called by the committee shall, as a general rule, be held outside of working hours.[9]

The statutes of the provisional government, inspired by the Menshevik and SR leaders of the soviet, were intended to bring about close collaboration between labor and management. They certainly did not include even a mention of the committee's right to assume managerial functions or control of the factory.[10]

Lenin was very quick to give vigorous support to the factory committees. Writing on May 17, he endorsed the slogan of "workers' control," declaring that "the workers must demand the immediate establishment of *genuine* control, to be exercized by the *workers themselves.*"[11]

To start with, unfortunately, the Bolsheviks had little influence in the factory committees. The Putilov armament factory, with thirty thousand workers, which throughout February had been seething with discontent and had staged several strikes and demonstrations, formed a "workers' committee" on February 28. On March 2, however, this committee placed the administration of the factory in the hands of the Peterhoff District Committee of the Petrograd Soviet, in which only eight or nine of the thirty elected members were Bolsheviks. During the first half of April, the Putilov workers, who were threatened with dismissal owing to a shortage of fuel, formed a factory committee of twenty-two, of whom only four were Bolsheviks.[12]

However, the factory committees, the focus of the rising revolutionary forces, were closer to the rank and file than the soviets and thus far to their left; as a result, they quickly came under the domination of the Bolshevik Party.

The First Conference of Petrograd Factory Committees, convened on May 30, was overwhelmingly influenced by the Bolsheviks. It was attended by 568 delegates from 236 factories employing 337,464 workers. Its agenda included reports on the state of industry in Petrograd, and discussions on the control and regulation of production, the supply of factories with required materials, and relations with the trade unions, cooperatives, and other workers' organizations.

The Menshevik minister of labor, Skobolev, opened the debate with a plea for state control of industry. He declared: "We find ourselves in the bourgeois stage of revolution. The transfer of enterprises into the hands of the people will not at the present time assist the revolution."

As the revolution was bourgeois, what was needed was the regulation of industry by the government in cooperation with the industrialists and the workers' organizations. "The regulation and control of industry," said Skobolev, "is not a matter for a particular class. It is a task for the state. Upon the individual class, especially the working class, lies the responsibility for helping the state in its organizational work."[13]

The Menshevik Chervanin, in the name of the Executive Committee of the Petrograd Soviet, elaborated further: "We can stop the growing catastrophe and restore economic life to normal only by planned interference of the state in economic life"; state regulation of the distribution of raw materials, fuel, and equipment to industry was necessary. Chervanin also called for state regulation of the distribution of consumer goods to the population, control over banking, and the compulsory formation of trusts in basic branches of industry. His resolution further demanded the fixing of prices, profits, and wages, and an increase in the taxation of the capitalists.[14]

In opposition to state control of industry, Zinoviev, for the Bolsheviks, moved a resolution on workers' control drafted by Lenin. It called for the institution of control "by means of a series of carefully considered measures, introduced gradually but without delay, leading to the complete regulation of production and distribution of goods by the workers." At least two-thirds of the votes in the organs of control would be reserved for the workers; commercial books were to be opened for inspection; a workers' militia and universal labor duty were to be instituted; and the war was to be brought to a swift conclusion. Economic control, moreover, was linked with political power, for Zinoviev also called for the transfer of the state to the soviets in order to assure the transfer of industrial control to the workers. The conference adopted Lenin's resolution, slightly amended, by 297 votes to 21, with 44 abstentions.[15]

As time passed, the factory committees' movement sharpened its conception of workers' control. Thus the Second Conference of Factory Committees of Petrograd and its environs, which took place on August 7–12, spelled out clearly the meaning of workers' control over production:

> It was the duty of the factory committee to…work out the rules of internal order—the organization of working time, wages, the hiring and firing and leave of workers and employees, etc.[16]

Factory committees should control the managers: they should have

> control over the composition of the administration, and over the dismissal of the members of the administration who cannot guarantee normal relations with the workers, or who are incompetent for other reasons.

A note adds:

> All members of the factory administration can enter into service only with the consent of the factory committee.[17]

The employers' offensive

After the defeat of the Bolsheviks in the July Days (see chapter 14 below), the employers thought that an opportunity was offered to cut the factory committees down to size. The metallurgical section of the Moscow Society of Manufacturers distributed a circular forbidding payment of wages for time spent in factory-committee work. In Petrograd, the owner of a smelting shop boldly announced that "there can be no workers' committee in the factory, and none will be recognized by the office," a declaration clearly in defiance of the decree of April 23 on the formation of factory committees. But such outright attempts to undermine the committees were rare, even during the reaction following the July demonstrations. Instead, the owners concentrated on curbing workers' control. They argued that the decree of April 23 had legalized the workers' committees, but had not given them the right to exercize control over production or, for that matter, to organize militias. In mid-July, the Petrograd Society of Manufacturers branded as "illegal" both workers' control and workers' demands that their militia be paid by the employers. Similar opinions were voiced by business organizations in other cities, notably in Kharkov, where opposition to workers' control was particularly intense.[18]

The newly formed All-Russian Central Society of Manufacturers resolved to issue "guiding instructions for the removal of factory-committee interference with the authority of the factory administration"; a Conference of Industrialists of Southern Russia maintained that the survival of industry was possible only if hiring and firing remained an exclusive right of the entrepreneur; and the Main Committee of United Industry forbade payment of wages to factory-committee members for time spent in committee work. Individual owners followed suit by withholding pay from committee members and by declining to provide space for committee meetings (in violation of the April 23 decree).[19]

The employers also undertook industrial sabotage—lockouts and factory closures. John Reed, who, as an American correspondent, had access to the most diverse circles, writes:

> The secretary of the Petrograd branch of the Cadet Party told me that the breakdown of the country's economic life was part of a campaign to discredit the revolution. An allied diplomat, whose name I promised not to mention, confirmed this from his own knowledge. I know of certain coal-mines near Kharkov which were fired and flooded by their owners, of textile factories at Moscow whose engineers put the machinery out of order when they left, of railroad officials caught by the workers in the act of crippling locomotives.[20]

Output in the Putilov factory fell very steeply, as can be seen from the following table[21]:

	June 1916	June 1917
	(tons)	(tons)
Mild steel	3,873	1,114
Cast steel	5,768	1,908
Pig iron	1,133	730
Copper	54	25
Steel goods	567	315

By the second half of October, some ten thousand Putilov workers were laid off.[22]

In Petrograd as a whole, twenty-five thousand workers lost their jobs in the first fortnight of September. In the Moscow and neighbouring *guberniias* fifty factories employing fifty thousand men closed down.[23] In Krivoi Rog and the Donetz basin, conflicts over workers' control and labor conditions, aggravated by a serious breakdown in transport and shortages of fuel, materials, and skilled workers, forced two hundred mines to cease operation by September.

The nation's output of steel fell off drastically.[24] Of sixty-five blast furnaces in the south, from only thirty-four to forty-four were in use, and even these were not working at full pressure. Of 102 Martin furnaces, only fifty-five were in use in October 1917. The rail-rolling works were only producing at 55 percent of their capacity.[25] The textile industry also approached a state of collapse.

A well-known industrialist, P.P. Riabushinsky, addressing a congress of businessmen in Moscow on August 3, let slip a phrase about "the bony hand of hunger," which "would grasp by the throat the members of the different committees and Soviets" and bring them to their senses. This phrase obtained wide circulation, and had an effect not unlike Marie Antoinette's "Let them eat cake!"

What answer to the employers' offensive was proposed by the leaders favoring compromise? Their solution was class collaboration. This fitted in perfectly with their attitude to state control of industry and their support of the war effort.

Conciliation between classes

On August 22, Skobolev issued a circular that stated:

> The right of hiring and firing of all...employees and workers belongs to owners of these plants.
>
> Coercive measures on the part of workers for purposes of dismissal or employment of certain persons are regarded as actions to be criminally punished.

He pointed out that, according to information reaching the Ministry of Labor, conferences and meetings were frequently held in many factories, mills, and mines during working hours, as a result of which work in the plants was disrupted. He notified the commissars and factory inspectors that, in accordance with the provisional government's law of April 23,

> conferences called by workers' committees must take place after working hours.... It is the duty of every worker to devote his energies to intensive labor and not to lose one minute of working time.... The Minister of Labor points out that the administration of plants must not allow workers' meetings during working hours which are detrimental to production in the plants. Moreover, the administration has

the right to make deductions from pay for loss of working time.[26]

Skobolev's two circulars, designed to curb the factory committees were issued on August 22 and 28, while General Kornilov was advancing on Petrograd! (See chapter 16 below.)

A few weeks later, the Special Council on Defense issued a circular stating:

> The owner of a plant is always at the head of the factory, and workers have no right to interfere with the actions of plant administration. Far less do they have the right to change them. In hiring and firing of workers, the existing statutes on this matter must be strictly adhered to.[27]

The acting minister of trade and industry, V. Stepanov, went a step further when he declared:

> [T]he use of the rights of strike and lockout should be suspended for the sake of the country's good. The conflicts should be made subject to a thorough analysis and solved by conciliatory institutions especially organized for the purpose.[28]

A similar conciliatory mitigation of the class struggle was proposed by *Izvestiia:*

> [T]he struggle between workers and employers under the circumstances of revolution and war cannot be conducted wholly in the same manner as under normal peacetime conditions.
>
> The point is that the wartime situation and the revolution force both sides to exercize extreme caution in utilizing the sharper weapons of class struggle—strikes and lockouts.
>
> These circumstances have made it necessary and possible to settle all disputes between employers and workers by means of negotiations and agreements, rather than by open conflict. Chambers of conciliation serve this purpose.... General problems must be resolved by an agreement reached between an association of employers and elected organs of the proletariat. Individual problems must be resolved by an agreement reached between the workers of the individual enterprises and their employers.... And both sides must abide unquestioningly by decisions delivered by the chambers.[29]

Imagine: revolution—the most extreme form of the class struggle—is not compatible with strikes and lockouts! Chambers of conciliation to contain the revolution!

The Skobolev circulars and the Kornilov insurrection prompted the Petrograd factory committees to summon a third all-city conference on September 10. Apart from the appearance of a new minister of labor, the Menshevik Kolokolnikov, the more moderate socialists were without a significant voice at the one-day gathering. With great

animosity, a Bolshevik speaker (Evdokimov) demanded the abrogation of the Skobolev circulars, condemned the decision of the Main
Committee of United Industry to suspend wages of men engaged in
factory-committee duties, and attacked Kolokolnikov for his negative policy on workers' control. Kolokolnikov's reply was virtually a
carbon copy of his predecessor's address to the First Petrograd Conference three months earlier. He declared that the present revolution
was not socialist but democratic, and thus could not move forward
from the capitalist mode of production to workers' control. Control
was required, Kolokolnikov admitted, but it had to be performed on
a statewide scale by "public-state organs." The hiring and firing of
labor was a right of management, and could be controlled by the
factory committees only if they became local trade-union organs.[30]

A Bolshevik resolution called for the nullification of Skobolev's
August circulars, the extension of factory-committee work, the rejec-
tion of the "fatal policy" of conciliation, and the removal from power
of the counterrevolutionary bourgeoisie.[31] It was almost unanimously
passed, with 198 votes for, 13 against, and 18 abstentions.[32]

The increasing "excesses" of workers

The workers were increasingly blaming the employers for the economic catastrophe the country was facing. They accused the entre-
preneurs of perpetuating a frightful war in order to reap huge profits,
even though such short-sighted avarice foredoomed the industrial
machine to eventual breakdown. The control commissions of factory
committees in Serpukhov (in Moscow province) disclosed that some
textile mills concealed the extent of their profits by keeping two sets
of books. Workers' committees elsewhere uncovered numerous cases
in which owners were speculating in the meager supplies of fuel, raw
materials, and equipment still available. Determined to weed out
such instances of "sabotage," the committees demanded the right to
make inventories of all available stores of goods and materials and to
inspect deliveries to and from the enterprises.

The lockouts and shutdowns often precipitated physical clashes
between labor and management. Violence against administrative
personnel took a curiously similar form in different parts of the
country. Members of the factory committee of the Volga mill in
Ivanovo-Voznesensk threw a sack over a mechanic and carted him
away in a wheelbarrow.[33] The director of a car plant in Moscow
and his assistant were also taken away in a wheelbarrow, while the

management threatened to close the shop.[34] The workers in a
Kharkov foundry seized their director, poured a bucket of heavy oil
mixed with lead over his head, and carried the unfortunate man
out of the plant amid shouts of "Hooray!"[35]

Industrialists were complaining more and more often that the
situation in the factories had reached a point "exceedingly close to
industrial anarchy."[36]

A conference of factory committees in the metal plants of
Kharkov decided on June 27 "to satisfy the demands of the workers with their own revolutionary power," adding:

> If the factory owners within the course of five days refuse to satisfy
> these demands, the directors are to be removed from the enterprises
> and are to be replaced by elected engineers.

When the management of the Helfferich-Sade factory, in the same
city, wanted to close the plant in September because of a labor dispute, the factory committee decided that work should continue,
under the direction of a special commission. And at the large locomotive factory in Kharkov more forceful measures were used. The harassed Kerensky received a telegram from the plant on September 20
to the effect that "the director and all the administrative personnel of
the factory have been arrested by the workers. The local military and
civil authorities are completely inactive." How often that last sentence must have been used during 1917, when formal legality and the
rights of private property were at a very great discount.[37]

In the Bokovo-Khrustalsk region of the Donetz coal basin, the
manager of a mine belonging to the Russian Anthracite Company,
engineer Pechuk, was beaten up at a session of the local Soviet of
Workers' Deputies, at the initiative and following the incitement of
the president of the soviet, Pereverzev. At the Mikhailov mine of
Donchenko in the same region, the same Pereverzev arrested one of
the owners, Iakovlev. There were widespread searches of the homes
of mine employees in the Bokovo-Khrustalsk region, and the employers were terrorized and left the mines. From other regions of
the Donetz basin came reports of increasing excesses, beating and
robbing of the mine owners, all suggesting that the anarchical and
riotous movement was spreading widely in the area. The local authorities were completely inactive.[38]

A list of workers' "excesses," compiled by a newspaper, indicated that the engineer, like the army officer or the landlord, sometimes received short shrift from mobs of enraged workers:

At the Lisva factory, the engineer Lepchukov was killed by a shot in the back. At the Sulinsk factory, at the demand of the workers, the managing director of the factory, engineer Gladkov, was arrested for refusing to increase wages by a hundred percent. In Makeevka, at the factory of the Russian Mining and Metallurgical Union Company, a worker in the foundry fired two shots at the chief of the foundry, a French citizen, the engineer Remy. At the factory of the Nikopol Mariupol Company, a mob of workers beat up the engineer Yasinsky and took him out on a wheelbarrow. At the Alexandrovsk factory of the Briansk Company in Ekaterinoslav province, the assistant director, Beneshevitch, the chief of the railroad department, Shkurenko, and some employees have been removed. At the factory of the Novorossisk Company in Yuzovka, the workers have cut off electrical lighting in the apartments of the senior employees and the factory management.[39]

By October, some form of workers' control existed in the great majority of Russian enterprises. There were even sporadic instances of factory committees ejecting their employers and engineers and then endeavoring to run the plants themselves, sending delegations in search of fuel, raw materials, and financial aid from workers' committees in other establishments.[40]

Lenin's policy

Basically Lenin's line was very simple indeed. It fitted perfectly the objective conditions, the economic disintegration of Russia, and the subjective experiences of the industrial workers. It echoed workers' feelings, and raised the instinctive urges of the workers to a generalized political level.

Decisive steps *must* be taken towards the overthrow of capitalism. They must be taken ably and gradually, relying *only* on the class-consciousness and organized activity of the overwhelming majority of the workers and poor peasants.

...cautious, gradual, well-considered, yet firm and direct steps towards socialism.[41]

What is necessary in Russia is not to invent "new reforms," not to make "plans" for "comprehensive" changes. Nothing of the kind. This is how the situation is depicted—deliberately depicted in a false light—by the capitalists, the Potresovs, the Plekhanovs, who shout against "introducing socialism" and against the "dictatorship of the proletariat." The situation in Russia in fact is such that the unprecedented burdens and hardships of the war, the unparalleled and very real danger of economic dislocation and famine have of themselves suggested the way out, have of themselves not only pointed out, but advanced reforms and other changes as absolutely necessary. These changes must be the grain monopoly, control over production and distribution, restriction of the issue of paper money, a fair exchange of grain for manufactured goods, etc.[42]

In a most systematic way, Lenin sums up his ideas on the way forward for the proletariat in the industrial field in his incisive pamphlet, "The Impending Catastrophe and How to Combat It," written between September 10 and 14. He starts by describing the objective situation in Russia.

> Unavoidable catastrophe is threatening Russia. The railways are incredibly disorganized and the disorganization is progressing. The railways will come to a standstill. The delivery of raw materials and coal to the factories will cease. The delivery of grain will cease. The capitalists are deliberately and unremittingly sabotaging (damaging, stopping, disrupting, hampering) production, hoping that an unparalleled catastrophe will mean the collapse of the republic and democracy, and of the Soviets and proletarian and peasant associations generally, thus facilitating the return to a monarchy and the restoration of the unlimited power of the bourgeoisie and the landowners.
>
> The danger of a great catastrophe and of famine is imminent.[43]
>
> Everybody says this. Everybody admits it. Everybody has decided it is so.
>
> Yet nothing is being done.
>
> Six months of revolution have elapsed. The catastrophe is even closer. Unemployment has assumed a mass scale. To think that there is a shortage of goods in the country, the country is perishing from a shortage of food and labor, although there is a sufficient quantity of grain and raw materials, and yet in such a country, at so critical a moment, there is mass unemployment! What better evidence is needed to show that after six months of revolution (which some call a great revolution, but which so far it would perhaps be fairer to call a rotten revolution), in a democratic republic, with an abundance of unions, organs, and institutions which proudly call themselves "revolutionary-democratic," absolutely *nothing* of any importance has actually been done to avert catastrophe, to avert famine? We are nearing ruin with increasing speed. The war will not wait and is causing increasing dislocation in every sphere of national life.[44]
>
> Control, supervision, and accounting are the prime requisites for combating catastrophe and famine. This is indisputable and universally recognized. And it is just what *is not being done* from fear of encroaching on the supremacy of the landowners and capitalists, on their immense, fantastic, and scandalous profits, profits derived from high prices and war contracts (and, directly or indirectly, nearly everybody is now "working" for the war), profits about which everybody knows and which everybody sees, and over which everybody is sighing and groaning.[45]

Control measures spelled out

The "control measures are known to all and easy to take."[46]

We shall see that all a government would have had to do, if its name of revolutionary-democratic government were not merely a joke, would have been to decree, in the very first week of its existence, the adoption of the principal measures of control, to provide for strict and severe punishment to be meted out to capitalists who fraudulently evaded control, and to call upon the population itself to exercise supervision over the capitalists and see to it that they scrupulously observed the regulations on control—and control would have been introduced in Russia long ago. These principal measures are:

1. Amalgamation of all banks into a single bank, and state control over its operations, or nationalization of the banks.

2. Nationalization of the syndicates, i.e., the largest, monopolistic capitalist associations (sugar, oil, coal, iron and steel, and other syndicates).

3. Abolition of commercial secrecy!

4. Compulsory syndication (i.e., compulsory amalgamation into associations) of industrialists, merchants, and employers generally.

5. Compulsory organization of the population into consumers societies, or encouragement of such organization, and the exercise of control over it.[47]

Nationalization of the banks:

Only by nationalizing the banks *can* the state *put itself in a position* to know where and how, whence and when, millions and billions of rubles flow. And only control over the banks, over the center, over the pivot and chief mechanism of capitalist circulation, would make it possible to organize real and not fictitious control over all economic life, of the production and distribution of staple goods, and organize that "regulation of economic life" which otherwise is inevitably doomed to remain a ministerial phrase designed to fool the common people.[48]

Nationalization of the syndicates:

The banks and the more important branches of industry and commerce have become inseparably merged. This means, on the one hand, that it is impossible to nationalize the banks alone, without proceeding to create a state monopoly of commercial and industrial syndicates (sugar, coal, iron, oil, etc.) and without nationalizing them. It means, on the other hand, that if carried out in earnest, the regulation of economic activity would demand the simultaneous nationalization of the banks and the syndicates.[49]

Abolition of commercial secrecy:

Unless commercial secrecy is abolished…control over production and distribution will remain an empty promise…. This is the very key to all control. Here we have the most sensitive spot of capital, which is robbing the people and sabotaging production.[50]

We usually do not even notice how thoroughly we are permeated by anti-democratic habits and prejudices regarding the "sanctity" of bourgeois property. When an engineer or banker publishes the income and expenditure of a worker, information about his wages, and the productivity of his labor, this is regarded as absolutely legitimate and fair. Nobody thinks of seeing it as an intrusion into the "private life" of the worker, as "spying or informing" on the part of the engineer. Bourgeois society regards the labor and earnings of a wage-worker as *its* open book, any bourgeois being entitled to peer into it at any moment, and at any moment to expose the "luxurious living" of the worker, his supposed "laziness," etc.

Well, and what about reserve control? What if the unions of employees, clerks, and *domestic servants* were invited by a *democratic* state to verify the income and expenditure of capitalists, to publish information on the subject and to assist the government in combating concealment of incomes?

What a furious howl against "spying" and "informing" would be raised by the bourgeoisie![51]

Regulation of consumption:

At a time when the country is suffering untold calamities, a revolutionary-democratic policy would not confine itself to bread cards to combat the impending catastrophe but would add, firstly, the compulsory organization of the whole population in consumers' societies, for otherwise control over consumption cannot be fully exercised; secondly, labor service for the rich, making them perform without pay, secretarial and similar duties for these consumers' societies; thirdly, the equal distribution among the population of absolutely all consumer goods, so as really to distribute the burdens of the war equitably; fourthly, the organization of control in such a way as to have the poorer classes of the population exercise control over the consumption of the rich.[52]

In point of fact, the whole question of control boils down to who controls whom, i.e., which class is in control and which is being controlled.... We must resolutely and irrevocably, not fearing to break with the old, not fearing boldly to build the new, pass to control *over* the landowners and capitalists *by* the workers and peasants.[53*]

---

* Lenin dealt disdainfully with the Mensheviks who promised to squeeze the capitalists dry but did not suggest workers' control. He quoted Skobelev's promise that he would "take the profits from the tills of the bankers," to the extent of "one hundred percent," and commented:

"Our party is much more moderate. Its resolution demands much less than this, namely, the mere establishment of control over the banks and the 'gradual (just listen, the Bolsheviks are for gradualness!) introduction of a more just progressive tax on incomes and properties.'"

"Our party is more moderate than Skobelev.

"Skobelev dispenses immoderate, nay, extravagant promises, without understanding the conditions required for their practical realization.

"That is the crux of the matter...

The struggle against economic catastrophe must be waged jointly with the struggle against the war and the struggle for workers' power.

> The war has created such an immense crisis, has so strained the material and moral forces of the people, has dealt such blows at the entire modern social organization that humanity must now choose between perishing or entrusting its fate to the most revolutionary class for the swiftest and most radical transition to a superior mode of production.[55]

For Lenin, the battle for workers' control of industry was part and parcel of the fight for workers' power. "The systematic and effective implementation of all these measures is possible only if all the power in the state passes to the proletarians and semi-proletarians."[56]

Again and again he repeats: "Control without power is an empty phrase."[57] "All power to the Soviets" was the slogan of the Bolsheviks in the political sphere, while "workers' control" was their slogan in the economic sphere.

For Lenin, the position was quite straightforward. In his own words describing the attitude of an enlightened Petrograd worker:

> The whole world is divided into two camps: "us," the working people, and "them," the exploiters.... "We squeezed 'them' a bit; 'they' won't dare to lord it over us as they did before. We'll squeeze again—and chuck them out altogether," that's how the worker thinks and feels.[58]

The rise in the influence of Bolshevism

The influence of the Bolsheviks rose very unevenly. They first achieved domination in the factory committees of Petrograd. From these, their influence spread into the workers' section of the soviet, and then to the soviet as a whole. At the same time, the influence of Bolshevism spread geographically, from Petrograd to the provinces.

At the First Conference of Factory Committees of Petrograd (May 31–June 5), as we have already pointed out, the Bolsheviks had an overwhelming influence; their main resolution was adopted by a large majority. Almost at the same time, at the Third Conference of Trade Unions assembled on June 20, the Bolsheviks ac-

---

"Less promises, Citizen Skobelev, and more practicalness. Less rhetoric and more understanding as to how to get down to business.

"And get down to business we can and should immediately, without a day's delay, if we are to save the country from an inevitable and terrible catastrophe. But the whole thing is that the...provisional government does not want to get down to business; and even if it wanted to, it could not, for it is fettered by a thousand chains which safeguard the interests of capital.'[54]

counted for 36.4 percent of the delegates.[59] At the All-Russian Congress of Soviets, which met on June 3, the Bolsheviks had 105 delegates out of a total of 777.

The unevenness between Petrograd and the provinces was also very great. At the Moscow Conference of Factory Committees, convened on July 23, the Bolsheviks were still a minority—they received 191 votes out of 682 for their policy.[60]

Because the Bolshevik influence was much greater among the industrial workers than in any other section of society, and because the factory committees were far closer to the rank and file than any other institution at the time, the Bolsheviks used the committees as a lever to influence other institutions—from the workers' section of the soviet to the soviet as a whole and the trade unions.

On the eve of the October Revolution, Lenin was coming to the view that the factory committees, and not the soviet, should serve as the instigators of insurrection. He told Ordzhonikidze:

> We must swing over the center of gravity to the factory committees. The factory committees must become the organs of insurrection. We must change our slogan, and say instead of "All power to the Soviets," "All power to the factory committees."[61]

Even though it turned out that the soviet did in fact play this role, the committees were of central importance to the victory of October.

Above all, for the Bolsheviks, the question of workers' control of industry was inseparable from the question of a proletarian seizure of power. This was stated very clearly by Trotsky in his speech to the All-Russian Conference of Factory Committees of October 17–22, a conference which Trotsky himself described as "the most direct and indubitable representation of the proletariat in the whole country."[62]*

> The proletariat must seize power. The army, the peasantry, and the navy all look to it with hope. And your organization, the factory committees, must become the champions of this idea. At the forthcoming Congress of Soviets, the questions of power, of peace, of land—all will be put point-blank. And when the Soviet gives the word, you in the localities must reply, "We are here!" Your reply must be a united "All power to the Soviets!"[63]

---

* Of the 167 delegates, 97 were Bolsheviks; there were 24 Socialist Revolutionaries (mostly left, who supported the Bolsheviks), 5 Maximalists, 1 Internationalist, and 21 non-party—all of these groups supporting the Bolsheviks; in opposition there were 13 Anarcho-syndicalists and 7 Mensheviks.

Lenin always considered the factory committees to be far more radical than the soviets and to the left of the Bolshevik Party. They were the main citadel of the proletariat.

The workers' movement that started after February, initially mainly by intensive organization accompanied by relatively fragmented conflicts on wages and hours, later developed into far more frequent and bitter strikes. The slogan of workers' control became increasingly put into practice by evictions and even arrests of unpopular factory managers and foremen, and by forcibly keeping open plants that the owners tried to close. Eventually the workers' industrial movement grew into the Bolshevik movement for proletarian political power.

CHAPTER 13

LENIN SUPPORTS THE REBELLIOUS
NATIONALITIES

The 1905 Revolution gave an impetus to national democratic revolutions in Persia, the Balkans, China, and India. The 1917 Revolution, with its much wider scope and depth, was inevitably bound to do the same, first and foremost within the borders of the Russian Empire itself.

In the tsarist empire, besides the seventy million Great Russians lived ninety million non-Russians; that is, 43 percent of the population was Russian and 57 percent non-Russian, including 7 percent Ukrainians, 6 percent Poles, and 4.5 percent White Russians. The oppression of the minority nationalities was harsh and crude, so much so as to make the national question in Russia an enormously explosive one.

The revolution, by bringing the masses into the arena, finally exhausted the patience of these oppressed groups. The establishment of formal national equality by the February Revolution brought out even more sharply the *actual* inequality, and spurred them on to fight even harder for their freedom. The continued existence of the same officials, the same law, enraged them as never before; and to be told, "Wait for the constituent assembly" only increased their irritation. Revolution is not a matter of patience. Why should the oppressed nationalities, who had suffered for centuries, trust the constituent assembly to be different in kind from the existing government and officials?

> During a revolution, millions and tens of millions of people learn in a week more than they do in a year of ordinary, somnolent life. For at the time of a sharp turn in the life of an entire people it becomes particularly clear what aims the various classes of the people are pursuing, what strength they possess, and what methods they use.[1]

The oppressed nationalities saw through the provisional government very easily. Its policy on nationalities, as in all other spheres, was vacillating and treacherous.

Finland

Finland became the first of the government's problems. Of all the nations in Russia, the Finland was the least underprivileged. At the end of the nineteenth century, Finland alone still retained a broad measure of self-rule. Indeed, in some respects, it had more democratic rights than Russia proper; Finland under the tsars presented the paradox of a subject nation possessing more political freedom than the people who ruled over it. It was a separate principality, which the Russian monarch governed in his capacity as Grand Duke. The Finns had complete control over the legislative institutions of the state. There was a bicameral legislative body, composed of a senate and a *Sejm*. The senate considered legislative projects and performed the function of the supreme court of the state. The *Sejm* was the highest legislative organ in the country. Called every five years on the basis of nationwide elections, it initiated and voted on legislation relevant to its domain. No law could become effective without its approval.[2]

The Finnish *Sejm* was the only parliament in the world in which the Social Democrats achieved a majority: 103 seats out of 200. On June 5, 1917, the *Sejm* issued a law declaring itself a sovereign power, except on questions of war and foreign policy.

At the All-Russian Congress of Soviets, a representative of the Finnish socialists appealed for support. He told the congress that the Finnish Social Democratic Party supported "the demand of the right to complete self-determination for Finland—in other words, the recognition by the Russian government of Finnish independence."

The Finnish people got no support from the provisional government.

> The provisional government has aroused the distrust of part of the Finns by delaying settlement of the question put forward by the senate, namely, that of increasing the right of the senate and the Finnish *Sejm*.

Formal equality was not enough, the Finnish socialist representative went on to say.

> The legal status has been reestablished in accord with the manifesto of March last, which assured us that our autonomy was secured. But this does not satisfy us. The Finnish people have been developed culturally, and the Finnish working class has become educated and class-conscious to such an extent that it cannot be satisfied with this declaration; it can-

not be satisfied with having achieved a legal status within the limits that already existed one hundred years.... Finland does not wish any longer to remain under Russia's protection and in the position of Russia's stepdaughter.... The Finnish people desire to be given the complete right of self-determination and, therefore, do not wish a Russian or English or German or any other imperialistic master.[3]

However, the Finnish Social Democrats did not receive a sympathetic response from the SR and Menshevik leaders of the soviet. The SR paper, *Volia Naroda,* said on July 16:

> [W]e reserve to the provisional government the right to accept and the right to reject any measures adopted by the Finnish *Sejm in so far as they go beyond the bounds permitted by autonomy and become measures the publication of which is the right only of a sovereign state.* Finland was not one of them. Likewise, the provisional government, both *de jure* and *de facto,* has the right to place its veto on all decisions of the *Sejm* that are obviously detrimental to the interests of the Russian state.... We recognize Finland's right to broad autonomy, the right to build its internal life independently. But in so far as this autonomy passes into a sovereign independence, in so far as the decisions of the *Sejm* contradict the interests of the Russian state and are to its detriment, we oppose and repudiate such attempts.[4]

Kerensky, who prided himself on being an "Iron Chancellor," spoke as follows:

> There are important circles in Finland which quite openly aspire to a complete separation from Russia and which imagine that it will be accomplished in the same way as the separation of Norway from Sweden, i.e., quite painlessly...this view is absolutely mistaken;.... Russia at the present moment is still sufficiently strong to defend the integrity of the remaining territory against anyone.[5]

And, trying to be more "diplomatic," to appear "liberal," he explained at a session of the soviet a couple of days later:

> [U]ntil the people's will has been expressed in the constituent assembly, the Russian provisional government cannot proclaim the independence of Finland because we do not consider ourselves as having autocratic power.[8]

In the face of the Finnish clamor for independence, on July 18, the provisional government dissolved the *Sejm. Izvestiia,* the paper of the executive of the soviet, hastened to justify the government's action:

> the leaders of the Finnish *Sejm* did not want to understand the sincerity of the provisional government's stand, they did not want to entrust the future of Finland to the Russian revolution, and they preferred to affirm the sovereign rights of Finland by an independent course....

> This may be the last time that the revolutionary democracy of Russia extends its fraternal hand to the Finnish people.[7]

The "fraternal hand" in the form of armed repression.

A general strike called by the Finnish Social Democrats brought sharply antagonistic comment from the SR and Menshevik leaders. Thus the Right Menshevik paper, *Den*, wrote:

> [I]nstead of lawfully appealing to the people, the Finnish socialists have suggested appealing to the rebellious instincts of the ignorant mob. They called on the workers [to start] a general strike, while the city mobs were solving the food question by attacking the warehouses.

The government reacted violently:

> Having heard the report of M.A. Stakhovich, Governor General of Finland, and bearing in mind that intense propaganda is being conducted in favor of an illegal convocation of the *Sejm*, the provisional government has authorized the Governor General of Finland to prevent in every possible way, [any] open disregard of Russia's interests, or [any] breach of peace and order in the state, and if necessary, to stop at nothing to restore the same. Similarly, no strikes must be permitted that may affect or undermine the military interests of Russia.[8]

The governor general, a Cadet, forbade the meeting of the dissolved *Sejm*, and ordered the doors of the building to be sealed. The Social Democratic members of the *Sejm* broke the seals, and sat for about two hours on September 15, passing controversial acts.

The conflict between the Finnish people and the provisional government continued until the latter was swept away by the October Revolution.

Ukraine

A second, and far larger, thorn in the flesh of the provisional government was the Ukraine. On March 4, a group of Ukrainian intellectuals formed a Central Ukrainian Council, or *Rada,* in Kiev. The first act of the Rada was to greet Prince Lvov and "dear comrade Kerensky."

> *To the President of the Council of Ministers, Prince Lvov:* We hail in your name the first ministry of free Russia. We wish you complete success in the struggle for democracy. We are confident that the just demands of the Ukrainian people and her democratic intelligentsia will be fully satisfied.
> *To the Minister of Justice, A.F. Kerensky:* In your name, dear comrade, we warmly hail the dawn of the fulfilment of the national

hopes. To you who from the tribune of the State Duma proclaimed the slogan of Ukrainian autonomy, we entrust the guarding of the just demands of the Ukrainian people and her democratic intelligentsia. We have faith that henceforth there shall be no disinherited peoples and that the time is not far distant when our ancient aspirations for a free federation of free peoples will be fulfilled.[9]

The provisional government reciprocated by granting one concession to the Ukrainian nation. On March 14, it authorized the use of the Ukrainian language in Ukrainian schools in the Kiev district.[10]

But the national movement of the Ukrainians did not stand still. To start with, its claims were quite moderate, and were limited to a request for autonomy *within* the Russian state. Thus the Congress of the Ukrainian Socialist Revolutionary Party on April 4–5 "expressed itself in favor of the quickest possible implementation of the national and territorial autonomy of the Ukraine, with the guarantee of rights to the national minorities."[11] A similarly moderate demand for national autonomy was put forward by the Conference of the Ukrainian Social Democratic Party.[12]

The Rada also put very modest demands to the provisional government:

> Taking into consideration the unanimous demand for an autonomous Ukraine advanced by the Ukrainian democracy, we hope that the provisional government will express in some act its sympathetic attitude, in principle, toward this slogan.
>
> In order to familiarize the government thoroughly with the attitudes in the Ukraine and with the demands of the Ukrainian population, also to render the government practical assistance in introducing various measures called for by the unique life of the region, the creation of the post of special Commissar on Ukrainian Affairs in the provisional government is urgently needed.
>
> The Ukrainization of the elementary schools, approved by the provisional government, should also be applied to the secondary and higher schools, in the language used as well as the subjects of instruction.
>
> [Officials in] responsible administrative posts in the Ukraine, both civil and clerical, should be replaced with people who enjoy the confidence of the population, who speak their language and are familiar with their way of life....
>
> In order to raise the fighting strength of the army and restore discipline, it is necessary to carry out the measure of separating the Ukrainians into separate army units in the rear as well as, so far as possible, at the front.[13]

The provisional government rejected these demands as going too far.

Early in June, Kerensky forbade the holding of a Ukrainian soldiers' congress convoked by the Rada. The compromising leaders of the Soviet supported Kerensky's ban. Thus *Izvestiia* wrote on June 2:

> [P]rior to the meeting of the constituent assembly we have, as all Russia has, [but] one aim—not to permit disunity or the dispersion of the forces of the revolution. Prior to the constituent assembly we will not undertake any steps to seize national rights by way of a *fait accompli*... The Russian revolutionary democracy must raise its voice and point out to the Ukrainians that in declaring his opposition to the propitiousness of the Ukrainian military congress, A.F. Kerensky was expressing the adamant will of the revolutionary and democratic masses of the population, [and], in particular, the will of the army.[14]

The Ukrainians did not submit to Kerensky's bullying, or to the admonitions of the Petrograd Soviet. The Ukrainian soldiers' congress went ahead on June 5–10, representing 993,400 organized soldiers. In order to save the face of the government, Kerensky legalized the congress *ex post facto,* sending a congratulatory telegram which the assembled deputies greeted with disrespectful laughter.

In its first official manifesto or *Universal,* issued on June 10, the Rada still did not propose a complete break with the Russian state.

> Let there be a free Ukraine. Without separating from all of Russia, without breaking away from the Russian State, let the Ukrainian people on their own territory have the right to manage their own life. Let a national Ukrainian assembly *(Sejm),* elected by universal, equal, direct, and secret suffrage, establish order and a regime in the Ukraine. Only our Ukrainian assembly is to have the right to issue all laws which are to establish this regime.
>
> Those laws which will establish the regime throughout the entire Russian state must be issued by the All-Russian parliament.[15]

The Cadets reacted by describing the Ukrainian leaders as German agents. The SR and Menshevik leaders admonished them. Thus *Izvestiia* of June 16 wrote:

> Regardless of the language the workers speak, [or] their ethnic affiliations, once they become aware of their interests they cannot [help] but stand for the indivisibility of the state.... The revolutionary democracy of Russia stands for the indivisibility of the state. To split up a great state, created by a thousand years of historical development, means taking a big step backward.[16]

The SR paper, *Volia Naroda,* of June 17, declared: "The democracy of Russia must brand the steps of the Central Ukrainian *Rada* as illegal, mistaken, and dangerous."[17]

Chernov published in the central organ of his party an attack on the "irresponsible actions" of the Rada, for usurping the rights of the future constituent assembly; the course of the Rada, he declared, was "Leninism in the national question."[18]

Naturally the Ukrainian SRs—forming the largest party in the Rada—did not take kindly to the policy of the Great Russian SR party.

In order to try to mend relations with the Ukrainians, the provisional government sent a delegation to Kiev, made up of Kerensky, Tsereteli, and Tereshchenko. In the heated atmosphere of the Ukraine, the delegation took some steps towards a compromise. A statement agreed to between the *Rada* and the provisional government was drafted.

> To appoint a special organ, the General Secretariat, in the capacity of a higher organ for the administration of regional affairs in the Ukraine.... The government shall work through the designated organ in carrying out measures dealing with the life and administration of the region. Considering that questions such as the national and political organization of the Ukraine and the methods of resolving the land question in the Ukraine within the framework of the general principle of transfer of land to the workers must be settled by the constituent assembly the provisional government shall respond favorably to the elaboration of bills by the Ukrainian *Rada*, in such forms as the *Rada* itself finds correspond most closely to the interests of the region...for the purpose of submitting these bills to the constituent assembly.[19]

The agreement, although in the nature of a compromise, represented quite an achievement for the Rada. First, and foremost, it was recognized as the institution authorized to speak for the Ukrainian people. However, after the July offensive against the Bolsheviks, the provisional government veered sharply to the right on the Ukrainian question, as well as others.

On July 16, the Rada drafted a proposal elaborating the agreement of July 3,[20] but the government rejected it out of hand on August 4.[21] The reaction of the Rada was very sharp. It declared that the position of the provisional government:

> (1) is dictated by distrust toward the aspirations of the entire democracy of the Ukraine; (2) is imbued with the imperialist tendencies of the Russian bourgeoisie toward the Ukraine; (3) violates the agreement of the Ukrainian Central *Rada* with the provisional government of July 3.[22]

"When the time came for the government to redeem its pledge," declared the head of the Rada, Vinnichenko, "it turned out that the provisional government...is a petty cheat, who hopes to get rid of a great historic problem by swindling."[23]

Neither the government nor the compromising leaders could check the rise of the national spirit in the Ukraine. The millions of peasants awakened by the revolution demanded land. They started making themselves heard, and the only language they could use was their native one—Ukrainian. In this way the agrarian revolution and the national revolution were interwoven.

Other nationalities

In the east there were nations that were much more cruelly exploited and oppressed than the Finns, Ukrainians, and White Russians in the more cultured west. The people and tribes along the Volga, in the Caucasus, in Central Asia, were startled by the revolution. But the February regime did not change their actual situation at all. The best lands continued to be in the hands of landlords and wealthy Russian peasants. These colonialists fought hard for the unity of the Russian state. They displayed the maximum hatred and chauvinism towards the downtrodden native population. National antagonisms intersected in all directions with class antagonisms. The inexorable pressure of the masses for national liberation bore down on the weak and tottering February regime.

Even the most modest claims of the moderate representatives of the oppressed nationalities went unheeded by the provisional government. What utterance could have been more moderate than the speech of A. Topchibashev, representing Muslim organizations, to the Moscow State Conference (of August 12–15)?

> No sooner had the sun of freedom appeared over Russia than the Muslim people, having thrown off the hated chains of despotism took heart, and, rejoicing in the hope for a better life, took their place in the ranks of the most fervent supporters of the new regime that is based on democratic principles. [They acted] not only as supporters but as defenders of the provisional government which personifies this system and decided to give every support to all the measures that the supreme power of the nation should undertake.... The day is close when free, democratic Russia will realize the equality and fraternity of peoples, Muslims among them, and will show the world an example, unparalleled in the history of mankind, of respect to the rights of all peoples, inviting European nations to liberate all their subjected peoples, including the Muslim peoples in Europe, Asia, and Africa, on the basis of free self-determination. Then we will proclaim enthusiastically, in one voice: *ex oriente lux*!![24]

After this declaration of love for the provisional government, the Estonian representative, Pipp, spoke:

> We state that in questions of a general nature we stand for the complete realization of the measures outlined by the Russian democracy, and we will give every support to the revolutionary provisional government in this direction. But we consider it necessary to make a special note of one question of tremendous importance to the state—the nationality question.
>
> First of all, we must point out that the statement made by the head of the provisional government harbors no kind words toward us. On the contrary, we, non-Russian peoples, are being reminded of the possible accounting and of the magnanimous forgiveness for the absence of friendship at a time of danger. We consider that this attitude toward us is profoundly unjust, for our desire to satisfy the most vital and urgent national demands is not a destructive or centrifugal phenomenon, but the only correct and sound principle of state construction.... We consider it necessary...to proceed to the resolution of the nationality question. There can be no delays. No people can live by promises alone. The vagueness of the situation can only increase the spontaneous unrest among the people. The basic needs of the people must be given timely satisfaction. At the same time, preliminary work must be started for reorganizing the state on principles providing the highest guarantee of freedom and national self-determination in a democratic Russian republic based on the federal principle of a friendly family of Russian peoples, where autonomous regions—Estonia among them—would constitute equal members.[25]

This timid reproach and humble request produced very little sympathetic response even from the left of the hall—the Mensheviks and SRs. As for the right, General Kaledin answered the representations of the oppressed nationalities in no uncertain terms: "Russia must be an indivisible whole. All separatist tendencies must be nipped in the bud."[26]

As an epitaph on the national policy of the provisional government, we can quote the draft constitution drawn up by a special commission a few days before the October Revolution: "The Russian state is one and indivisible."[27]

Lenin's sympathy

Lenin felt a deep sympathy for the oppressed nationalities. He detested chauvinism, and especially abhorred the Great Russian variety. Above all, he was profoundly aware of the enormous revolutionary potential of the national movement against oppression.

He hated with the oppressed, loved with the oppressed, and

hoped and fought with the oppressed. He supported the struggle of the minority nationalities for freedom with all his strength of feeling while at the same time forging an international, united party of the proletariat.

With what passion Lenin attacked the role of the Great Russians as tyrants over the Ukrainian people:

> Accursed Tsarism made the Great Russians executioners of the Ukrainian people, and fomented in them a hatred for those who even forbade Ukrainian children to speak and study in their native tongue.
>
> Russia's revolutionary democrats, if they want to be truly revolutionary and truly democratic, must break with that past, must regain for themselves, for the workers and peasants of Russia, the brotherly trust of the Ukrainian workers and peasants. This cannot be done without full recognition of the Ukraine's rights, including the *right* to free secession.[28]

His clear, sharp policy on the national question was summed up in the resolution he wrote for the April Conference of the Bolsheviks:

> The right of all the nations forming part of Russia freely to secede and form independent states must be recognized. To deny them this right, or to fail to take measures guaranteeing its practical realization, is equivalent to supporting a policy of seizure or annexation. Only the recognition by the proletariat of the right of nations to secede can ensure complete solidarity among the workers of the various nations and help to bring the nations closer together on truly democratic lines.
>
> The conflict which has arisen at the present time between Finland and the Russian provisional government strikingly demonstrates that denial of the right to free secession leads to a direct continuation of the policy of Tsarism.[29]

However, Lenin did not find it very easy to win the day at this conference. He had to fight again and again among the ranks of his own party for the right of nations to self-determination. We have seen how, during the years 1912–16, Lenin had to argue against those Bolshevik leaders who in the name of internationalism opposed the right of oppressed nations to self-determination, including separation (see chapter 3). Now, during the revolution of 1917, he had to fight the same battle again. At the April Conference G.L. Piatakov argued against the slogan of national self-determination:

> [F]rom an economic point of view, national independence represents an antiquated, obsolete, impossible object. The demand for independence is taken out of another historical epoch, is reactionary for it desires to turn back the march of history.[30]

F.E. Dzerzinsky practically accused Lenin of supporting the "point of view of Polish, Ukrainian, and other chauvinists."[31]

Lenin responded to these attacks:

> In no nation does hatred of Russia sit so deep as with the Poles; no nation dislikes Russia so intensely as the Poles.... The Polish Social Democratic comrades have rendered a great historic service by advancing the slogan of internationalism and declaring that the fraternal union of the proletariat of all countries is of supreme importance to them and that they will never go to war for the liberation of Poland. This is to their credit, and this is why we have always regarded only these Polish Social Democrats as socialists. The others are patriots, Polish Plekhanovs. But this peculiar position, when, in order to safeguard socialism, people were forced to struggle against a rabid and morbid nationalism, has produced a strange state of affairs: comrades come to us saying that we must give up the idea of Poland's freedom, her right to secession.[32]

Lenin's resolution was carried by the conference, but against quite widespread opposition. fifty-six delegates voted for it, sixteen against, and eighteen abstained. Piatakov's resolution got eleven votes, with forty-eight against, and nineteen abstentions. A resolution similar to Piatakov's put by the Georgian Makhiaradze, received twenty-one votes, with forty-two opposing, and fifteen abstentions.[33]

A few days before the October insurrection, Lenin wrote again on the national question, crossing the t's and dotting the i's.

> When we win power, we shall immediately and unconditionally recognize this right for Finland, the Ukraine, Armenia, and any other nationality oppressed by Tsarism (and the Great Russian bourgeoisie). On the other hand, we do not at all favor secession. We want as vast a state, as close an alliance of the Great Russians; we desire this in the interests of democracy and socialism, to attract into the struggle of the proletariat the greatest possible number of the working people of different nations. We desire *proletarian revolutionary* unity, *unification,* and not secession. We desire *revolutionary* unification.... We want *free* unification; that is why we must recognize the right to secede (without freedom to secede, unification cannot be called free).[34]

His unambiguous, decisive policy on the national question, as on other questions, cut through the equivocations of the February regime, and helped to destroy the wealth, power, and influence of the Great Russian bourgeoisie, upheld by the provisional government and the compromising leadership. Lenin's policy on nationalities was among the important levers of the October Revolution.

CHAPTER 14

THE JULY DAYS

The storm rising in Petrograd

The regime based on dual power was one of permanent and deepening crisis. When the thunder of revolution had awakened millions, procrastination became intolerable. In a revolutionary period, more than at any other time, the masses cannot tolerate a cleavage between words and action. Aroused at last, after centuries, the people would not wait patiently and passively for the compromising leaders to satisfy their hunger for bread, land, peace, and freedom for the nationally oppressed.

On June 18, Kerensky launched a military offensive against Germany and Austria. The bourgeoisie and the general staff looked to it as a way of unifying the deeply divided people behind a national purpose. As we have already seen, Kerensky announced the offensive on June 16, with a great fanfare, before the participating troops. On June 18, units of the Seventh and Eleventh Russian Armies on the southwestern front moved forward into attack in the direction of Austrian-held Lvov.

The offensive was officially announced in Petrograd on June 19. The next day, several garrison regiments of the capital received orders to be ready to move to the front. The First Machine Gun regiment was given seven days to furnish five hundred machine guns, and on June 21 was presented with a "reorganization plan," according to which about two-thirds of its personnel were to be sent to the front. This enraged the soldiers who well remembered the provisional government's promise that units participating in the February Revolution would not be disarmed or removed from Petrograd. The machine gunners later made it clear that they had decided "to go not to the German front, against the German proletariat, but against their own capitalist ministers."

On June 30, the regiment received a further order for a particularly large transfer of men and machine guns, and there were rumors that this was a prelude to the complete disbanding of the regiment. The unit initiated a massive demonstration on July 2. The leaders of the Bolshevik Military Organization were apparently instrumental in fanning the flames of revolt.

On July 3, at a meeting of the regiment,

> the soldiers I.M. Golovin, I. Kazakov, K.N. Romanov, and I. Ilinsky (all members of the Bolshevik Military Organization collective) spoke out in favor of an immediate *coup d'etat*. Ilinsky promised that as a member of the Military Organization, he would take upon himself responsibility for the mobilization of the rest of the garrison.... First Machine Gunners carrying mandates signed by Golovin and in many cases by members of the unit's Military Organization fanned out across the city and its environs. As nearly as can be determined, delegations were sent to, among others, the Moskovsky, Grenadier, First Infantry, 180th Infantry, Pavlovsky, Izmailovsky, Finliandsky, and Petrogradsky Reserve regiments and to the Sixth Engineer battalion and the Armored Car division, to such Vyborg district factories as Novyi Parviainen, Novyi Lessner, Russkii Reno, Erikson and Baranovsky, and to the Putilov works in the Narva district. Additional delegations were sent to the military installations in Kronstadt, Oranienbaum, Strelna, and Peterhoff. The machine gunners generally arrived in trucks mounted with machine guns between 3 and 5 p.m. and hurriedly organized mass meetings either on their own or through regimental and factory committees.... By mid-evening the Moskovsky, 180th Reserve Infantry, Finliandsky, Grenadier, and Pavlovsky regiments, as well as the Sixth Engineer battalion, could probably be counted as having joined the insurrection. On the Vyborg side, factories stopped operating as soon as trucks bearing the machine gunners appeared, and workers in many of them scurried for their weapons almost immediately. Something like ten thousand armed sailors in Kronstadt and thirty thousand workers in the Putilov factory were soon to follow suit.[1]

None of this was to Lenin's liking.[2]

Lenin warns against impatience and adventurism

While rank-and-file Bolsheviks in the First Machine Gun regiment and other army units, and in the factories, as well as leaders of the Bolshevik Military Organization, were pressing for armed demonstrations, and even talking about overthrowing the provisional government, Lenin warned again and again that what was necessary was to continue patiently to win workers, soldiers, and peasants to Bolshevism.

On June 13 he wrote:

> The socialist proletariat and our party must be as cool and collected as possible, must show the greatest staunchness and vigilance. Let the future Cavaignacs begin first.... The workers of Petrograd will bide their time, gathering their forces and preparing for resistance *when* those gentlemen decide to turn from words to action.[3]

On June 21 he repeated:

> This general and basic fact, the trust of the majority in the petty-bourgeois policy of the Mensheviks and the Socialist-Revolutionaries which is dependent on the capitalists, determines our party's stand and conduct.
>
> We shall keep up our efforts to expose government policy, resolutely warning the workers and soldiers, as in the past, against pinning their hopes on uncoordinated and disorganized actions. It is a question of a phase in the people's revolution...a phase of petty-bourgeois illusions and petty-bourgeois phrases, which serve to disguise the same old cynical imperialism.
>
> This phase must be brought to an end. Let us help to end it as speedily and as painlessly as possible. This will rid the people of the *last* petty-bourgeois illusions and bring about the transfer of power to the revolutionary class.[4]

But his calls for patience were less and less heeded by many hot-headed Bolshevik cadres. At a Bolshevik military conference on June 20, one participant recalled

> the spirit prevailing in some party circles to the effect that there was no point in waiting, that it was now time to seize power. Lenin came out hotly and sharply against such views. For a large part of the conference his views were received with disappointment or even dissatisfaction.[5]

Another described Lenin's speech as a "cold shower" for the "hotheads." Here is the passage in it which was directed against the growing movement toward an immediate uprising:

> We must be especially attentive and careful, so as not to be drawn into a provocation.... One wrong move on our part can wreck everything... If we were now able to seize power, it is naive to think that having taken it we would be able to hold it....
>
> What is the exact weight of our fraction in the Soviet? Even in the Soviets of both capitals, not to speak now of the others, we are an insignificant minority. And what does this fact show? It cannot be brushed aside. It shows that the majority of the masses are wavering but still believe the SRs and Mensheviks....
>
> ...[I]n order to gain power seriously (not by Blanquist methods), the proletarian party must fight for influence inside the Soviet, pa-

tiently, unswervingly, explaining to the masses from day to day the error of their petty-bourgeois illusions....

Events should not be anticipated. Time is on our side.[6]

The Petersburg committee impatient on Lenin's left

On June 20, the Petersburg Committee met in an emergency session to review the situation. The discussion showed clearly that only a minority of the committee agreed with Lenin. First there was an extremist group that was for an immediate overthrow of the government. One of its members, I.K. Naumov, severely criticized the party for "an absence of leadership" and urged that the Bolsheviks present the soviet with an ultimatum: either take power or the Bolsheviks will be duty-bound to take command of the developing movement. "We will testify to our own political bankruptcy if we avoid taking political action.... The temporizing policy of the Central Committee," claimed Naumov, "cannot withstand criticism." Other members of the extreme left group were M.Ia. Latsis, I.N. Stukov, P.A. Zalutsky, and A. Dylle.

There was also a significant middle group, which suggested that decisive action against the provisional government should be postponed for a few days until the inevitable breakdown of the government's offensive. The leaders of this group were M.P. Tomsky and V.V. Volodarsky.[7]

The military organization straining at the leash

On June 22, an unofficial meeting of some members of the Central Committee, the Petersburg Committee, and the Military Organization took place. All the Petrograd Military Organization unit leaders were impatient with the Central Committee line of restraint. Most interesting are the statements of Semashko of the First Machine Gun regiment, and Sakharov of the First Reserve Infantry regiment.

> Semashko, *de facto* commander of over fifteen thousand machine gunners, evidently spoke for the majority when he said that the Petersburg and Central Committees lacked "a clear understanding" of the party's strength. He declared, "Almost the whole garrison is with us." "In general," observed Sakharov, "the speeches of the soldiers boil down to the fact that they all demand active operations and are against limiting themselves to resolutions. The soldiers say these lead nowhere." Among Military Organization unit representatives only M.M. Lashevich, an old Bolshevik and non-commissioned officer in the First Machine Gun regiment who was a member of the Petrograd Soviet, spoke

in support of the Central Committee position. "We must now be especially careful and restrained in our tactics," he argued, "but in the
speeches of the last few days this is precisely what is missing. Frequently," said Lashevich, not without sarcasm, "it is impossible to
make out where the Bolshevik ends and the Anarchist begins."[8]

Pravda and *Soldatskaia pravda*

Pravda was the daily paper of the Central Committee, then
under the direct control of Lenin. *Soldatskaia pravda* was the daily
of the Bolshevik Military Organization, which enjoyed virtual autonomy. In the last days of June and the first few days of July, the
two papers diverged radically.

While *Pravda* was very cautious in its approach in the days after
the offensive was launched, *Soldatskaia pravda* had a very sharp and
unrestrained tone. Nowhere did it refer to the fact that the Bolsheviks
had still to win the majority of the proletariat. Instead it called for direct action immediately. Thus, on the very eve of the July Days (indeed, after organization of the movement had already begun), at a
time when *Pravda* was focusing attention on the campaign to win
control of the Petrograd Soviet, *Soldatskaia pravda* published an in-
flammatory front-page article by L. Chubunov, which concluded:

> Comrades! Enough of sacrificing ourselves for the welfare of the
> bourgeoisie. The time has come not to sleep but to act. Comrades!
> Chase the bourgeoisie from power and since they cry "war to com-
> plete victory," away to the front with the whole damn lot of them. All
> of us are worn out by this awful war which has already taken away
> the lives of millions, which has made millions cripples, and which has
> brought with it unheard-of poverty, destruction, and hunger.
>
> Wake up, whoever is asleep. The SRs and the Mensheviks want to
> fool you.... I appeal to you to be ready at any minute to repulse the
> counter-revolution. It stalks Nevskii Prospect led by Plekhanov and
> Rodzianko. Soon the "Black Hundreds" will come out, but you, com-
> rades, with all your strength protect the freedom that has been won.
> All power must pass into the hands of the workers, soldiers, and peas-
> ants. Remove from power the bourgeoisie and all its sympathizers.
>
> Hail all power to the Soviets of Workers' and Soldiers' Deputies![9]

Indiscipline among party members

According to the Stalinist legend, the Bolsheviks, with a very
few insignificant exceptions, always followed the will of Lenin; the
party was practically a monolith. But nothing was further from the
truth. Again and again, Lenin had to fight to win over his party

members. Whereas in April his main problem was to overcome the conservatism of the top leadership of the party, at the end of June and the beginning of July he had to contend with the revolutionary impatience of rank-and-file leaders and members.

In many cases party members acted against the spirit of Central Committee instructions without openly challenging party discipline. At a meeting of the Petersburg Committee on August 27, for instance, M.I. Kalinin suggested that at the beginning of July, Bolshevik agitators, while appearing to be restraining the masses, had actually been urging them to act.[10]

Similarly Nevsky, leader of the Military Organization, in a memorial article many years after the event, could write:

> Some comrades at the present time ask the question: who initiated the July events—the Central Committee or the Military Organization—or did the movement erupt spontaneously?.... [T]here is no need now to hide the fact that we, the responsible leaders of the Military Organization, i.e., especially Podvoisky, myself, Mekhonoshin, Beliakov, and other active workers, through our agitation, propaganda, and enormous influence and authority in the military units, promoted the spirit that aroused the demonstration...thus when the Military Organization, having learned (on 1 July) of the machine gunners' demonstration, sent me as the more or less most popular Military Organization orator to talk the masses into not going out, I talked to them, but in such a way that only a fool could come to the conclusion that he should not demonstrate.[11]

Lenin in the July Days

On July 4, as many as half a million soldiers and workers went out into the streets carrying banners with slogans like, "Down with the provisional government," "Down with the ten capitalist ministers," "All power to the Soviets of Workers' and Soldiers' Deputies." The Central Committee summoned Lenin to Petrograd from the place in Finland where he was resting, and on the morning of July 4, he came straight to Kshesinskaia Mansion, the headquarters of the Bolsheviks.

When a mass of Kronstadt sailors came and called on Lenin to speak, he did so, though very briefly. He started by apologizing for confining himself to a few words because of illness. He sent "greetings" to the revolutionary people of Kronstadt, on behalf of the Petrograd workers. Finally, he expressed his "confidence that our slogan 'All power to the Soviets' must and will win despite all the zigzags of history," then appealed for "firmness, steadfastness, and vigilance."[12] The audience was disappointed.

A Kronstadt Bolshevik recalls that for many of the sailors, Lenin's emphasis on the necessity for a peaceful demonstration at that time was unexpected. He writes that not only the anarchists but some of the Bolsheviks could not see how a column of armed men, craving to rush into battle, could limit itself to an armed demonstration![13]

The paradox of the July demonstration

The demonstration could easily have overthrown the provisional government, which at the time had no reliable troops in the capital at all. But if the Bolsheviks had taken power, could they have retained it?

When in October they did take power, they found that the greatest difficulties occurred *after* the insurrection. The masses needed to be profoundly convinced that there was no alternative to Bolshevik power. In July even the Petrograd proletariat was not ready for such a trial. While able to seize power, they still offered it to the Executive Committee of the Soviets. It was not until August 31 that the Bolsheviks became a majority in the Soviet of Petrograd. Even the party had no clear idea of the route by which it was possible to reach power. Lenin wrote:

> The real mistake of our party on 3–4 July, as events now reveal, was...that the party *still* considered a peaceful development of political changes possible through an alteration in the Soviets' policies, whereas in reality the Mensheviks and SRs had become so much entangled and bound by compromising with the bourgeoisie, and the bourgeoisie had become so counter-revolutionary, that peaceful development was no longer possible.[14]

If the proletariat was not sure and steadfast, the troops were even less so. On July 5, when the government's slander of Lenin as being a German spy was disseminated, the troops from Petrograd kept their distance from the Bolsheviks. The situation was even worse in the active army, where the "Bolshevism" of many soldiers was spontaneous—agreeing with the Bolsheviks' slogan of "Land, peace, and bread," but in no way identifying themselves with the party.

The provinces lagged very much behind Petrograd, as even Moscow did. Thus, during the July Days,

> In the session of the Moscow committee of the Bolsheviks, stormy debates arose. Individuals belonging to the extreme left wing of the

party—such as, for example, Bubnov—proposed that they occupy the post office, the telegraph, and telephone stations, the editorial offices of *Russkoe Slovo*—that is, that they take the road of insurrection. The committee, very moderate in its general spirit, decisively rejected these proposals, considering that the Moscow masses were not in the least ready for such action. It was nevertheless decided to hold a demonstration in spite of the veto of the Soviet. A considerable crowd of workers marched to Skobelevsky Square with the same slogans as in Petrograd, but with far from the same enthusiasm. The garrison reacted by no means unanimously; individual units joined the procession, but only one of them came fully armed.[15]

The majority of workers and soldiers did not respond to the Bolshevik summons to demonstrate.

By far the greatest paradox of the July Days lay in the contradictory consciousness of the masses supporting the Bolsheviks in Petrograd itself: calling for soviet power and nursing illusions about the possibility of the SR and Menshevik Soviet leaders taking power, which was precisely what they refused to do. This paradox expressed itself in the cry of a fist-shaking worker to Victor Chernov: "Take power, you son-of-a-bitch, when it is given to you."[16]

> Running into this armed resistance from the very institution to which they wished to turn over the power [Trotsky writes] the workers and soldiers lost a clear sense of their goal. From their mighty mass movement the political axis had been torn out.[17]

Lenin was absolutely right in refusing to seize power in the July Days, as he could easily have done. As he wrote in retrospect, two months after the events:

> It would have been wrong if the Bolsheviks had aimed to seize power on 3-4 July, since neither the majority of the people nor even the majority of the workers at that time had yet actually experienced the counter-revolutionary policies of the generals in the army, of the landowners in the countryside, and of the capitalists in the town.[18]

Reaction goaded revolution. The workers needed the experience of Kornilov's counterrevolutionary coup to steel them for the seizure of power.

Lenin teaches how to retreat

Believing that the armed demonstration should not end in an insurrection, Lenin argued that it was necessary to call it off, once the masses had learned from their own experience that it could not end in decisive victory. No one could force the Menshevik and SR soviet leaders to take power if they were mortally afraid of the workers and soldiers and of the responsibility of power. Therefore on July 5, the Central Committee of the Bolshevik Party issued a leaflet calling for an end to the demonstration.

> Comrades! On Monday you came out on the streets. On Tuesday you decided to continue the demonstration. We called you to a peaceful demonstration yesterday. The object of this demonstration was to show to all the toiling and exploited masses the strength of our slogans, their weight, their significance, and their necessity for the liberation of the peoples from war, hunger, and ruin.
>
> The object of the demonstration was achieved. The slogans of the vanguard of the working class and of the army were imposingly and worthily proclaimed. The scattered firing of the counter-revolutionaries on the demonstrators could not disturb the general character of the demonstration.
>
> Comrades! For the present political crisis, our aim has been accomplished. We have therefore decided to end the demonstration. Let each and every one peacefully and in an organized manner bring the strike and the demonstration to a close.
>
> Let us await the further development of the crisis. Let us continue to prepare our forces. Life is with us, the course of events shows the correctness of our slogans.[19]

However, not all the Bolshevik leaders accepted the necessity of retreat. Among those who did not was Latsis, who the same evening, at a meeting of several members of the Petersburg Committee, advocated in the name of the Vyborg District Committee that the party should rejuvenate the uprising by means of a general strike.

When members of the Executive Commission of the Petersburg Committee met Lenin at the watchmen's hut of the Reno factory where he had temporarily taken refuge, he was vehement in his opposition to the declaration of a general strike. Treating the Executive Commission like a group of ill-behaved schoolboys, he wrote the following categorical back-to-work appeal in its name:

> The Executive Commission of the Petersburg Committee RSDLP, in compliance with the Central Committee's decision published in the 6 July *Listok pravdy* (a decision also signed by the Petersburg Committee), calls on workers to resume work beginning tomorrow, that is, beginning on the morning of 7 July.[20]

Could the Bolsheviks have remained aloof from the July demonstration?

Once the mass of the soldiers and workers had held an armed demonstration, against the wish of the Central Committee of the Bolshevik Party, should the party have stood aside? Lenin had no doubt that it could not abstain, could not stand apart from the masses.

Had our party refused to support the 3–4 July mass movement, which burst out spontaneously despite our attempts to prevent it, we should have actually and completely betrayed the proletariat, since the people were moved to action by their well founded and just anger at the protraction of the imperialist war, which is a predatory war conducted in the interests of the capitalists, and at the inaction of the government and the Soviets in regard to the bourgeoisie, who are intensifying and aggravating economic disruption and famine.[21]

Two years after the July Days Lenin wrote:

Mistakes are inevitable when the masses are fighting, but the communists *remain with the masses,* see these mistakes, explain them to the masses, try to get them rectified, and strive perseveringly for the victory of class-consciousness over spontaneity.[22]

The Bolshevik Party could not wash its hands of responsibility for the actions of the workers and soldiers. It would rather suffer defeat *with* them than leave them without leadership, to be slaughtered by the counterrevolutionaries. Thanks to the Bolshevik Party's taking its place at the head of the movement, the blow struck at the masses by reaction during the July Days and after, although considerable, was not mortal. The victims were counted in tens and not tens of thousands. The working class emerged from the struggle more experienced, more mature, more sober.

The lessons of the July Days

With clarity and incisiveness, and without wavering, Lenin summarized the lessons of the July Days shortly afterwards. In an article written on July 7 and entitled "Three Crises," he started by comparing the three political crises, April 20 and 21, June 10 and 18, and July 3–4. "What is common to all three is a mass dissatisfaction overflowing all bounds, a mass resentment with the bourgeoisie and *their* government."

But this mass dissatisfaction expressed itself differently on each occasion. The first crisis of April "was stormy and spontaneous and completely unorganized." In the June crisis, "the demonstration was called by the Bolsheviks, and was cancelled after a stern ultimatum and direct ban by the Congress of Soviets; then, on June 18, came a general demonstration in which the Bolshevik slogans clearly predominated." "The third crisis broke out spontaneously on July 3 despite the Bolsheviks' efforts on July 2 to check it. Reaching its climax on July 4, it led to a furious outburst of counter-revolution on July 5 and 6."

Lastly,

> perhaps the most instructive conclusion to be drawn from considering the events in their interconnection is that *all* three crises manifested some form of demonstration that is new in the history of our revolution, a demonstration of a more complicated type in which the movement proceeds in waves, a sudden drop following a rapid rise, revolution and counter-revolution becoming more acute, and the middle elements being eliminated for a more or less extensive period.
>
> In all three crises, the movement took the form of a *demonstration*. An anti-government demonstration—that would be the most exact, formal description of events. But the fact of the matter is that it was not an ordinary demonstration; it was something considerably more than a demonstration, but less than a revolution. It was an outburst of revolution and counter-revolution *together,* a sharp, sometimes almost sudden elimination of the middle elements, while the proletarian and bourgeois elements made a stormy appearance.[23]

Lenin drew another important lesson from the July Days: the tactics and the slogans must now be quickly changed, in accordance with the general change in the objective situation.

> Too often has it happened that, when history has taken a sharp turn, even progressive parties have for some time been unable to adapt themselves to the new situation and have repeated slogans which had formerly been correct but had now lost all meaning—lost it as "suddenly" as the sharp turn in history was "sudden"....
>
> Unless this is understood, it is impossible to understand anything of the urgent questions of the day. Every particular slogan must be deduced from the totality of specific features of a definite political situation. And the political situation in Russia now, after 4 July, differs radically from the situation between 27 February and 4 July.[24]

Above all, the possibility of a peaceful transfer of power to the working class no longer existed.

> The movement on 3 and 4 July was the last attempt by means of a demonstration to induce the Soviets to take power. That was when the Soviets, i.e., the Socialist Revolutionaries and Mensheviks controlling them, virtually handed over power to the counter-revolution

by summoning counter-revolutionary troops to Petrograd, disarming and disbanding revolutionary regiments and the workers, approving and tolerating acts of tyranny and violence against the Bolsheviks, the introduction of the death penalty at the front, etc.[25]

All hopes for a peaceful development of the Russian revolution have vanished for good. This is the objective situation: either complete victory for the military dictatorship, or victory for the workers' armed uprising; the latter victory is only possible when the insurrection coincides with a deep, mass upheaval against the government and the bourgeoisie caused by economic disruption and the prolongation of the war.

The slogan "All power to the Soviets!" was a slogan for peaceful development of the revolution which was possible in April, May, June, and up to 5–9 July, i.e., up to the time when actual power passed into the hands of the military dictatorship. This slogan is no longer correct.[26]

...[P]ower can no longer be taken peacefully. It can be obtained only by winning a decisive struggle against those actually in power at the moment, namely, the military gang, the Cavaignacs, who are relying for support on the reactionary troops brought to Petrograd and on the Cadets and monarchists.

The Soviets no longer had any power, Lenin said. They were mere "figureheads, puppets."[27]

The present Soviets have failed, have suffered complete defeat, because they are dominated by the Socialist Revolutionary and Menshevik parties. At the moment, these Soviets are like sheep brought to the slaughterhouse and bleating pitifully under the knife. The Soviets *at present* are powerless and helpless against the triumphant and triumphing counter-revolution. The slogan calling for the transfer of power to the Soviets might be construed as a "simple" appeal for the transfer of power to the present Soviets, and to say that, to appeal for it, would now mean deceiving the people. Nothing is more dangerous than deceit.[28]

Bending the stick

Lenin's description of the change in the position of the soviets after the July Days was correct. His realistic grasp of the altered situation was in this case magnificently demonstrated. The evidence collected years later proved how far the soviets did deteriorate after the July Days.

"The entire work of our Soviet, running in the Menshevik and Social Revolutionary channel," writes the Saratov Bolshevik, Antonov, "lost all meaning.... At a meeting of the Executive Committee we would yawn from boredom till it became indecent. The Social Revolutionary-Menshevik talking-mill was empty and trivial."

The sickly Soviets were becoming less and less able to serve as a support to their Petrograd center. The correspondence between Smolny and the localities was going into a decline: there was nothing to write about, nothing to propose; no prospects remained, and no tasks.[29]

The soviet, being basically an organization for the struggle for power, could not survive without this struggle.

However, Lenin bent the stick too far. The soviet did not die after the July Days. And the assumption subsequently made at the Sixth Congress of the party, that the soviets were completely powerless, that dual power had ended, proved wrong. If they did nothing else, the Kornilov days showed that the soviets were still full of life.

After months of emphasizing slow, patient propaganda, Lenin now, after the July Days, in the difficult conditions resulting from the semi-legality of the party, and knowing that a new turn towards direct struggle would be needed for the seizure of state power, had to "bend the stick" to straighten the party out, to put the emphasis on the key issue of the day.

To minimize the significance of the changes after the July Days would have been much more dangerous for Bolshevism than exaggerating them. And so Lenin turned to his old method of stick bending...

Above all, he learned a very important lesson from the July Days: for the first time he concluded that it was necessary for the Bolsheviks to seize power directly, and in the not too distant future.

The new turn Lenin suggested was first considered at an expanded Central Committee meeting of July 13–14, where it was rejected.[30] But he got his way at the Sixth Party Congress in July–August.[31]

However, as we shall see, this was not a complete victory. To accept the *principle* of insurrection is one thing; to be ready to dare to actually seize power is another thing altogether. Every revolutionary situation is an equation with many unknowns; this is especially true of an act of insurrection. Conservatism and timidity are at a great advantage under such circumstances. But we are jumping ahead of the story.

CHAPTER 15

REACTION ON THE MOVE

On July 4, the provisional government, with the consent of the Soviet Executive Committee, authorized General Polovtsev, commander of the Petrograd Military District, to rid Petrograd of armed mobs, to disarm the First Machine Gun regiment, and to occupy the Ksheshinskaia Mansion.

At dawn on July 5, a detachment of soldiers went to *Pravda*'s printing works. They arrived too late to catch Lenin, who had just left the premises for his first pre-October hideout. The army detachment wrecked the *Pravda* plant, and arrested the workers and soldiers on duty there.

During the day, patrols of officers, soldiers, and Cossacks began mopping-up operations. They confiscated armed trucks and disarmed suspicious-looking workers, soldiers, and sailors, who were prevented from escaping behind barricades in the workers' districts because the bridges on the Neva either remained raised or were under heavy guard.

At a late-night meeting of cabinet ministers on July 6, it was resolved that

[a]nyone guilty of inciting officers, soldiers, and other military ranks during wartime to disobey the laws in effect under the new democratic system in the army and the orders of the military authorities consistent with them is to be punished as for state treason.[1]

This decree was followed by orders for the arrest of such leading Bolsheviks as Lenin, Zinoviev, and Kamenev, and a few days later the leaders of the Mezhraiontsy, Trotsky and Lunacharsky.

On July 7, the provisional government ordered the military units that had participated in the July Days to be disbanded, and their personnel distributed at the discretion of the war and navy minister.

Extreme measures by the right

The Bolsheviks were persecuted. The entire Bolshevik press was closed down. Hundreds of Bolsheviks were arrested, and a number of workers were killed. The intensity of the reaction was such that even non-Bolsheviks were alarmed. Thus the Menshevik Voytinsky remembers:

> The pendulum swung to the right. Reactionary forces that had taken no part in quelling the riots now tried to capitalize on the failure of the revolt. "Vigilantes" roamed the city, breaking into private apartments in search of suspects. Public opinion demanded drastic measures.[2]

> First of all the new government energetically continued the searches, arrests, disarmings, and persecutions of all kinds that had already been begun. Self-appointed groups of officers, military cadets, and I think the gilded youth too, rushed to the "help" of the new regime, which was obviously trying to present itself as a "strong government." It was not only the mutinous regiments and battalions that were disarmed; almost more attention was devoted to the working-class districts, where the workers' Red Guard was disarmed. Enormous quantities of arms were collected.
>
> Every Bolshevik that could be found was seized and imprisoned. Kerensky and his military friends were definitely trying to wipe them off the face of the earth.[3]

After destroying the Bolshevik organizations the counterrevolutionaries went on the offensive against other working-class groups. As Stalin described the situation at the time:

> From attacking the Bolsheviks they are now proceeding to attack all the Soviet parties and the Soviets themselves. They smash the Menshevik district organizations in Petradskaia Storona and Okhta. They smash the metal-workers' union branch in Nevskaia Zastava. They invade a meeting of the Petrograd Soviet and arrest its members (Deputy Sakharov). They organize special groups on the Nevskii Prospect to track down members of the Executive Committee.[4]

Plundering, violence, and in some cases shooting went on in various parts of the city. Only in the workers' districts could the Bolsheviks move safely and freely.

In the provinces, land committees were arrested *en masse*. On July 17, Tsereteli, minister of the interior, sent out instructions for the taking of "quick and energetic measures to put a stop to all arbitrary actions in the field of land relations."[5]

On July 8, General Kornilov, commander in chief of the southwestern front, gave orders to open fire on retreating soldiers with machine guns and artillery.[6] On July 12, the death penalty was restored at the front.[7]

As we have already described (see pp. 183–85), on July 16 Kerensky called a conference of top army commanders at headquarters, at which a general attack on army committees, on the soviets, and on Order No. 1 was launched by all present, and where Kerensky declared that he differed from the generals only in believing that the attack should be carried out in stages and not at one fell swoop (see chapter 10). On July 18, Kornilov became commander in chief of the whole Russian army. Chauvinistic Great Russian attacks on Ukrainians and Finns received a new stimulus (see chapter 13). Factory managers started a massive campaign of suppression of factory committees and lockouts of workers (see chapter 12). The Congress of Trade and Industry, the central organization of capitalists in Russia, declared on July 19:

> The government, during the past months, has permitted the poisoning of the Russian people and the Russian army and the disruption of all discipline, thereby following the Soviets of Workers' and Soldiers' Deputies, who must bear the responsibility for the disgrace and humiliation of Russia and the Russian army. Only by a radical break by the government with the dictatorship of the Soviet, which leads to disintegration...can Russia be saved.... If a dictatorial power is needed to save the motherland, such a power can only be a genuinely national power which is above parties and above classes, born of national enthusiasm.[8]

V.M. Purishkevich, the old leader of the Black Hundreds, dared to come out of his hole and, after introducing himself by saying, "I am a thoroughly convinced monarchist, and I will not alter my convictions," went on to declare, "It is necessary that the government be a government; it is necessary to put in its place and to dissolve the Soviet of Workers' and Soldiers' Deputies."[9]

The conciliators plumb new depths

The Mensheviks and SR leaders became even more cringing after the July Days than they had been since February. As Lenin graphically put it:

> Down the ladder, step by step. Having once set foot on the ladder of compromise with the bourgeoisie, the Socialist Revolutionaries and Mensheviks slid irresistibly downwards, to rock bottom. On 28 February, in the Petrograd Soviet, they promised conditional support to the bourgeois government. On 6 May, they saved it from collapse and allowed themselves to be made its servants and defenders by agreeing

to an offensive. On 9 June, they united with the counter-revolutionary bourgeoisie in a campaign of furious rage, lies, and slander against the revolutionary proletariat. On 19 June, they approved the resumption of the predatory war. On 3 July, they consented to the summoning of reactionary troops, which was the beginning of their complete surrender of power to the Bonapartists. Down the ladder, step by step.

This groveling of the compromisers before the capitalists and the army chiefs was not coincidental. After all, the attitude is inherent in the nature of the petty bourgeoisie.

> Everybody, of course [Lenin wrote], has seen the small owner bend every effort and strain every nerve to "get on in the world," to become a real master, to rise to the position of a "strong" employer, to the position of a bourgeois. As long as capitalism rules the roost, there is no alternative for the small owner other than becoming a capitalist (and that is possible at best in the case of one small owner out of a hundred), or becoming a ruined man, a semi-proletarian, and ultimately a proletarian. The same is true in politics: the petty-bourgeois democrats, especially their leaders, tend to trail after the bourgeoisie. The leaders of the petty-bourgeois democrats console their people with promises and assurances about the possibility of reaching agreement with the big capitalists; at best, and for a very brief period, they obtain certain minor concessions from the capitalists for a small upper section of the working people; but on every decisive issue, on every important matter, the petty-bourgeois democrats have always tailed after the bourgeoisie as a feeble appendage to them, as an obedient tool in the hands of the financial magnates.[10]

However, although the compromisers were doing their best to ingratiate themselves with the right, they were also extremely afraid of it. The Menshevik and SR leaders would have been ready to permit the complete annihilation of the Bolshevik Party, if only they had not feared that after dealing with the Bolsheviks, the officers, Cossack and Black Hundred heroes, would turn on the compromisers themselves. The Cadets, as well as the generals, made it increasingly clear that they wanted to sweep away not only the Bolsheviks, but also the soviets. One has only to recall the words spoken at the conference at Stavka on July 16 (see p 183). Again, *Rech*, the Cadet paper, after the July Days viciously attacked Chernov and Tsereteli as "Zimmerwaldists" and "traitors." The SR and Menshevik press warned repeatedly of the danger of "counterrevolution."

On July 17, while forbidding all demonstrations in the streets, a move against the left, Tsereteli also warned the right against excesses: "The government cannot tolerate any further demonstrations of anarchy such as the treacherous blow dealt the revolution during the days of July 3–5."

> Nevertheless, the provisional government is well aware of the danger
> with which the country is threatened by the counter-revolution which
> is rearing its head in an attempt to take advantage of the internal dis-
> cord and of misfortunes at the front in order to turn the country
> back, to deprive the people of the fruits of their revolutionary strug-
> gle, and to restore the system under which, in the interests of a few,
> the most basic interests of the country, and the wide popular masses
> were betrayed and sold.
>
> Rigorous suppression of both anarchical and counter-revolutionary
> undertakings constitutes one of the most important tasks of the gov-
> ernment.[11]

The result of the hesitation, the vacillation of the compromisers
between Miliukov and Lenin, was that the job of suppressing Bolshevism was botched. "At the beginning of July," the liberal Nabokov
wrote later, "there was one short moment when the authority of the
government seemed again to lift its head; that was after the putting
down of the first Bolshevik uprising. But the provisional government
was unable to make use of this opportunity, and let slip the favorable
conditions of the moment. It was never repeated."[12]

The bark of the provisional government against the revolutionary left was much worse than its bite. Vacillation is not an effective
way to achieve a successful counterrevolution.

Let us consider the disbanding of the military units that had participated in the armed demonstrations of July. General C.D. Romanovsky, chief of the general staff, suggested the following plan:
regiments of the Petrograd garrison should be divided into three
categories depending on the extent of their involvement in the July
movement. To the first category were assigned units having participated in the demonstrations in full or close to full strength. Included
in this group were the Grenadier regiment; the First, Third, 176th,
and 180th Reserve Infantry regiments; and the First Machine Gun
regiment, together constituting the core of Military Organization
strength in the garrison. These units were to be completely and per-
manently disbanded, their personnel (with the exception of those in
jail) to be transferred to duty at the front. The second category included the units in which only individual companies had taken part
in the demonstration. The Moskovsky, Pavlovsky, Third Rifle, and
Second Machine Gun regiments and the South Engineer battalion
were assigned to this group. Only guilty elements in these units were
scheduled to be dissolved. Finally, the third category was composed

of units that had not been actively involved in the demonstrations, but contained guilty individuals. This group, which was ordered to conduct a thorough purge of subversive elements, accounted for all the remaining regiments in the garrison. By this plan, Romanovsky proposed to reduce the garrison by one hundred thousand of its most unreliable elements.[13]

The government's implementation of this plan was only very half-hearted.

> The policy of dissolving unreliable regiments was apparently limited to the transfer to the front of reinforcement companies presumably composed of the most subversive elements. This seems to have been at least partly because allocating one hundred thousand particularly unruly soldiers was more easily said than done—quite naturally most field commanders were not at all interested in receiving such replacements. In any event, troops belonging to the Grenadier regiment and the First and 180th Reserve Infantry regiments, classed as "category one," were still in the capital at the time of the October revolution. Similarly, except for the First Machine Gun regiment, the 180th Reserve Infantry regiment, and the Grenadier regiment, it appears that the proposed disarmament of insurgent troops was never carried out. Moreover, no significant punitive measures were taken against either participating Kronstadt units or the vessels of the Baltic fleet.
>
> Also unfulfilled were the government's plans for disarming civilians. Most factories evidently followed a suggestion of the Bolshevik Central Committee issued on 7 July and hid their weapons instead of turning them over to government troops. In addition, some stores of arms passed into the hands of the workers from garrison regiments threatened with disarmament.[14]

In France, according to Engels, the workers had emerged armed from every revolution: "[T]herefore, the disarming of the workers was the first commandment for the bourgeoisie, who were at the helm of the state."[15] Unfortunately for the Russian bourgeoisie, the Russian proletariat was far too well organized and led to let its arms be taken away!

Almost on the same day as Tsereteli issued instructions for energetic measures to be taken against the anarchistic activities of land committees, the government promulgated a decree limiting the sale of land.[16] This belated half-measure made the right grind their teeth.

The Bolsheviks after the July Days

The main propaganda weapon used against the Bolsheviks after July 5 was the accusation that Lenin was a German agent. Docu-

ments to "prove" this were produced: the testimony of a certain Er-
molenko (former agent of the intelligence service), and of a merchant, Z. Burshtein, that the Polish revolutionaries Ganetsky and
Kozlovsky had financial transactions with Parvus, the former revolutionary, who was now an ardent defensist.

Lenin, Zinoviev, and Kamenev repudiated the accusations in a
letter published in Gorky's paper, *Novaia Zhizn (Pravda* had been
closed down) on July 11. They pointed out that as early as 1915 the
Bolshevik paper *Sotsial-Demokrat* had denounced Parvus as a
"renegade, licking the boots of Hindenburg." The authors of the letter asserted that they had "never received a kopek from Kozlovsky
or Ganetsky, either personally or for the party." Lenin also repudiated Ganetsky as a party comrade in a special leaflet issued on July
6, in which he asserted: "Ganetsky and Kozlovsky are not Bolsheviks, but members of the Polish Social Democratic Party. The Bolsheviks received no money either from Ganetsky or Kozlovsky."

One of the first decisions Lenin had to make was whether to appear in court to defend himself.

"Now they will shoot us all..." he said to Trotsky. "[F]or them
it is the best moment."[17] After some hesitation he made up his mind
that he would not allow himself to be imprisoned, but would go
into hiding, together with Zinoviev.

From the letter of Pereverzev, the former Minister of Justice, published on Sunday in *Novoe Vremia*, it became perfectly clear that the
"espionage" "case" of Lenin and others was quite deliberately
framed by the party of the counter-revolution.

Pereverzev has openly admitted that he took advantage of uncon-
firmed accusations to work up (his actual expression) the soldiers
against our party. This is admitted by the former Minister of Justice,
a man who only yesterday called himself a socialist! Pereverzev is
gone, but whether the new Minister of Justice will hesitate to adopt
Pereverzev's and Alexinsky's methods, nobody can venture to say.

The counter-revolutionary bourgeoisie are trying to create a new
Dreyfus case. They believe in our "espionage" as much as the leaders of
Russian reaction, who framed the Beilis case, believed that Jews drink
children's blood. There are no guarantees of justice in Russia at present.

At present there can be no legal basis in Russia, not even such constitutional guarantees as exist in the orderly bourgeois countries. To
give ourselves up at present to the authorities would mean putting
ourselves into the hands of the Miliukovs, Alexinskys, Pereverzevs, of
rampant counter-revolutionaries who look upon all the charges
against us as a simple civil war episode.[18]

In order to grasp the meaning of the phrase "civil war episode," it is enough to recall the fate of Karl Liebknecht and Rosa Luxemburg. Lenin knew how to think ahead.

Many, even among the left leaders, felt Lenin was wrong to go into hiding. Trotsky thought the decision unfortunate.

> He thought that Lenin had nothing to hide, that, on the contrary, he had every interest in laying his record before the public, and that in this way he could serve his cause better than by flight, which would merely add to any adverse appearances by which people might judge him. Kamenev shared Trotsky's feelings and decided to submit to imprisonment.[19]

At the Sixth Party Congress, July 13–14, a number of delegates expressed the view that Lenin should come out of hiding, including Volodarsky, Manuilsky, and Lashevich. Manuilsky stated:

> We should make another Dreyfus case from the trial of Lenin. We should go into the fight with a raised visor.... This is demanded by the interests of the revolution and the prestige of our party.[2]

However the congress adopted a resolution that Lenin should not appear in court.[21]

Lenin, in bending the stick, was ready to believe the worst about the ruthlessness of the enemy at the time. He was not about to fall into the trap of "constitutional illusions."

His attitude was far removed from the way of thinking of such people as Sukhanov, who were convinced that Lenin was not guilty of the accusations against him, but could not understand why he avoided the court:

> However biased the court, however minimal the guarantees of justice—nevertheless Lenin risked absolutely nothing but imprisonment.... This was something quite special, unexampled, and incomprehensible. Any other mortal would have demanded an investigation and trial even in the most unfavorable conditions. Any other mortal would personally and publicly have done everything possible, as energetically as he could, to rehabilitate himself.... In the whole world, only he could have behaved thus.[22]

Many others have indeed made the mistake of playing up to "public opinion," and thus would have risked their lives in this situation.

From July 6 until October 25, i.e., until the day of the October Revolution, Lenin was in hiding. He first spent a number of weeks camping with Zinoviev in the area surrounding Petrograd, and in a forest near Sestroretsk. They had to spend the nights and shelter from rain in haystacks. Disguised as a fireman, Lenin then crossed the Finnish border in a locomotive, and concealed himself in the apartment of a Helsingfors police chief, a former Petrograd worker. Afterwards he moved nearer the Russian border, to the Finnish town of Vyborg. From the end of September, he lived secretly in Petrograd, and on the day of the insurrection, appeared in the open after almost four months' absence.

The Bolshevik Party survived the persecution relatively unscathed. It is true that some rank-and-file members were badly confused and startled by the accusation against Lenin. Thus the Executive Committee of the Bolshevik organization in the huge Vyborg district Metallist factory passed a resolution pledging full support to the soviet and placed the local party organization under its control. It demanded that the Bolshevik Central and Petersburg Committees divest themselves of authority and turn themselves over to the courts in order to demonstrate that "one hundred thousand Bolshevik workers are not German agents." Finally, the measure pronounced the factory committee independent of higher party organizations until a conference could be convened to elect new Central and Petersburg Committees. This resolution was passed by a vote of sixteen to four with four abstentions.[23]

The Tiflis Bolsheviks also expressed confidence in the Central Executive Committee of the soviet on July 7, and joined the compromising parties in protesting against "any unsanctioned demonstrations, armed or unarmed."[24]

The influx of new recruits into the party was severely checked and the mood of the workers in all districts was very depressed, as is clearly shown in the minutes of the meeting of the Petersburg Committee of July 10.[25] The slander against Lenin was quite effective among workers not in the party. At the meeting, one delegate after another also said that workers were leaving the party, but on a very small scale. A delegate from Vyborg said: "No mass flight from the party." The same words were repeated by a delegate from the Second Gorodsky district. A delegate from Nerva district reported: "The exit from the party can be characterized as one of solitary cases."[26]

The representative for the Nevsky district complained that the majority of workers in his area were relying on rumors and the "boulevard press," while a delegate from the Kolpinsky district declared that from the moment the demonstrations were crushed, "the mood of the workers turned against us." The Porokhovsky district representative (he was one of six Bolsheviks thrown out of his factory in the aftermath of the July Days) complained of "slander" against the Bolsheviks and of their being "watched," and characterized the workers of his district as a "stagnant swamp."[27]

The Bolsheviks did disastrously badly in the municipal elections in Nevsky district on August 13: out of more than 42,000 votes, they got only 4,822, as against the SRs' 31,980.[28]

Latsis wrote in his diary:

> 9 July. All our printing plants in the city are destroyed. Nobody dares print our papers and leaflets. We are compelled to set up an underground press. The Vyborg district has become an asylum for all. Here have come both the Petrograd Committee and the persecuted members of the Central Committee. In the watchman's room of the Renaud factory, there is a conference of the committee with Lenin. The question is raised of a general strike. A division occurs in the committee. I stand for calling the strike. Lenin, after explaining the situation, moves that we abandon it.... 12 July. The counter-revolution is victorious. The Soviets are without power. The junkers, running wild, have begun to raid the Mensheviks too. In some sections of the party there is a loss of confidence. The influx of members has stopped.... But there is not as yet a flight from our ranks.[29]

From Kolomna, it was reported to the Moscow Regional Committee of the Bolsheviks that "after July 3–5 there was a disarray in the ranks of the organized comrades. Resignations from the organization took place." In Vyselki there prevailed a "pogrom mood. The organization was in flames"; in the Latvian section "a split, few left to join the Mensheviks."[30]

In Moscow, it was reported from one district of the city: "We had 1,500 members, of whom 560 were steadfast. The slander of Lenin did affect the workers."[31] On July 15, it was reported at the Moscow Committee: "There were deserters from the besieged camp...5 percent left."[32] In Serpukhov district, "135 left the party."[33]

On July 16, a delegate from Vassilievsky Ostrov reported at a Bolshevik city conference that the mood in his district was "in general" hearty, with the exception of a few factories. "In the Baltic factories, the Social Revolutionaries and Mensheviks are crowding us out." Here the reaction was extreme: the factory committee decreed that the Bolsheviks should attend the funeral of the slain Cossacks, which they did. The official loss in membership of the party was admittedly insignificant. In the whole district, out of four thousand members not more than a hundred openly withdrew. But a far greater number in those first days quietly stood apart. "The July Days," a worker, Minichev, subsequently remembered, "showed us that in our ranks too there were people who, fearing for their own skin, 'chewed up' their party cards, and denied all connection with the party." "But there were not many of them," he adds reassuringly. "The July events," writes Shliapnikov, "and the whole accompanying campaign of violence and slander against our organization interrupted that growth of our influence which by the beginning of July had reached enormous proportions.... The very party became semi-illegal, and had to wage a defensive struggle, relying in the main upon the trade unions and the shop and factory committees."

> The charge that the Bolsheviks were in the service of Germany [explains Trotsky] could not but create an impression even upon the Petrograd workers—at least upon a considerable number of them. Those who had been wavering, drew off. Those who were about to join, wavered. Even of those who had already joined, a considerable number withdrew.[34]

The situation in Moscow was not very different. "The attacks of the bourgeois press," remembers Piatnitsky, "produced a panic even in certain members of the Moscow committee." The organization weakened numerically after the July Days. "I will never forget," writes the Moscow worker, Ratekhin,

> one mortally hard moment. A plenary session was assembling (of the Zamoskvoretsky district Soviet).... I saw there were none too many of our comrade Bolsheviks.... Steklov, one of the energetic comrades, came right up close to me and, barely enunciating the words, asked: "Is it true they brought Lenin and Zinoviev in a sealed train? Is it true they are working on German money...?" My heart sank with pain when I heard those questions. Another comrade came up—Konstantinov: "Where is Lenin? He has beat it, they say.... What will happen now?" And so it went.

This vivid picture accurately reflects the experience of the advanced workers at the time. "The appearance of the documents published by Alexinsky, ["proving" Lenin to be a foreign agent]" writes the Moscow gunner, Davidovsky, "produced a terrible confusion in the brigade. Even our battery, the most Bolshevik, wavered under the blow of this cowardly lie.... It seemed as though we had lost all faith."

"After the July Days," writes V. Yakovleva, at that time a member of the Central Committee and a leader of the work in the extensive Moscow region,

> all the reports from the localities described with one voice not only a sharp decline in the mood of the masses, but even a definite hostility to our party. In a good number of cases, our speakers were beaten up. The membership fell off rapidly, and several organizations, especially in the southern provinces, even ceased to exist entirely.[35]

In the period immediately following the July Days, the influence of Bolshevism was very badly affected in some places, but hardly at all in others. In general, reaction among workers and soldiers was not deep or lasting. Let us begin by quoting some facts about areas in which the Bolsheviks did very badly:

In the Kiev municipal elections on July 26, out of 174,492 votes, the Bolsheviks got only 9,520 (or 5 percent), while the SR-Menshevik bloc gained 63,576 votes; the Ukrainian SRs 35,238 votes; and the Cadets 15,078.[36] In the Vladimir municipal elections on July 30, the SRs won 22 seats; the Mensheviks, 10; the Cadets, 15; and the Bolsheviks only 6.[37]

In Iaroslav on the same day, out of 103 seats, the SRs got 35; the Mensheviks, 34; and the Bolsheviks, 12.[38]

In Odessa on August 10, the SRs won 66 seats; the Cadets, 15; the Jewish bloc, 14; the Menshevik-Bund bloc, 8; the Ukrainian Socialists, 5; and the Internationalists and Bolsheviks, 3.[39] In Samara, on August 15, in eleven wards in which elections took place, the SRs won 13,800 votes, while the Bolsheviks got only 4,900.[40] In Tula on July 30, the Menshevik-SR bloc got 85 seats; the Cadets, 7; and the Bolsheviks, only 5.[41] Two days later, the Soviet of Workers' and Soldiers' Deputies in Tula banned Bolshevik agitation in the garrison.[42]

Things were very different, however, in other areas of the country. In Petrograd, on July 26, six thousand Putilov workers attended a meeting and passed a unanimous resolution supporting the Bolsheviks in their struggle against the counterrevolutionary policy of the SR and Menshevik leaders.[43] On August 8, an even larger meeting of more than eight thousand workers in Putilov passed a unanimous resolution of support for the Central Committee of the Bolsheviks in its opposition to the Moscow State Conference.[44]

In elections to the sickness funds on August 3 in Novyi Lessner and Staryi Lessner, the Bolsheviks won 80 percent of the seats; the SRs, 15; and the Mensheviks, 5. Until then, the Mensheviks had had a majority. In the Erikson telephone factory, out of 60 seats, the Bolsheviks won 38; the SRs, 14; and the Mensheviks, 7. In Treugolnik factory, the Bolsheviks won 70 out of 100 seats. Until then, the SRs had had the majority there.[45]

In the municipal elections in Petrograd on August 20, the Bolsheviks received 184,000 votes, against the SRs' 205,000; the Cadets' 114,000; and the Mensheviks' 24,000.[46]

The SRs kept the first place with 37 percent of the votes [writes

Sukhanov]; in comparison with the May elections, however, this was no victory but a substantial setback. The victors of July, the Cadets, had also held their ground since the district elections: they got one-fifth of all the votes. Our Menshevik list got a wretched 23,000 votes.... But who was the sole real victor? It was the Bolsheviks, so recently trampled into the mud, accused of treason and venality, utterly routed morally and materially, and filling till that very day the prisons of the capital. Why, one would have thought them annihilated forever. People had almost ceased to notice them. Then where had they sprung up from again? What sort of strange, diabolical enchantment was this?[47]

In many other centers besides Petrograd, Bolshevism held its own immediately after the July Days. On August 6, a meeting in Kronstadt of 15,000 workers, soldiers, sailors, and peasants protested against the arrest of Bolshevik leaders, and against the counter-revolutionary government.[48] On the same day, a meeting of similar size in Helsingfors passed a unanimous resolution against the counter-revolutionary policy of the provisional government and in support of the transfer of power to the soviets, workers' control of industry, etc.[49]

In the Lugansk municipal elections on August 6, the Bolsheviks won 29 seats out of a total of 75.[50] In Reval, on August 6, out of 69,681 votes, the Bolsheviks got 21,648 (or 31 percent), the SRs 15,198 (22 percent), and the Mensheviks, 8,273 (12 percent).[51]

In Nizhni-Novgorod, at the August 3–4 session of the Soviet of Workers' Deputies, there were 54 SRs, 36 Mensheviks, 10 Bundists, and 28 Bolsheviks.[52]

In the municipal elections in Tver, on August 20, out of 36,355 votes the Bolsheviks got 10,661 (or 29 percent).[53]

On August 27 in Ivanovo-Voznesensk, out of 33,709 votes, they got 20,164 (or 60 percent).[54]

At the Second Congress of the Soviet of Workers' and Soldiers' Deputies of the Urals, representing 505,780 workers and soldiers, which met on August 17–21, the Bolshevik faction was made up of 77 deputies, as against the Menshevik defensist faction, which had only 23.[55]

The Bolshevik Party continued to march ahead, despite the persecution. It was steeled by it. Lenin found in the slander against Bolshevism a badge of honor.

> The Bolsheviks in particular have had the honor of experiencing these methods of persecution used by the republican imperialists.
> In general, the Bolshevik might apply to himself the well-known

words of the poet:

> He hears the voice of approbation
> Not in the dulcet sounds of praise,
> But in the savage cries of indignation!

...[F]or the fierce hatred of the bourgeoisie is often the best proof of faithful and honest service to the cause of the proletariat by the slandered, baited, and persecuted.[56]

Bonapartism

After the great change in the balance of forces, and the events of the July Days, Lenin was quick to redefine the political regime. In an article called "The Beginning of Bonapartism," published in *Rabochii i soldat* on July 29, he wrote:

> Kerensky's cabinet is undoubtedly a cabinet taking the first steps towards Bonapartism.
> We see the chief historical symptom of Bonapartism: the maneuvering of state power, which leans on the military clique (on the worst elements of the army) for support, between two hostile classes and forces which more or less balance each other out.[57]

The soil in which Bonapartism grew was that of extreme social tensions verging on civil war.

> The class struggle between the bourgeoisie and the proletariat has reached the limit and on 20 and 21 April, as well as on 3–5 July, the country was within a hair's breadth of civil war. This socio-economic condition certainly forms the classical basis for Bonapartism. And then, this condition is combined with others that are quite akin to it; the bourgeoisie are ranting and raving against the Soviets, but are *as yet* powerless to disperse them, while the Soviets, prostituted by Tsereteli, Chernov, and Co., are *now* powerless to put up serious resistance to the bourgeoisie.
> The landowners and peasants, too, live as on the eve of civil war: the peasants demand land and freedom, they can be kept in check, if at all, only by a Bonapartist government capable of making the most unscrupulous promises to all classes without keeping any of them.
> Add to this the situation created by a foolhardy offensive and military reverses, in which fancy phrases about saving the country are particularly fashionable (concealing the desire to save the imperialist program of the bourgeoisie), and you have a perfect picture of the socio-political setting for Bonapartism.[58]

Bonapartism was not rendered impossible by the existence of democracy. On the contrary:

It would be a very big mistake to think that a democratic situation rules out Bonapartism. On the contrary, it is exactly in a situation like this (the history of France has confirmed it twice) that Bonapartism emerges, given a certain relationship between classes and their struggle.[59]

However, Kerensky's Bonapartism was very different from that of Napoleon I or his nephew, Napoleon III; it was much less stable and enduring.

The Russian Bonapartism of 1917 differs from the beginnings of French Bonapartism in 1799 and 1849 in several respects, such as the fact that not a single important task of the revolution has been accomplished here. The struggle to settle the agrarian and the national questions is only just gathering momentum.[60]

Kerensky's Bonapartism was a caricature.

Kerensky and the counter-revolutionary Cadets who use him as a pawn can neither convoke the constituent assembly on the appointed date, nor postpone it, without in both cases promoting the revolution. And the catastrophe engendered by the prolongation of the imperialist war keeps on approaching with even greater force and speed than ever.

The advance contingents of the Russian proletariat succeeded in emerging from our June and July Days without losing too much blood. The proletarian party has every opportunity to choose the tactics and form, or forms, of organization that will in any circumstances prevent unexpected (seemingly unexpected) Bonapartist persecutions from cutting short its existence and its regular messages to the people.

Let the party loudly and clearly tell the people the whole truth that Bonapartism is beginning; that the "new" government of Kerensky, Avksenteev, and Co. is merely a screen for the counter-revolutionary Cadets and the military clique which is in power at present; that the people can get no peace, the peasants no land, the workers no eight-hour day, and the hungry no bread unless the counter-revolution is completely stamped out.[61]

The Moscow state conference

If Lenin's analysis of the Kerensky regime after the July Days as a Bonapartist regime needed confirmation, this was amply given by the Moscow State Conference. A demonstration of Bonapartism in one show!

To muster public support for its policy, the provisional government assembled a State Conference in Moscow on August 12–15. This was conceived as a consultative conference, where representatives of every class and profession could express their views. Among the 2,414 delegates who took part in its sessions, the largest delegations were from members of the four tsarist Dumas (488), from the cooperatives (313), from the trade unions (176), from commercial and industrial organizations and banks (150), from municipalities (147), from the Executive Committee of the United Soviets of Workers', Soldiers', and Peasants' Deputies (129), from the army and navy (117), and from the Soviets of Workers' and Soldiers' and of Peasants' Deputies (each of which received 100 places). An effort was made to balance the conference carefully between the right and the left. However, it was a symptom of the post-July reaction that the organizations of the propertied classes were granted representation out of all proportion to their numerical weight in the population.

The Bolsheviks decided to boycott the conference. But to make their presence felt they called a general strike in Moscow, which was very successful indeed, as *Izvestiia* had to admit on August 13.

> The conference opens under rather unusual conditions. Street cars are not running; coffee houses and restaurants are closed. At yesterday's meeting of the Soviet, it was resolved to ask the Moscow proletariat not to strike; but the attitude of the Moscow proletariat toward the conference is so hostile that late at night there was a meeting of the Central Trade Union, attended by delegates of all the wards, representing about 400,000 proletarians. This delegation voted, almost unanimously, to strike.[62]

Similar stoppages took place in other towns in the Moscow province, as well as in places further afield, such as Kiev, Kostroma, and Tsaritsin.

This was convincing proof, if such were needed, to the delegates at the State Conference that Bolshevism was very much alive, even if its voice was not to be heard in the opera house where the conference was held. The new Petrograd organ of the Bolsheviks, *Proletari,* managed before it was closed down to put a question to the conference: "From Petrograd you went to Moscow—where will you go from there?"[63]

In his opening speech, Kerensky showed clearly that he was trying to strike a balance between the right and left. Without directly naming the Bolsheviks, he began with a stab in their direction: any new attempt against the government "will be put down with blood and iron." Both wings of the conference joined in strong applause. Then he made a supplementary threat in the direction of Kornilov, who had not yet arrived. "Whatever ultimatums no matter who may present to me, I will know how to subdue him to the will of the supreme power, and to me, its supreme head." This evoked ec-static applause, but only from the left half of the conference.[64]

Following Kerensky, a number of speeches were heard from the extreme right. General Kornilov, commander in chief,

> ascends the rostrum and is met by a prolonged storm of applause from the whole audience, with the exception of the left section of the aisles. The whole audience, with the exception of representatives of the Soviets of Workers' and Soldiers' Deputies, rises from the seats and applauds the Supreme Commander, who has ascended the rostrum. Growing shouts of indignation are heard from different corners of the audience, addressed to those on the left who remain sitting…. Shouts ring out: "Cads!" "Get up!" No one rises from the left benches, and a shout is heard from there: "Serfs!" The noise, which has been continuous, grows even louder.[65]

Kornilov described the anarchy in the army and the disciplining measures he had taken.

> The army is conducting a ruthless struggle against anarchy, and anarchy will be crushed…. By a whole series of legislative measures passed after the revolution by people whose understanding and spirit were alien to the army, this army was converted into the most reckless mob, which values nothing but its own life…there can be no army without discipline. Only an army welded by iron discipline, only an army that is led by the single, inflexible will of its leaders, only such an army is capable of achieving victory and is worthy of victory…. The prestige of the officers must be enhanced…. There is no army without a rear…. The measures that are adopted at the front must also be adopted in the rear.[66]

General Kaledin was even more frank and brutal than Kornilov.

> We have outlined the following principal measures for the salvation of the native land: (1) The army must be kept outside of politics (applause from the right; cries: "Bravo!") (Note: According to *Russkoe Slovo*: strong commotion on the left; cries: "This is a counter-revolution"; the chairman rings the bell)…both in the army and in the rear (cries from the right; "Right!" "Bravo!"; noise from the left), with the exception of regimental, company, battery, and Cossack troop (committees) whose rights and duties must be limited strictly to the sphere of internal routine (applause from the right; cries: "Right!" "Bravo!"); (3) the Declaration of Soldiers' Rights must be revised (applause from the right; cries "Right!" noise from the left) and supplemented with a declaration of his duties (cries: "Bravo!" "True!"; applause); (4) discipline in the army must be raised and strengthened by the most resolute measures (noise; cries from the right: "Right!"); (5) the rear and the front are an indivisible whole guaranteeing the fighting efficiency of the army, and all measures nec-

essary for strengthening the discipline at the front must likewise be implemented in the rear (cries: "Right!" "Bravo!"); (6) the disciplinary rights of the commanding personnel must be restored (cries from the right: "Bravo!" "Right!"; storm of applause, noise and whistles from the left); the leaders of the army must be given full powers (cries from the right: "Right!"; applause).

In the menacing hour of grave ordeals at the front and complete internal collapse from the political and economic disorganization, the country can be saved from ultimate ruin only by a really strong government in the capable and experienced hands (cries from the right: "Bravo, bravo!") of persons who are not bound by narrow party or group programs (cries from the right: "Right!"; applause), who are free from the necessity of looking over their shoulders after every step they take to all kinds of committees and Soviets (applause from the right; cries: "Right!").... There must be one single power for the central and local levels. The usurpation of state power by central and local committees and by the Soviets must be immediately and abruptly brought to an end. (Note: In *Russkoe Slovo* there follows: Storm of protest from the left. Cries are heard: "Out with him!" "Counter-revolutionary!" Storm of applause from the right).[67]

Then came a speech from the left, by Chkheidze, president of the soviet,

who was met with a storm of prolonged applause from the left benches. His appearance on the rostrum was accompanied by cries of "Long live the leader of the revolution!"; applause. "Citizens: In spite of the fact that it has just been proclaimed that democratic institutions must be immediately abolished—and the Central Executive of the Soviets of Workers' and Soldiers' Deputies and the Executive Committee of the Soviets of Peasants' Deputies are such organizations—I must begin my speech with a reference to these institutions."[68]

At the end of his speech it is reported that there was "Loud applause. The deputies of the left and part of the center give a stormy ovation to Comrade Chkheidze."[69]

A speech from the president of the Moscow guberniia *Zemstvo* Board from the right was balanced by a speech of the guberniia *Zemstvo* representative from the left.[70] A speech from a right-wing representative of the navy—Commander Kallistov[71]—was balanced by one from the representative of the Navy Central Committee, Abramov.[72] Abramov went out of his way to attack General Kaledin.

In contrast to General Kaledin's declaration on behalf of the Cossacks, which contained the points demanding the immediate abolition of the Soviets of Soldiers' and Workers' Deputies and the immediate abolition of the military organizations in the army, we declare that this may only be accomplished when the Russian navy ceases to exist.[73]

Towards the very end of the conference, an incident occurred revealing the deep split even in that group which was considered the
model of unity and loyalty to the state, the Cossacks. Nagaiev, a young
Cossack officer in the Soviet delegation, declared that the working
Cossacks were not with Kaledin. The Cossacks at the front, he said, do
not trust the Cossack leaders. That was true, and touched the conference upon its sorest point. The newspaper accounts here report the
stormiest of all the scenes at the conference. The left ecstatically ap-
plauded Nagaiev and shouts were heard: "Hurrah for the revolutionary Cossacks!" Indignant protests from the right: "You will answer for
this!" A voice from the officers' benches: "German marks!" In spite of
the inevitability of these words as the last argument of patriotism, they
produced an effect like an exploding bomb. The hall was filled with a
perfectly hellish noise. The Soviet delegates jumped from their seats,
threatening the officers' benches with their fists. There were cries of
"Provocateurs!" The president's bell clanged continually. Another moment and it seemed as though a fight would begin.[74]

In his concluding address, Kerensky did his best to paper over
the cracks.

Is it not clear to you, citizens, from what you have heard here, that it
is so difficult, sometimes almost impossible, to reconcile the various
points of view, the various interests, and to establish a common understanding of things?.... It is precisely this that constitutes the un-
bearable difficulty for the government which honestly strives only for
this common will and these common aims.... I will not summarize
the opinions that have been voiced here. I must only state that everything that has been expressed here will be taken into consideration by
the provisional government for guidance and coordination in the
name of the interests of the country and her salvation. (Loud applause).... Every person, according to his perception and awareness,
spoke only of the state, of the native land, of her ills, and appealed
only for the common, united cause of saving what is so profoundly
dear to us, that which is of immeasurable value to us, which has no
name, because one speaks too often of the native land.[75]

At this point the dishonesty of the February regime reached its
peak. Unable to stand the strain, Kerensky ended with a melodra-
matic wail of despair:

Let my heart turn to stone, let all the chords of my faith in men fade
away, let all the flowers of my dreams for man wither and die. (Cry
from above: "Don't let this happen!") These have been scorned and
stamped upon today from this rostrum. Then I will stamp on them
myself. They will cease to be. (Cry from above: "You cannot do
this—your heart will not permit you this.") I will cast away the keys
to this heart that loves the people and I will think only of the state.[76]

The days immediately following the Moscow State Conference

proved how right Lenin was when he said at the beginning of September that Kerensky's Bonapartist regime was instability incarnate.

> All efforts, in fact, must be directed towards keeping up with events and doing on time our work of explaining to the workers, and to the working people in general, as much as we can, the changes in the situation and in the course of the class struggle. This is still the main task of our party; we must explain to the people that the situation is extremely critical, that every action may end in an explosion, and that therefore a premature uprising may cause the greatest harm. At the same time, the critical situation is inevitably leading the working class—perhaps with catastrophic speed—to a situation in which, due to a change in events beyond its control, it will find itself compelled to wage a determined battle with the counter-revolutionary bourgeoisie and to gain power.[77]

CHAPTER 16

THE KORNILOV COUP

A plot of the extreme right

The Moscow State Conference clearly demonstrated that however hard the compromisers tried, the conditions of dual power were inevitably leading to civil war, to the elimination of one part of the diarchy by the other. The showdown was accelerated by events at the front. Whereas the June 18 offensive had led to the spontaneous armed demonstration by the left on July 3–4, defeats at the front now fueled the plotting of the right.

On August 21, Riga fell into the hands of the Germans. The fulfillment of Kornilov's prediction at the Moscow conference became a signal for a general attack by the bourgeois press against "soldiers who will not fight," and "workers who will not work."

> "The Bolsheviks," writes Stankevich, "had already begun to spread rumors that the city was surrendered to the Germans on purpose, because the officers wanted to get rid of that nest and nursery of Bolshevism. These rumors could not but win belief in the army, which knew that essentially there had been no defense or resistance." The fact is that as early as December 1916, Generals Ruzsky and Brusilov had complained that Riga was "the misfortune of the northern front," that it was "a nest of propaganda," which could only be dealt with by the method of executions.[1]

Both workers and soldiers suspected that the counterrevolutionaries would be happy to sacrifice Petrograd—the heart of the revolution—to the Germans. And they had evidence for their suspicions. Thus Rodzianko, a former chairman of the Duma, declared in *Utro Rossii* that the taking of Petrograd by the Germans would be a blessing, because it would destroy the soviets and get rid of the revolutionary Baltic fleet:

Petrograd is in danger. I say to myself, "Let God take care of Petrograd." They fear that if Petrograd is lost the central revolutionary organizations will be destroyed. To that I answer that I rejoice if all these organizations are destroyed; for they will bring nothing but disaster upon Russia....

   With the taking of Petrograd, the Baltic fleet will also be destroyed.... But there will be nothing to regret; most of the battleships are completely demoralized.[2]

John Reed, a most reliable witness of the revolution, testified that a considerable proportion of the propertied classes did express their preference for a German victory over that of the revolution. "One evening I spoke at the house of a Moscow merchant," he related, among other examples. "During tea, we asked the eleven people at the table whether they preferred 'Wilhelm or the Bolsheviki.' The vote was ten to one for Wilhelm."[3] He also spoke to an officer on the northern front who "frankly preferred a military defeat to working with the soldiers' committees."

On August 19, Kornilov telegraphed Kerensky: "I insistently assert the necessity of subordinating to me the Petrograd district." The general was openly stretching out his hand towards the capital.

"On August 22," writes Kerensky, "Savinkov went to headquarters at my direction in order, among other things, to demand of General Kornilov that he place a cavalry corps at the disposal of the Government." Savinkov explained his mission to Kornilov thus:

To get from General Kornilov a cavalry corps for the actual inauguration of martial law in Petrograd and for the defense of the provisional government against any attempt whatever, in particular an attempt of the Bolsheviks who...according to information received from a foreign intelligence service, were again preparing an attack in connection with a German siege and an insurrection in Finland.[4]

The fact that Kerensky was plotting with Kornilov to bring military rule into Petrograd can hardly be better substantiated than by General Alekseev, who was a party to the plot. In a letter to Miliukov on September 12, he wrote:

Kornilov's action was no mystery for the members of the government. The question was discussed with Savinkov, with Filonenko—and through them, with Kerensky.... The participation of Kerensky is beyond question.... The advance of the 3rd Cavalry Corps' division on Petrograd was made upon Kerensky's instructions, which had been transmitted by Savinkov. To what degree the agreement (which finds its explanation in the expected action of the Bolsheviks) had been worked out and established can be demonstrated to you by the following brief telegram:

"27 August. 2hr. 30min. To the Assistant Minister of War. The corps will concentrate in the outskirts of Petrograd toward the evening of 28 August. I request you to declare Petrograd under martial law on 29 August 6394. General Kornilov."

I think that it would be superfluous to explain the significance of this telegram. The members of the government who participated in the action and who, for some reason, withdrew from it at the decisive moment had decided during the night of 26–27 August, i.e., almost on the very hour when Kornilov was writing his telegram No. 6394, to remove him from the post of Supreme Commander. But then it was already impossible to stop the movement of the troops and to abandon the action.[5]

Prime Minister Kerensky, behind the back of part of his government, behind the back of the soviets that had given him power, and in secrecy from the SR Party to which he belonged, had conspired with the highest generals of the army for a radical change in the regime. But at the last minute, he began to fear that the military dictatorship would deliver him into the hands of the general.

Kerensky, just like Kornilov [writes Sukhanov], had set himself the goal of introducing a bourgeois dictatorship (even though, also like Kornilov, he didn't understand this).

These two...had fallen out over the question of which could be the bearer of this dictatorship. One represented the stock exchange, capital, and the rentiers; the other the same, plus the still to a large extent indeterminate groups of petty-bourgeois democratic artisans, intelligentsia, the third estate, and the paid managers of home industry and commerce.

But Kornilov and Kerensky each needed the other.... Each was trying to use the other for his own aims. Kornilov was striving for a pure dictatorship of finance, capital, and rentiers, but had to accept Kerensky as hostage of the democracy. Kerensky was aiming at a dictatorship of a bloc of the big and petty bourgeoisie, but had to pay heavy tribute to his ally as the *wielder of the real power*. And each was trying to ensure that at the finishing post he would be the actual and formal master of the situation.[6]

Kerensky "was a Kornilovite—on condition that he himself head the Kornilov rising."[7]

Unfortunately for the plot, at the last moment, before Kornilov's troops got the order to march on Petrograd, Kerensky stepped out of the general's embrace and turned against him. On August 27, he issued the following national declaration:

On August 26, General Kornilov sent to me a member of the State Duma, Vladimir Lvov, with a demand for the surrender by the provisional government of all civil and military power, so that he may form, at his personal discretion, a *new government* to administer the country....

I am taking all necessary measures to protect the liberty and order of the country, and the population will be informed in due time with regard to such measures....

I order herewith:

1. General Kornilov to surrender the post of Supreme Commander to General Klembovskii, the Commander in Chief of the northern front, which bars the way to Petrograd; and General Klembovskii to assume temporarily the post of Supreme Commander, while remaining at Pskov.

2. The city and *uezd* of Petrograd under martial law, extending to it the regulations for regions declared under martial law.[8]

General Kornilov's response made it clear that his efforts were directed to ridding Russia not only of Bolshevism, but also of the soviets. He issued a declaration to the people:

People of Russia! Our great motherland is dying. The hour of her death is near. Forced to speak openly, I, General Kornilov, declare that under the pressure of the Bolshevik majority of the Soviets, the provisional government acts in complete harmony with the plans of the German general staff, and simultaneously with the forthcoming landing of the enemy forces on the Riga shores, it is killing the army and undermines the very foundation of the country.[9]

The general was confident that he would easily win: after all, *all* the top generals supported him, as well as big business and the foreign embassies, headed by the British and French.

On August 28, Prince G.N. Trubetskoi, the representative of the Ministry of Foreign Affairs at Stavka, telegraphed the following to the minister:

A sober appraisal of the situation forces us to admit that the entire commanding personnel, the overwhelming majority of the officers, and the best combat units of the army will follow Kornilov. In the rear, the entire Cossack host, the majority of the military schools, and the best combat units will go over to Kornilov's side. Added to the physical strength is the superiority of the military organization over the weakness of the government organs, moral support of all nonsocialist elements of the population, a growing discontent among the lower classes with the existing order. The majority of the popular and urban masses have grown indifferent to the existing order and will submit to any cracking of the whip. Undoubtedly, the overwhelming number of the March socialists will not hesitate to go over on their side.[10]

General Krasnov, who was to command the Fifth Caucasian Cavalry division, one of the units involved in the expedition on Petrograd, was assured before he left Moghilev that "no one will defend Kerensky. This is only a promenade."[11] Had it been merely a question of defending Kerensky, Kornilov might have encountered very little resistance. But Prince Trubetskoi, in the seclusion of Stavka, completely misjudged the mood of the masses. So did General Krasnov.

Lenin's clear lead

The Bolshevik Party, in a state of semi-legality, suppressed and persecuted by the Kerensky government, and with its leaders viciously slandered as German agents by the same body, did not hesitate for a moment to take steps to form a practical alliance with its jailers and slanderers—Kerensky, Tsereteli, and company—in order to fight Kornilov.

Lenin's writings during these decisive days are his clearest and sharpest by far. In a letter to the Central Committee, he wrote:

> The Kornilov revolt is a most unexpected (unexpected at such a moment and in such a form) and downright unbelievably sharp turn in events. Like every sharp turn, it calls for a revision and change of tactics.[12]

However, when a radical change in tactics was needed, Lenin warned, one "must be extra cautious not to become unprincipled." There must be no concealment of principled disagreements, no weakening of the criticism of the position of the temporary ally, no covering up of differences.

> It is my conviction that those who become unprincipled are people who (like Volodarsky) slide into defensism or (like other Bolsheviks) into a *bloc* with the SRs, into *supporting* the provisional government. Their attitude is absolutely wrong and unprincipled. We shall become defensists *only after* the transfer of power to the proletariat, *after* a peace offer, *after* the secret treaties and ties with the banks have been broken—*only afterwards*. Neither the capture of Riga *nor the capture of Petrograd* will make us defensists. (I should very much like Volodarsky to read this.) Until then we stand for a proletarian revolution, we are against the war, and we are *no* defensists.
>
> *Even now* we must not support Kerensky's government. This is unprincipled. We may be asked: aren't we going to fight against Kornilov? Of course we must! But this is not the same thing; there is a dividing line here, which is being stepped over by some Bolsheviks who fall into compromise and allow themselves to be *carried away* by the course of events.
>
> We shall fight, we are fighting against Kornilov, *just as* Kerensky's *troops do*, but we do not support Kerensky. *On the contrary*, we expose his weakness. There is the difference. It is rather a subtle differ-

ence, but it is highly essential and must not be forgotten.... We must relentlessly fight against phrases about the defense of the country, about a united front of revolutionary democrats, about supporting the provisional government, etc., etc., since they are just empty *phrases*. We must say: now is the time for *action;* you SR and Menshevik gentlemen have long since worn these phrases threadbare. Now is the time for *action;* the war against Kornilov must be conducted in a revolutionary way, by drawing the masses in, by arousing them, by inflaming them (Kerensky is *afraid* of the masses, *afraid* of the people).

What then constituted the change in Bolshevik tactics brought about by the Kornilov revolt?

We are changing the *form* of our struggle against Kerensky. Without in the least relaxing our hostility towards him, without taking back a single word said against him, without renouncing the task of overthrowing him, we say that we must *take into account* the present situation. We shall not overthrow Kerensky right now. We shall approach the task of fighting against him *in a different way*, namely, we shall point out to the people (who are fighting against Kornilov) Kerensky's *weakness* and *vacillation*. This has been done in the past *as well*. Now, however, it has become the *all-important* thing and this constitutes the change.

The change in Bolshevik tactics in response to the Kornilov revolt must involve the putting forward as the central theme of party agitation a number of

"partial demands" to be presented to Kerensky: arrest Miliukov, arm the Petrograd workers, summon the Kronstadt, Vyborg, and Helsingfors troops to Petrograd, dissolve the Duma, arrest Rodzianko, legalize the transfer of the landed estates to the peasants, introduce workers' control over grain and factories, etc., etc. We must present these demands not only to Kerensky, and *not so much* to Kerensky, as to the workers, soldiers, and peasants who have been *carried away* by the course of the struggle against Kornilov. We must keep up their *enthusiasm*, encourage them to deal with the generals and officers who have declared for Kornilov, urge *them* to demand the immediate transfer of land to the peasants, suggest to *them* that it is necessary to arrest Rodzianko and Miliukov, dissolve the Duma, close down *Rech* and other bourgeois papers, and institute investigations against them. The "left" SRs must be especially urged on in this direction.

In all these tactical changes Lenin repeatedly emphasized that the central issue of the revolution must never for a second be forgotten:

It would be wrong to think that we have moved farther away from the task of the proletariat winning power. No. We have come very close to it, *not directly*, but from the side. *At the moment* we must campaign not so much directly against Kerensky, as *indirectly* against him, namely, by demanding a more and more active, truly revolutionary war against Kornilov. The development of this war alone can lead *us* to power, but we must *speak* of this as little as possible in our propaganda.[13]

With such simplicity and economy of expression, the most fundamental and sharpest turn in strategy was enunciated.

The Bolshevik agitation, following the line put so clearly by Lenin, was crucial in the defeat of the Kornilov coup. On August 27, the Bolshevik fraction in the Executive Committee of the Soviet declared that the current struggle between the coalition government and the Kornilov generals was a struggle between two methods of liquidation of the revolutionary conquests. The declaration listed a number of demands: the removal of all counterrevolutionary generals, and their replacement by elections carried out by the revolutionary soldiers; the immediate transfer of all landlords' land to the peasants' committees; eight hours a day by law, and the organization of democratic control over factories, plants, and banks; immediate abolition of all secret treaties, and the offer of terms for general democratic peace; and last, but not least, the transfer of all power to the revolutionary workers, peasants, and soldiers.[14]

Opposing Kornilov did not in any way mean supporting Kerensky, argued the Moscow Bolshevik daily, *Sotsial-Demokrat,* on August 30. "The revolutionary proletariat cannot tolerate either the dictatorship of Kornilov or of Kerensky."[15]

The collapse of the Kornilov coup

At first it looked as if Kornilov was moving from one success to another.

From hour to hour came the messages [writes Trotsky], one more threatening than the other, of the approach of Kornilov's troops. The bourgeois press seized them hungrily, expanded them, piled them up, creating an atmosphere of panic. At 12:30 p.m. on 28 August: "The troops sent by General Kornilov have concentrated themselves in the vicinity of Luga." At 2:30 in the afternoon: "Nine new trains containing the troops of Kornilov have passed through the station Oredezh. In the forward train is a railroad engineering battalion." At 3 p.m.: "The Luga garrison has surrendered to the troops of General Kornilov and turned over all its weapons. The station and all the government buildings of Luga are occupied by the troops of Kornilov." At 6 in the evening: "Two echelons of Kornilov's army have broken through from Narva and are within half a *verst* of Gatchina. Two more echelons are on the road to Gatchina." At two o'clock in the morning of the 29th: "A battle has begun at the Antropshino station (33 kilometers from Petrograd) between government troops and the troops of Kornilov. Killed and wounded on both sides." By nightfall comes the news that Kaledin has threatened to cut off Petrograd and Moscow from the grain-growing south of Russia.[16]

But, at a meeting of the Central Executive Committee of the Soviets, frightened for his own skin,

> the right Menshevik Weinstein had proposed, in the name of his fraction, that a special "committee for the struggle against the counterrevolution" be formed.... The Menshevik resolution was of course passed. Later the new body received the name of Military Revolutionary Committee. It was this institution that bore the whole brunt of the struggle against the Kornilov campaign.

What should this committee do? "Its initiators were not quite clear about that. In any case, it must give every kind of technical aid to the official organs of government in the struggle against Kornilov."[17]

The Bolsheviks' attitude was decisive.

> It was precisely the Bolsheviks who were to define its whole character, fate, and role.... The Military Revolutionary Committee, in organizing the defense, had to set in motion the masses of workers and soldiers, and these masses, in so far as they were organized, were organized by the *Bolsheviks* and followed them. At that time, theirs was the only organization that was large, welded together by elementary discipline, and united with the democratic rank and file of the capital. *Without* them the Military Revolutionary Committee was impotent.... *With* the Bolsheviks...the Military Revolutionary Committee had at its disposal all organized worker-soldier strength, of whatever kind.[18]

> ...[D]espite their being in the minority it was quite clear that in the Military Revolutionary Committee *control was in the hands of the Bolsheviks.* This followed from the nature of things. First of all, if the committee wanted to act *seriously,* then it had to act *revolutionarily,* that is, independently of the provisional government, of the existing constitution, of the acting official institutions. Only the Bolsheviks could operate like this, not the Soviet compromisers. Secondly, only the Bolsheviks had the material means for revolutionary activity, in the form of control of the masses.[19]

The most effective measure taken by the Military Revolutionary Committee was the arming of the workers.

> It goes without saying not only that this was on the initiative of the Bolsheviks but also that they issued an ultimatum on the subject. As far as I know, it was a condition of their participation in the Military Revolutionary Committee. The majority of the committee could not help accepting this condition.... The democratic, military, and trade

union organizations in the suburbs of Petersburg wired the Military
Revolutionary Committee their readiness to place themselves completely at its disposition. Without any superfluous words that Kronstadt Soviet eliminated the post-July authorities and installed their
own commander in the fortress. The Central Committee of the fleet
also went over to a revolutionary position and was ready for battle—
on sea or land—at the first demand from the Central Ex. Com.

That same night [August 28] and early morning, the Bolsheviks
had begun to display a feverish activity in the workers' districts.
Their military apparatus organized mass meetings in all the barracks.
Everywhere instructions were given, and obeyed, to remain under
arms, ready to advance. By and large, Smolny was meeting Kornilov
with all its lights blazing.[20]

Factory committees all over Petrograd swiftly organized detachments of Red Guards consisting largely of Bolsheviks—encompassing
as many as forty thousand workers. The Shlüsselburg Gunpowder
works sent a barge-load of grenades to the capital, which the Central
Council of Petrograd Factory Committees distributed among the
workers of the Vyborg district.[21]

> The giant Putilov factory became the center of resistance in the Peter-
> hoff district. Here fighting companies were hastily formed; the work
> of the factory continued day and night; there was a sorting out of
> new cannon for the formation of proletarian artillery divisions. The
> worker, Minichev, says: "In those days we worked sixteen hours a
> day.... We got together about 100 cannon." Without resort to force,
> with not a shot fired, Kornilov's conspiracy disintegrated, crumbled.

> The newly formed Vikzhel [the All-Russian Executive of the rail-
> waymen's trade union] received a prompt baptism of war. The rail-
> road workers had a special reason to dread the victory of Kornilov,
> who had incorporated in his program the inauguration of martial
> law on the railroads.... The railroad workers tore up and barricaded
> the tracks in order to hold back Kornilov's army.[22]

> The railroad workers in those days did their duty. In a mysterious
> way, echelons would find themselves moving on the wrong roads.
> Regiments would arrive in the wrong division, artillery would be sent
> up a blind alley, staffs would get out of communication with their
> units. All the big stations had their own soviets, their railroad work-
> ers' and their military committees. The telegraphers kept them in-
> formed of all events, all movements, all changes. The telegraphers
> also held up the orders of Kornilov. Information unfavorable to the
> Kornilovists was immediately multiplied, distributed, pasted up,
> passed from mouth to mouth. The machinists, the switchmen, the
> oilers, became agitators. It was in this atmosphere that the Kornilov
> echelons advanced—or what was worse, stood still.[23]

The coup collapsed after four days. "The insurrection," Trotsky wrote, "had rolled back, crumbled to pieces, been sucked up by the earth." In the army itself, Kornilov and his co-plotters found themselves completely isolated.

> The fronts did not support headquarters. Only the south-western made a somewhat serious attempt. Denikin's staff had adopted preparatory measures in good season. The unreliable guards at the staff were replaced by Cossacks. The printing presses were seized on the night of the 27th. The staff tried to play the role of self-confident master of the situation, and even forbade the committee of the front to use the telegraph. But the illusion did not last more than a few hours. Delegates from various units began to come to the committee with offers of support. Armored cars appeared, machine guns, field artillery. The committee immediately asserted its control of the activity of the staff.... By three o'clock on the 28th, the power on the south-western front was wholly in the hands of the committees. "Never again," wept Denikin, "did the future of the country seem so dark, our impotence so grievous and humiliating."[24]

Things were not very different on the other fronts.

All in all, as Miliukov had to admit in his *History of the Russian Revolution,* Kornilov failed because he was isolated from the soldiers.

> The question was actually decided not so much by troop movements, or by the strategic and tactical successes of either the government's or Kornilov's detachments, as by the mood of the troops. The question was decided—here, as well as on the front—not by the leaders of regiments, but by the soldiers.[25]

After Kornilov, a peaceful way to workers' power?

The day after the collapse of Kornilov's coup Lenin called for an examination of the new situation. And in an article entitled, "On Compromises," he argued:

> The Russian revolution is experiencing so abrupt and original a turn that we, as a party, may offer a voluntary compromise—true, not to our direct and main class enemy, the bourgeoisie, but to our nearest adversaries, the "ruling" petty-bourgeois-democratic parties, the Socialist Revolutionaries, and Mensheviks.
>
> We may offer a compromise to these parties only by way of exception, and only by virtue of the particular situation, which will obviously last only a very short time. And I think we should do so. The compromise on our part is our return to the pre-July demand of all power to the Soviets and a government of SRs and Mensheviks responsible to the Soviets.
>
> Now, and only now, perhaps *during only a few days* or a week or two, such a government could be set up and consolidated in a per-

fectly peaceful way. In all probability it could secure the peaceful *advance* of the whole Russian revolution, and provide exceptionally good chances for great strides in the world movement towards peace and the victory of socialism.[26]

What compromise should the Bolsheviks offer?

The Bolsheviks, without making any claim to participate in the government (which is impossible for the internationalists unless a dictatorship of the proletariat and the poor peasants has been realized), would refrain from demanding the immediate transfer of power to the proletariat and the poor peasants and from employing revolutionary methods of fighting for this demand. A condition that is self-evident and not new to the SRs and Mensheviks would be complete freedom of propaganda and the convocation of the constituent assembly without further delays or even at an earlier date.

The Mensheviks and SRs, being the government bloc, would then agree (assuming that the compromise had been reached) to form a government wholly and exclusively responsible to the Soviets, the latter taking over all power locally as well. This would constitute the "new" condition.

The compromise Lenin suggested could work only on condition that both parties—the Bolsheviks on the one hand and the compromisers on the other—saw some benefit in it for themselves.

The Bolsheviks would gain the opportunity of quite freely advocating their views and of trying to win influence in the Soviets under a really complete democracy…. The Mensheviks and SRs would gain in that they would at once obtain every opportunity to carry out *their* bloc's program with the support of the obviously overwhelming majority of the people and in that they would secure for themselves the "peaceful" use of their majority in the Soviets.

"Would it work?" Lenin asks, and he answers: "We cannot know, experience will show."

No matter how difficult this compromise may be at present (after July and August, two months equivalent to two decades in "peaceful," somnolent times), I think it stands a small chance of being realized. This chance has been created by the decision of the SRs and Mensheviks not to participate in a government together with the Cadets! …[I]f there is even one chance in a hundred, the attempt at realizing this opportunity is still worthwhile.[27]

In all tactical changes one must avoid sacrificing principle and falling into opportunism. One of the main dangers involved in the slogan "Power to the Soviets," was that it could degenerate simply into a call for a "Cabinet of the parties of the Soviet majority." It must mean much more than that. It must entail a radical change in the nature of state power:

> A "Cabinet of the parties of the Soviet majority" means a change of individual ministers, with the entire old government apparatus left intact—a thoroughly bureaucratic and thoroughly undemocratic apparatus incapable of carrying out serious reforms, such as are contained even in the SR and Menshevik programs.
>
> "Power to the Soviets"...means removing this apparatus and substituting for it a new, popular one, i.e., a truly democratic apparatus of Soviets, i.e., the organized and armed majority of the people—the workers, soldiers, and peasants. It means allowing the majority of the people initiative and independence not only in the election of deputies, but also in state administration, in effecting reforms and various other changes.[28]

The slogan must mean confidence in "people's initiative and independence."

> Put your faith in their revolutionary organizations, and you will see *in all* realms of state affairs the same strength, majesty, and invincibility of the workers and peasants as were displayed in their unity and their fury against Kornilov.[29]

In line with the compromise offered by Lenin, at the Democratic Conference on September 18, the Bolshevik group made a statement including the following:

> [W]e consider it necessary to declare once again, here in the hearing of the whole country, that in fighting for power so that its program can be carried out, our party has never sought and is not seeking to take power against the organized will of the majority of the working masses of the country. If all power passed to the Soviets, neither the class struggle nor the struggle between parties within the democratic camp would be abolished. But *under conditions of full and unlimited freedom of agitation* and with the Soviets constantly renewed from below, the struggle for influence and power would take place within the boundaries of Soviet organizations.[30]

After Kornilov

However, a week later Lenin could justifiably write: "[T]he Socialist Revolutionaries and Mensheviks had rejected our offer of a compromise."[31] They continued to support the provisional government even after the defeat of the Kornilov coup.

The policy of the government was as reactionary as ever. Kerensky tried energetically, although very unsuccessfully, to restore discipline in the army and to suppress peasant rebellion, as if the events of August 26–31 had never happened.

On August 30, he was compelled to dismiss Savinkov as governor general of Petrograd, because he was deeply implicated in the
Kornilov plot and had been expelled a few days earlier from the SR
Party. But a political equivalent of Savinkov was immediately appointed to the post—Palchinsky, who started his term of office by
closing down the Bolshevik paper *Rabochii* and Maxim Gorky's
paper *Novaia Zhizn.*

On September 3, as supreme commander (replacing Kornilov),
Kerensky issued an order to the army and the fleet in conjunction
with General Alekseev, formerly chief of staff under the tsar and
now holding the same office again, stating:

> As a result of General Kornilov's revolt, normal life in the army is
> completely disrupted.
>
> For the restoration of order I command: The cessation of all politi-
> cal struggle among the troops.... All troop organizations and commis-
> sars to function in a correct manner, free from political intolerance
> and suspicion and from any interference.... The cessation immediately
> of arrests of superiors, inasmuch as the right to such action belongs
> exclusively to investigative authorities, prosecutors, and the Extraor-
> dinary Investigating Commission, organized by me, which has already
> begun its work. The cessation altogether of the replacement and dis-
> missal of commanders from their posts, inasmuch as this right belongs
> only to the authorized organs of authority and is by no means within
> the competency of committee organizations. The discontinuation im-
> mediately of the arbitrary formation of detachments under the pretext
> of combatting counter-revolutionary action.[32]

Kerensky's order brought a protest from the moderate paper of
the compromisers, *Izvestiia.*

> What shall we say to yesterday's order by Kerensky to disband at once
> all the committees that waged war on counter-revolution, the same
> committees that came to life in those terrible days and became at once
> the center of all the public forces that were loyal to the revolution?...
>
> To disband them now, when there is yet so much to do to quiet the
> soldier and to inspire him with confidence that no one will cover up
> counter-revolutionary plots...to disband them now, when only thanks
> to them the revolutionary masses are organized and disciplined, to dis-
> band them now shows little understanding of conditions.[33]

An interdistrict conference of the soviets in Petrograd adopted a
resolution: "Not to dissolve the revolutionary organizations of
struggle with the counter-revolution." The pressure from below
was so strong that the compromising Military Revolutionary Committee decided not to obey the order, and summoned its local

branches "in view of the continued alarming situation to work with their former energy and restraint." Kerensky took this in silence. "There was nothing else for him to do."[34]

On the other hand, the top compromising leadership—the Central Executive Committee of the Soviets—gave the order open support on September 3.

> Soldiers of the Russian revolution. Control your wrath. Let there be no reprisals or lynchings of officers. The vast majority of them are our comrades of the revolution....
>   In the interest of the revolution, refrain from lynchings.
>   Use self-restraint, soldiers!
>   Put an end to lynchings![35]

The peasant movement was growing fast. How did the government deal with it? On October 7, a new minister of the interior, the Menshevik A.M. Nikitin, issued a circular calling for the strengthening of the militia by "reliable elements."

> The ever-worsening internal situation of the country induces me to address myself to the [oblast, guberniia, and municipal] commissars with an appeal to rally all the sound elements of the population for the purpose of fighting the anarchy which is developing and which is irrepressibly driving the country to ruin!.... If you consider that local conditions render it expedient, I suggest that you create and attach to yourselves a special committee for fighting anarchy, consisting of the representatives of the town and Zemstvo self-government, of the commander of the local garrison, and the representative of the judicial authority. Take urgent measures for an adequate organization of the militia; reinforce its cadres by selected reliable men [drawn] from the servicemen now being discharged from the service or released for the purpose of reinforcing the militia, in accordance with the order issued to the commanders of the military districts by the Minister of War.[36]

Four days later, on October 11, the new minister of war, Major General Verkhovskii, issued a further order to supplement Nikitin's.

> The militia now existing is not in a position to guarantee this foremost preoccupation of the state. The army has the duty to come to the assistance of the government commissars and the town and Zemstvo organizations with all its means and all its experience.
>   The anarchy which grows in the country compels the urgent execution of the task, without the delay of even one day..., I authorize the assignment for duty in the militia, at the request of town and Zemstvo self-governments, of the best soldiers, preferably Cavaliers of St. George and those who have been wounded.

The Cavaliers of St. George had been among Kornilov's few reliable supporters!

> For the purpose of guarding the railways, the best officers and men, preferably Cavaliers of St. George who have been in battle and received wounds, are to be placed at the disposal of railway authorities.... For the purpose of organizing mounted guards, I authorize the district commanders to assign from cavalry units, at the request of government commissars or the local self-governments, the best officers and men (with horses), preferably Cavaliers of St. George having been in combat action and having been wounded.
>
> The officers and men assigned for this service shall be immediately returned to the ranks of the army at the slightest evasion of duty or the slightest infringement of strict order or military discipline.[37]

Unfortunately, the government had little power to impose real discipline.

The disintegration of the February regime

The process of disintegration of the army was greatly accelerated by the events of the last days of August. Stankevich summed up the situation in the days after the Kornilov coup:

> The authority of the commanders was destroyed once for all. The masses of soldiers, seeing how a General, Commander in Chief, had gone against the revolution, felt themselves surrounded by treason on all sides and saw in every man who wore epaulettes a traitor. And whoever tried to argue against this feeling also seemed a traitor.[38]

The Menshevik commissar in the army, Voytinsky, gave a similar account:

> The Kornilov affair had a disastrous effect on the morale of the army. It opened the old wound—distrust between the enlisted men and officers. All our efforts to reconcile the two groups had been wiped out!.... Soldiers made no distinction between Kerensky and Kornilov, between their immediate commanders and generals playing politics in Mogilev. To them, all officers were members of the same gang.[39]

A military intelligence report from the commander of the Sixth Siberian corps and the Third Siberian division for the days September 7–18 stated:

> [O]pen hostility and animosity are manifest on the part of the soldiers; the most insignificant event may provoke unrest. Soldiers say among themselves that all the officers are followers of General Kornilov and partisans of the old regime, and that for this reason they should be destroyed.... There is a complete lack of authority and no force that could compel the fulfilment of service duty.[40]

On September 11, the minister of war addressed the Central Committee of the Socialist Revolutionary Party:

> General Verkhovskii gave a vivid picture of the disintegration of the army as a result of the Kornilov action, particularly in the light of the fact that on the heels of declaring Kornilov a rebel, the army received instructions from the government to continue to execute his operative orders. Nobody wanted to believe that an order in such contradiction to the preceding instruction could be true. In general there was an increase of attacks on officers by soldiers, shootings, and throwing of grenades through the windows of officers' meetings, etc.[41]

But like King Canute, Kerensky had an answer to the rising tide of soldiers' revolution: discipline. On September 18, he sent an order dissolving the Central Committee of the Baltic fleet.

The sailors answered: "The order dissolving the Centroflot, being unlawful, is to be considered inoperative, and its immediate annulment is demanded." The Executive Committee intervened, and supplied Kerensky with a formal pretext for annulling his decision three days later.

Kerensky's quixotism knew no bounds. Five days before he was swept away by the October Revolution he wrote a decree on "Stricter Disciplinary Measures":

> Those individual military units and their subdivisions (companies, battalions, etc.) in which serious repeated or mass breaches of duty, order, and military discipline occur, in the form of refusal to obey the lawful authorities, failure to carry out battle orders, unwillingness to discharge duties, acts of violence or similar acts, are placed, in view of the overt and grave nature of the aforesaid breaches, on a special disciplinary footing by authority of the commander of the army (Chief Commander of the Military District) or the Commander in Chief of the armies of the front, by agreement with the corresponding military commissars and appropriate army committees, or by authority of the Supreme Commander and War Minister. A unit or command placed on a disciplinary footing receives, in addition to its name, the term of "penal" unit and shall be deprived of the right to have elective military organizations, as a result of which all committees and disciplinary courts of this unit end their activity, and disciplinary authority is handed over to commanders.[42]

This was farcical. Those whom the gods condemn they rob of their senses first!

The farce of the Democratic Conference

To paper over the cracks in the government and in an attempt to demonstrate the existence of popular support for it, the compromising leaders decided to call a Democratic Conference on September 14–19.

The Bolsheviks were gaining more and more support in the soviets, and as their struggle for a soviet government was gaining in popularity, the Menshevik and SR leaders decided to establish this Democratic Conference to rival the Congress of Soviets. They were trying to create a new base for themselves—by an artificial combination of all kinds of organizations. The delegacies were apportioned very arbitrarily, but following one rule—that the organizations of the higher strata of society were far better represented than the lower. The *Zemstvos* and cooperatives enormously outweighed the soviets.

However, even the Democratic Conference could not prevent the collapse of the February regime. It rather demonstrated its utter bankruptcy.

At the conference, 766 deputies voted for a coalition government, against 688, with 38 abstaining.[43] The two camps were evenly balanced. An amendment excluding the Cadets from the coalition got a majority of 595 to 493, with 72 abstentions. Without the Cadets, however, as the SR leader Gots stated, "a coalition is impossible."

The collapse of the policy of the compromisers is clearly shown by the votes of the soviet representatives at the conference on the question of the coalition.

Groups	For	Against	Not Voting
Soviet of Workers' and Soldiers' Deputies	83	192	4
Soviets of Peasants' Deputies	102	70	12
TOTAL	185	262	16

Among the "non-Russian groups," opponents of coalition constituted a majority of forty votes against fifteen. Kerensky's policy of violence towards the oppressed nationalities had borne fruit.

Before dispersing, the conference set up a permanent body composed of 15 percent of the membership of each of its constituent groups—about 350 delegates in all. The institutions of the property-owning classes were to receive an additional 120 seats. The government in its own name added 20 seats for the Cossacks. All these together were to constitute a Council of the Republic, or pre-parliament, which was to represent the nation until the constituent assembly. This pre-parliament was destined to stagger along until the October Revolution got rid of it, together with all the other institutions of the February regime.

Bolshevism sweeps all before it

On August 31, the Bolsheviks won a majority in the Petrograd Soviet. Trotsky became its president. On September 5, the Moscow Soviet, the second strongest in the country, passed into the hands of the Bolsheviks, and a vote of no confidence in the provisional government was passed by 335 votes to 254. Kiev, the capital of the Ukraine, followed suit a few days later, and so did Kazan, Baku, Nikolaev, and a host of other industrial towns. Finnish Soviets gave even more wholehearted support to the Bolsheviks.

As early as September 1, the Bolshevik newspaper *Rabochii* announced that 126 soviets had requested the Soviet Central Executive Committee to take over power. The committee, elected at the first Congress of soviets and dominated by Mensheviks and Socialist Revolutionaries, had no intention of complying with this request; but the mood of the local soviets was nonetheless significant. On September 5, a Congress of Soviets in the radical Siberian center of Krasnoiarsk revealed a Bolshevik majority; on the following day a message from Ekaterinburg, the main city of the Urals, announced that power had passed into the hands of the soviets in this important mining and industrial region. In the large Briansk factory in Ekaterinoslav, in the Ukraine, the workers were passing a resolution to the effect that "we cannot recognize the provisional government." The same swing of the pendulum to the left was evident in the Volga towns in the Donetz basin. It was no longer possible to assume, as it had been in the summer, that the more conservative provinces would oppose a revolutionary blow struck in Petrograd.

Still more significant, because closer to the nerve center of the Kerensky regime, was the trend in the Baltic fleet and in Finland. On September 10, a regional congress of soviets in Finland adopted Bolshevik resolutions by big majorities. The Socialist Revolutionaries who were elected to the congress were almost all members of the left wing of the party, which was now growing steadily in strength and often voted and acted with the Bolsheviks.

The Baltic fleet, always a pacemaker in agitation against the provisional government, took a stand of sharp opposition after the

Kornilov affair. Its attitude toward its nominal commander in chief, Kerensky, was pungently expressed in a published resolution of a congress of the Baltic fleet, which contained the following sentiments:

> We demand the removal from the ranks of the provisional government of the political adventurer, Kerensky, as a person who, by his shameless political trickery in favor of the bourgeoisie, disgraces the great revolution, and, along with it, the whole revolutionary people. To you, betrayer of the revolution, Bonaparte Kerensky, we send our curses.[44]

In Saratov, the soldiers' section of the soviet before the Kornilov coup was represented by 260 SR delegates, 90 Mensheviks, and 50 Bolsheviks. After the Kornilov affair, they were represented by 60 SRs, 4 Mensheviks, and 156 Bolsheviks.

> Perhaps the most drastic turnround in the country took place among the soldiers of the Moscow garrison in the interval between the two municipal elections of June and September. On the first occasion, the garrison had given 70 percent of its vote to the SRs; on the second, 90 percent went to the Bolsheviks.[45]

Millions were moving towards a spontaneous Bolshevism.

> In the reports of local authorities, both military and civil [wrote Trotsky], Bolshevism had become in these days a synonym for every kind of mass activity, every decisive demand, every resistance against exploitation, every forward motion—in a word, it had become another name for revolution. Does that mean that all these things *are* Bolshevism? the strikers would ask themselves—and the protesting sailors, and the dissatisfied soldiers' wives, and the *muzhiks* in revolt. The masses were, so to speak, compelled from above to identify their intimate thoughts and demands with the slogans of Bolshevism. Thus the revolution turned to its own use a weapon directed against it.[46]

If the July Days jolted the counterrevolution forward, the failure of the Kornilov coup provided a spur for Bolshevism. As Sukhanov put it: "[A]fter the Kornilov revolt, Bolshevism began blossoming luxuriantly and put forth deep roots throughout the country."[47]

CHAPTER 17

STATE AND REVOLUTION

The central problem of all revolutions is that of state power. Which class is to hold it? There can be no revolutionary movement without revolutionary theory—as Lenin many times reiterated—so it is not surprising that he spent the months of August and September, while in hiding, preparing a work on the subject of state and revolution.

He had been studying the subject systematically during the last few months of 1916. On February 17, 1917, while still in Switzerland, he wrote to Alexandra Kollontai: "I am preparing (have almost got the material ready) an article on the question of the attitude of marxism to the state."[1]

Lenin left this manuscript in Stockholm on his way to Russia. Apparently it was practically ready for publication, as can be deduced from his letter to Kamenev, written between July 5 and July 7:

> *Entre nous:* if they do me in, I ask you to publish my notebook: "Marxism on the State" (it got left behind in Stockholm). It's bound in a blue cover. It contains a collection of all the quotations from Marx and Engels, likewise from Kautsky against Pannekoek. There are a number of remarks and notes, and formulations. I think it could be published after a week's work. I believe it to be important... . The condition: all this is absolutely *entre nous!*[2]

It is clear from this, firstly, that the work was practically ready even before the February Revolution, and secondly that Lenin thought it to be of paramount importance. And there is no doubt that this work, the final draft of which was written a couple of months before the October insurrection and published under the title *State and Revolution,* has proved to be among his most significant.

It addresses itself to some of the most momentous questions of theory and practice facing the revolutionary movement, questions that have certainly not lost their importance over time, but rather the contrary.

Reviving the Marxist theory of the state

The "Marxists" of the Second International, including their chief theoretician, Kautsky, castrated and vulgarized the Marxist theory of the state.

> What is now happening to Marx's theory [Lenin writes] has, in the course of history, happened repeatedly to the theories of revolutionary thinkers and leaders of oppressed classes fighting for emancipation. During the lifetime of great revolutionaries, the oppressing classes constantly hounded them, received their theories with the most savage malice, the most furious hatred, and the most unscrupulous campaigns of lies and slander. After their death, attempts are made to convert them into harmless icons, to canonize them, so to say...while at the same time robbing the revolutionary theory of its substance, blunting its revolutionary edge, and vulgarizing it. Today, the bourgeoisie and the opportunists within the labor movement concur in this doctoring of marxism. They omit, obscure, or distort the revolutionary side of this theory, its revolutionary soul.[3]

The reformists distorted Marxism in general, but especially the Marxist concept of the state. The "Marxism" of Kautsky was mechanical, fatalistic. It was passive and nonrevolutionary. A long period of purely evolutionary, reformist activity had led Kautsky to adopt a critical position on various individual aspects of the capitalist state, but not to oppose it totally. Reform of aspects of the capitalist state, not its overthrow, became the *leitmotiv*. For Kautsky, Marxism was a theory of the class struggle. But for Marx himself, it was the development of the class struggle *to the dictatorship of the proletariat*. Thus in a letter to Weydemeyer dated March 5, 1852, Marx stated:

> And now as to myself, no credit is due to me for discovering the existence of classes in modern society or the struggle between them. Long before me, bourgeois historians had described the historical development of this class struggle and bourgeois economists, the economic anatomy of the classes. What I did that was new was to prove: (1) that the *existence of classes* is only bound up with *particular, historical phases in the development of production*, (2) that the class struggle necessarily leads to the *dictatorship of the proletariat*, (3) that this dictatorship itself only constitutes the transition to the *abolition of all classes* and to a *classless society*.[4]

Thus, according to Marx, an acceptance of the concept of the class struggle does not go beyond bourgeois limits; the dictatorship of the proletariat does.

For Kautsky and his associates, the capitalist state was taken as given, to be adapted, even while fighting particular aspects of it. In the *Erfurt Program* (1891), Kautsky wrote:

> This revolution (i.e., the seizure of political power by the proletariat) may take the most diverse forms, depending on the conditions in which it occurs. *It is in no way inseparable from violence and bloodshed.*
>
> We have already seen cases, in the history of the world, of ruling classes who were intelligent enough, weak enough, or cowardly enough to surrender voluntarily in the face of necessity.[5]

Kautsky's theory bore fruit in the years after the First World War. In a work published in 1922, he wrote:

> In his famous article criticizing the Social Democratic Party's program, Marx says: *"Between capitalist and communist society, there lies the period of the revolutionary transformation of the one into the other. Corresponding to this is a period of political transition in which the state can be nothing but the revolutionary dictatorship of the proletariat."* Given our experiences over the last few years, we can now alter this passage on the kind of government we want, and say: *"Between the period of a purely bourgeois state and a purely proletarian state, there lies a period of the transformation of one into the other. Corresponding to this there is also a period of political transition, in which the state will usually take the form of a coalition government."*[6]

In a later book, *The Materialist Concept of History,* Kautsky went so far as to completely deny the need for armed struggle in the revolution:

> When you have a democratic state (the existing bourgeois state), a consolidated democracy, armed struggle no longer plays any role in the solution of social conflicts. These conflicts are resolved by peaceful means, by propaganda, and the vote. Even the mass strike, as a means of pressure by the working class, is of decreasing utility.[7]

The state is a neutral body:

> The modern democratic state differs from preceding types in that utilization of the government apparatus by the exploiting classes is no longer an essential feature of it, no longer inseparable from it. On the contrary, the democratic state tends not to be the organ of a minority, as was the case in previous regimes, but rather that of the majority of the population, in other words of the toiling classes. Where it is, however, the organ of a minority of exploiters, the reason for this does not

lie in its own nature; it is rather that the toiling classes themselves lack unity, knowledge, independence, or fighting ability—all qualities which in their turn are a result of the conditions in which they live.

Democracy offers the possibility of cancelling the political power of the exploiters, and today, with the constant increase in the number of workers, this in fact happens more and more frequently.

The more this is the case, the more the democratic state ceases to be a simple instrument in the hands of the exploiting classes. The government apparatus is already beginning, in certain conditions, to turn against the latter—in other words to work in the opposite direction to that in which it used to work in the past. From being an instrument of oppression, it is beginning to change into an instrument of emancipation for the workers.[8]

Kautsky was, of course, not as openly antirevolutionary before 1917, but the basic characteristic of reformist adaptation to the state, never raising the question of the need to smash it by revolution, was already detectable in his thinking.

Smashing the capitalist state

In *State and Revolution*, Lenin starts by making it clear that the question of the state is the central question for war and revolution. First, "our prime task is to *reestablish* what Marx really taught on the subject of the state."[9]

The state is a product and a manifestation of the *irreconcilability* of class antagonisms. The state arises where, when and insofar as class antagonisms objectively *cannot* be reconciled. And, conversely, the existence of the state proves that the class antagonisms are irreconcilable.[10]

...[T]he state is an organ of class *rule*, an organ for the *oppression* of one class by another.

In October–November 1918, in his book *The Proletarian Revolution and the Renegade Kautsky*, Lenin underlined even more heavily the class nature of parliamentary democracy.

Bourgeois democracy, although a great historical advance in comparison with medievalism, always remains, and under capitalism is bound to remain, restricted, truncated, false, and hypocritical, a paradise for the rich and a snare and deception for the exploited, for the poor[11]

...[D]eceit, violence, corruption, mendacity, hypocrisy, and oppression of the poor is hidden beneath the civilized, polished, and perfumed exterior of modern bourgeois democracy.[12]

Kautsky's distortion of Marxism was subtle:

Theoretically, it is not denied that the state is an organ of class rule, or that class antagonisms are irreconcilable. But what is overlooked or glossed over is this: if the state is the product of the irreconcilability of class antagonisms, if it is a power standing *above* society and *"alienating* itself *more and more* from it," it is obvious that the liberation of the oppressed class is impossible not only without a violent revolution, *but also without the destruction* of the apparatus of state power which was created by the ruling class...it is this conclusion which Kautsky has "forgotten" and distorted[13]...all previous revolutions perfected the state machine, whereas it must be broken, smashed.

This conclusion is the chief and fundamental point in the marxist theory of the state. And it is precisely this fundamental point which has been completely *ignored* by the dominant official Social Democratic parties and, indeed, *distorted* (as we shall see later) by the foremost theoretician of the Second International, Karl Kautsky.[14]

Dictatorship of the proletariat

The smashing of the capitalist state apparatus and the crushing of the bourgeoisie are necessary, because the bourgeoisie will never give up its effort to reestablish its economic and political dominance.

The theory of the class struggle, applied by Marx to the question of the state and the socialist revolution, leads as a matter of course to the recognition of the *political rule* of the proletariat, of its dictatorship, i.e., of undivided power directly backed by the armed force of the people. The overthrow of the bourgeoisie can be achieved only by the proletariat becoming the *ruling class,* capable of crushing the inevitable and desperate resistance of the bourgeoisie, and of organizing *all* the working and exploited people for the new economic system.

The proletariat needs state power, a centralized organization of force, an organization of violence, both to crush the resistance of the exploiters and to *lead* the enormous mass of the population—the peasants, the petty bourgeoisie, and semi-proletarians—in the work of organizing a socialist economy.[15]

To confine marxism to the theory of the class struggle means curtailing marxism, distorting it, reducing it to something acceptable to the bourgeoisie. A marxist is solely someone who *extends* the recognition of the class struggle to the recognition of the *dictatorship of the proletariat.*[16]

On the basis of the experience of the Paris Commune of 1871, Marx and Engels had drawn clear conclusions about what kind of state should replace the capitalist state, what form the dictatorship of the proletariat should take. In Marx's words:

The first decree of the Commune...was the suppression of the standing army, and its replacement by the armed people.... The Commune was formed of the municipal councillors, chosen by universal suffrage in the various wards of Paris, responsible and revocable at any time. The majority of its members were naturally working men, or acknowledged representatives of the working class...The police, which until then had been the instrument of the government, was at once stripped of its political attributes, and turned into the responsible and at all times revocable instrument of the Commune. So were the officials of all other branches of the administration. From the members of the Commune downwards, public service had to be done at *workmen's wages*. The privileges and the representation allowances of the high dignitaries of state disappeared along with the dignitaries themselves.... Having once got rid of the standing army and the police, the instruments of the physical force of the old government, the Commune proceeded at once to break the instrument of spiritual suppression, the power of the priests.... The judicial functionaries lost that sham independence...they were thenceforward to be elective, responsible, and revocable.[17]

Lenin quotes these words and concludes:

The Commune...appears to have replaced the smashed state machine "only" by fuller democracy: abolition of the standing army; all officials to be elected and subject to recall. But as a matter of fact this "only" signifies a gigantic replacement of certain institutions by other institutions of a fundamentally different type...the abolition of all representation allowances, and of all monetary privileges to officials, the reduction of the remuneration of *all* servants of the state to the level of *"workmen's wages."*[18]

Under capitalism, the executive (civil servants, etc.) hides behind the parliamentary facade.

"The Commune was to be a working, not a parliamentary, body, executive and legislative at the same time."

"A working, not a parliamentary, body"—this is a blow straight from the shoulder at the present-day parliamentarians and parliamentary "lap dogs" of Social Democracy! Take any parliamentary country, from America to Switzerland, from France to Britain, Norway and so forth—in these countries the real business of "state" is performed behind the scenes and is carried on by the departments, chancelleries, and general staffs. Parliament is given up to talk for the special purpose of fooling the "common people."[19]

Bolshevik policy was a practical policy.

We are not Utopians, we do not "dream" of dispensing *at once* with all administration, with all subordination. These anarchist dreams, based upon incomprehension of the tasks of the proletarian dictatorship, are totally alien to marxism, and, as a matter of fact, serve only to postpone the socialist revolution until people are different. No, we want the socialist revolution with people as they are now, with people who cannot dispense with subordination, control and "foremen and accountants."

The subordination, however, must be to the armed vanguard of all the exploited and working people, i.e., to the proletariat. A beginning can and must be made at once, overnight, to replace the specific "bossing" of state officials by the simple functions of "foremen and accountants," functions which are already fully within the ability of the average town dweller and can well be performed for "workmen's wages."

We, the workers, shall organize large-scale production on the basis of what capitalism has already created, relying on our own experience as workers, establishing strict, iron discipline backed up by the state power of the armed workers. We shall reduce the role of state officials to that of simply carrying out our instructions as responsible, revocable, modestly paid "foremen and accountants" (of course, with the aid of technicians of all sorts, types, and degrees). This is *our* proletarian task, this is what we can and must *start* with in accomplishing the proletarian revolution. Such a beginning, on the basis of large-scale production, will of itself lead to the gradual "withering away" of all bureaucracy, to the gradual creation of an order—an order without inverted commas, an order bearing no similarity to wage slavery—an order under which the functions of control and accounting, becoming more and more simple, will be performed by each in turn, will then become a habit and will finally die out as the *special* functions of a special section of the population.[20]

The transition from capitalism to communism

In Lenin's writings, as in those of Marx before him, there is very little about the future socialist society. Neither Marx nor Lenin were Utopian socialists and they believed that socialism could be achieved only through the practical struggle of humanity. To postulate the features of socialism before it was achieved would be dogmatic, empty playacting. But both were quite explicit on the process of the class struggle against capitalism for socialism.

During the *transition* from capitalism to communism suppression is *still* necessary, but it is now the suppression of the exploiting minority by the exploited majority. A special apparatus, a special machine for suppression, the "state," is *still* necessary, but this is now a transitional state. It is no longer a state in the proper sense of the word; for the suppression of the minority of exploiters by the majority of the wage slaves of *yesterday* is comparatively so easy, simple, and natural a task that it will entail far less bloodshed than the suppression of the risings of slaves, serfs, or wage-laborers, and it will cost mankind far less. And it is compatible with the extension of democracy to such an overwhelming majority of the population that the need for a *special machine* of suppression will begin to disappear. Naturally, the exploiters are unable to suppress the people without a highly complex machine for performing this task, but *the people* can suppress the exploiters even with a very simple "machine," almost without a "machine," without a special apparatus, by the simple *organization of the armed people* (such as the Soviets of Workers' and Soldiers' Deputies, we would remark, running ahead).[21]

Democracy for the vast majority of the people, and suppression by force, i.e., exclusion from democracy, of the exploiters and oppressors of the people—this is the change democracy undergoes during the transition from capitalism to communism.

Only in communist society, when the resistance of the capitalists has been completely crushed, when the capitalists have disappeared, when there are no classes (i.e., when there is no distinction between the members of society as regards their relation to the social means of production), *only* then "the state...ceases to exist," and "*it becomes possible to speak* of freedom."[22]

Lastly, only communism makes the state absolutely unnecessary, for there is *nobody* to be suppressed—"nobody" in the sense of a *class;* of a systematic struggle against a definite section of the population. We are not Utopians, and do not in the least deny the possibility and inevitability of excesses on the part of *individual persons,* or the need to stop *such* excesses. In the first place, however, no special machine, no special apparatus of suppression, is needed for this; this will be done by the armed people themselves, as simply and as readily as any crowd of civilized people, even in modern society, interferes to put a stop to a scuffle or to prevent a woman from being assaulted. And, secondly, we know that the fundamental social cause of excesses, which consist in the violation of the rules of social intercourse, is the exploitation of the people, their want, and their poverty. With the removal of this chief cause, excesses will inevitably begin to "*wither away.*" We do not know how quickly and in what succession, but we do know they will wither away. With their withering away the state will also *wither away.*[23]

For Lenin the question of the transition from capitalism to communism on the economic level was also a political question. Here again he was practical, realistic to the end, trying to gauge the combination of elements of the past and the future—of capitalism and communism—in the transition period. In the immediate post-revolutionary society, there would be a combination of elements of the old and the new.

The means of production are no longer the private property of individuals. The means of production belong to the whole of society. Every member of society, performing a certain part of the socially necessary work, receives a certificate from society to the effect that he has done a certain amount of work. And with this certificate he receives from the public store of consumer goods a corresponding quantity of products. After a deduction is made of the amount of labor which goes to the public fund, every worker, therefore, receives from society as much as he has given to it.

"Equality" apparently reigns supreme.[23]

However, there is no real equality:

"Equal right," says Marx, we certainly do have here; but it is *still* a "bourgeois right," which, like every right, *implies inequality*. Every right is an application of an *equal* measure to *different* people who in fact are not alike, are not equal to one another. That is why "equal right" is a violation of equality and an injustice. In fact, everyone, having performed as much social labor as another, receives an equal share of the social product (after the above-mentioned deductions).

But people are not alike: one is strong, another is weak; one is married, another is not; one has more children, another has less, and so on. And the conclusion Marx draws is:

"With an equal performance of labor, and hence an equal share in the social consumption fund, one will in fact receive more than another, one will be richer than another, and so on. To avoid all these defects, right would have to be unequal rather than equal. The first phase of communism, therefore, cannot yet provide justice and equality: differences, and unjust differences, in wealth will still persist, but the *exploitation* of man by man will have become impossible.[25]

And so, in the first phase of communist society (usually called socialism) "bourgeois right" is *not* abolished in its entirety, but only in part, only in proportion to the economic revolution so far attained, i.e., only in respect of the means of production. "Bourgeois right" recognizes them as the private property of individuals. Socialism converts them into *common* property. To that extent—and to that extent alone—"bourgeois right" disappears.

However, it persists as far as its other part is concerned; it persists in the capacity of regulator (determining factor) in the distribution of products and the allotment of labor among the members of society. The socialist principle, "He who does not work shall not eat," is *already* realized; the other socialist principle, "An equal amount of products for an equal amount of labor," is also *already* realized. But this is not yet communism, and it does not yet abolish "bourgeois right," which gives unequal individuals, in return for unequal (really unequal) amounts of labor, equal amounts of products.[26]

To the extent that "bourgeois rights" remain,

there still remains the need for a state, which, while safeguarding the common ownership of the means of production, would safeguard equality in labor and in the distribution of products. The state withers away insofar as there are no longer any capitalists, any classes, and, consequently, no *class* can be *suppressed*. But the state has not yet completely withered away, since there still remains the safeguarding of "bourgeois right," which sanctifies actual inequality. For the state to wither away completely, complete communism is necessary.[27]

Even though the workers differ from one another in skill, in their needs and those of their families, etc., in one thing they must be *absolutely equal* in order that the same amount of labor that every worker gives to society in one form be received back in another: in the ownership of the means of production. The growth of production, the increase of the amount of means of production belonging to society, i.e., owned equally by all the workers, will progressively undermine equal rights in the distribution of the products. This in turn will progressively increase equality among the people. And thus does the bourgeois right of the transition period include its own negation.

Bourgeois right in the transition period, while it lays down that every worker will receive means of consumption from society according to the labor he gives it, is based on social equality as regards the means of production, and thereby will wither away of itself.[28]

The dictatorship of the proletariat and the abolition of private property of the means of production are not enough, according to Marx and Lenin, to overcome bourgeois law and the bourgeois state inherited from a barbarous class society. A whole period of progress of the productive forces, plus intellectual and moral transformation of the most important productive force—the working people—are necessary for the transition to real human freedom.

The period of the dictatorship of the proletariat will be a long one of very hard class struggle, in which the proletariat will have to fight on the economic, cultural, and political fronts against the powers of the past, above all the habits and traditions of capitalism that have burdened the consciousness of the masses.

The seizure of political power by the proletariat is only the first step towards the economic construction and cultural revolution that are necessary to achieve real communism.

In conclusion

Throughout history, the ruling classes have created a mystique around the state, describing it as supreme and omnipotent, so that the oppressed classes should accept their inferiority in face of it. Lenin's task was to remove all mystification and to reveal the class nature of the state.

The intimate relation between his theory and practice is most clearly shown in the few words from his postscript to *State and Revolution* written on November 30, 1917:

> [T]he writing of the second part of the pamphlet ("The Experience of the Russian Revolutions of 1905 and 1917") will probably have to be put off for a long time. It is more pleasant and useful to go through the "experience of the revolution" than to write about it.[29]

While attributing to his work the very modest goal of reviving the genuine "teaching of Marx about the state" in the light of the actual experience and needs of the revolution, Lenin in fact gave Marx's ideas a new concreteness and hence a new development. The whole of Lenin's teaching is in *State and Revolution,* above all his complete confidence in the creative potential of the masses—a confidence that was the theme of all his work and struggles. To quote from just one article which he wrote in 1906:

> It is just the revolutionary periods which are distinguished by wider, richer, more deliberate, more methodical, more systematic, more courageous, and more vivid making of history than periods of philistine, Cadet, reformist progress. But the liberals turn the truth inside out! They palm off paltriness as magnificent making of history. They regard the inactivity of the oppressed or downtrodden masses as the triumph of "system" in the work of bureaucrats and bourgeois. They shout about the disappearance of intellect and reason when, instead of the picking of draft laws to pieces by petty bureaucrats and liberal *penny-a-liner* journalists, there begins a period of direct political activity of the "common people," who simply set to work without more ado to smash all the instruments for oppressing the people, seize power, and take what was regarded as belonging to all kinds of robbers of the people—in short, when the intellect and reason of millions of downtrodden people awaken not only to read books, but for action, vital human action, to make history.[30]

And again:

> The organizing abilities of the people, particularly of the proletariat, but also of the peasantry, are revealed a million times more strongly, fully, and productively in periods of revolutionary whirlwind than in periods of so-called calm (dray-horse) historical progress.[31]

State and Revolution was influenced by the struggles of 1917 and in turn influenced them. It is a perfect synthesis of theory and practice. The point of departure of this work is revolutionary practice and its final aim is also revolutionary practice—the connecting link is revolutionary theory. The theory in turn is immediately integrated with practice.

In *State and Revolution* there is a remarkable combination of scientific sobriety and real will for action. It is the apex of Lenin's writing—his real testament. It became the guide for the first victorious proletarian revolution and is bound to grow in importance in future revolutionary struggles. The destiny of this masterpiece is also of historical importance in another sense: its spirit is bound to be invoked against the bureaucratic degeneration associated with the rise of Stalinist state capitalism and the development of hyper-bureaucratic regimes elsewhere.

CHAPTER 18

THE PROLETARIAT CAN WIELD
STATE POWER

Obstacles in the path of workers' power

As a complement to his *State and Revolution*, Lenin wrote another important pamphlet, called *Can the Bolsheviks Retain State Power?* It was written between late September and October 1, and its main aim was to expose the age-old prejudices that the masses of the downtrodden and oppressed were too ignorant to be able to wield political power, that the state apparatus was too complicated an instrument for simple mortals to handle.

Where *State and Revolution* deals with the above problem *in general terms,* this second pamphlet is much more concerned with the immediate issue of seizing power in Russia in October 1917. One argument against the seizure of power by the proletariat was that

> the proletariat "will not be able technically to lay hold of the state apparatus".... It deserves most attention...also because it indicates one of the most *serious* and *difficult* tasks that will confront the victorious proletariat. There is no doubt that these tasks will be very difficult, but if we, who call ourselves socialists, indicate this difficulty only to *shirk* these tasks, in practice the distinction between us and the lackeys of the bourgeoisie will be reduced to nought. The difficulty of the tasks of the proletarian revolution should prompt the proletariat's supporters to make a closer and more definite study of the means of carrying out these tasks.[1]

Obstacles were not an excuse for running away, but impediments to be overcome.

It was true that the proletariat would meet with resistance from the capitalists as well as of high officialdom. "This resistance will have to be *broken*."

> We can do this, for it is merely a question of breaking the resistance of

an insignificant minority of the population, literally a handful of people, over each of whom the employees' unions, the trade unions, the consumers' societies, and the Soviets will institute such *supervision* that every [one] will be *surrounded*.... We know these...by name: we only have to consult the lists of directors, board members, large shareholders, etc. There are several hundred, at most several thousand of them in the *whole* of Russia, and the proletarian state, with the apparatus of the Soviets, of the employees' unions, etc., will be able to appoint ten or even a hundred supervisors to each of them, so that instead of "breaking resistance" it may even be possible, by means of *workers' control* (over the capitalists), to make all resistance *impossible*.

The important thing will not be even the confiscation of the capitalists' property, but country-wide, all-embracing workers' control over the capitalists and their possible supporters. Confiscation alone leads nowhere, as it does not contain the element of organization, of accounting for proper distribution. Instead of confiscation, we could easily impose a *fair* tax...taking care, of course, to preclude the possibility of anyone evading assessment, concealing the truth, evading the law. And this possibility can be *eliminated only* by the workers' control of the *workers' state*....

We must not only "terrorize" the capitalists, i.e., make them feel the omnipotence of the proletarian state and give up all idea of actively resisting it. We must also break *passive* resistance, which is undoubtedly more dangerous and harmful. We must not only break resistance of every kind. We must also *compel the capitalists to work* within the framework of the new state organization. It is not enough to "remove" the capitalists; we must (after removing the undesirable and incorrigible "resisters") employ them *in the service of the new state*. This applies both to the capitalists and to the upper section of the bourgeois intellectuals, office employees, etc.... "He who does not work, neither shall he eat"—this is the fundamental, the first, and most important rule the Soviets of Workers' Deputies can and will introduce when they become the ruling power.[2]

The proletariat can operate the state machine

Another argument that Lenin deals with is that the proletariat will not be able to set the state apparatus in motion. And he replies:

Since the 1905 Revolution, Russia has been governed by 130,000 landowners, who have perpetrated endless violence against 150,000,000 people, heaped unconstrained abuse upon them, and condemned the vast majority to inhuman toil and semi-starvation. Yet we are told that the 240,000 members of the Bolshevik Party will not be able to govern Russia, govern her in the interests of the poor and against the rich. These 240,000 are already backed by no less than a million votes of the adult population, for this is precisely the proportion between the number of party members and the number of votes cast for the party that has been established by the experience of Europe and the experience of Russia as shown, for example, by the elections to the Petrograd City Council last August. We therefore already have a "state apparatus" of *one million* people devoted to the socialist state for the sake of high ideals and not for the sake of a fat sum received on the 20th of every month.

In addition to that, we have a "magic way" to enlarge our state apparatus *tenfold* at once, at one stroke, a way which no capitalist state ever possessed or could possess. This magic way is to draw the working people, to draw the poor, into the daily work of state administration.

To explain how easy it will be to employ this magic way and how faultlessly it will operate, let us take the simplest and most striking example possible.

The state is to forcibly evict a certain family from a flat and move another in. This often happens in the capitalist state, and it will also happen in our proletarian or socialist state.

The capitalist state evicts a working-class family which has lost its breadwinner and cannot pay the rent. The bailiff appears with police, or militia, a whole squad of them. To affect an eviction in a working-class district a whole detachment of Cossacks is required. Why? Because the bailiff and the militiaman refuse to go without a very strong military guard. They know that the scene of an eviction arouses such fury among the neighbors, among thousands and thousands of people who have been driven to the verge of desperation, arouses such hatred towards the capitalists and the capitalist state, that the bailiff and the squad of militiamen run the risk of being torn to pieces at any minute. Large military forces are required, several regiments must be brought into a big city, and the troops must come from some distant, outlying region so that the soldiers will not be familiar with the life of the urban poor, so that the soldiers will not be "infected" with socialism.

The proletarian state has to forcibly move a very poor family into a rich man's flat. Let us suppose that our squad of workers' militia is fifteen strong, two sailors, two soldiers, two class-conscious workers (of whom, let us suppose, only one is a member of our party, or a sympathizer), one intellectual, and eight from the poor working people, of whom at least five must be women, domestic servants, unskilled laborers, and so forth. The squad arrives at the rich man's flat, inspects it and finds that it consists of five rooms occupied by two men and two women—"You must squeeze up a bit into two rooms this winter, citizens, and prepare two rooms for two families now living in cellars. Until the time, with the aid of engineers (you are an engineer, aren't you?), we have built good dwellings for everybody, you will have to squeeze up a little. Your telephone will serve ten families. This will save a hundred hours of work wasted on shopping, and so forth. Now in your family there are two unemployed persons who can perform light work: a citizeness fifty-five years of age and a citizen fourteen years of age. They will be on duty for three hours a day supervising the proper distribution of provisions for ten families and keeping the necessary account of this. The student citizen in our squad will now write out this state order in two copies and you will be kind enough to give us a signed declaration that you will faithfully carry it out."

This, in my opinion, can illustrate how the distinction between the old bourgeois and the new socialist state apparatus and state administration could be illustrated.

We are not Utopians. We know that an unskilled laborer or a cook cannot immediately get on with the job of state administration. In this we agree with the Cadets, with Breshkovskaya, and with Tsereteli. We differ, however, from these citizens in that we demand an immediate break with the prejudiced view that only the rich, or officials chosen from rich families, are capable of *administering* the state, of performing the ordinary, everyday work of administration. We demand that *training* in the work of state administration be conducted by class-conscious workers and soldiers and that this training be begun at once, i.e., that a beginning be made at once in training all the working people and all the poor, for this work.[3]

The potentialities of the proletariat

What confidence Lenin had in the potential power and initiative of the oppressed masses! Nevertheless, the Bolsheviks were realistic, and knew that workers would make mistakes.

It goes without saying that this new apparatus is bound to make mistakes in taking its first steps.... Is there any way other than practice by which the people can learn to govern themselves and to avoid mistakes? Is there any way other than by proceeding immediately to genuine self-government by the people? The chief thing now is to abandon the prejudiced bourgeois-intellectualist view that only special officials, who by their very social position are entirely dependent upon capital, can administer the state.... The chief thing is to imbue the oppressed and the working people with confidence in their own strength, to prove to them in practice that they can and must themselves ensure the *proper*, most strictly regulated and organized distribution of bread, all kinds of food, milk, clothing, housing, etc., in *the interests of the poor*. Unless this is done, Russia *cannot* be saved from collapse and ruin. The conscientious, bold, universal move to hand over administrative work to proletarians and semi-proletarians will, however, rouse such unprecedented revolutionary enthusiasm among the people, will so multiply the people's forces in combating distress, that much that seemed impossible to our narrow, old, bureaucratic forces will become possible for the millions, who will *begin* to work *for themselves* and not for the capitalists, the gentry, the bureaucrats, and not out of fear of punishment.[4]

[Another] plea is that the Bolsheviks will not be able to retain power because "the situation is exceptionally complicated."... O wise men! They, perhaps, would be willing to reconcile themselves to revolution if only the "situation" were not "exceptionally complicated."

Such revolutions never occur, and sighs for such a revolution amount to nothing more than the reactionary wails of a bourgeois intellectual. Even if a revolution has started in a situation that seemed to be not very complicated, the development of the revolution itself *always* creates an *exceptionally* complicated situation. A revolution, a real, profound, a "people's" revolution, to use Marx's expression, is the incredibly complicated and painful process of the death of the old and birth of the new social order, of the mode of life of tens of millions of people.... There is nothing to discuss in [this] plea, because there is no economic, political, or any other meaning whatever in it. It contains only the yearning of people who are distressed and frightened by the revolution....

I had a conversation with a wealthy engineer shortly before the July Days. This engineer had once been a revolutionary, had been in the Social Democratic movement and even a member of the Bolshevik Party. Now he was full of fear and rage at the turbulent and indomitable workers. "If they were at least like the German workers," he said (he is an educated man and has been abroad), of course, "I understand that the social revolution is, in general, inevitable, but here, when the workers' level has been so reduced by the war...it is not a revolution, it is an abyss."

He was willing to accept the social revolution if history were to lead to it in the peaceful, calm, smooth, and precise manner of a German express train pulling into a station. A sedate conductor would open the carriage door and announce: "Social Revolution station! *Alle Aussteigen!* [All change!]" In that case, he would have no objection to changing his position of engineer under the Tit Tityches to that of engineer under the workers' organizations. That man has seen strikes. He knows what a storm of passion the most ordinary strike arouses even in the most peaceful times. He, of course, understands how many million times more furious this storm must be when the class struggle has aroused *all* the working people of a vast country, when war and exploitation have driven almost to desperation millions of people who for centuries have been tormented by the landowners, for decades have been robbed and downtrodden by the capitalists and the Tsar's officials. He understands all this "theoretically," he only pays *lip service* to this, he is simply terrified by the "exceptionally complicated situation."[5]

The revolution, for Lenin, is the drama in which the masses enter the arena of history by means of their independent actions, defying all established norms. It is a time when everyone wants *to know,* to learn, to decide.... As John Reed described so well:

In every city, in most towns, along the front, each political faction had its newspaper—sometimes several. Hundreds of thousands of pamphlets were distributed by thousands of organizations, and poured into the armies, the villages, the factories, the streets. The thirst for education, so long thwarted, burst with the revolution into a frenzy of expression. From Smolny Institute alone, the first six months, went out every day tons, car-loads, train-loads of literature, saturating the land. Russia absorbed reading matter like hot sand drinks water, insatiable. And it was not fables, falsified history, diluted religion, and the cheap fiction that corrupts—but social and economic theories, philosophy, the works of Tolstoy, Gogol, and Gorky....

Then the talk, beside which Carlyle's flood of French speech was a mere trickle. Lectures, debates, speeches—in theaters, circuses, school-houses, clubs, Soviet meeting-rooms, union headquarters, barracks.... Meetings in the trenches at the front, in village squares, factories.... What a marvellous sight to see Putilovsky Zavod [the Putilov factory] pour out its forty thousand to listen to Social Democrats, Socialist Revolutionaries, Anarchists, anybody, whatever they had to say, as long as they would talk! For months in Petrograd, and all over Russia, every street-corner was a public tribune. In railway trains, street-cars, always the spurting up of impromptu debate, everywhere.[6]

The intelligence of the masses was harnessed along with their courage; their warmheartedness was accompanied by forceful action. The revolution, Reed writes, "had not come as they expected it would come, nor as the intelligentsia desired it; but it had come—rough, strong, impatient of formulas, contemptuous of sentimentalism; *real.*"[7]

Maxim Gorky

As a banner-bearer and symbol of the intelligentsia who for years had longed for a revolution, and then could not stomach the one that actually took place, no one could surpass Maxim Gorky, for many years a close friend of Lenin. In 1917, Gorky represented everything Lenin argued against in the pamphlet we are considering. He did not see social revolution, but only an explosion of "zoological anarchism," aroused by the call "rob the robbers!" On April 20, he wrote in *Novaia Zhizn:*

Politics is the soil in which the nettle of poisonous enmity, evil suspicions, shameless lies, slander, morbid ambitions and disrespect for the individual grows rapidly and luxuriantly. Name anything bad in man and it is precisely in the soil of political struggle that it grows with particular liveliness and abundance.[8]

On May 6, Gorky approvingly quoted a letter he had received:

Doesn't one become frightened when one sees how dirty hands and pocket interests are seizing the great and sacred banner of socialism... ? The peasantry, greedy for property, will receive land and turn away, having torn up for leggings the banner of Zhelyabov and

Breshkovskaya.... Soldiers willingly take up the banner of "peace for the whole world"; however, they strive for peace not in the name of the idea of international democracy, but in the name of their own selfish interests: preservation of life and hoped-for personal prosperity.[9]

This was his reaction to the July Days:

The disgusting scenes of the madness which seized Petrograd the day of 4 July will remain in my memory for the rest of my life.

There, bristling with rifles and machine guns, a truck flashes by like a mad hog; it is tightly packed with motley members of the "revolutionary army."[10]

And this was what Gorky had to say on the "role of the Leninists":

I detest and abhor people who arouse the dark instincts of the masses, no matter what names these people bear and no matter how considerable their service to Russia may have been in the past.[11]

The Bolshevik preparation for insurrection aroused these feelings in his breast:

All the dark instincts of the crowd irritated by the disintegration of life and by the lies and filth of politics will flare up and fume, poisoning us with anger, hate, and revenge; people will kill one another, unable to suppress their own animal stupidity.[12]

The essentially aristocratic disdain for the "dark masses" is expressed by this "stormy petrel," who for two decades had been in the revolutionary movement!

Lenin's pamphlet, *Can the Bolsheviks Retain State Power?* was a reply to the Gorkys of his time. It was a concentrated and economical statement of revolutionary optimism, of confidence in the creative abilities of the organized proletariat, the warm humanity and courage of the millions who for centuries had had their personalities stunted, and now were standing up and fighting.

CHAPTER 19

LENIN CALLS UP THE INSURRECTION

With the increasing breakdown in industry, the peasant war spreading, the national movement growing bitter, the army disintegrating, the provisional government becoming more and more paralyzed, and Bolshevik influence gaining massively, the question of state power inevitably became increasingly central and urgent.

As soon as the Bolsheviks gained control of the soviets of the two capitals, Petrograd and Moscow, Lenin said: "Our hour has come." But he found it very difficult indeed to persuade the party—and especially its leadership—of the need to seize state power.

In April, June, and July, Lenin's role was to check the impatient masses. He had to restrain the vanguard of the working class and the soldiers from moving too far ahead too quickly, before the more backward sections had the chance to catch up. Now he had to put his foot on the accelerator.

In August, Lenin prepared for the new stage theoretically; and from the middle of September onwards he stressed more and more forcibly the urgent need to seize state power directly.

The Bolshevik Party Military Organization was particularly cautious and conservative. Having been to the left of Lenin in June and July, and having burnt their fingers badly during the July Days, its leaders now, in September and October, insisted on the absolute necessity of thorough preparation before taking the offensive against the provisional government.[1]

Referring to the situation in his memoirs, Nevsky records that "some comrades felt then that we [the leaders of the Military Organization] were too cautious.... But our experience (especially in the July Days) showed us what an absence of thorough preparation and preponderance of strength means."[2] And of course the role of the Military Organization was crucial for any move towards taking power.

Lenin found it even harder to convince the top leaders of the party—the Central Committee members. It was as though the April Days had returned—Lenin was again isolated in the Central Committee. Again the committee appears to have been too passive, too compromising in its attitude to the Menshevik and Socialist Revolutionary leaders, too accommodating towards the provisional government. Admittedly the relentless criticism of Lenin on the one hand and pressure from the rank-and-file workers on the other did force it to change course radically in April. But conservatism and the urge to adapt are not eliminated by a single instance of admitting one's error. Lenin had to overcome his lieutenants again and again.

Insurrection demands the greatest daring, and the conservatism of leadership therefore appeared in an even more extreme form now than in April. It was no accident that a few days before the October Revolution Lenin found himself obliged to demand the expulsion from the party of two of his closest former collaborators, Zinoviev and Kamenev.

In April, he used the pressure of the workers, whom he believed to be considerably to the left of the party. Now the advanced sections of the proletariat were more cautious. There was a mood of depression among the Petrograd proletariat as a result of having waited so long. The workers began to doubt even the Bolsheviks. Who knew, perhaps they too were not really prepared to go beyond talk? While rearming the party in September and October, Lenin found it very difficult to mobilize mass pressure on the compromising Bolshevik leaders. However, once the battle signal was given, the wariness of the waiting masses disappeared in a flash.

The Bolsheviks must assume power

This was the heading of a letter Lenin wrote sometime between September 12–14. It was addressed both to the Central Committee and to the Petrograd and Moscow Committees of the Bolsheviks, and demonstrates his method of putting pressure on the Central Committee through lower party bodies. "The Bolsheviks, having obtained a majority in the Soviets of Workers' and Soldiers' Deputies of both capitals, can and *must* take power into their own hands."

The Bolsheviks could seize power because

the active majority of revolutionary elements in the two chief cities is large enough to carry the people with it, to overcome the opponent's resistance, to smash him, and to gain and retain power. For the Bolsheviks, by immediately proposing a democratic peace, by establishing the democratic institutions and liberties which have been mangled and shattered by Kerensky, will form a government which *nobody* will be able to overthrow.[3]

The task was urgent, although Lenin did not yet in this letter tackle the technicalities of the insurrection—as he was to do in a few days' time.

We are concerned now not with the "day," or "moment" of insurrection in the narrow sense of the word. That will be only decided by the common voice of those who are in *contact* with the workers and soldiers, with the *masses.*

The point is that now, at the Democratic Conference, our party has virtually *its own congress* and this congress (whether it wishes to or not) *must* decide the *fate of the revolution.*

The point is to make the *task* clear to the party. The present task must be an *armed uprising* in Petrograd and Moscow (with its region), the seizing of power and the overthrow of the government.[4]

A day or two later, Lenin wrote another letter to the Central Committee, on "Marxism and Insurrection." In it he compared the situation prevailing in mid-September with that during the July Days. His aim was to overcome the inertia of the Bolshevik leadership, which, having bent the stick in one direction in July, was too conservative and timid to change course now.

The Bolsheviks were right not to have taken power in July, but now things were different, Lenin argued. In July

an insurrection on 3–4 July would have been a mistake; we could not have retained power either physically or politically. We could not have retained it physically even though Petrograd was at times in our hands, because at that time our workers and soldiers would not have *fought and died* for Petrograd. There was not at the time that "savageness," or fierce hatred *both of* the Kerenskys *and of* the Tseretelis and Chernovs. Our people had still not been tempered by the experience of the persecution of the Bolsheviks in which the Socialist Revolutionaries and Mensheviks participated.

We could not have retained power politically on 3–4 July because, *before the Kornilov revolt,* the army and the provinces could and would have marched against Petrograd.[5]

But it was necessary to be both sober and bold. To seize power one must deal seriously with the techniques of insurrection.

To be successful, insurrection must rely not upon conspiracy and not upon a party, but upon the advanced class. That is the first point. Insurrection must rely upon a *revolutionary upsurge of the people*. That is the second point. Insurrection must rely upon that *turning point* in the history of the growing revolution when the activity of the advanced ranks of the people is at its height, and when the *vacillations* in the ranks of the enemy and in *the ranks of the weak, half-hearted, and irresolute friends of the revolution* are strongest. That is the third point.... Once these conditions exist, however, to refuse to treat insurrection as an *art* is a betrayal of marxism and a betrayal of the revolution.[6]

Once it is understood that the armed insurrection is the climax of the revolution, which has to relate to the general mass movenent, its specifically technical aspect must be considered. This demands serious study and application. Lenin gives some technical suggestions for immediate action:

[W]ithout losing a single moment, organize a *headquarters* of the insurgent detachments, distribute our forces, move the reliable regiments to the most important points, surround the Aleksandrinsky theater, occupy the Peter and Paul fortress, arrest the general staff and the government, and move against the officer cadets and the savage division those detachments which would rather die than allow the enemy to approach the strategic points of the city. We must mobilize the armed workers and call them to fight the last desperate fight, occupy the telegraph and the telephone exchange at once, move *our* insurrection headquarters to the central telephone exchange and connect it by telephone with all the factories, all the regiments, all the points of armed fighting, etc.

Of course, this is all by way of example, only to *illustrate* the fact that at the present moment it is impossible to remain loyal to marxism, to remain loyal to the revolution *unless insurrection is treated as an art.*[7]

The reference to the need to surround the Aleksandrinsky theater is very revealing. It was there that the Democratic Conference was assembled on September 14–19. Clearly Lenin was aiming at an immediate seizure of power! In all probability, this particular suggestion was intended not so much to convince the Bolshevik leaders about the specific technique to be adopted, as to force them into a radical change of attitude to the question of insurrection; by bending the stick to shake the leadership out of its passivity, lethargy, and willingness to go along with the provisional government.*

How did the Central Committee react to Lenin's letters? In the committee itself, he found no support whatsoever. In 1921, Bukharin, with characteristic exaggeration, described the episode:

---

* We have Stalin's word for the fact that after the revolution Lenin himself acknowledged that the above-mentioned plan for seizure of power was not appropriate.[8]

The letter [of Lenin] was written with extraordinary force and threat-ened us with all sorts of punishments. We all gasped. Nobody had yet posed the question so abruptly.... At first all were bewildered. After-wards, having talked it over, we made a decision. Perhaps that was the sole case in the history of our party when the Central Committee unan-imously decided to burn a letter from Lenin.... Although we believed unconditionally that in Petersburg and Moscow we should succeed in seizing power, we assumed that in the provinces we could not yet hold out, that having seized power and dispersed the Democratic Conference we would not be able to fortify ourselves in the rest of Russia.[9]

Some members of the Central Committee were absolutely opposed to the idea of insurrection; others, like Trotsky, Sverdlov, and Bukharin, thought that the time of the Democratic Conference was the least favorable moment for it; others simply vacillated and preferred to wait. The decision to burn the letter was, in fact, not reached unani-mously, but with six votes for, four against, and six abstentions.[10]

The minutes of the Central Committee go on to say:

Comrade Kamenev moved the adoption of the following resolution: After considering Lenin's letters, the CC rejects the practical propos-als they contain, calls on all organizations to follow CC instructions alone and affirms once again that the CC regards any kind of demon-stration in the streets as quite impermissible at the present moment. At the same time, the CC makes a request to comrade Lenin to elabo-rate in a special brochure on the question he raised in his letters of a new assessment of the current situation and the party's policy.

The resolution is rejected.

In conclusion, this decision is adopted:

CC members in charge of work in the Military Organization and the Petersburg Committee are instructed to take measures to prevent demonstrations of any kind in barracks and factories.[11]

The party adapts to constitutionalism

We have already mentioned that, as the Democratic Conference was drawing to a close, it appointed a permanent Council of the Republic, or pre-parliament, from among its members, which was to represent the nation until the constituent assembly met.

The question of the attitude to be taken to the pre-parliament became a crucial tactical issue for the Bolsheviks. Lenin thought that revolutionaries ought to participate in parliamentary institu-tions, so long as the immediate overthrow of the regime was not on the agenda. Thus the debate about the pre-parliament in the party was linked with the discussion of the insurrection.

First, Lenin sharply criticized the behavior of the Bolsheviks at the Democratic Conference:

> [N]ow I come to the errors of the Bolsheviks. To have confined them-
> selves to ironic applause and exclamations at such a moment was an
> error.... The Bolsheviks should have walked out of the meeting in
> protest and not allowed themselves to be caught by the conference trap
> set to divert the people's attention from serious questions. The Bolshe-
> viks should have left two or three of their 136 delegates for "liaison
> work," that is, to report by telephone the moment the idiotic babbling
> came to an end and the voting began. They *should not have allowed
> themselves to be kept busy* with obvious nonsense for the obvious pur-
> pose of deceiving the people with the obvious aim of *extinguishing* the
> growing revolution by wasting time on trivial matters.
>
> Ninety-nine percent of the Bolshevik delegation ought to have
> gone to the factories and barracks; that was the proper place for dele-
> gates who had come from all ends of Russia and who...could see the
> full depth of the Socialist Revolutionary and Menshevik rottenness.
> There, closer to the masses, at hundreds and thousands of meetings
> and talks, they ought to have discussed the lessons of this farcical
> conference whose obvious purpose was only to give a respite to the
> Kornilovite Kerensky and make it easier for him to try new variations
> of the "ministerial leapfrog" game.... How it happened can be under-
> stood—history made a *very* sharp turn at the time of the Kornilov re-
> volt. The party failed to keep pace with the incredibly fast tempo of
> history at this turning point. The party allowed itself to be diverted,
> for the time being, into the trap of a despicable talking-shop.... Par-
> liamentarism should be used, especially in revolutionary times, not to
> waste valuable time over representatives of what is rotten, but *to use
> the example of what is rotten to teach the masses.*[12]

The Bolshevik leadership, unfortunately, did not heed his argu-
ment and took a compromising attitude towards the Democratic
Conference and the pre-parliament. The minutes of the Central
Committee of September 21 reported:

> On the subject of the Democratic Conference, it is decided not to
> withdraw from it but merely to recall members of our party from the
> Presidium. Where the pre-parliament is concerned, a decision not to
> go into it was passed by 9 votes to 8. But since the vote was divided
> almost equally, the final decision was referred to the party meeting
> being organized right now from the group gathered at the Democra-
> tic Conference. Two reports—by comrade Trotsky and comrade
> Rykov—are planned.
>
> At the meeting, participation in the pre-parliament was approved
> by 77 votes to 50, a decision which the CC also confirmed.[13]

The next day Lenin wrote an article called "From a Publicist's
Diary: The Mistakes of Our Party." In it, he showed that decisions
about the tactics of participation or boycott of parliamentary insti-

tutions should be reached by way of an analysis of objective class relations, the rise or decline of the revolution, and the relation between extraparliamentary and parliamentary means of struggle.

In October 1905, the Bolsheviks had called for the boycott of the Bulygin Duma. Why was this move correct? "Because it was in accordance with the objective alignment of social forces in their development. It provided the maturing revolution with a slogan for the overthrow of the old order."[14]

In 1907, the ultraleft Bolsheviks again called for the boycott of the Duma.[15] Why were such tactics wrong?

> Because they were based only on the "catchiness" of the boycott slogan and on the revulsion felt towards the brutal reaction of the 3 June "pigsty." The objective situation, however, was such that...the revolution was in a state of collapse and declining fast. For the upsurge of the revolution a parliamentary base (even inside a "pigsty") was of tremendous political importance, since extra-parliamentary means of propaganda, agitation, and organization were almost nonexistent or extremely weak.[18]

From the experience of the past, Lenin went on to the immediate issue of the present.

> Participation in the pre-parliament is an *incorrect* tactic, that does not correspond to the objective relations of classes, to the objective conditions of the moment.... We must boycott the pre-parliament. We must leave it and go to the Soviets of Workers,' Soldiers,' and Peasants' Deputies, to the trade unions, to the masses in general. We must call on *them* to struggle. We must give *them* a correct and clear slogan: disperse the Bonapartist gang of Kerensky and *his* fake pre-parliament, with this Tsereteli-Bulygin Duma.[17]

He singled Trotsky out for praise for his sharp opposition to participation in the pre-parliament:

> Trotsky was for the boycott. Bravo, Comrade Trotsky!
> Boycottism was defeated in the Bolshevik group at the Democratic Conference.
> Long live the boycott![16]

Lenin then continued:

> There is not the slightest doubt that at the "top" of our party there are noticeable vacillations that may become *ruinous,* because the struggle is developing; under certain conditions, at a certain moment, vacillations may *ruin* the cause.... Not all is well with the "parliamentary" leaders of our party; greater attention must be paid to them, there must be greater workers' supervision over them; the competency of parliamentary groups must be more clearly defined.

> Our Party's mistake is obvious. The fighting party of the advanced class need not fear mistakes. What it should fear is persistence in a mistake, refusal to admit and correct a mistake out of a false sense of shame.[19]

At last, on October 5, the Central Committee bent to Lenin's will and resolved, with only one voice of dissent (Kamenev), to withdraw from the pre-parliament on its first day.[20] On October 7, Trotsky read out a fighting statement at the pre-parliament which ended with the words:

> Petrograd is in danger. The revolution and the people are in danger. The government is intensifying this danger, and the ruling parties are helping it. Only the people can save themselves and the country. We address the people: "Long live an immediate, honest, democratic peace. All power to the Soviets, all land to the people. Long live the constituent assembly."[21]

Then all the Bolsheviks stood up and walked out of the assembly hall to the accompaniment of shouts of "Go to your German trains!"

That the Bolsheviks' departure from the pre-parliament meant that they were committing themselves to the goal of insurrection was clear to both their friends and their opponents.

> There was only one road for them out of the pre-parliament [wrote Sukhanov]—to the barricades. If they cast away the "electoral ballot," they must take up the rifle. And that, indeed, is what happened.[22]

The Petrograd Soviet's report on the Bolshevik withdrawal from the pre-parliament ended with the cry: "Long live the direct and open struggle for revolutionary power in the country!" That was on October 9.

Spurring Smilga on

The urgency of the issue, of the need to take immediate steps towards the seizure of power, was so overwhelming that Lenin left no stone unturned in his efforts to convince, and if need be to circumvent, the Central Committee. Party formalities dwindled in significance under such conditions. This explains the tone of his letter of September 27 to I.T. Smilga, the young chairman of the Regional Committee of the Army, Navy, and Workers of Finland. He wrote:

> What are we doing? We are only passing resolutions. We are losing time. We set "dates" (20 October, the Congress of Soviets—is it not ridiculous to put it off so long? Is it not ridiculous to rely on that?).

The Bolsheviks are *not* conducting regular work to prepare their *own* military forces for the overthrow of Kerensky.[23]

He called on Smilga to act:

Now about your role. It seems to me we can have *completely* at our disposal only the troops in Finland and the Baltic fleet and only they can play a *serious* military role. I think you must make the most of your high position...give *all your attention* to the *military* preparation of the troops in Finland plus the fleet for the impending overthrow of Kerensky. Create a *secret* committee of absolutely *trustworthy* military men, discuss matters *thoroughly* with them, collect (and *personally* verify) the most precise data on the composition and the location of troops near and in Petrograd, the transfer of the troops from Finland to Petrograd, the movement of the fleet, etc.... It is obvious that we can *under no circumstances* allow the troops to be moved from Finland. Better *do anything,* better decide on an uprising, on the seizure of power, later to be transferred to the Congress of Soviets. I read in the papers today that in two weeks the danger of a landing will be nil. Obviously, you have very little time left for preparation.[24]

It seems to me that in order to prepare people's minds properly we must immediately circulate the following slogan: transfer power now to the Petrograd Soviet *which will transfer it* to the Congress of Soviets. Why should we tolerate three more weeks of war and Kerensky's "Kornilovite preparations"?[25]

Smilga was a member of the extreme left wing of the party, and even in July had been inclined to carry the struggle through to the end. Now Lenin entered into a sort of conspiracy with him.

The crisis is ripe

Two days after his letter to Smilga, Lenin wrote a document with the above title, which was in the nature of a declaration of war on the Central Committee. To maximize its effectiveness, he sent it not only to Central Committee members, but also to members of the Petrograd Committee, the Moscow Committee, and the soviets of the capitals.

What, then, is to be done? We must *aussprechen was ist,* "state the facts," admit the truth that there is a tendency, or an opinion, in our Central Committee and among the leaders of our party which favors *waiting* for the Congress of Soviets, and is *opposed* to taking power immediately, is *opposed* to an immediate insurrection. That tendency, or opinion, must be *overcome.*

Otherwise, the Bolsheviks will cover themselves with eternal *shame* and *destroy themselves* as a party.

For to miss such a moment and to "wait" for the Congress of Soviets would be *utter idiocy,* or *sheer treachery...*for it would mean
losing *weeks* at a time when weeks and even days decide *everything.*
It would mean faint-heartedly *renouncing* power, for on 1–2 November it will have become impossible to take power (both politically
and technically, since the Cossacks would be mobilized for the day of
the insurrection so foolishly "appointed"). (Note: To "convene" the
Congress of Soviets for 20 October in order to decide upon "taking
power"—how does that differ from foolishly "appointing" an insurrection? It is possible to take power now, whereas on 20–29 October
you will not be given a chance to.)
To "wait" for the Congress of Soviets is idiocy, for the Congress
will give nothing, and can give nothing![26]

He then put forward a plan for a military campaign to seize
power.

The Bolsheviks are now *guaranteed* the success of the insurrection:
we can (if we do not "wait" for the Soviet Congress) launch a *surprise* attack from three points—from Petrograd, from Moscow, and
from the Baltic fleet.... [W]e are technically in a position to take
power in Moscow (where the start might even be made, so as to
catch the enemy unawares).[27]

To increase the pressure he was applying, Lenin went beyond
criticizing the leaders of the party. As an expression of protest, he
resigned from the Central Committee, explaining why:

In view of the fact that the Central Committee has *even left unan-
swered* the persistent demands I have been making for such a policy
ever since the beginning of the Democratic Conference, in view of the
fact that the central organ is *deleting* from my articles all references
to such glaring errors on the part of the Bolsheviks as the shameful
decision to participate in the pre-parliament, the admission of Mensheviks to the Presidium of the Soviet, etc. etc.—I am compelled to
regard this as a "subtle" hint at the unwillingness of the Central
Committee even to consider this question, a subtle hint that I should
keep my mouth shut, and as a proposal for me to retire.
I am compelled to *tender my resignation from the Central Committee,* which I hereby do, reserving for myself freedom to campaign
among the *rank and file* of the party and at the Party Congress.[28]

The records do not show what happened next. In any event,
Lenin did not leave the Central Committee.
A couple of days later, on October 1, he wrote another letter to
the Central Committee, the Moscow and Petrograd Committees,
and the Bolshevik members of the Petrograd and Moscow Soviets.

Delay is criminal. To wait for the Congress of Soviets would be a childish game of formalities, a disgraceful game of formalities, and a betrayal of the revolution.

The Moscow Soviet should take power into its hands:

Victory in Moscow is guaranteed, and there is no need to fight. Petrograd can wait. The government cannot do anything to save itself; it will surrender.[29]

A few days later, Lenin issued his *Theses for the Conference of the Petrograd Organizations, also for a Resolution and Instructions to Those Elected to the Party Congress.* The document was written in a tone of furious criticism of the leadership.

Vacillations are to be noted at the top levels of our party, a "fear," as it were, of the struggle for power, a tendency to substitute resolutions, protests, and congresses for this struggle.... To insist on connecting this task with the Congress of Soviets, to subordinate it to this congress, means *to be merely playing at insurrection* by setting a definite date beforehand, by making it easier for the government to prepare troops, by confusing the masses with the illusion that a "resolution" of the Congress of Soviets can solve a task which only the insurrectionary proletariat is capable of solving by force.... [T]he Soviet of Workers' and Soldiers' Deputies is a reality only as an organ of insurrection, as an organ of revolutionary power. Apart from this, the Soviets are a meaningless plaything that can only produce apathy, indifference, and disillusion among the masses, who are legitimately disgusted by the endless repetition of resolutions and protests.[30]

On October 2, he wrote to the Petrograd City Conference, repeating his plan for armed insurrection—to start from Moscow as a base:

We must appeal to the Moscow comrades, persuade them to seize power in Moscow, declare the Kerensky government deposed, and declare the Soviet of Workers' Deputies in Moscow the provisional government of Russia in order to offer immediate peace and save Russia from the conspiracy. Let the Moscow comrades raise the question of the uprising in Moscow immediately.[31]

Reading this correspondence, one is deeply impressed by the persistence and urgency with which Lenin hammered at one and the same theme: the Bolsheviks must seize state power.

Advice from an onlooker

How galling it must have been for Lenin to have been away from the field of struggle, to be compelled to live an underground existence, to express himself largely *after* decisions had already been reached in Petrograd. In an article called "Advice of an Onlooker," written on October 8, he addressed the comrades assembling at the Congress of the Northern Soviets and developed Marx's idea that "insurrection is an art."

> Of the principal rules of this art, Marx noted the following:
>
> 1. *Never play* with insurrection, but when beginning it realize firmly that you must *go all the way.*
>
> 2. Concentrate a *great superiority of forces* at the decisive point and at the decisive moment, otherwise the enemy, who has the advantage of better preparation and organization, will destroy the insurgents.
>
> 3. Once the insurrection has begun, you must act with the greatest *determination*, and by all means, without fail, take the offensive. "The defensive is the death of every armed rising."
>
> 4. You must try to take the enemy by surprise and seize the moment when his forces are scattered.
>
> 5. You must strive for *daily* successes, however small (one might say hourly, if it is the case of one town), and at all costs retain "*moral superiority.*"
>
> Marx summed up the lessons of all revolutions in respect to armed uprising in the words of "Danton, the greatest master of revolutionary policy yet known: *de l'audace, de l'audace, encore de l'audace.*"[32]*

Lenin then went on to sketch a military plan for the seizure of power. What was needed, he wrote, was

> a simultaneous offensive on Petrograd, as sudden and as rapid as possible, which must without fail be carried out from within and from without, from the working-class quarters and from Finland, from Reval, and from Kronstadt, an offensive of the *entire* navy....
>
> Our *three* main forces—the fleet, the workers, and the army units must be so combined as to occupy without fail and to hold *at any cost*: (a) the telephone exchange; (b) the telegraph office; (c) the railway stations; (d) and above all, the bridges.
>
> The *most determined* elements (our "shock forces" and *young workers,* as well as the best of the sailors) must be formed into small detachments to occupy all the more important points and to *take part* everywhere in all important operations, for example: to encircle and cut off Petrograd; to seize it by a combined attack of the sailors, the workers, and the troops—a task which requires *art and triple audacity*; to form detachments from the best workers, armed with rifles and bombs, for the purpose of attacking and surrounding the enemy's "centers" (the officers' schools, the telegraph office, the telephone exchange, etc.).

---

* The words Lenin quotes are from *Revolution and Counter-revolution in Germany,* which was published in instalments in the *New York Daily Tribune* in 1851and 1852. It bore Marx's signature, but in fact was written by Engels.

He ended his letter with these words: "The success of both the Russian and the world revolution depends on two or three days' fighting."[33] One of the members of the Vyborg District Committee, Sveshnikov, remembers:

> Ilyich from underground was writing and writing untiringly, and Nadezhda Konstantinovna [Krupskaya] often read these manuscripts to us in the District Committee.... The burning words of the leader would redouble our strength.... I remember as though it were yesterday the bending figure of Nadezhda Konstantinovna in one of the rooms of the district administration, where the typists were working, carefully comparing the copy with the original, and right alongside stood Uncle and Gene demanding a copy each.

"Uncle" and "Gene" were old conspirative pseudonyms for two leaders of the district. "Not long ago," relates the district worker Naumov, "we got a letter from Ilyich for delivery to the Central Committee...We read the letter and gasped. It seems that Lenin had long ago put before the Central Committee the question of insurrection. We raised a row. We began to bring pressure on them."[34] It signified enormous confidence in the proletariat and the party, as well as serious mistrust of the Central Committee, for Lenin to go over the heads of the latter on his own personal responsibility, from the underground, and begin agitation for an armed insurrection. But he was never one to shirk responsibility and challenge.

However, the Congress of the Northern Soviets, though dominated by the Bolsheviks, did not carry out his bidding. It was convened for October 11, sat for three days, and dispersed, having limited itself to passing the usual general revolutionary resolutions.

At last the Central Committee moves

On October 10, the celebrated meeting of the Central Committee took place at which Lenin flatly posed the question of the armed insurrection—and won. Sukhanov wrote,

> Oh, the novel jokes of the merry muse of History! This supreme and decisive session took place in my own home, still at the Karpovka. But—without my knowledge.

The Menshevik Sukhanov's wife was a Bolshevik.

> As before I would very often spend the night somewhere near the office or Smolny, that is about eight *versts* from the Karpovka. This time special steps were taken to have me spend the night away from

home: at least my wife knew my intentions exactly and gave me a piece of friendly, disinterested advice—not to inconvenience myself by a further journey after work. In any case, the lofty assemblage had a complete guarantee against my arrival.[35]

Eleven of the twenty-one members of the Central Committee were present (plus one candidate member). Lenin came in wearing a wig and spectacles, and without a beard. It was the first meeting of the Central Committee he had attended since going underground. The session lasted ten hours, until about three o'clock in the morning. It started with an organizational report by Sverdlov, which prepared the ground for Lenin's resolution:

> Representatives who have arrived from armies on the northern front assert that there is something shady going on on that front to do with the withdrawal of troops into the interior.
>
> There is information from Minsk that a new Kornilov-type plot is being prepared there. Because of the character of the garrison, Minsk is surrounded by Cossack units. Some suspicious talks are going on between the headquarters and Supreme Command. Agitators are at work against the Bolsheviks among the Osset and certain other units of the troops. On the front, though, the mood is *for* the Bolsheviks, they follow them against Kerensky.[36]

Lenin immediately took the offensive:

> [S]ince the beginning of September a certain indifference to the question of insurrection has been noticeable. Yet if we are seriously promoting the slogan of a seizure of power by the Soviets, this cannot be allowed. That is why attention should have been given to the technical side of the matter long ago. Now, apparently, considerable time has been lost.
>
> Nonetheless, the question is urgent and the decisive moment is near. The international situation is such that we must take the initiative.
>
> What is being done to surrender as far as the Narva and to surrender Peter makes it even more imperative for us to take decisive action.
>
> The political position is also working impressively in this direction.
>
> On 3–5 July, positive action on our part would have failed because the majority was not behind us. Since then we have gone up in leaps and bounds.
>
> Absenteeism and indifference among the masses can be explained by the fact that the masses are fed up with words and resolutions. The majority is now behind us. Politically, the situation is completely ripe for a transfer of power.
>
> The agrarian movement is going in the same direction, for it is clear that it would need heroic forces to quell this movement. The slogan for all land to be transferred has become the general slogan of the peasants. So the political circumstances are ripe. We have to talk about the technical side. That is the crux of the matter. Yet we, in the

wake of the defensists, are inclined to regard the systematic preparation of an insurrection as something akin to a political sin.

It is senseless to wait for the constituent assembly, which will clearly not be on our side, for this means complicating our task. The Regional Congress and the proposal from Minsk must be used as the starting point for decisive action.[37]

Then he moved a resolution:

Recognizing...that an armed rising is inevitable and that its time has come, the CC suggests that all party organizations be guided by this and approach the discussion and solution of all practical issues from this point of view (the Congress of Northern Region Soviets, the withdrawal of troops from Peter, the action of our people in Moscow and Minsk, etc.).[38]

There were ten votes in favor (nine members of the CC and one candidate) and two (Zinoviev and Kamenev) against.

Zinoviev's and Kamenev's dissent

Immediately after the meeting, Zinoviev and Kamenev issued a statement, which they circulated among the members of the Petrograd Committee, the Moscow Committee, the Moscow Regional Committee, and the Regional Finnish Committee, arguing against the Central Committee decision.

We are deeply convinced that to proclaim an armed insurrection now is to put at stake not only the fate of our party but also the fate of the Russian and the international revolution....

Our party's chances in the constituent assembly are excellent.... With the right tactics, we can get a third of the seats in the constituent assembly, or even more....

The constituent assembly cannot by itself, of course, change the real relationship between social forces. But it will prevent this relationship being disguised as at present. There is no getting rid of the Soviets, which have taken root in the life we live. Already the Soviets in practice exercise power in a number of places.

The constituent assembly too, can only rely on the Soviets in its revolutionary work. The constituent assembly plus the Soviets—here is that mixed type of state institution we are going towards....

We have not forgotten, and still must not forget, that between us and the bourgeoisie stands a huge third camp: the petty bourgeoisie. This camp aligned itself with us in the days of the Kornilov revolt and brought us victory.... There is no doubt that now this camp is far nearer to the bourgeoisie than it is to us.... And it only takes one careless step, some ill-considered move which makes the whole fate of the revolution depend on an immediate insurrection, for the proletarian party to push the petty bourgeoisie into Miliukov's arms *for a long time.*

They say: (1) The majority of the people in Russia are already on our side and (2) the majority of the international proletariat is on our side. Alas! Neither one nor the other is true, and that is the whole point.

In Russia, we have the majority of the workers and a considerable section of the soldiers on our side. But all the rest are doubtful. We are all convinced, for example, that if things now get as far as the constituent assembly elections, the peasants will vote in the main for the SRs.

And now we come to the second assertion—that the majority of the international proletariat now supports us. Unfortunately, it is not so.... [I]f we stake everything now and suffer defeat, we shall also be striking a cruel blow at the international proletarian revolution, which is growing extremely slowly but undoubtedly growing all the same. But, so long as the choice depends on us, we can and must confine ourselves now to a *defensive position....* In the constituent assembly, we shall be so strong as an opposition party that, with universal suffrage in the country, our opponents will be forced to yield to us at every step, or we shall form a ruling bloc with the left SRs, the non-party peasants, and others which will basically have to promote our program....

We do not have the right before history, before the international proletariat, before the Russian revolution and the Russian working class to stake the whole future on the card of an armed insurrection now...at this moment the most harmful thing of all would be to underestimate the enemy's strength and overestimate our own. The strength of the opposition is greater than it seems. Petrograd is the key and in Petrograd the enemies of the proletarian party have amassed considerable forces: 5,000 junkers *magnificently* armed, *organized,* eager (because of their class position) and knowing how to fight, then the headquarters staff, the shock troops, the Cossacks, an important section of the garrison, and a large amount of artillery deployed in a fan round Peter [Petersburg]. Then our opponents, with the help of the TsIK [Executive Committee of the Soviets], will almost certainly try to bring forces from the front.

The workers and soldiers were not in a fighting mood.

Even those who advocate action declare that the mood among the masses of workers and soldiers is far from reminiscent of, say, the feelings before 3 July. If a militant mood for street demonstrations existed deep among the masses of the city's poor, it would serve as a guarantee that once they had started to act, they would also carry along behind them those very large and important organizations (the railway and post and telegraph unions, etc.) where our party's influence is weak. But since this mood does not even exist in the factories and barracks, to calculate on it would be to deceive ourselves....

Under these conditions, it would be a grave historical error to put the question of transferring power into the hands of the proletarian party in the terms: now or never!

No! The party of the proletariat will grow and its program will be made clear ever more widely to the masses.[39]

Lenin's slashing attack

Lenin's anger knew no bounds. Two of his closest comrades had now emerged as the main opponents of the insurrection. On October 17, he wrote a long and sharp "Letter to Comrades":

> [S]ince the revolutionary party has no right to tolerate vacillations on such a serious question, and since this pair of comrades, who have scattered their principles to the winds, might cause some confusion, it is necessary to analyze their arguments, to expose their vacillations, and to show how shameful they are.[40]

Zinoviev and Kamenev had said: "We are not strong enough to seize power, and the bourgeoisie is not strong enough to hinder the convening of the constituent assembly." Lenin retorted sharply:

> [T]he confusion of its authors and their fear of the bourgeoisie are expressed in terms of pessimism in respect of the workers and optimism in respect of the bourgeoisie. If the officer cadets and the Cossacks say that they will fight against the Bolsheviks to the last drop of blood, this deserves full credence; if, however, the workers and soldiers at hundreds of meetings express full confidence in the Bolsheviks and affirm their readiness to defend the transfer of power to the Soviets, then it is "timely" to recall that voting is one thing and fighting another.

Lenin dealt with Zinoviev's and Kamenev's argument that "[t]he Soviets must be a revolver pointed at the head of the government with the demand to convene the constituent assembly and stop all Kornilovite plots."

> This is how far one of the two sad pessimists has gone.... Someone has very pointedly retorted to our pessimist: "Is it a revolver with no cartridges?".... If, however, it is to be a revolver "with cartridges," this cannot mean anything but *technical* preparation for an uprising; the cartridges have to be procured, the revolver has to be loaded—and cartridges alone will not be enough.[41]

Zinoviev and Kamenev wrote: "We are becoming stronger every day. We can enter the constituent assembly as a strong opposition; why should we stake everything?" Lenin retorted:

> This is the argument of a philistine who has "read" that the constituent assembly is being called, and who trustingly acquiesces in the most legal, most loyal, most constitutional course.
>
> It is a pity, however, that *waiting* for the constituent assembly does

not solve either the question of famine or the question of surrendering Petrograd. This "trifle" is forgotten by the naive or the confused or those who have allowed themselves to be frightened. The famine will not wait. The peasant uprising did not wait. The war will not wait. The admirals who have disappeared did not wait.

Will the famine agree to wait, because we Bolsheviks *proclaim* faith in the convocation of the constituent assembly? Will the admirals who have disappeared agree to wait? Will the Maklakovs and Rodziankos agree to stop the lockouts and the sabotaging of grain deliveries, or to denounce the secret treaties with the British and the German imperialists?

This is what the arguments of the heroes of "constitutional illusions" and parliamentary cretinism amount to. The living reality disappears, and what remains is only a *paper* dealing with the convocation of the constituent assembly; there is nothing left but to hold elections.[42]

Again he quoted Zinoviev and Kamenev: "Were the Kornilovites to start again, we would show them! But why should we take risks and start?" and replied:

History does not repeat itself, but if we turn our *backs* on it, contemplate the first Kornilov revolt and repeat: "If only the Kornilovites would start"—if we do that, what excellent revolutionary strategy it would be. How much like a waiting game it is! Maybe the Kornilovites will start again at an inopportune time. Isn't this a "weighty" argument? What kind of an earnest foundation for a proletarian policy is this?

And what if the Kornilovites of the second draft will have learned a thing or two? What if they *wait* for the hunger riots to begin, for the front to be broken through, for Petrograd to be surrendered, *before they begin?* What then?

It is proposed that we build the tactics of the proletarian party on the possibility of the Kornilovites' repeating one of their old errors!... Here you have the "marxist" tactics! Wait, ye hungry! Kerensky has promised to convene the constituent assembly.[43]

"As everybody reports, the masses are not in a mood that would drive them into the streets. Among the signs justifying pessimism may be mentioned the greatly increasing circulation of the pogromist and Black Hundred press," Zinoviev and Kamenev had claimed. Lenin had this to say about the mood of the masses:

[A]nd this is at present the main thing the spineless people forget to add:
that "everybody" reports it as a tense and expectant mood;
that "everybody" agrees that, called upon by the Soviets for the defense of the Soviets, the workers will rise to a man;
that "everybody" agrees that the workers are greatly dissatisfied with the indecision of the centers concerning the "last decisive strug-

gle," the inevitability of which they clearly recognize;

that "everybody" unanimously characterizes the mood of the broadest masses as close to desperation and points to the anarchy developing therefrom;

that "everybody" also recognizes that there is among the class-conscious workers a definite unwillingness to go out into the streets *only* for demonstrations, *only* for partial struggles, since a general and not a partial struggle is in the air, while the hopelessness of individual strikes, demonstrations, and acts to influence the authorities has been seen and is fully realized.

And so forth.

Zinoviev and Kamenev "conveniently" forget, of course, that a firm party line, its unyielding resolve, is *also* a mood-creating *factor*, particularly at the sharpest revolutionary moments. It is sometimes very "convenient" for people to forget that the responsible leaders, by their vacillations and by their readiness to burn their yesterday's idols, cause the most unbecoming vacillations in the mood of certain strata of the masses.[44]

Those who, in arguing about the mood of the masses, blame the masses for their own personal spinelessness, are in a hopeless position. The masses are divided into those who are consciously biding their time and those who unconsciously are ready to sink into despair; but the masses of the oppressed and the hungry are *not* spineless.[45]

What is needed for an uprising is...on the one hand, a conscious, firm, and unswerving resolve on the part of the class-conscious elements to fight to the end; and on the other, a mood of despair among the broad masses who *feel* that nothing can now be saved by half-measures; that you cannot "influence" anybody; that the hungry will "smash everything, destroy everything, even anarchically," *if* the Bolsheviks are not able to lead them in a decisive battle.[46]

Zinoviev and Kamenev had said, "On the other hand, the Marxist party cannot reduce the question of an uprising to that of a military conspiracy." Lenin accused them of trying to identify insurrection with Blanquism.

Military conspiracy is Blanquism, *if* it is organized not by a party of a definite class, *if* its organizers have not analyzed the political moment in general and the international situation in particular, *if* the party has not on its side the sympathy of the majority of the people, as proved by objective facts, *if* the development of revolutionary events has not brought about a practical refutation of the conciliatory illusions of the petty bourgeoisie, *if* the majority of the Soviet-type organs of revolutionary struggle that have been recognized as authoritative or have shown themselves to be such in practice have not been won over, *if* there has not matured a sentiment in the army (if in war-time) against the government that protracts the unjust war against the will of the whole people, *if* the slogans of the uprising (like "All power to the Soviets," "Land to the peasants," or "Immediate offer of a democratic peace to all the belligerent nations, with an immediate abrogation of all secret treaties and secret diplomacy," etc.) have not become widely known and popular, *if* the advanced workers are not sure of the desperate situation of the masses and of the support of the countryside, a support proved by a serious peasant movement or by an uprising against the landowners and the government that defends the landowners, *if* the country's economic situation inspires earnest hopes for a favorable solution of the crisis by peaceable and parliamentary means.

This is probably enough.[47]

Events were unfortunately to prove that Lenin was right when he wrote about Zinoviev and Kamenev: "[T]he skeptics can *always* 'doubt' and cannot be refuted by anything but experience."[48]

The Petrograd leadership vacillates

On October 15, there was a meeting of the Petrograd Committee together with active leaders of the Bolshevik Party. Throughout the discussion hesitancy and lack of clarity prevailed.

Nevsky: As a representative of the Military Organization, I must call your attention to a number of difficulties confronting us. The Military Organization has suddenly begun to move to the right.

We must distinguish two questions: those of (1) fundamental principles, and (2) their practical realization. With reference to the resolution of the Central Committee [of 10 October], the Military Organization pointed out that this resolution has left unconsidered a number of conditions, namely, that the poor peasants are also taking a part in the revolution. Instead of the village turning away from us it has only begun to come to us. We receive information from numerous places that the Bolsheviks are beginning to become popular. The decisive factor in the revolution is, of course, the working class.... But we must not on that account neglect the spirit of the peasant masses; if we do we shall not win the victory. In quite a number of *guberniias*...the peasants say that in case of an insurrection they will not give us any bread. Absolutely nothing has been done to stir up the village. An armed uprising of the proletariat here in Petersburg is a feasible thing. The whole garrison will come out at the call of the Soviet.... But we cannot confine the insurrection to Petersburg. How will Moscow and the provinces react to this? Can the Central Committee give us an assurance that Russia as a whole will support us? We all realize that the moment is ripe. But are we ready? Have we the majority which will guarantee freedom? From the report, it is quite clear that we are not ready, and the question stands thus: If we should come out, we shall find ourselves isolated from the rest of Russia. We have no data concerning the situation on the railroads.

And are you sure that the 5th Army will not be sent against us?...
Neither the military organization nor the Central Committee has this
assurance.... The military organization will come out [for us] any
time, but I cannot tell what this will accomplish.... The resolution of
the Central Committee which raised the question [of insurrection]
with such urgency should have considered the other question of the
preparedness of the masses. The Petrograd Committee must call the
attention of the Central Committee to the necessity of preparing the
provinces....

Kharitonov: ... The joint session of the Petrograd Committee, the
Central Committee, the district committee, and the Moscow district
[disclosed] that there is a general lack of enthusiasm. In Krasnoe Selo,
where we have a large organization of some 5,000 members, only
500 may be expected to come here [Petrograd]; the rest will remain
in Krasnoe Selo undecided. Krasnoe Selo is living through a mood of
depression. Drunkenness is prevalent even among our comrades.
From a military point of view, the sailors are a very poor lot. A good
many of them have been sent back from the front because they did
not know how to handle arms. As for the post and telegraph employees, we have in our organization from 140 to 150 members.... The
telegraph operators are mostly Cadets and have very little sympathy
with us. At a decisive moment, there may be sufficient force to occupy the telegraph and other important positions.

Slutskaia [woman representative of the Vasilevsky Ostrov district]:
Regarding the military situation in our district, I can say that military
instruction is being given in the factories and industrial plants. There
is not much desire to take part in the insurrection.

Latsis (Vyborg district): A serious concentration of interest in
events is observable among the masses. In addition to the district
committees a new central organization has grown up from the bottom.... The masses will support us.

Kalinin (Lesnovsky sub-district): We have decided to investigate
conditions; as yet the business is badly managed. We have decided to
get in contact with the army units. We receive telegrams from Finland
and from the front protesting against the uprising of the Bolsheviks.
On the other hand, over the head of the army organization, delegates
are arriving from the front, and their demands clearly indicate a militant frame of mind. It proves that the army committees are not with
us, and that they do not express the wishes of the masses. We have a
Red Guard; only 84 rifles.

Naumov (Vyborg district): There is a marked dissatisfaction among
the masses...and a feeling of suppressed indignation in connection
with the evacuation [of Petrograd] and the paying off of the workmen.

Menzhinskaia [woman representative of the first city district]:
With regard to arms, conditions are very bad. In the committee, there
are only 6 rifles, in one factory 100, in another 20. It is difficult to estimate the spirit of the workers.

Pakhemov (second city district): The frame of mind is better than it was on 3 to 5 July. The Red Guard is badly organized. We have 50 rifles, 3,000 cartridges. From 60 to 80 are receiving [military] instruction.

Ravich (Moscow district): In the factories there is a turbulent state of feeling. The masses will rise only at the call of the Soviet, but very few will respond to the call of our party. The organs created during the Kornilov days are still intact....

Gessen (Narva district): In general, there is no desire to rise. Where our influence is strong, the spirit is cheerful and eager. Among the backward masses there is an indifference to politics. But our party has not lost its authority.... We have several hundred rifles, but there is no concentration point and our military forces are scattered....

Vinokurov (Neva district): The state of mind is in our favor. The masses are alert. We have no Red Guard.

Comrade from the Obukhov factory: Previously the Obukhov factory stood for the defensists. But now there is a break in our favor. The attendance at our mass meetings is 5-7,000.... [W]e have 2,000 in the Red Guard, 500 rifles, 1 machine gun, and 1 armored car. We have organized a revolutionary committee. The factory will no doubt respond to the call of the Petrograd Soviet.

Pervukhin (Okhtensky district): There is no desire among the workers to rise. In the factories the Black Hundreds have raised their heads.

Prokhorov (Petersburg district): Where our influence is strong the attitude is one of watchfulness—otherwise the masses are apathetic.... Generally there is a complete disorganization in the district. Even if the Soviet should issue a call for an uprising, certain factories (ours for example) will not respond.

Axelrod (Rozhdestvensky district): The attitude is one of watchfulness. In case of an offensive on the part of the counter-revolution, we shall offer resistance, but to a call to insurrection the workers will hardly respond. There is discouragement due to the paying off of workers in connection with the evacuation of factories. The influence of the anarchists is considerably on the increase.

Porokhovski district: ... Before the Kornilov events the Mensheviks and the Socialist Revolutionaries predominated. But now the feeling is in our favor.... The committee in the factory is quite ready to lead the masses if there should come a call for the uprising....

Shlüsselburg district: Our district is small; 200 members in all. But the majority of the masses will go with us. A Red Guard has been organized, but the enlistment is not popular. The workers have taken upon themselves the defense of the factories. The masses will come out at the call of the Soviet.

Railroad section: Dissatisfaction with the provisional government is manifest.... Our propaganda does not go outside the limits of Petersburg. Now we have connections with Moscow.... We have sent 13 comrades into the provinces to establish connections with railroad workers there. Some of them have come back with reports that political conditions are not so good....

Trade unions: There are no signs of an aggressive spirit among the masses. If there should be an offensive of the counter-revolution, resistance would be offered, but the masses by themselves will not take the offensive. The masses might respond to the call of the Soviet.

Rakhia (Finnish district): The Finns all feel that the sooner the better....

(A discussion of general principles followed.)

Kalinin: That resolution of the Central Committee is the best it has ever passed. The resolution summons our organization to direct political action. We are confronted with an armed insurrection but our stumbling-block is the practical aspect of the situation. When that insurrection will take place, we cannot say—possibly in a year's time.[49]

It is interesting to note that the hotheads of the July Days— above all the leaders of the Military Organization, like Nevsky, were very cautious this time. Of the nineteen district representatives at the Petersburg Committee meeting on October 15, only eight felt that the masses were in a "fighting mood," and ready to act immediately; six viewed the prevailing spirit as indefinite; while five referred explicitly to the lack of any desire to "come out."

A couple of days later, Lenin sent for the leaders of the Military Organization, to discuss the situation with them. The meeting is described in Podvoisky's memoirs:

Antonov-Ovseenko declared that while he had no basis for judging the Petrograd garrison, he was sure that the fleet would come out at the first call, but it could hardly arrive at Petrograd in time. Nevsky and Podvoisky indicated that the mood of the troops of the garrison was clearly sympathetic to the uprising, but that nevertheless a certain delay of ten to fifteen days was necessary in order to present this question directly and decisively in each military unit, and to prepare technically for the uprising, the more so since the units that came out in the month of July...had been partly discharged and partly demoralized, and would come out only if they were sure of a move by other units, while the readiness for a move on the part of other units which had formerly been reactionary had to be tested. The point was also made by Podvoisky that Kerensky could rely on special combined units and other reactionary units from the front that were capable of obstructing the success of the uprising.

Comrade Nevsky indicated that as regards the sailors from Helsingfors and elsewhere there could be no doubt but that the movement of the fleet to Petrograd would meet with colossal difficulties, for the uprising would certainly evoke counteraction by the officers and consequently their arrest, and then the sailors taking their place would have a hard time navigating the ships through the minefields and doing battle at Petrograd.

In general, all agreed on the idea of postponing the insurrection a few weeks, believing it necessary to use this time for the most energetic preparations for the uprising in Petrograd, in the provinces, and at the front....

However, none of these conclusions convinced or shook Vladimir Ilyich in any way.[50]

Only ten days before the insurrection, the leaders of the Bolshevik Military Organization were still prevaricating.

The Central Committee continues to waver

On October 16, i.e., nine days before the insurrection, the Central Committee still showed signs of nervousness, hesitation, and vacillation. The minutes of the enlarged meeting of the Central Committee (including as well as Central Committee members, the Executive Commission of the Petersburg Committee, the Military Organization, the Petrograd Soviet, the leaders of the Bolsheviks in the trade unions, the factory committees, the Petrograd Area Committee, and the railway workers) are really astonishing. It is hard to believe that with such leadership the revolution still emerged victorious.

Comrade Boky of the Petrograd Committee...gives information district by district:

Vasilevskii Island—mood not militant, military preparations being made.

Vyborg district the same but they are preparing for an insurrection; a military council has been formed; if there were action, the masses would be in support. They consider that the initiative ought to come from above.

1st city district	*The mood is difficult to assess....*
2nd [city district]	*A better mood.*
Moscow district	*A reckless mood, will come out if the Soviet calls but not the party.*
Narva district	*Not eager for action but no falling off in the party's authority...*
Neva district	*The mood has swung sharply in our favor. Everyone will follow the Soviet.*
Okhten district	*Things are bad.*
Petersburg district	*An expectant mood.*
Rozhdestvensk district	*Doubt here, too, on whether they will rise....*
Porokhov district	*The mood has improved in our favor.*
Schlüsselburg	*Mood in our favor.*

Comrade Krylenko of the Military Bureau announces that they differ sharply in their assessment of the mood. Personal observations of the mood in the regiments indicate that they are ours to a man, but information from comrades working in the districts differs; they say that they would have to be positively stung by something for a rising, that is: the withdrawal of troops. The Bureau believes that morale is falling. Most of the Bureau thinks there is no need to do anything in practice to intensify things, but the minority thinks that it is possible to take the initiative oneself.

Comrade Stepanov of the Area Organization: In Sestroretsk, Kolpino, the workers are arming, the mood is militant and they are preparing for a rising. In Kolpino, an anarchist mood is developing. The atmosphere in Narva is grave because of the dismissals. 3,000 have already been dismissed.

Where the garrisons are concerned, the mood is depressed but Bolshevik influence is very strong (2 machine gun regiments). Work in the regiment in Novyi Peterhoff has fallen off a lot and the regiment is disorganized. Krasnoe Selo—176th regiment is completely Bolshevik, the 172nd regiment nearly, but apart from that the cavalry is there. Luga—a garrison of 30,000; the Soviet is defensist. A Bolshevik mood and there are elections ahead. In Gdov—the regiment is Bolshevik.

Comrade Boky adds that according to the information he has, matters are not so good in Krasnoe Selo. In Kronstadt, morale has fallen and the local garrison there is no use for anything in a militant sense.

Comrade Volodarsky from the Petrograd Soviet: The general impression is that no one is ready to rush out on the streets but everyone will come if the Soviet calls.

Comrade Ravich confirms this and adds that some have indicated that also at the party's call.

Shmidt of the trade unions reports:

The mood is one where active demonstrations cannot be expected, especially because of the fear of dismissals.... Comrade Shliapnikov adds that Bolshevik influence predominates in the metal workers' union but a Bolshevik rising is not popular; rumors of this even produce panic.... Comrade Skrypnik from the factory committees... states that a craving for practical results has been noted everywhere; resolutions are no longer enough. It is felt that the leaders do not fully reflect the mood of the masses; the former are more conservative; a growth of anarcho-syndicalist influence is noted, particularly in the Narva and Moscow districts.

Miliutin states that,

personally, he believes that we are not ready to strike the first blow. We are unable to depose and arrest the authorities in the immediate future.... Comrade Shotman says the mood was far more pessimistic at the City Conference and in the Petrograd Committee and the *Voenka* [Bolshevik Military Organization]. He shows that we are unable to take action but must prepare ourselves.

Comrade Lenin argues against Miliutin and Shotman and demonstrates that it is not a matter of armed forces, not a matter of fighting against the troops but of a struggle between one part of the army and another. He sees no pessimism in what has been said here. He shows that the bourgeoisie do not have large forces on their side. The facts show that we have the edge over the enemy. Why is it not possible for the CC to begin? No reason emerges from all the facts.

Then a number of comrades argued that the October 10 resolution should be taken as a matter of *general orientation,* rather than a directive for immediate action:

Comrade Kalinin does not interpret the resolution as meaning a rising tomorrow but as taking the matter out of the realm of policy into that of strategy and appealing for specific action.

Sokolnikov said:

On the subject of the resolution, there is absolutely no point in interpreting it as an order to act.

If it turns out that events give us a respite then we will, of course, make use of it. It is possible that the congress will be earlier. If the congress adopts all power to the Soviets, it will be necessary then to deal with the question of what to do, appeal to the masses or not....

Comrade Miliutin: The resolution was not written in the sense it has been given here; it is being interpreted to mean that we should orient ourselves towards an insurrection.... We gained from the fact that there was no insurrection on 3-5 [July] and if there is not one now, it will not be the end of us. The resolution must be for internal consumption.

Comrade Volodarsky: If the resolution is an order then it has already been disobeyed. If the question of an insurrection is put in terms of tomorrow, we must say straight out that we have nothing to do with it. I made speeches daily but I must say that the masses met our appeal with bewilderment; this week, a change has occurred.... A concrete motion: to continue to make technical preparations and to bring the question before the congress, but not to regard the moment as having arrived already.

A much harder line was taken by a number of others present.

Comrade Diadia (Latsis): It is lamentable that the resolution has not been put into effect so far.... I took the floor to amend the assessment given of the mood of the masses. The eagerness with which the masses seize on arms is an indication of how they feel. Our strategy is also strange. When they talk of junkers, I have already said they can be crossed off.

Comrade Skrypnik: If we do not have the strength now, we are not going to have any more later; if we will not retain power now, it will be even worse then.... Now we are talking too much when we should act. The masses are appealing to us and if we do not give them anything, they will regard it as a crime. What is needed is preparation for insurrection and an appeal to the masses.

Krylenko: ... [T]he mood described here is the result of our mistakes. He differs from V.I. [Lenin] on the subject of who will start it and how. He considers it unnecessary to enter into the technical details of the insurrection too much and, on the other hand, also regards it as inadvisable to make a definite date for it. But the issue of withdrawing the troops is crucial, the very moment to give rise to a fight. It will be argued at the Cheremisov conference that it is necessary for the troops to retreat; we shall not be able to make an answer to this but must reply that even if it is necessary, it will not be done because there is no faith in the generals: thus, the offensive against us is already a fact and it can be used. Agitation cannot be diminished and there is no point in worrying about who is to begin since a beginning already exists.

Stalin, elaborating on Krylenko's words:

The Petrograd Soviet has already taken its stand on the road to insurrection by refusing to sanction the withdrawal of the troops. The navy has already rebelled since it has gone against Kerensky. Comrade Rakhia shows that the masses are consciously preparing for an uprising. If the Petersburg proletariat had been armed, it would have been on the streets already regardless of any CC resolutions. There is no sign of pessimism. There is no need to wait for a counterrevolutionary attack for it already exists. The masses are waiting for slogans and weapons. They will erupt into the streets because famine awaits them. Apparently, our rallying cry is already overdue for there is doubt whether we are going to live up to our exhortations. It is not our task to reconsider but, on the contrary, to reinforce.

Trotsky was not present at the meeting; Zinoviev and Kamenev came out again against the insurrection. Lenin moved the following resolution:

The meeting unreservedly welcomes and entirely supports the CC resolution, calls on all organizations and all workers and soldiers to make comprehensive and intensive preparations for an armed insurrection and to support the center created for this by the Central Committee and expresses its full confidence that the CC and the Soviet will be timely in indicating the favorable moment and the appropriate methods of attack.

Comrade Lenin's resolution voted on in principle. In favor 20, against 2, abstained 3.

Zinoviev, obviously relying on the fact that the Bolsheviks from the provinces lagged behind those of Petrograd, moved the following resolution:

While going ahead with the work of reconnaissance and preparation, to consider that any demonstrations in advance of a conference with the Bolshevik section of the Congress of Soviets are inadmissible.

This mild and prevaricating resolution received considerable support—six for, fifteen against, and three abstentions.[51]

A bombshell

On October 18, Kamenev, in association with Zinoviev, published an article in a nonparty paper, *Novaia Zhizn,* attacking the idea of insurrection.

> Not only comrade Zinoviev and I but also a number of comrades with experience in the field consider it would be inadmissible, and fatal for the proletariat and the revolution, for us to initiate an armed insurrection at the present moment, with the prevailing relationship of social forces, independently of and only a few days before a Congress of Soviets.... [I]nsurrection, in Marx's expression, is an art. And that is just why we believe that it is our duty now, in the present circumstances, to speak out against any attempt to initiate an armed insurrection which would be doomed to defeat and would bring in its train the most disastrous consequences for the party, for the proletariat, for the destiny of the revolution. To stake all this on a rising in the coming days would be an act of despair. And our party is too strong, it has too great a future, to take such desperate steps.[52]

Lenin was beside himself with rage. The same day, he wrote a letter to the Central Committee demanding the expulsion of the two as traitors. The next day he wrote a further letter, elaborating:

> No self-respecting party can tolerate strike-breaking and blacklegs in its midst. That is obvious. The more we reflect upon Zinoviev's and Kamenev's statement in the non-party press, the more self-evident it becomes that their action is strike-breaking in the full sense of the term.[53]

> The Executive Committee of a trade union, after a *month* of deliberation, decides that a strike is inevitable, that the time is ripe, but that the date is to be concealed from the employers. After that, two members of the Executive Committee appeal *to the rank and file,* disputing the decision, and are defeated. Thereupon these two come out in the press and with a slanderous lie betray the decision of the Executive Committee to the capitalists, thus more than half wrecking the strike, or delaying it to a less favorable time by warning the enemy. Here we have strike-breaking in the full sense of the term.

> There can and must be only one answer to that: an immediate decision of the Central Committee:

> "The Central Committee, regarding Zinoviev's and Kamenev's statement in the non-party press as strike-breaking in the full sense of the term, expels both of them from the Party."

> It is not easy for me to write in this way about former close com-

rades. But I should regard any hesitation in this respect as a crime, for otherwise a party of revolutionaries which does not punish prominent blacklegs would perish.[54]

To add to the confusion, the editors of the official Bolshevik newspaper came out with a statement criticizing "[t]he sharp tone of Comrade Lenin's article [which] does not change the fact that, fundamentally, we remain of one mind." The editors at that time were Stalin and Sokolnikov. The Central Committee minutes read: "Comrade Sokolnikov reports that he had no part in the editorial statement on the subject of Kamenev's letter, etc., and considers this statement a mistake."[55]

It thus became clear that Stalin alone was responsible for the ambiguous attitude towards Zinoviev's and Kamenev's blacklegging. All this was happening four days before the insurrection!

When Kamenev offered his resignation from the Central Committee on October 20,[56] Stalin spoke against acceptance, arguing that "our whole position is contradictory"; in other words, he took it on himself to defend confusion and vacillation. Kamenev's resignation was accepted by five votes to three. By six votes, against Stalin's opposition, a decision was taken forbidding Kamenev and Zinoviev to carry on a struggle against the policy of the Central Committee. The minutes read: "Comrade Stalin announces that he is leaving the editorial board." In order not to complicate an already difficult situation, the Central Committee refused to accept Stalin's resignation. Neither did it accept Lenin's demand that Zinoviev and Kamenev should be expelled from the party.

Lenin had to go on prodding the party leadership even on the eve of the insurrection, he still did not trust the political courage of the Central Committee. On October 24—the day the insurrection actually started—he wrote:

> I am writing these lines on the evening of the 24th. The situation is critical in the extreme. In fact, it is now absolutely clear that to delay the uprising would be fatal.... History will not forgive revolutionaries for procrastinating when they could be victorious today (and they certainly will be victorious today), while they risk losing much tomorrow, in fact, they risk losing everything.... The seizure of power is the business of the uprising; its political purpose will become clear after the seizure.... The government is tottering. It must be *given the death-blow* at all costs. To delay action is fatal.[57]

So wrong on the technicalities of the uprising

While Lenin was proved absolutely correct on the strategic decision—the need for an armed insurrection to seize power—his technical suggestions, the particulars of the plans he drafted, were very defective.

Let us consider the suggestion that the revolution should be started in Moscow. As matters turned out, even after the success of the uprising in Petrograd, the Moscow Bolsheviks found the going extremely difficult. The Moscow insurrection took much longer and entailed far greater sacrifice. It is a fact that *after* the victory of the Bolsheviks in Petrograd on October 25, it still took eight long days for the Bolsheviks to achieve power in Moscow, through a very bloody battle.... For several reasons, Moscow before October was more difficult to win over to Bolshevism than Petrograd. It was more isolated from the front, it did not have Petrograd's rebellious soldiers and sailors, it suffered much less from food supply difficulties. The Moscow proletariat was dispersed among smaller factories, compared with the Petrograd giants.[58] The proletariat of Moscow was far less class-conscious than that of Petrograd: up to 40 percent of the Moscow workers had plots of land in the countryside, and 22.8 percent owned farms. (The corresponding figures for Petrograd were 16.5 and 7.8 percent.)[59] In the years during which Bolshevism became a mass workers' party, 1912–14, Moscow lagged far behind Petersburg. During the war, as we pointed out earlier,[60] less than 9 percent of the workers involved in political strikes were in Moscow, whereas 74 percent were in Petrograd.

As late as October 1917, the Socialist Revolutionaries had a mass following among the workers of Moscow, while their influence among the workers of Petrograd was practically nonexistent. In addition, both the proletariat and the troops in Petrograd had experienced the baptism of the February Revolution, while in Moscow they had not had to fight for that victory. The revolutionary spirit of the Petrograd garrison was fanned by the threat to transfer regiments to the front. The Moscow garrison was not subjected to this pressure.

Finally, the Bolshevik leadership in Petrograd was superior to that in Moscow. The most brilliant leaders of Bolshevism, including Lenin, Trotsky, and Lunacharsky, were in Petrograd. The Moscow leadership was split (as was that of Petrograd). Bukharin took the same line as Lenin and Trotsky, while Nogin and Rykov vacillated. It was only on October 25 that a Military Revolutionary Committee was established in Moscow. Thus Lenin's technical advice about the conduct of the insurrection was not at all sound.

Discarding the plan for a coup in Moscow first, Lenin then, as we have seen, proposed that the rising should begin in Helsingfors, and develop into an offensive from the north against Petrograd. But this was also impractical.

Lenin's method was basically right. The approach to insurrection as an art must be consistent and concrete. But, having been in hiding and out of touch with the practicalities of the situation, he could not judge it correctly. It is also possible that his emphasis on the strategic decision—his accustomed stick-bending—made it difficult for him to grasp the particulars. Concentrating on the key link, on the strategic choice, and absent from the scene of the struggle, Lenin was almost bound to make serious tactical miscalculations.

An even more important error than the suggestions of starting the uprising in Moscow, or arresting the government during the State Conference, was his view that the uprising should be prepared and carried out through party channels and in the name of the party, and should be sanctioned by the Congress of Soviets only after victory had been achieved.

Soviet legality

Lenin's main opponent on this issue was Trotsky, who was equally dedicated to the idea of the insurrection. History has shown that on this issue Trotsky was absolutely right.

The reports of the Bolshevik Petrograd Committee, as well as the Central Committee, repeat the refrain: the troops and the workers will come out if summoned by the soviets; but it is less certain that they will do so if summoned by the party. The very fact that the local party leaders, organizers, and agitators, in estimating the state of mind of the masses, always alluded to the distinction between the soviet and the party shows that it was a matter of great importance which institution was to call for the insurrection.

> The party set the Soviets in motion [Trotsky wrote], the Soviets set in motion the workers, soldiers, and to some extent the peasantry. What was gained in mass was lost in speed. If you represent this conducting apparatus as a system of cog-wheels—a comparison to which Lenin had recourse at another period on another theme—you may say that the impatient attempt to connect the party wheel directly with the gi-

gantic wheel of the masses—omitting the medium-sized wheel of the Soviets—would have given rise to the danger of breaking the teeth of the party wheel, and nevertheless not setting sufficiently large masses in motion.[61]

All the necessary work for the conquest of power—the political as well as the military and technical—went ahead at full speed under the auspices of the Soviets. Trotsky made brilliant use of the set up under the dual power born of the February Revolution to carry out the preparations for October.

Immediately after its establishment, the provisional government gave an undertaking not to disarm and not to remove from Petrograd those army units that had taken part in the February Revolution. The major upheavals of April, June, and July, the Kornilov coup and its liquidation repeatedly raised the same question of the subordination of the Petrograd garrison to the Petrograd Soviet. At the beginning of October, the government saw the German threat as an excellent excuse to rid the capital once and for all of the unruly elements in the garrison.[62] On October 5, Kerensky directed Polkovnikov, commander of the Petrograd Military District, to prepare the troops for transfer to the front.

On October 6, a rumor concerning a counterrevolutionary conspiracy was discussed in the Soldiers' Section of the Petrograd Soviet. It was that the government was preparing its flight from Petrograd, and intended to abandon the heart of the revolution to the approaching Germans. Trotsky made a momentous decision when he immediately took advantage of the rumor. In the Bolshevik declaration to the pre-parliament, he painted a grim picture of the deadly danger that now threatened the capital: Kerensky was going to transfer the government to Moscow, was going to evacuate the troops from Petrograd, the city would be abandoned to the German army so as to smother the revolution.[63]

Kerensky's denial that he had any intention of evacuating Petrograd did not convince the masses. As John Reed put it:

> In the relations of a weak government and a rebellious people there comes a time when every act of the authorities exasperates the masses, and every refusal to act excites their contempt....
> The proposal to abandon Petrograd raised a hurricane; Kerensky's public denial that the government had any such intention was met with hoots of derision.[64]

On October 9, the Petrograd Soviet resolved to establish a Revolutionary Military Committee, to guide the troops in their resistance to the counterrevolutionary plot of the provisional government. On October 13, the committee was set up with Trotsky as president. It constituted the immediate leadership of the garrison as well as the Red Guard. The task of the committee was to establish the size of the garrison needed for the defense of the capital; to keep in touch with the troops on the northern front, the Baltic fleet, the Finnish garrison, etc.; to assess the manpower and the stocks of munitions available; to work out a plan of defense; and to maintain discipline in the civilian population.

On October 21, the Petrograd Soviet provoked a showdown with Polkovnikov.

On 21 October [*Izvestiia* reported], the Petrograd Soviet recognized the Military Revolutionary Committee as the leading organ of the troops of the capital.

On the night of 22 October, the members of the Military Revolutionary Committee presented themselves at district headquarters and demanded that they be permitted to control the orders of the headquarters with the right to a deciding voice.

Colonel Polkovnikov, the commander of the troops, replied to this demand with an emphatic refusal.

The Petrograd Soviet then called a meeting of representatives of regiments, [to be held] at Smolny Institute. From this meeting, telephoned telegrams were dispatched to all units [stating] that the headquarters has refused to recognize the Military Revolutionary Committee and, by so doing, has severed [relations] with the revolutionary garrison and with the Petrograd Soviet of Workers' and Soldiers' Deputies, and has become a direct instrument of the counter-revolutionary forces.

"Soldiers of Petrograd," the telephoned telegram read, "the protection of the revolutionary order against the counter-revolutionary attacks falls upon you under the leadership of the Military Revolutionary Committee. Any orders to the garrison that are not signed by the Military Revolutionary Committee are not valid. All orders of the Petrograd Soviet for today, the day of the Petrograd Soviet and Workers' and Soldiers' Deputies, shall remain in full force. It is the duty of every officer of the garrison to exercize vigilance, self-control, and strict discipline. The revolution is in danger. Long live the revolutionary garrison."

The Commander of the Military District called a separate meeting, with the participation of representatives of the Central Committee and the commissar attached to the Military District headquarters. Representatives of the Petrograd garrison were called out from the Smolny Institute to attend the same meeting. A delegation, headed by Second Lieutenant Dashkevich, came to the district headquarters. Dashkevich announced that he was authorized by the garrison to inform the district headquarters that henceforth all the orders issued by it must be countersigned by the Military Revolutionary Committee of the Petrograd Soviet. To this, Second Lieutenant Dashkevich added that he had not been authorized to say anything more, and the delegation departed.[65]

Most of the regiments placed themselves under the command of the Revolutionary Military Committee; the Cossacks remained neutral.

Now the only thing needed was to entice the government into an act of open provocation against the revolution, so that a defensive mantle could be thrown over the activities of the Military Revolutionary Committee.

The government fell easily into the trap: on October 24, Colonel Polkovnikov sent a squad of soldiers to close down the printing press of the Bolshevik Party. The Revolutionary Military Committee reacted very sharply, in a declaration stating:

Soldiers! Workers! Citizens!

The enemies of the people have gone over to the offensive during the night. The Kornilovites at headquarters are trying to pull cadets and shock battalions in from the outskirts. The Oranienbaum cadets and the shock troops at Tsarskoe Selo have refused to move. A traitorous blow is being devised against the Petrograd Soviet of Workers' and Soldiers' Deputies. The newspapers *Rabochi put* and *Soldat* have been closed and the printing plant sealed up. The campaign of the counter-revolutionary plotters is directed *against the All-Russian Congress of Soviets* on the eve of its opening, *against the constituent assembly, against the people.* The Petrograd Soviet of Workers' and Soldiers' Deputies is standing up to defend the revolution. The Revolutionary Military Committee is leading the resistance to the attack of the plotters. The whole garrison and the whole proletariat of Petrograd are ready to deal a crushing blow to the enemies of the people.

The Revolutionary Military Committee decrees:

1. All regimental, company, and crew committees, together with the commissars of the Soviet, and all revolutionary organizations must meet in constant session, and concentrate in their hands all information about the plans and actions of the plotters.

2. Not a single soldier shall become separated from his unit without the permission of the committee.

3. Two representatives from each unit and five from each district Soviet shall immediately be sent to the Smolny Institute.

4. Report all actions of the plotters immediately to the Smolny Institute.

5. All members of Petrograd Soviet and all delegates to the All-Russian Congress of Soviets are summoned immediately to the Smolny Institute for a special session.

The counter-revolution has raised its criminal head.

All the gains and hopes of the soldiers, workers, and peasants are

threatened with great danger. But the forces of the revolution immeasurably surpass the forces of its enemies.
The people's cause is in firm hands. The plotters will be crushed. No vacillation or doubts. Firmness, steadfastness, perseverance, decisiveness. Long live the revolution![66]

How easy it was to reopen the Bolshevik printing press closed by order of Colonel Polkovnikov; Trotsky recounts:

A worker and a working-girl from the Bolshevik printing plant ran panting to Smolny and there found Podvoisky and Trotsky. If the committee would give them a guard against the junkers, the workers would bring out the paper. A form was soon found for the first answer to the government offensive. An order was issued to the Litovsky regiment to send a company immediately to the defense of the workers' press. The messengers from the printing-plant insisted that the 6th battalion of sappers be also ordered out: these were near neighbors and loyal friends. Telephonograms were immediately sent to the two addresses. The Litovtsi and the sappers came out without delay. The seals were torn from the building, the moulds again poured, and the work went on. With a few hours' delay the newspaper suppressed by the government came out under the protection of the troops of a committee which was itself liable to arrest. That was insurrection. That is how it developed.[67]

All in all, the "legality" imparted by soviet involvement played a very important role in the success of the rising. As Trotsky put it years after the event:

From the moment when we, as the Petrograd Soviet, invalidated Kerensky's order transferring two-thirds of the garrison to the front, we had actually entered a state of armed insurrection...the outcome of the insurrection of 25 October was at least three-quarters settled, if not more, the moment that we opposed transfer of the Petrograd garrison; created the Military Revolutionary Committee (October 16); appointed our own commissars in all army divisions and institutions, and thereby completely isolated not only the general staff of the Petrograd zone, but also the government. As a matter of fact, we had here an armed insurrection—an armed though bloodless insurrection of the Petrograd regiments against the provisional government—under the leadership of the Military Revolutionary Committee and under the slogan of preparing the defense of the Second Soviet Congress, which would decide the ultimate fate of the state power.[68]

As a result of the way in which the Military Revolutionary Committee planned the insurrection, it was relatively easy to synchronize the seizure of power with the opening of the Second Soviet Congress on October 26. The fact that on the day of the insurrection, October 25, the resistance of the government was reduced to defending the Winter Palace demonstrates how successful Trotsky's direction of the preparation and carrying out of the final insurrection had been. As Sukhanov describes the insurrection:

> [N]o resistance was shown. Beginning at 2 in the morning the stations, bridges, lighting installations, telegraphs, and telegraphic agency were gradually occupied by small forces brought from the barracks. The little groups of cadets could not resist and didn't think of it. In general, the military operations in the politically important centers of the city rather resembled a changing of the guard. The weaker defense force, of cadets, retired; and a strengthened defense force, of guards, took its place.... [T]he decisive operations that had begun were quite bloodless; not one casualty was recorded. The city was absolutely calm. Both the center and the suburbs were sunk in a deep sleep, not suspecting what was going on in the quiet of the cold autumn night.... The operations, gradually developing, went so smoothly that no great forces were required. Out of the garrison of 200,000, scarcely a tenth went into action, probably much fewer. Because of the presence of the workers and sailors, only volunteers could be led out of the barracks.[69]

Sukhanov could quite rightly refer to the "meticulously executed October insurrection."[70]

"Compared with the classical revolutionary scheme," wrote one historian, "October was quite unique. There were no great street processions in Petrograd that day, no mass demonstrations, no baton charges—not even a marked rise in popular agitation, and barely any victims."[71*]

Victor Serge in his moving account of the revolution writes:

> The revolution did, indeed, go off in proletarian style—with organization. That is why, in Petrograd, it won so easily and completely.... The rational element of coordination, the superb organization of the rising as a military operation conducted along the rules of the warmaking art, is clearly demonstrated here, and forms a striking contrast with the spontaneous or ill organized movements which have been so numerous in the history of the proletariat.[72]

We have already mentioned that Trotsky agreed with Lenin on the urgency of insurrection. But he differed on the method, especially over the idea that the party should stage the insurrection in its own name, and on its own responsibility. History gave a clear verdict on this disagreement.

Trotsky's scheme implied a certain delay in carrying out the

---

* The only casualties in the whole of Petrograd fell during the assault on the Winter Palace; all five came from among the insurrectionists.

plan of action. Lenin feared any such delay. His attention was focused on the outright opponents of the insurrection in the party leadership—Zinoviev, Kamenev, Nogin, and Rykov. He suspected that any delay would result in concessions to the irresolute, a loss of time through vacillation.

Trotsky was the supreme organizer of the October insurrection. To quote only a few witnesses, Stalin, in an article called "The Role of the Most Eminent Party Leaders," written on November 6, 1918, had this to say:

> All the work of practical organization of the insurrection was conducted under the immediate leadership of the chairman of the Petrograd Soviet, Trotsky. It is possible to declare with certainty that the swift passing of the garrison to the side of the Soviet and the bold execution of the work of the Military Revolutionary Committee, the party owes principally and above all to comrade Trotsky.

A footnote in Lenin's *Collected Works* reads:

> After the majority in the Petrograd Soviet passed into the hands of the Bolsheviks, [Trotsky] was elected its chairman and in that position organized and led the insurrection of 25 October.[73]

In addition, Sukhanov wrote:

> Trotsky, tearing himself away from work on the revolutionary staff, personally rushed from the Obukhovsky plant to the Trubochny, from the Putilov to the Baltic works, from the riding-school to the barracks; he seemed to be speaking at all points simultaneously. His influence, both among the masses and on the staff, was overwhelming. He was the central figure of those days and the principal hero of this remarkable page of history.[74]

Lenin, the party, and the revolution

Consciousness and planning are bound to play a central role in the proletarian revolution. A revolutionary party is therefore a fundamental, indispensible instrument of the revolution. Nevertheless, the question history puts squarely before us is, How did it happen that the Bolshevik Party and its leadership, in two key turning points in 1917—the morning after the February Revolution, and the eve of October—so lagged behind the needs of the struggle that they threatened the success of the whole affair?

The Bolshevik Party had great advantages. It had been steeled by its bitter struggle against tsarism. Its cadres, selected, trained, and tempered, were extremely tough and self-sacrificing. Its politics of independence from the liberals and their hangers-on (from the Mensheviks to the Socialist Revolutionaries) were principled; it had assimilated the experience of 1905, including active participation in the organization of an armed insurrection; its policies were grounded on very firm, broad theoretical foundations, and on serious study of the international experience of the workers' revolutionary movement from 1848 to 1871 and onwards; its leadership had been selected and tested over years of hard and heroic struggle.

And yet, both in April and in September–October, the party leadership was prey to extreme vacillation. How is this to be explained?

First of all, every party, including the most revolutionary, inevitably produces its own organizational conservatism—without routine there is no stability. Of course, in a revolutionary organization, discipline must be combined with initiative and daring. As Lenin so many times repeated: at every turning point the party faces the danger of clinging to yesterday's methods, slogans, and actions, which become an impediment to the adoption of the new ones now demanded. Both routinism and initiative are most concentrated in the top leadership of the party.

In addition, even the most revolutionary party is subject to pressure from alien social forces. The main psychological support of the social *status quo* is the belief of the ruling class, of the petty bourgeoisie, which transmits its influence, and of the workers that the oppressed classes are intrinsically inferior, impotent, and ignorant. To isolate the revolutionary party from bourgeois public opinion, to cut any link with the bourgeoisie and the petty-bourgeois milieu, to insulate the party from these alien influences was a goal for which Lenin fought all his life. (This incidentally is why he insisted that no party member could work as a journalist on a bourgeois paper.)[75] But no party can free itself completely from the pressure of the petty-bourgeois environment.

The sharpest turning point, at which the pressure of bourgeois disbelief in the potential of the oppressed is also most strongly exerted, is the moment when the revolutionary party has to progress from the work of preparation, of propaganda, agitation, and organization, to the immediate struggle for state power, to the armed insurrection.

A revolutionary party develops over a whole historical period, during which experience convinces its members that on the whole the correlation of class forces is such as to give the capitalist class power over the working class. While the workers may be stronger in individual parts of the battlefield, on the whole they are weaker than their opponents. If this was not the case, the rule of the capitalists would be long past. Any revolutionary party that did not control its impatience over the years in the light of this fact would condemn itself to adventurism and to its own destruction. But the moment comes—and this is the meaning of revolution—when the habit of considering the enemy as stronger becomes the main obstacle on the road to victory. "At this moment, the most harmful thing of all would be to underestimate the enemy's strength and overestimate our own," wrote Zinoviev and Kamenev on October 11.

Another serious obstacle hinders the attempt to turn the party sharply towards the insurrection: the state of mind of the proletariat on the eve of the armed uprising. The masses may be waiting, listless, and not ready for spontaneous action. In Russia, the experience of April, June, July, and the Kornilov episode brought the masses to the conclusion that isolated, uncoordinated actions were useless. Between the exuberant mood of early days and the confidence born out of the well-led, relentless struggle of the masses directed by a clear revolutionary leadership, there was a pause, a lull.

Lenin played a crucial role in rearming the Bolsheviks both in April and in September–October, for which he was certainly well qualified.

His genius was first of all rooted in his absolute confidence in the magnificent potential of the proletariat. He identified passionately with the hatreds and hopes of the oppressed.

Secondly, Lenin's Marxism was neither fatalistic, mechanical, nor voluntaristic. Its basis was materialist dialectics and the principle that the masses discern their own abilities only through action. While a sober assessment of the real class forces is necessary, the revolutionary party itself is one of the key factors in an uncertain situation, especially at a time of revolution. The boldness of the party will give confidence to the workers, while irresolution may lead the masses into passivity and a mood of depression.

Thirdly, Lenin had uncanny intuition. In a period of great changes, the number of unknown factors, not only in the enemy camp, but also in our own, is so great that sober analysis alone will not suffice. An unsurpassed ability to detect the mood of the masses was Lenin's most important gift.

Finally, the years of heroic struggle, and above all the experience of 1905, had trained and tempered Lenin for the battle of 1917. In 1905, he shaped and developed the rules of action for the party and the class in an armed insurrection. He made clear the inter-relation between a mass movement and the planned armed insur-rection, the necessary balance between political leadership and technical planning.[76]

Now, in 1917, he was ready for the challenge. In the same way as Marx and Engels in the years of dull "normalcy" looked back again and again to 1848 as the point from which to determine the future pattern of the revolutionary workers' movement, so Lenin in the years after 1905 looked back to 1905. The mass revolutionary struggle of that period was the point of departure for his formula-tion and reformulation of the strategy and tactics of Bolshevism. As I have written elsewhere:

> The 1905 revolution threw into sharp relief not only the relation of the vanguard party to the class, but also that of the party leader to the party. In 1905, Lenin's leadership of his own faction was on the whole incontestable. But it demanded from him a continuous effort of thought and organization—he had, in a sense, to reaffirm his lead-ership and reconquer his party every day. On the evidence of 1905... one could write instructive chapters on what happened to the leader-ship of the Leninists without Lenin. If 1905 steeled the Bolsheviks, even more so did it steel Lenin. His ideas, program, and tactics were put to the stiffest test during those days.[77]

In 1917, Lenin managed to rearm the party and to raise it to meet the needs of the day, because he had immense capital to rely on. He had strong support in the party ranks, prepared by the whole history of Bolshevism. Lenin was the founder of the party, and its leader throughout its long, hard struggle. The crucible of October furnished the supreme test of his strategy and of the cal-iber of his leadership of the party and the class.

Lenin's character—his confidence in the power of the working class, his direct thinking, and plain speaking—is epitomized in the first words he spoke to the Congress of Soviets on the day after the victorious uprising: "We shall now proceed to construct the socialist order."[78]

CHRONOLOGY

Events occurring in Russia are dated according to the Julian calendar; events occurring abroad are dated according to both the Julian and (Western) Gregorian calendars.

1914

July 19/August 1: First World War begins.

July 23/August 4: German Social Democratic Party votes war credit.

July 26/August 8: Lenin arrested in Nowy Targ (Poland).

August 23/September 5: Lenin arrives in Berne (Switzerland).

October 12/November 4: Bolshevik deputies in the Duma arrested and sent to Siberia.

August 24–26/September 6–8: Lenin reports on the attitude towards the war at a conference of the Bolsheviks in Berne. His theses on the war are adopted as a resolution of the Social Democratic group.

1915

February 14–27/February 19–March 4: Conference of Bolshevik groups abroad in Berne.

March 13–15/March 26–28: International Socialist Women's Conference in Berne.

March 22–24/April 4–6: International Socialist Youth Conference in Berne.

August 23–26/September 5–8: Antiwar Zimmerwald Conference.

1916

December 1915–June 1916: Lenin works on *Imperialism: The Highest Stage of Capitalism*.

April 11–17/April 24–30: Antiwar Kienthal Conference.

December 16–17/December 29–30: Assassination of Rasputin.

December 1916–February 1917: Lenin works in the Zurich library on the Marxist attitude towards the state. His notes from Marx and Engels, together with his own comments and conclusions, are gathered together under the title "Marxism on the State."

1917

January 9: Street meetings and a printers' strike celebrate the anniversary of "Bloody Sunday."

February 14: The last State Duma assembles.

February 23: Celebration of International Women's Day begins the revolution.

February 24: 200,000 workers on strike in Petrograd.

February 25: General strike in Petrograd. Shootings and arrests of revolutionists.

February 26: Duma dissolved by the tsar. The deputies disperse but decide not to leave town. Tens of thousands of workers in the streets.

February 27: Mutiny of the guard regiments. Formation of the Soviet of Workers' Deputies. Formation of the Provisional Committee of the Duma.

February 28: Arrest of the tsar's Ministers. Capture of Schlüsselberg Prison. First issue of *Izvestiia*, "The News of the Soviet."

March 1: "Order No. 1" is issued to the soldiers. Formation of the Soldiers' Section of the Soviet. First session of the Moscow Soviet.

March 2: The tsar abdicates in favor of the Grand Duke Mikhail. The provisional government is formed by the Provisional Committee of the Duma, with the support of the soviet and with Kerensky as minister of justice.

March 3: The Grand Duke Mikhail abdicates. The provisional government announces the revolution to the world by radio.

March 5: The first issue of *Pravda*, central organ of the Bolshevik Party.

March 6: The provisional government declares an amnesty for political prisoners.

March 7/March 26: Lenin writes his "Letters from Afar."

March 8: The tsar arrested at Moghiliev.

March 14: Address of the soviet "to the people of the whole world" declaring for peace without annexations or indemnities.

March 23: Funeral of martyrs of the revolution.

March 29: All-Russian Conference of the Soviets.

March 28–April 4: All-Russian Conference of the Bolshevik Party.

April 3: Lenin, Zinoviev, and the other Bolsheviks arrive from Switzerland.

April 4: Lenin's *April Theses* outlining his policy of proletarian revolution.

April 14–22: Petrograd City Conference of the Bolshevik Party.

April 18: Celebration of the international socialist holiday of May 1. Foreign Minister Miliukov sends a note to the allies promising war to victory on the old terms.

April 20: Armed demonstrations of protest against the note of Miliukov—the "April Days."

April 24–29: The Seventh (April) All-Russian Conference of the Bolsheviks.

May 1: The Petrograd Soviet votes for a coalition government.

May 2: Miliukov resigns.

May 4: Trotsky arrives from America seconding the policies of Lenin. An All-Russian Congress of Peasants' Deputies opens in Petrograd.

May 5: A coalition government is organized with Kerensky as minister of war.

May 17: The Kronstadt Soviet declares itself the sole governing power in Kronstadt.

May 25: All-Russian Congress of the Socialist Revolutionary Party.

May 30: First conference of factory and shop committees opens in Petrograd.

June 3: First All-Russian Congress of Soviets.

June 9: Bolsheviks call off antigovernment demonstration in Petrograd.

June 18: Russian offensive in Galicia begins. Mass meetings in Petrograd organized by the Soviet turn into pro-Bolshevik demonstrations.

July 3–4: Violent antigovernment demonstrations in Petrograd.

July 5: Arrest of Bolshevik leaders ordered.

July 7: Lenin goes into hiding.

July 8: Prince Lvov resigns; Kerensky appointed head of an interim government.

July 12: The provisional government reestablishes the death sentence at the front.

July 16: General Kornilov appointed commander in chief of the

Russian Army.

July 23: Trotsky arrested by the provisional government.

July 24: Kerensky forms a new coalition government.

July 26/August 3: Sixth Congress of the Bolshevik Party.

August 12–15: State Conference in Moscow, and general protest strike.

August 20: Bolshevik success in Petrograd municipal elections.

August 21: The Germans occupy Riga.

August–September: Lenin writes *State and Revolution*.

August 27–30: Abortive counterrevolutionary putsch led by General Kornilov.

September 1: The Petrograd Soviet carries a Bolshevik motion.

September 4: Trotsky freed on bail.

September 5: The Moscow Soviet carries a Bolshevik motion.

September 9: The leaders of the Petrograd Soviet go over to Bolshevism.

September 10–14: Lenin writes *The Impending Catastrophe and How to Combat It*.

September 15: The Central Committee discuss Lenin's letters "The Bolsheviks must assume power" and "Marxism and insurrection," which it circulated among the major Bolshevik organizations.

September 14–21: A "Democratic Conference" meets in Petrograd.

September 24: Kerensky forms a third and last coalition government. Bolshevik victory in the Moscow municipal elections.

End of September–October 1: Lenin writes *Can the Bolsheviks Retain State Power?*

October 7: Opening of pre-parliament; Bolsheviks refuse to participate.

October 9: Formation of Military Revolutionary Committee of the Petrograd Soviet.

October 10: Central Committee of the Bolshevik Party declares for an armed insurrection.

October 15: The soldiers' section of the Petrograd Soviet votes to transfer all military authority from headquarters to a Military Revolutionary Committee.

October 13: An enlarged Conference of the Petrograd Committee of Bolsheviks discusses, in the main unenthusiastically, the prospect of insurrection.

October 16: An enlarged plenum of the Central Committee, the

Executive Commission of the Petrograd Committee, the Military Organization, members of the Petrograd Soviet, trade unions, factory committees, Petrograd Area Committee, and the railway workers. Decision on insurrection reaffirmed.

October 18: Zinoviev's and Kamenev's letter to Gorky's paper opposing the insurrection.

October 19: Lenin demands the expulsion of Zinoviev and Kamenev from the party.

October 20: The Military Revolutionary Committee begins actual preparations for insurrection.

October 22: A review of soviet forces in Petrograd under the guise of huge meetings.

October 23: The Peter and Paul fortress, last important obstacle to the success of the insurrection, declares for the Petrograd Soviet.

October 24: The provisional government issues orders for the arrest of the Military Revolutionary Committee, suppression of Bolshevik papers, replacement of Bolshevik-propagandized troops in Petrograd with loyal troops; Kerensky delivers his last speech to the Council of the Republic; Lenin comes to Smolny, Bolshevik headquarters, at night.

October 25: October Revolution begins (2 a.m.). Troops of the Military Revolutionary Committee close Council of the Republic (12 noon). Lenin comes out of hiding; appears at a session of the Petrograd Soviet (3 p.m.); is introduced by Trotsky. Operations against the Winter Palace (seat of the provisional government) begin (9 p.m.). Second All-Russian Congress of Soviets opens (11p.m.).

NOTES

FOREWORD

1   L. Trotsky, *History of the Russian Revolution*, London 1934, p. 975.

CHAPTER 1: THE WAR

1   N.K. Krupskaya, *Memories of Lenin*, London 1970, pp. 240–41.
2   O.H. Gankin and H.H. Fisher, *The Bolsheviks and the World War: The Origins of the Third International*, Stanford 1940, p. 59.
3   C.E. Schorske, *German Social Democracy, 1905–1917: The Development of the Great Schism*, Cambridge, Mass., 1955, p. 286.
4   J.P. Nettl, *Rosa Luxemburg*, London 1966, vol. 2, p. 604.
5   L. Trotsky, *My Life*, New York 1960, p. 236.
6   S.F. Cohen, *Bukharin and the Bolshevik Revolution*, London 1974, p. 22.
7   Nettl, p. 609.
8   G.L. Shklovsky, "The Berne Conference 1915," *Proletarskaia Revoliutsiia*, no. 5 (40), 1925, in Gankin and Fisher, p. 143.
9   V. I. Lenin, *Collected Works*, translated from the 4th Russian edition, vol. 21, pp. 347–78.
10 Lenin, *Collected Works*, vol. 21, pp. 33–34.
11 Lenin, *Collected Works*, vol. 21, p. 276.
12 Lenin, *Collected Works*, vol. 21, p. 144.
13 Lenin, *Collected Works*, vol. 21, p. 315.
14 Lenin, *Collected Works*, vol. 21, p. 163.
15 Lenin, *Collected Works*, vol. 21, p. 278.
16 Lenin, *Collected Works*, vol. 22, p. 169.
17 Lenin, *Collected Works*, vol. 22, p. 176.
18 Lenin, *Collected Works*, vol. 22, p. 140.
19 Lenin, *Collected Works*, vol. 23, pp. 77–79.

20 Lenin, *Collected Works*, vol. 23, p. 96.
21 Lenin, *Collected Works*, vol. 21, p. 40.
22 Lenin, *Sochineniia*, 4th edition, vol. 11, p. 330.
23 Lenin, *Sochineniia*, 4th edition, vol. 15, pp. 173–76.
24 Schorske, p. 69.
25 Schorske, p. 72.
26 Schorske, pp. 77–78.
27 Schorske, p. 199.
28 Schorske, pp. 244–45.
29 Schorske, p. 245.
30 Schorske, p. 54.
31 K. Kautsky, *The Road to Power*, Chicago 1910, p. 95.
32 Schorske, p. 247.
33 Lenin, *Collected Works*, vol. 21, p. 161.
34 Lenin, *Collected Works*, vol. 35, p. 165.
35 Lenin, *Collected Works*, vol. 35, pp. 167–78.
36 Lenin, *Collected Works*, vol. 43, p. 613.
37 Lenin, *Collected Works*, vol. 21, pp. 40–41.
38 Trotsky, *My Life*, p. 249.
39 J. Braunthal, *History of the International, 1914–1943*, London 1967, vol. 2, pp. 47–48.
40 Gankin and Fisher, p. 332.
41 Gankin and Fisher, p. 334.
42 Braunthal, vol. 2, p. 50.
43 Braunthal, vol. 2, p. 51.
44 Braunthal, vol. 2, p. 51.
45 A.E. Senn, *The Russian Revolution in Switzerland, 1914–1917*, Madison 1971, p. 41.
46 Senn, pp. 41–42.
47 Senn, pp. 204–18.
48 Senn, p. 83.
49 Krupskaya, p. 254.
50 Krupskaya, p. 260.
51 Senn, p. 45.
52 Senn, p. 233.
53 Senn, p. 32.
54 Lenin, *Collected Works*, vol. 43, p. 448.
55 Lenin, *Collected Works*, vol. 43, p. 486.
56 Lenin, *Collected Works*, vol. 37, p. 624.
57 Lenin, *Collected Works*, vol. 36, p. 365.
58 Lenin, *Collected Works*, vol. 35, p. 236.
59 Lenin, *Collected Works*, vol. 37, p. 535.
60 Krupskaya, p. 268.
61 Krupskaya, p. 267.

62 Lenin, *Collected Works*, vol. 43, p. 602.
63 Lenin, *Collected Works*, vol. 43, p. 609.
64 Gankin and Fisher, p. 170.
65 Trotsky, *The War and the International*, Colombo 1971, pp. 20–21.
66 Lenin, *Collected Works*, vol. 21, p. 353.
67 Lenin, *Collected Works*, vol. 21, p. 216.
68 Lenin, *Collected Works*, vol. 30, p. 32.

CHAPTER 2: THE BOLSHEVIK PARTY IN THE TEST OF THE WAR

1   L. Trotsky, *Stalin*, London 1947, p. 168.
2   F.I. Kalinychev, *Gosudarstvennaia duma v Rossii: Sbornik dokumentakh i materialakh*, Moscow 1957, pp. 595–96.
3   Trotsky, *Stalin*, p. 168.
4   D.A. Baevsky, *Ocherki po istorii oktiabrskoi revoliutsii*, vol. 1, Moscow 1927, p. 379.
5   A.G. Shliapnikov, *Kanun semnadtsatogo goda*, Moscow-Petrograd 1923, vol. 1, p. 29.
6   *Sotsial-Demokrat*, no. 51, February 29, 1916.
7   *Revoliutsionnoe Byloe*, no. 3, 1924, quoted in Baevsky, p. 384.
8   Gankin and Fisher, p. 151.
9   T. Dan in J. Martow, *Geschichte der russischen Sozialdemokratie*, Berlin 1926, p. 283.
10 Lenin, *Collected Works*, vol. 21, p. 171.
11 Lenin, *Collected Works*, vol. 21, p. 172.
12 *Sbornik Sotsial Demokrata*, no. 1, October 1916, p. 57.
13 Letter by Kamenev written on April 23, 1915, quoted in "On the correspondence of the Russian Bureau of the CC with abroad in the war years (1914–1916)," *Proletarskaia revoliutsiia*, nos. 7–8 (102–3), 1930.
14 Krupskaya, p. 247.
15 I.P. Khonianko, "In the underground and in emigration 1911–1917," *Proletarskaia revoliutsiia*, no. 4 (16), 1923.
16 Gankin and Fisher, p. 148.
17 Shliapnikov, vol. 1, pp. 10–11.
18 R.G. Suny, *The Baku Commune, 1917–1918*, Princeton 1972, p. 59.
19 See, for instance, O. Chadaev, ed., *Bolsheviki v gody imperialisticheskoi Voiny, 1914–Fevral 1917*, Moscow 1939; or N.P. Donii, ed., *Bolsheviki Ukrainy v period mezhdu pervoi i vtoroi burshuazno-demokraticheskimi revoliutsiiami*, Kiev 1960, pp. 554–650.
20 Trotsky, *History of the Russian Revolution*, p. 56.
21 A. Kiselev, "In July 1914," *Proletarskaia revoliutsiia*, no.7 (30), 1924.
22 Trotsky, *My Life*, p. 233.
23 *Sotsial-Demokrat*, December 12, 1914.

24 I.P. Leiberov and O.I. Shkaratan, "Concerning the social composition of the Petrograd industrial workers in 1917," *Voprosy Istorii*, no. 1, 1961.
25 K. Sidorov, "The labour movement in Russia during the years of the imperialist war," in M.N. Pokrovsky, ed., *Ocherki po istorii oktiabrskoi revoliutsii*, Moscow-Leningrad 1927, vol. 1, p. 261.
26 Sidorov, in Pokrovsky, p. 270.
27 V.L. Meller and A.M. Pankratova, eds., *Rabochee dvizhenie v 1917 g.*, Moscow-Leningrad 1926, p. 16.
28 Meller and Pankratova, pp. 17, 20.
29 Sidorov, in Pokrovsky, vol. 1, p. 287.
30 Leiberov and Shkaratan.
31 M. Cherniavsky, ed. and trans., *Prologue to Revolution. Notes of A.N. Iakhontov on the secret meetings of the Council of Ministers, 1915*, New York 1967, pp. 100–01.
32 Cherniavsky, pp. 233–34.
33 Cherniavsky, pp. 236–37.
34 C.E. Vuillamy and A.L. Hynes, *The Red Archives: Russian State Papers and Other Documents Relating to the Years 1915–1918*, London 1929, pp. 62–63.
35 Vuillamy and Hynes, p. 66–67.
36 Vuillamy and Hynes, p. 68.
37 Cherniavsky, p. 45.
38 Cherniavsky, p. 48.
39 A.E. Badaev, *Bolsheviki v gosudarstvennoi dume*, Leningrad 1939, p. 361.
40 Cherniavsky, p. 183.
41 Kiselev.
42 M.G. Fleer, ed., *Peterburgskii Komitet bolshevikov v gody voiny 1914–17*, Leningrad 1927, pp. 19–20.
43 Fleer, p. 19.
44 *Sotsial-Demokrat*, no. 41, May 1, 1915.
45 *Partiia bolshevikov v gody mirovoi imperialisticheskoi voiny 1914–17*, Moscow 1963, p. 235.
46 *Partiia bolshevikov v gody mirovoi imperialisticheskoi voiny 1914–17*, p. 232.
47 I.P. Leiberov, "V.I. Lenin and the Petrograd organization of the Bolsheviks during the First World War (1914–1916)," *Voprosy Istorii KPSS*, no. 6, 1960.
48 Fleer, p. 409.
49 I.I. Mints, *Istoriia Velikogo Oktiabria*, Moscow 1967, vol. 1, p. 259.
50 Fleer, p. 91.
51 Fleer, p. 91.
52 Petrograd Committee letter to the CC before October 31, 1916.

Revoliutsionnoe dvizhenie v armii a na flote v gody pervoi mirovoi voiny 1914–17, Moscow 1961, pp. 218–19.

53 Shliapnikov, vol. 1, p. 292.
54 *Istoriia KPSS,* Moscow 1963; Baevsky in Pokrovsky, vol. 1, p. 458.
55 Shliapnikov, vol. 1, p. 54.
56 Mints, p. 319.
57 *Revoliutsionnoe dvizhenie v armii a na flote v gody pervoi mirovoi voiny 1914–17,* p. 435.
58 Shliapnikov, vol. 2, p. 49.
59 M. Ia. Latsis, "Underground work in Moscow (1914–1916)," *Proletarskaia revoliutsiia,* no. 10 (45), 1925.
60 Antonov-Saratovskii, "Saratov in the Years of the Imperialist War (1914–1916) and *Nasha Gazeta,*" *Proletarskaia revoliutsiia,* no. 4, (16), 1923.
61 Shliapnikov, vol. 1, pp. 152, 259.
62 K. Pechak, "The Social-Democracy of Latvia (Communist Party of Latvia) in the period 1909 to 1915," *Proletarskaia revoliutsiia,* no. 12, 1922.
63 Shliapnikov, vol. 1, p. 51.
64 Shliapnikov, vol. 1, p. 74.
65 Shliapnikov, vol. 1, p. 248.
66 *Sbornik Sotsial Demokrata,* no. 2, p. 82.
67 Fleer, p. 259.
68 M. Balabanov, *Ot 1905 k 1917 godu,* Moscow-Leningrad 1927, p. 411.
69 Fleer, p. 262.
70 G. Zinoviev and V.I. Lenin in "Socialism and War," Lenin, *Collected Works,* vol. 21, p. 319.
71 L. Kochan, *Russia in Revolution, 1890–1918,* London 1970, p. 183.
72 Mints, vol. 1, pp. 277–83.
73 *Partiia bolshevikov v gody mirovoi imperialisticheskoi voiny 1914–17,* p. 141.
74 Mints.
75 Shliapnikov, vol. 1, pp. 99–119, 128–36.
76 Shliapnikov, vol. 1, pp. 99–119, 128–36.
77 Mints, p. 279.
78 Mints, p. 279.
79 Gankin and Fisher, p. 193.
80 S.O. Zagorsky, *State Control of Industry in Russia during the War,* New Haven 1928, p. 165.
81 Lenin, *Collected Works,* vol. 21, p. 176.
82 *Krasnaia Letopis,* no. 7, 1923.

Chapter 3: Lenin and the National Question

1 *Verhandlungen des Gesamtparteitages der Sozialdemokratie in oester-reich*, Vienna 1899, p. xiv.
2 *Verhandlungen des Gesamtparteitages*, p. 15.
3 *Verhandlungen des Gesamtparteitages*, p. 107.
4 O. Bauer, *Die Nationalitätensfrage und die Sozialdemokratie*, Vienna 1907.
5 R. Pipes, *The Formation of the Soviet Union*, Harvard University Press 1954, p. 28.
6 Pipes, p. 28.
7 Lenin, *Collected Works*, vol. 19, pp. 532–33.
8 *Przeglad Socjaldemokratyczny* (theoretical organ of the SDKPL), 1908, no. 6.
9 *Neue Zeit*, 1895–96, p. 466.
10 Gankin and Fisher, pp. 219–20.
11 Lenin, *Collected Works*, vol. 24, p. 298.
12 Lenin, *Collected Works*, vol. 20, p. 412.
13 Lenin, *Collected Works*, vol. 20, pp. 422–23.
14 Lenin, *Collected Works*, vol. 20, p. 413.
15 Lenin, *Collected Works*, vol. 22, p. 346.
16 Lenin, *Collected Works*, vol. 20, p. 427.
17 Lenin, *Collected Works*, vol. 22, p. 333.
18 Lenin, *Collected Works*, vol. 22, pp. 355–57.
19 Lenin, *Collected Works*, vol. 23, p. 60.
20 "From the correspondence of the Bureau of the CC with abroad in the years of the war (1915–1916)," *Proletarskaia revoliutsiia*, nos. 7–8 (102–3), 1930.
21 See T. Cliff, *Lenin: Building the Party*, London 1975, pp. 34–40.
22 Lenin, *Collected Works*, vol. 31, p. 453.

Chapter 4: Imperialism, the Highest Stage of Capitalism

1 Lenin, *Collected Works*, vol. 32, pp. 266–67.
2 Lenin, *Collected Works*, vol. 32, p. 277.
3 Lenin, *Collected Works*, vol. 32, p. 298.
4 Lenin, *Collected Works*, vol. 32, p. 302.
5 Lenin, *Collected Works*, vol. 32, p. 281.
6 Lenin, *Collected Works*, vol. 32, p. 301.
7 Lenin, *Collected Works*, vol. 32, p. 194.
8 Lenin, *Collected Works*, vol. 32, p. 302.
9 Lenin, *Collected Works*, vol. 32, p. 295.

10 L.G. Churchwood, "Towards the understanding of Lenin's *Imperialism*," *The Australian Journal of Politics and History*, May 1959.

CHAPTER 5: CRISIS AND COLLAPSE OF THE
TSARIST REGIME

1 Lenin, *Collected Works*, vol. 21, pp. 213–14.
2 Cherniavsky, p. 2.
3 Cherniavsky, p. 3.
4 I.V. Gessen, *V dvukh vekakh; Arkhiv Russkoi Revoliutsii*, vol. 22, Berlin 1937, p. 355.
5 V.I. Gurko, *Features and Figures of the Past*, Stanford 1939, p. 546.
6 Cherniavsky, p. 147.
7 Cherniavsky, pp. 147–48.
8 Cherniavsky, p. 148.
9 Cherniavsky, p. 169.
10 Cherniavsky, p. 241.
11 Cherniavsky, p. 128.
12 Cherniavsky, pp. 141–42.
13 Cherniavsky, p. 7.
14 J. Buchanan, *My Mission to Russia*, London 1923, vol. 1, p. 165.
15 M. Paléologue, *An Ambassador's Memoirs*, London 1923–25, vol. 2., p. 14.
16 Buchanan, vol. 2, p. 3.
17 Paléologue, vol. 2, p. 166.
18 Cherniavsky, p. 245.
19 R.K. Massie, *Nicholas and Alexandra*, London 1968, p. 367.
20 Gurko, p. 545.
21 Gurko, p. 551.
22 Gurko, pp. 552–53.
23 Buchanan, vol. 2, p. 6.
24 B. Pares, ed., *Letters of the Tsaritsa to the Tsar, 1914–1916*, London 1923, p. 297.
25 A. Knox, *With the Russian Army, 1914–1917*, New York 1921, p. 412.
26 Massie, p. 325.
27 Pares, pp. 394–95.
28 Pares, p. 398.
29 Pares, p. 428.
30 A. Kerensky, *The Crucifixion of Liberty*, New York 1934, p. 218.
31 Buchanan, vol. 2, p. 51.
32 Trotsky, *History of the Russian Revolution*, p. 82.
33 Pares, pp. 86–87.
34 Pares, p. 390.

35 Pares, p. 221.
36 Pares, p. 377.
37 Pares, p. 382.
38 Pares, p. 411.
39 W.H. Chamberlin, *The Russian Revolution*, New York 1935, vol. 1, p. 68.
40 Chamberlin, p. 73.
41 Cherniavsky, p. 154.
42 Cherniavsky, p. 225.
43 Cherniavsky, p. 88.
44 Cherniavsky, p. 18.
45 G. Katkov, *Russia 1917: The February Revolution*, London 1969, p. 257.
46 A. Kerensky, *Russia and History's Turning Point*, New York 1965, p. 150.
47 Rodzianko's memoirs, *Arkhiv Russkoi Revoliutsii*, vol. 17, pp. 82 ff. in F. Golder, ed., *Documents of Russian History*, New York 1927, pp. 82–121.
48 Paléologue, vol. 3, p. 157.
49 Buchanan, vol. 2, p. 141.
50 R.P. Browder and A.F. Kerensky, *The Russian Provisional Government 1917—Documents*, Stanford 1961, vol. 3, p. 1276.
51 Kerensky, *Russia—History's Turning Point*, p. 152.
52 Lenin, *Collected Works*, vol. 23, p. 301.

Chapter 6: From the February Revolution to Dual Power

1   Browder and Kerensky, vol. 1, p. 34.
2   Browder and Kerensky, vol. 1, pp. 34–35.
3   Browder and Kerensky, vol. 1, pp. 35–36.
4   Chamberlin, vol. 1, p. 77.
5   Browder and Kerensky, vol. 1, pp. 38–39.
6   N.N. Sukhanov, *The Russian Revolution 1917: A Personal Record.* London 1955, p. 36.
7   I.A. Aluf, "On some problems of the February Revolution," *Voprosy istorii KPSS*, no. 1, 1967.
8   Trotsky, *History of the Russian Revolution*, p. 122.
9   Sukhanov, p. 5.
10 General E.K. Klimovich, *Padenie tsarskogo rezhima*, Leningrad 1927, vol. 1, p. 98.
11 V. Kaiurov, "Six days of the February Revolution," *Proletarskaia revoliutsiia*, no. 1 (13), 1923.
12 A.G. Shliapnikov, *Semnadtsatyi god*, Moscow-Petrograd 1923,

vol. 1, p. 86.
13 Browder and Kerensky, vol. 1, pp. 37–38.
14 Trotsky, *History of the Russian Revolution*, p. 171.
15 Cherniavsky, p. 199.
16 Sukhanov, p. 18.
17 Sukhanov, pp. 54–55.
18 Sukhanov, p. 67.
19 Sukhanov, p. 77.
20 V.V. Kutuzov, ed., *Velikaia Oktiabrskaia Sotsialisticheskaia Revoliutsiia—Khronika Sobytii*, Moscow 1957, vol. 1, p. 219.
21 Sukhanov, pp. 85–86.
22 Sukhanov, p. 308.
23 Sukhanov, pp. 6–7.
24 Sukhanov, p. 8.
25 Sukhanov, pp. 8–9, 12.
26 Sukhanov, p. 258.
27 Sukhanov, p. 105.
28 Sukhanov, pp. 55–56.
29 Sukhanov, p. 119.
30 Sukhanov, pp. 124–25.
31 V.B. Stankevich, *Vospominaniia, 1914–19 gg*, Berlin 1920, pp. 70–71.
32 V.V. Shulgin, *Dni*, Belgrade 1925; Golder, pp. 263–64, 270.
33 Sukhanov, p. 330.
34 Shliapnikov, *Semnadtsatyi god*, vol. 1, pp. 193–94.
35 A.L. Sidorov, et al., eds., *Velikaia oktiabrskaia sotsialisticheskaia revoliutsiia: Dokumenty i materialy*, Moscow 1957, vol. 1, p. 283.
36 M. Ferro, *The Russian Revolution of February 1917*, London 1972, p. 169.
37 A.V. Lukashev, "The struggle of the Bolsheviks for a revolutionary policy in the Moscow soviet of workers' deputies during the dual power," *Voprosy istorii KPSS*, no. 8, 1967.
38 Sukhanov, p. 228.
39 Sukhanov, pp. 346–47.
40 Sukhanov, p. 167.
41 Sukhanov, p. 327.
42 Shliapnikov, *Semnadtsatyi god*, vol. 2, p. 236.
43 Sukhanov, p. 326.
44 K. Marx and F. Engels, *Selected Correspondence, 1846–1895*, London 1941, pp. 433–34.
45 Lenin, *Collected Works*, vol. 24, pp. 61–62.
46 Lenin, *Collected Works*, vol. 24, p. 62.
47 Lenin, *Collected Works*, vol. 24, p. 60.
48 Lenin, *Collected Works*, vol. 24, p. 61.

49 Lenin, *Collected Works,* vol. 24, p. 22.

CHAPTER 7: LENIN REARMS THE PARTY

1 Kutuzov, vol. 1, p. 5.
2 Shliapnikov, *Semnadtsatyi god,* vol. 2, p. 175.
3 P.F. Kudelli, ed., *Pervyi legalnyi Peterburgskii komitet bolshevikov v 1917 g.,* Moscow-Leningrad 1927, p. 16.
4 Sukhanov, p. 195.
5 Sukhanov, pp. 107–08.
6 Shliapnikov, *Semnadtsatyi god,* vol. 1, pp. 167–85.
7 Kudelli, p. 19.
8 Shliapnikov, *Semnadtsatyi god,* vol. 1, p. 240.
9 Shliapnikov, *Semnadtsatyi god,* vol. 1, p. 255.
10 Shliapnikov, *Semnadtsatyi god,* vol. 1, p. 209; Kudelli, p. 11.
11 *KPSS v borbe za pobedu sotsialisticheskoi revoliutsii v period dvoevlastii 27 fevrali–4 iulia 1917 g. Sbornik dokumentov,* Moscow 1957, p. 171.
12 *KPSS v borbe,* p. 172.
13 Kudelli, pp. 19–20.
14 Kudelli, p. 27.
15 D.A. Longley, "The divisions in the Bolshevik Party in March 1917," *Soviet Studies,* July 1972.
16 Sidorov, vol. 1, pp. 3–4.
17 Kudelli, p. 11.
18 Sidorov, vol. 1, p. 106; Trotsky, *The Stalin School of Falsification,* New York 1937, pp. 240–41.
19 Kudelli, pp. 24–26.
20 Sukhanov, p. 227.
21 *Pravda,* March 15, quoted in Browder and Kerensky, vol. 2, p. 868.
22 Shliapnikov, *Semnadtsatyi god,* vol. 2, p. 185.
23 Sidorov, vol. 1, p. 111.
24 Kudelli, pp. 49–52.
25 Sidorov, vol. 1, p. 520.
26 Sidorov, vol. 1, p. 528.
27 Sidorov, vol. 1, p. 63.
28 Sidorov, vol. 1, p. 463.
29 Sidorov, vol. 1, p. 163.
30 Sidorov, vol. 1, p. 532.
31 R.G. Suny, *The Baku Commune, 1917–1918,* Princeton 1972, pp. 72–75.
32 For a long time the only full report of this conference was in the minutes published by Trotsky as an appendix to his book *The Stalin School of Falsification.* After the death of Stalin these were published

in Russia, in *Voprosy istorii KPSS*, 1962, no. 5, pp. 106–25; no. 6, pp. 130–52. These correspond exactly, except that: (1) they contain material not in Trotsky's work, and (2) they omit the last day, when Lenin presented the *April Theses* to the conference.

33 See note 32.
34 Trotsky, *History of the Russian Revolution*, p. 316.
35 Lenin, *Collected Works*, vol. 21, p. 435.
36 Lenin, *Collected Works*, vol. 21, p. 403.
37 Lenin, *Collected Works*, vol. 21, p. 379.
38 Lenin, *Collected Works*, vol. 21, p. 380.
39 Lenin, *Collected Works*, vol. 21, p. 436.
40 Lenin, *Collected Works*, vol. 35, pp. 309–10.
41 Lenin, *Collected Works*, vol. 35, p. 313.
42 Lenin, *Collected Works*, vol. 23, pp. 304–05.
43 Lenin, *Collected Works*, vol. 23, pp. 306–07.
44 Lenin, *Collected Works*, vol. 23, p. 307.
45 Lenin, *Collected Works*, vol. 23, p. 308.
46 Lenin, *Collected Works*, vol. 23, p. 310.
47 Lenin, *Collected Works*, vol. 23, pp. 325–26.
48 Lenin, *Collected Works*, vol. 23, p. 323.
49 Lenin, *Collected Works*, vol. 23, p. 334.
50 Lenin, *Collected Works*, vol. 23, pp. 337–38.
51 Lenin, *Collected Works*, vol. 23, pp. 340–41.
52 Krupskaya, pp. 287–88.
53 *Leninski Sbornik,* vol. 2, p. 376–77.
54 W. Hahlweg, *Lenins Rückkehr nach Russland 1917*, Leiden 1957, p. 13.
55 Hahlweg, pp. 76–77.
56 Senn, p. 231.
57 Quoted in Hahlweg, pp. 11–12.
58 Quoted in Hahlweg, p. 11.
59 Quoted in Hahlweg, p. 25.
60 D. Lloyd George, *War Memoirs*, London 1936, vol. 5, p. 2530.
61 F.F. Raskolnikov, *Kronstadt i Piter V 1917 godu*, Moscow-Leningrad 1925, p. 54.
62 Sukhanov, pp. 272–74.
63 Sukhanov, p. 280.
64 Sukhanov, pp. 281–82.
65 Sukhanov, p. 286.
66 Sukhanov, p. 287.
67 Sukhanov, pp. 287–88.
68 Lenin, *Collected Works*, vol. 24, pp. 21–24.
69 Sukhanov, p. 289.
70 Lenin, *Collected Works*, vol. 21, p. 33.

71 Cliff, pp. 205–06.
72 Lenin, Collected Works, vol. 8, p. 314.
73 Lenin, Collected Works, vol. 24, p. 43.
74 Lenin, Collected Works, vol. 24, pp. 44–46.
75 Lenin, Collected Works, vol. 24, p. 38.
76 Lenin, Collected Works, vol. 24, p. 50.
77 Trotsky, "Results and Prospects," The Permanent Revolution, London 1962, pp. 201, 203, 233–34.
78 Sidorov, vol. 2, pp. 15–16.
79 Sukhanov, pp. 225–26.
80 Sukhanov, p. 230.
81 Trotsky, History of the Russian Revolution, p. 326.
82 Trotsky, Stalin, p. 198.
83 Kudelli, p. 88.
84 Sukhanov, p. 288.
85 Browder and Kerensky, vol. 3, p.1210.
86 Sedmaia (Aprelskaia) Vserossiiskaia konferentsiia RSDRP (bolshevikov) (hereafter referred to as Sedmaia konferentsiia), Moscow 1958, pp. 14–18.
87 Sedmaia konferentsiia, p. 37.
88 Kudelli, pp. 99–100, 103.
89 Sedmaia konferentsiia, p. 80.
90 Sedmaia konferentsiia, p. 106.
91 Sedmaia konferentsiia, pp. 91–92.
92 Sedmaia konferentsiia, pp. 241–43.
93 Sedmaia konferentsiia, p. 177.
94 Sedmaia konferentsiia, p. 373.
95 Sedmaia konferentsiia, p. 195.
96 Sedmaia konferentsiia, p. 372.
97 Sedmaia konferentsiia, p. 228.
98 Sedmaia konferentsiia, p. 322.
99 I.V. Stalin, Na putiakh k Oktobriu, Moscow 1924, p. viii.
100 Trotsky, History of the Russian Revolution, p. 343.
101 Sukhanov, p. 290.
102 Trotsky, Diary in Exile, London 1958, pp. 53–54.
103 The Bolsheviks and the October Revolution. Minutes of the Central Committee of the Russian Social-Democratic Labour Party (bolsheviks) August 1917–February 1918, London 1974, p. 11.
104 Minutes of the Central Committee, p. 49.
105 Shestoi sezd RSDRP (bolshevikov), avgust 1917 goda: Protokoly, Moscow 1958, p. 252.
106 Leninskii sbornik, vol. 4, p. 303.
107 Lenin, Sochineniia, 1st ed., vol. 14, p. 488.
108 Leninskii sbornik, vol. 4, p. 290.

CHAPTER 8: LENIN, THE PARTY, AND THE PROLE-TARIAT

1 Lenin, *Collected Works*, vol. 24, pp. 63–65.
2 Lenin, *Collected Works*, vol. 24, pp. 65–66.
3 Lenin, *Collected Works*, vol. 24, p. 65.
4 Lenin, *Collected Works*, vol. 24, p. 59.
5 Lenin, *Collected Works*, vol. 24, p. 67.
6 Lenin, *Collected Works*, vol. 24, p. 80.
7 Lenin, *Collected Works*, vol. 24, pp. 82–84.
8 Lenin, *Collected Works*, vol. 24, p. 75.
9 Lenin, *Collected Works*, vol. 13, p. 65.
10 Lenin, *Collected Works*, vol. 11, p. 346.
11 *Sedmala konferentsiia*, p. 355.
12 Kutuzov, vol. 2, p. 45.
13 *KPSS v borba za pobedu sotsialisticheskoi revoliutsii v period dvo-evlastii*, pp. 62–63.
14 Kutuzov, vol. 2, p. 84.
15 *Krasnaia Letopis*, no. 1 (10), 1924, p. 47.
16 Kutuzov, vol. 2, p. 170.
17 *Shestoi sezd*, pp. 317–90.
18 W.G. Rosenberg, "The Russian municipal Duma elections of 1917," *Soviet Studies*, 1969.
19 Lenin, *Collected Works*, vol. 24, p. 543.
20 V.V. Anikeev, "Data on the Bolshevik organizations from March to December 1917," *Voprosy istorii KPSS*, nos. 2 and 3, 1958.
21 Kutuzov, vol. 2, pp. 111, 185, 189, 194, 219.
22 Kutuzov, vol. 2, pp. 225, 251, 256, 276, 301, 337, 358, 362, 383, 443–45, 462.
23 Kutuzov, vol. 3, pp. 15, 95, 179, 482, 489, 497, 509, 516.
24 Anikeev, in *Voprosy istorii KPSS*, nos. 2 and 3, 1958.
25 Anikeev, in *Voprosy istorii KPSS*, nos. 2 and 3, 1958.
26 Anikeev, in *Voprosy istorii KPSS*, nos. 2 and 3, 1958.
27 K.T. Sverdlova, *Iakov Mikhailovich Sverdlov*, Moscow 1960, p. 252.
28 Sverdlova, p. 253.
29 Trotsky, *On Lenin*, London 1971, pp. 73–74.
30 Trotsky, *History of the Russian Revolution*, p. 1212.
31 Shliapnikov, *Kanun semnadtsatogo goda*, vol. 1, Moscow-Petrograd 1923, p. 248.
32 B. Zaslavsky, I. Sazonov, and Kh. Astrakhan, *"Pravda" 1917 goda*, Moscow 1962, p. 10.
33 *Perepiska sekretariata TsK RSDRP(b) s mestnymi partiinymi organizatsiiami: Sbornik dokumentov*, vol. 1, Moscow 1957.
34 *Perepiska sekretariata*, p. 50.

35 Zaslavsky et al., pp. 54–55.
36 *Shestoi sezd*, p. 40.
37 Kutuzov, vol. 2, p. 107.
38 Kutuzov, vol. 2, p. 181.
39 Anikeev, "Some new data on the history of the October Revolution," *Voprosy istorii KPSS*, no. 9, 1963.
40 *Minutes of the Central Committee*, p. 77.
41 Anikeev, in *Voprosy istorii KPSS*, no. 2, 1958.
42 Anikeev, in *Voprosy istorii KPSS*, no. 9, 1963.
43 Anikeev, in *Voprosy istorii KPSS*, no. 9, 1963.
44 See *Perepiska sekretariata*, vol. 1.
45 *Shestoi sezd*, pp. 74–75.
46 *Shestoi sezd*, pp. 20–21.
47 *Shestoi sezd*, p. 25.
48 *Shestoi sezd*, p. 40.
49 *Shestoi sezd*, p. 40.
50 *Shestoi sezd*, p. 37.
51 *Shestoi sezd*, pp. 26–27; Stalin, *Collected Works*, vol. 3, pp. 180–81.
52 *Minutes of the Central Committee*, pp. 44–45.
53 *Minutes of the Central Committee*, p. 272.
54 J. Keep, "October in the provinces," in R. Pipes, ed., *Revolutionary Russia*, Cambridge, Mass., 1967, pp. 188–90.
55 Cohen, pp. 49–50.
56 *Minutes of the Central Committee*.
57 *Minutes of the Central Committee*, p. 85.
58 *Minutes of the Central Committee*, pp. 88–89.
59 *Minutes of the Central Committee*, p. 109.
60 Trotsky, *Stalin*, p. 232.
61 *Minutes of the Central Committee*, p. 97.
62 *Shestoi sezd*, p. 36.
63 *Sedmoi Sezd RSDRP (bolshevikov): Protokoly*, Moscow 1918, p. 20.
64 Cliff, p. 93.
65 D. Lane, *The Roots of Russian Communism*, Assen 1969, p. 12.
66 Cliff, p. 358.
67 Mints, p. 319.
68 "VKP(b)," in *Bolshaia Sovetskaia Entsiklopediia*, 1930, vol. 11, p. 537.
69 E. Smitten, *Sotsialnyi i natsionalnyi sostav VKP(b)*, Moscow-Leningrad 1928, p. 13.
70 Kutuzov, vol. 3, p. 183.
71 *Shestoi sezd*, pp. 319–90.
72 Trotsky, *History of the Russian Revolution*, p. 808.
73 Kutuzov, vol. 2, p. 318.
74 See Cliff, pp. 180–81.

75 Lenin, *Collected Works*, vol. 43, p. 613.
76 *Shestoi sezd*, p. 295.
77 *Shestoi sezd*, pp. 296–97.
78 *Shestoi sezd*, pp. 298–300.
79 *Shestoi sezd*, pp. 147–150.
80 A.M. Pankratova, *Istoriia proletariata SSSR*, Moscow 1935, p. 168.
81 *Krasnyi Arkhiv*, no. 64, 1934, p. 140.
82 *Perepiska sekretariata*, vol. 1, p. 287.
83 Lenin, *Collected Works*, vol. 31, p. 26.
84 Lenin, *Collected Works*, vol. 31, pp. 24–25.
85 Cliff, pp. 255–56.
86 Lenin, *Collected Works*, vol. 31, pp. 68–69.
87 Lenin, *Collected Works*, vol. 31, p. 74.
88 Cliff, pp. 257–58.
89 Lenin, *Collected Works*, vol. 31, p. 58.
90 Lenin, *Collected Works*, vol. 33, p. 227.
91 Lenin, *Collected Works*, vol. 30, p. 60.
92 Lenin, *Collected Works*, vol. 30, p. 258.
93 Lenin, *Collected Works*, vol. 30, p. 262.
94 Lenin, *Collected Works*, vol. 27, p. 274.
95 Lenin, *Collected Works*, vol. 33, p. 302.
96 Lenin, *Collected Works*, vol. 31, p. 57.
97 K. Radek, "V.I. Lenin," in *Dvadtsat piat let RKP*, Tver 1923, p. 234.
98 Lenin, *Collected Works*, vol. 31, pp. 95–96.

CHAPTER 9: LENIN LOWERS THE TEMPERATURE

1 Lenin, *Collected Works*, vol. 24, p. 364.
2 N.K. Krupskaya, *Lenin i partiia*, Moscow 1963, p. 118.
3 Browder and Kerensky, vol. 2, pp. 1044–45.
4 Browder and Kerensky, vol. 2, p. 1046.
5 Browder and Kerensky, vol. 2, p. 1098.
6 Browder and Kerensky, vol. 3, p. 1238.
7 W.S. Woytinsky, *Stormy Passage*, New York 1961, pp. 270–71.
8 Browder and Kerensky, vol. 3, p. 1858.
9 Trotsky, *History of the Russian Revolution*, p. 353.
10 Lenin, *Works*, vol. 24, pp. 184–85; Sidorov, vol. 2, p. 726.
11 *Sedmaia konferentsiia*, p. 204.
12 A. Rabinowitch, *Prelude to Revolution: The Petrograd Bolsheviks and the July Uprising*, Indiana 1968, pp. 44–45.
13 Lenin, *Collected Works*, vol. 24, p. 146.
14 Lenin, *Collected Works*, vol. 24, p. 211.
15 Lenin, *Collected Works*, vol. 24, pp. 244–45.
16 Lenin, *Collected Works*, vol. 24, p. 223.

17   Lenin, *Collected Works*, vol. 32, p. 34.
18   Lenin, *Collected Works*, vol. 24, p. 211.
19   Sukhanov, p. 323.
20   Kutuzov, vol. 2, p. 408.
21   O.H. Radkey, *The Agrarian Foes of Bolshevism*, New York 1958, p. 243.
22   Kutuzov, vol. 2, p. 16.
23   Kutuzov, vol. 2, p. 163.
24   Lenin, *Collected Works*, vol. 25, p. 129.
25   Trotsky, *History of the Russian Revolution*, p. 374.
26   Browder and Kerensky, vol. 3, p. 1257.
27   Browder and Kerensky, vol. 3, p. 1269.
28   Browder and Kerensky, vol. 3, p. 1282.
29   Browder and Kerensky, vol. 3, pp. 1283–84.
30   Browder and Kerensky, vol. 2, p. 942.
31   Sidorov, vol. 3, pp. 483–84.
32   Sidorov, vol. 3, p. 485.
33   Sidorov, vol. 3, p. 486.
34   Sidorov, vol. 3, p. 486.
35   Kudelli, pp. 136–45.
36   Kudelli, p. 157.
37   Kudelli, p. 158.
38   Browder and Kerensky, vol. 3, pp. 1312–13.
39   Browder and Kerensky, vol. 3, p. 1314.
40   Kudelli, p.156.
41   Quoted in Rabinowitch, p. 264.
42   Kudelli, pp. 158–66.
43   M. Ia. Latsis, "The July Days in Petrograd: From an agitator's diary,' *Proletarskaia revoliutsiia*, no. 5 (17), 1923.
44   Kudelli, p. 158.
45   *Pravda*, June 10, Sidorov, vol. 3, p. 498.
46   Rabinowitch, pp. 79–80.
47   Latsis, in *Proletarskaia revoliutsiia*, no. 5 (17), 1923; Kudelli, p. 164.
48   Kudelli, pp. 153–68.
49   Lenin, *Collected Works*, vol. 25, p. 79.
50. Lenin, *Collected Works*, vol. 25, pp. 80–81.
51   Kudelli, pp. 157–58.
52   Kudelli, pp. 159–61.
53   Kudelli, p. 163.
54   Sidorov, vol. 3, p. 518.
55   Kudelli, pp. 178–84.
56   Sukhanov, pp. 416–17.
57   Trotsky, *History of the Russian Revolution*, p. 463.
58   Sidorov, vol. 3, pp. 541–51.

59 Lenin, *Collected Works*, vol. 25, pp. 109–10.
60 Lenin, *Collected Works*, vol. 25, p. 83.

Chapter 10: Lenin and the Soldiers' Mutinies

1 Trotsky, *History of the Russian Revolution*, p. 875.
2 Marx and Engels, *Correspondence*, vol. 2, Paris 1931, p. 228.
3 Shliapnikov, *Semnadtsatyi god*, vol. 2, p. 102.
4 Browder and Kerensky, vol. 1, p. 51.
5 Sukhanov, p. 76.
6 Quoted in Trotsky, *History of the Russian Revolution*, p. 264.
7 Stankevich, p. 72.
8 Browder and Kerensky, vol. 2, p. 860.
9 Browder and Kerensky, vol. 2, p. 860.
10 Radkey, p. 343.
11 Browder and Kerensky, vol. 2, pp. 855–56.
12 Browder and Kerensky, vol. 2, p. 845.
13 Browder and Kerensky, vol. 2, pp. 849–50.
14 Browder and Kerensky, vol. 2, pp. 848–49.
15 Trotsky, *History of the Russian Revolution*, p. 291.
16 Sukhanov, p. 114.
17 A. Wildman, "The February Revolution in the Russian Army," *Soviet Studies*, July 1970.
18 Sukhanov, p. 129.
19 Browder and Kerensky, vol. 2, pp. 851–52.
20 Browder and Kerensky, vol. 2, p. 853.
21 Browder and Kerensky, vol. 2, p. 882.
22 Browder and Kerensky, vol. 2, p. 886.
23 N.N. Golovine, *The Russian Army in the World War*, New Haven 1931, pp. 124–25.
24 Browder and Kerensky, vol. 2, p. 925.
25 Browder and Kerensky, vol. 2, p. 887.
26 Browder and Kerensky, vol. 2, pp. 959–61, 968–69.
27 Browder and Kerensky, vol. 2, p. 991.
28 Browder and Kerensky, vol. 2, p. 1009.
29 Browder and Kerensky, vol. 2, p. 981.
30 Browder and Kerensky, vol. 2, p. 996.
31 Browder and Kerensky, vol. 2, p. 1000.
32 Browder and Kerensky, vol. 2, pp. 997–98.
33 Browder and Kerensky, vol. 2, p. 985.
34 Browder and Kerensky, vol. 2, pp. 992–93.
35. Browder and Kerensky, vol. 2, pp. 995–96.
36 Browder and Kerensky, vol. 2, p. 993.

37   Browder and Kerensky, vol. 2, p. 996.
38   Browder and Kerensky, vol. 2, p. 1003.
39   Browder and Kerensky, vol. 2, p. 1007.
40   Browder and Kerensky, vol. 2, p. 1019.
41   Lenin, *Collected Works,* vol. 24, pp. 100–01.
42   Lenin, *Collected Works,* vol. 24, p. 165.
43   Lenin, *Collected Works,* vol. 24, p. 318.
44   Lenin, *Collected Works,* vol. 24, p. 268.
45   Kutuzov, vol. 2, p. 446.
46   O.H. Radkey, *The Sickle Under the Hammer,* New York 1967, pp. 278–79.
47   Ferro, p. 252.
48   Sukhanov, p. 534.
49   Anikeev, in *Voprosy istorii KPSS,* nos. 2 and 3.
50   Stankevich, pp. 182–84, 186–90.
51   Sidorov, vol. 2, pp. 481–565, and vol. 3, pp. 329–89; Ferro, p. 364.
52   *Shestoi sezd,* p. 85.
53   Sidorov, vol. 3, p. 358.
54   *Shestoi sezd,* p. 147.
55   Lenin, *Collected Works,* vol. 25. p. 232.
56   A.A. Brusilov, *Moi vospominaniia,* Moscow-Leningrad 1929, p. 214.

Chapter 11: The Peasantry in the Revolution

1   Sukhanov, pp. 328–29.
2   M. Ferro, "The Aspirations of Russian Society," in Pipes, *Revolutionary Russia,* p. 149.
3   Quoted in V. Chernov, *The Great Russian Revolution,* New York 1966, p. 256.
4   Quoted in Lenin, *Collected Works,* vol. 24, p. 365.
5   Browder and Kerensky, vol. 2, p. 582.
6   K.G. Kotelnikov and C.V.L. Meller, *Krestianskoe dvizhenie v 1917 godu,* Moscow-Leningrad 1927, Appendix.
7   M. Miliutin, *Agrarnaia revoliutsiia,* Moscow 1927, p. 172.
8   Browder and Kerensky, vol. 2, p. 593.
9   Browder and Kerensky, vol. 2, p. 576.
10   Browder and Kerensky, vol. 2, p. 525.
11   Browder and Kerensky, vol. 2, pp. 527–28.
12   Radkey, *The Agrarian Foes of Bolshevism,* p. 253.
13   Radkey, *The Agrarian Foes of Bolshevism,* p. 255.
14   Radkey, *The Agrarian Foes of Bolshevism,* p. 448.
15   Browder and Kerensky, vol. 2, p. 527.
16   Browder and Kerensky, vol. 2, pp. 583–84.

17 Chernov, pp. 256–57.
18 Browder and Kerensky, vol. 2, p. 584.
19 Browder and Kerensky, vol. 2, pp. 567–68.
20 Kotelnikov and Meller, pp. 420–21.
21 Miliutin, p. 182.
22 Kotelnikov and Meller, pp. 420–21.
23 Chernov, pp. 262–63.
24 Radkey, *The Agrarian Foes of Bolshevism*, p. 246.
25 Radkey, *The Agrarian Foes of Bolshevism*, pp. 257–58.
26 Radkey, *The Agrarian Foes of Bolshevism*, pp. 438–39.
27 Radkey, *The Agrarian Foes of Bolshevism*, p. 192.
28 Lenin, *Collected Works*, vol. 9, p. 315.
29 Lenin, *Collected Works*, vol. 24, p. 167.
30 Lenin, *Collected Works*, vol. 24, p. 285.
31 Lenin, *Collected Works*, vol. 25, p. 227.
32 Lenin, *Collected Works*, vol. 24, p. 72.
33 Lenin, *Collected Works*, vol. 10, p. 411.
34 Lenin, *Collected Works*, vol. 10, p. 191.
35 Lenin, *Collected Works*, vol. 24, p. 168.
36 Lenin, *Collected Works*, vol. 24, pp. 501–02.
37 Lenin, *Collected Works*, vol. 25, pp. 122–25.
38 Lenin, *Collected Works*, vol. 24, p. 169.
39 Lenin, *Collected Works*, vol. 24, p. 502.
40 Lenin, *Collected Works*, vol. 25, pp. 275–76.
41 Lenin, *Collected Works*, vol. 25, p. 276.
42 Lenin, *Collected Works*, vol. 26, pp. 260–61.
43 *Delo Naroda*, November 17, 1917.
44 Lenin, *Collected Works*, vol. 28, p. 175.
45 *Protokoll des Zweite Weltkongresses der Kommunistische Internationale*, Hamburg 1921, p. 318; Lenin, *Sochineniia*, vol. 25, p. 359; E.H. Carr, *The Bolshevik Revolution*, London 1952, vol. 2, p. 166.
46 Sukhanov, p. 371.
47 Sukhanov, pp. 371–72.
48 Sukhanov, p. 635.
49 Sukhanov, pp. 201–02.
50 Sukhanov, p. 553.
51 See Cliff, pp. 216–19.
52 Lenin, *Collected Works*, vol. 25, p. 42.
53 R. Luxemburg, *The Russian Revolution*, New York 1940, pp. 18–21.

CHAPTER 12: LENIN AND WORKERS' CONTROL

1 P. Avrich, "Russian factory committees in 1917," *Jahrbücher für Geschichte Osteuropas,* June 1963, pp. 161–62.
2 Ferro, p. 115.
3 *Izvestiia,* March 6; Browder and Kerensky, vol. 2, p. 709.
4 Ferro, p. 181.
5 Avrich, p. 163.
6 C. Goodey, "Factory committees and the dictatorship of the poletariat 1918," *Critique,* no. 3, 1974, p. 30.
7 P.N. Amosov et al. *Oktiabrskaia Revoliutsiia i Fazavkomy,* Moscow 1927, vol. 1, pp. 27–28.
8 Avrich, p. 164.
9 Browder and Kerensky, vol. 2, pp. 719–20.
10 Amosov, vol. 1, pp. 22–24.
11 Lenin, *Collected Works,* vol. 24, p. 428.
12 M. Dewar, *Labor Policy in the USSR, 1917–1928,* London 1956, p. 6.
13 Amosov, vol. 1, p. 83.
14 Amosov, vol. 1, p. 95.
15 Amosov, vol. 1, p. 108.
16 Amosov, vol. 1, p. 242.
17 Amosov, vol. 1, p. 243.
18 Avrich, pp. 170–71.
19 Avrich, pp. 175–76.
20 J. Reed, *Ten Days that Shook the World,* London 1961, p. 7.
21 Zagorsky, p. 191.
22 M. Mitelman, *1917 god na putilovskom zavoda,* Leningrad 1939, p. 141.
23 Meller and Pankratova, p. 286.
24 Avrich, p. 170.
25 Zagorsky, p. 192.
26 Browder and Kerensky, vol. 2, p. 722.
27 Browder and Kerensky, vol. 2, p. 723.
28 Browder and Kerensky, vol. 2, p. 675.
29 Browder and Kerensky, vol. 2, pp. 741–42.
30 Amosov, vol. 2, pp. 16–20.
31 Amosov, vol. 2, pp. 20–28.
32 Amosov, vol. 2, pp. 118–19.
33 Avrich, p. 171.
34 Sidorov, vol. 4, p. 358.
35 Sidorov, vol. 4, pp. 339–40.
36 Meller and Pankratova, pp. 126–27.
37 Chamberlin, vol. 1, pp. 269–70.
38 Meller and Pankratova, pp. 229–30; Chamberlin, vol. 1, p. 270.

39 Chamberlin, vol. 1, p. 271.
40 Avrich, *The Russian Anarchists*, Princeton 1967, p. 149.
41 Lenin, *Collected Works,* vol. 24, pp. 36–37.
42 Lenin, *Collected Works,* vol. 25, p. 371.
43 Lenin, *Collected Works,* vol. 25, p. 323.
44 Lenin, *Collected Works,* vol. 25, pp. 323–24.
45 Lenin, *Collected Works,* vol. 25, p. 324.
46 Lenin, *Collected Works,* vol. 25, p. 327.
47 Lenin, *Collected Works,* vol. 25, pp. 328–29.
48 Lenin, *Collected Works,* vol. 25, p. 331.
49 Lenin, *Collected Works,* vol. 25, p. 335.
50 Lenin, *Collected Works,* vol. 25, p. 338.
51 Lenin, *Collected Works,* vol. 25, pp. 355–56.
52 Lenin, *Collected Works,* vol. 25, p. 348.
53 Lenin, *Collected Works,* vol. 25, p. 342.
54 Lenin, *Collected Works,* vol. 24, p. 425.
55 Lenin, *Collected Works,* vol. 25, pp. 363–64.
56 Lenin, *Collected Works,* vol. 24, p. 515.
57 Lenin, *Collected Works,* vol. 24, p. 231.
58 Lenin, *Collected Works,* vol. 26, p. 120.
59 A. Abolin, *The October Revolution and the Trade Unions,* Moscow 1933, p. 13.
60 Amosov, vol. 1, p. 271.
61 G.K. Ordzhonikidze, *Izbrannie Stati i Rechi, 1911–1937,* Moscow 1939, p. 124.
62 Trotsky, *History of the Russian Revolution,* p. 935.
63 Amosov, vol. 2, pp. 158–60.

CHAPTER 13: LENIN SUPPORTS THE REBELLIOUS NATIONALITIES

1   Lenin, *Collected Works,* vol. 25, p. 225.
2   Pipes, *The Formation of the Soviet Union,* pp. 3–4.
3   Browder and Kerensky, vol. 1, pp. 341–42.
4   Browder and Kerensky, vol. 1, pp. 349–50.
5   Browder and Kerensky, vol. 1, p. 340.
6   Browder and Kerensky, vol. 1, p. 341.
7   Browder and Kerensky, vol. 1, pp. 354–55.
8   Browder and Kerensky, vol. 1, pp. 357–58.
9   Browder and Kerensky, vol. 1, p. 370.
10 Browder and Kerensky, vol. 1, p. 370.
11 Browder and Kerensky, vol. 1, p. 371.
12 Browder and Kerensky, vol. 1, pp. 371–72.
13 Browder and Kerensky, vol. 1, pp. 375–76.

14   Browder and Kerensky, vol. 1, pp. 381–82.
15. Browder and Kerensky, vol. 1, p. 383.
16   Browder and Kerensky, vol. 1, p. 388.
17   Browder and Kerensky, vol. 1, p. 387.
18   Radkey, *The Agrarian Foes of Bolshevism*, pp. 274–75.
19   Browder and Kerensky, vol. 1, pp. 389–90.
20   Browder and Kerensky, vol. 1, pp. 394–96.
21   Browder and Kerensky, vol. 1, pp. 396–97.
22   Browder and Kerensky, vol. 1, p. 398.
23   Trotsky, *History of the Russian Revolution*, p. 895.
24   Browder and Kerensky, vol. 3, p. 1500.
25   Browder and Kerensky, vol. 3, pp. 1500–01.
26   Browder and Kerensky, vol. 3, p. 1480.
27   Browder and Kerensky, vol. 1, p. 319.
28   Lenin, *Collected Works*, vol. 25, pp. 91–92.
29   Lenin, *Collected Works*, vol. 24, p. 302.
30   *Sedmaia konferentsia*, p. 213.
31   *Sedmaia konferentsia*, p. 219.
32   Lenin, *Collected Works*, vol. 24, pp. 297–98.
33   *Sedmaia konferentsia*, p. 227.
34   Lenin, *Collected Works*, vol. 36, pp. 175–76.

CHAPTER 14: THE JULY DAYS

1   Rabinowitch, pp. 146–48.
2   The whole fascinating story of the conflicts between Lenin, on the
    one hand, and on the other, the Bolshevik Military Organization,
    some leading members of the Petersburg Committee, and some lead-
    ing Bolsheviks in the barracks and in the factories is told very graphi-
    cally in Alexander Rabinowitch's book.
3   Lenin, *Collected Works*, vol. 25, p. 83.
4   Lenin, *Collected Works*, vol. 25, pp. 113–14.
5   Rabinowitch, p. 121.
6   Rabinowitch, pp. 121–22.
7   Kudelli, pp. 185–99.
8   Kudelli, pp. 200–05; Rabinowitch, p. 129.
9   Rabinowitch, pp. 131–34.
10 Kudelli, pp. 244–45.
11 Rabinowitch, pp. 137–38.
12 Lenin, *Collected Works*, vol. 25, p. 210.
13 Rabinowitch, p. 184.
14 Lenin, *Collected Works*, vol. 25, p. 313.
15 Trotsky, *History of the Russian Revolution*, pp. 581–82.
16 P.N. Miliukov, *Istoriia vtoroi russkoi revoliutsii*, Sofia 1921, vol. 1,

p. 244.
17 Trotsky, *History of the Russian Revolution*, p. 576.
18 Lenin, *Collected Works*, vol. 25. p. 312.
19 Browder and Kerensky, vol. 3, pp. 1354–55.
20 Rabinowitch, pp. 215–16.
21 Lenin, *Collected Works*, vol. 25, p. 312.
22 Lenin, *Collected Works*, vol. 29, p. 396.
23 Lenin, *Collected Works*, vol. 25, pp.170–71.
24 Lenin, *Collected Works*, vol. 25, p. 183.
25 Lenin, *Collected Works*, vol. 25, p. 215.
26 Lenin, *Collected Works*, vol. 25, p. 177.
27 Lenin, *Collected Works*, vol. 25, pp. 186–87.
28 Lenin, *Collected Works*, vol. 25, pp. 189–90.
29 Trotsky, *History of the Russian Revolution*, p. 800.
30 A.M. Sovokin, "Enlarged Meeting of the Central Committee of the RSDLP(b) 13–14 July 1917," *Voprosy istorii KPSS*, no. 4, 1959.
31 *Shestoi sezd*, pp. 110–146.

CHAPTER 15: REACTION ON THE MOVE

1 Browder and Kerensky, vol. 3, p. 1358.
2 Woytinsky, pp. 306–07.
3 Sukhanov, p. 486.
4 Stalin, *Collected Works*, vol. 3, p. 112.
5 Browder and Kerensky, vol. 2, pp. 562–63.
6 Golder, p. 515.
7 Browder and Kerensky, vol. 2, p. 982.
8 Browder and Kerensky, vol. 3, p. 1404.
9 Browder and Kerensky, vol. 3, p. 1409.
10 Lenin, *Collected Works*, vol. 25, pp. 237–38.
11 Browder and Kerensky, vol. 3, pp. 1437–38.
12 Trotsky, *History of the Russian Revolution*, p. 625.
13 Rabinowitch, pp. 221–22.
14 Rabinowitch, p. 223.
15 Engels, "Introduction to K. Marx's *The Civil War in France*," in Marx-Engels *Selected Works*, Moscow 1962, vol. 1, p. 475.
16 Browder and Kerensky, vol. 2, p. 556.
17 Trotsky, *History of the Russian Revolution*, p. 75.
18 Lenin, *Collected Works*, vol. 25, pp. 181–82.
19 I. Deutscher, *The Prophet Armed*, London 1954, p. 274.
20 *Shestoi sezd*, p. 33.
21 *Shestoi sezd*, p. 270.
22 Sukhanov, pp. 471–72.
23 *Izvestiia*, July 16; Rabinowitch, p. 220.

24 Suny, p. 106.
25 Kudelli, pp. 210–16.
26 Sidorov, vol. 4, pp. 162–63.
27 Kudelli, p. 210; Rabinowitch, p. 219.
28 Kutuzov, vol. 3, p. 182.
29 Latsis, in *Proletarskaia revoliutsiia*, no. 5 (17), 1923.
30 Sidorov, vol. 5, pp. 58–59.
31 Sidorov, vol. 5, p. 112.
32 Sidorov, vol. 5, p. 187.
33 *Shestoi sezd*, p. 330.
34 Trotsky, *History of the Russian Revolution*, pp.757–58.
35 Trotsky, *History of the Russian Revolution*, pp. 760–61.
36 Kutuzov, vol. 3, p.16.
37 Kutuzov, vol. 3, p. 44.
38 Kutuzov, vol. 3, p. 44.
39 Kutuzov, vol. 3, p. 155.
40 Kutuzov, vol. 3, p. 207.
41 Kutuzov, vol. 3, p. 44.
42 Kutuzov, vol. 3, p. 71.
43 Kutuzov, vol. 3, p. 29.
44 Kutuzov, vol. 3, p. 127.
45 Kutuzov, vol. 3, p. 79.
46 Kutuzov, vol. 3, p. 248.
47 Sukhanov, p. 497.
48 Kutuzov, vol. 3, p. 107.
49 Kutuzov, vol. 3, p. 107.
50 Kutuzov, vol. 3, p. 112.
51 Kutuzov, vol. 3, p. 107.
52 Kutuzov, vol. 3, p. 85.
53 Kutuzov, vol. 3, p. 252.
54 Kutuzov, vol. 3, p. 309.
55 Kutuzov, vol. 3, p. 226.
56 Lenin, *Collected Works*, vol. 25, pp. 257–58.
57 Lenin, *Collected Works*, vol. 25, p. 220.
58 Lenin, *Collected Works*, vol. 25, p. 220.
59 Lenin, *Collected Works*, vol. 25, p. 221.
60 Lenin, *Collected Works*, vol. 25, p. 221.
61 Lenin, *Collected Works*, vol. 25, p. 222.
62 Golder, pp. 489–90.
63 Trotsky, *History of the Russian Revolution*, p. 659.
64 Trotsky, *History of the Russian Revolution*, p. 670.
65 Browder and Kerensky, vol. 3, p. 1474.
66 Browder and Kerensky, vol. 3, pp. 1475–77.
67 Browder and Kerensky, vol. 3, pp. 1479–80.

68 Browder and Kerensky, vol. 3, pp. 1480–81.
69 Browder and Kerensky, vol. 3, p. 1488.
70 Browder and Kerensky, vol. 3, p. 1497.
71 Browder and Kerensky, vol. 3, pp. 1501–02.
72 Browder and Kerensky, vol. 3, pp. 1504–05.
73 Browder and Kerensky, vol. 3, p. 1505.
74 Trotsky, *History of the Russian Revolution*, pp. 690–91.
75 Browder and Kerensky, vol. 3, pp. 1511, 1514.
76 Browder and Kerensky, vol. 3, p. 1514.
77 Lenin, *Collected Works*, vol. 25, p. 314.

Chapter 16: The Kornilov Coup

1   Trotsky, *History of the Russian Revolution*, p. 694.
2   Reed, pp. 22–23.
3   Reed, p. 7.
4   Trotsky, *History of the Russian Revolution*, pp. 704–05.
5   Browder and Kerensky, vol. 3, p. 1604.
6   Sukhanov, p. 503.
7   Sukhanov, p. 509.
8   Browder and Kerensky, vol. 3, pp. 1572–73.
9   Browder and Kerensky, vol. 3, p. 1573.
10 Browder and Kerensky, vol. 3, pp. 1573–74.
11 Chamberlin, vol. 1, p. 213.
12 Lenin, *Collected Works,* vol. 25, p. 285.
13 Lenin, *Collected Works,* vol. 25, pp. 285–89.
14 Sidorov, vol. 5, pp. 476–77.
15 Sidorov, vol. 5, p. 572.
16 Trotsky, *History of the Russian Revolution*, p. 724.
17 Sukhanov, p. 504.
18 Sukhanov, p. 505.
19 Sukhanov, p. 506.
20 Sukhanov, pp. 507–508.
21 Amosov, vol. 2, p. 48.
22 Trotsky, *History of the Russian Revolution*, p. 736.
23 Trotsky, *History of the Russian Revolution*, pp. 744–45.
24 Trotsky, *History of the Russian Revolution*, pp. 746–47.
25 Miliukov, vol. 2, p. 263.
26 Lenin, *Collected Works,* vol. 25, p. 306.
27 Lenin, *Collected Works,* vol. 25, pp. 306–308.
28 Lenin, *Collected Works,* vol. 25, p. 368.
29 Lenin, *Collected Works,* vol. 25, p. 370.
30 *Minutes of the Central Committee,* p. 54.
31 Lenin, *Collected Works,* vol. 26, p. 49.

32   Browder and Kerensky, vol. 3, p. 1614.
33   *Izvestiia*, September 19; Golder, p. 582.
34   Trotsky, *History of the Russian Revolution*, p. 829.
35   Browder and Kerensky, vol. 3, p. 1615.
36   Browder and Kerensky, vol. 3, p. 1649.
37   Browder and Kerensky, vol. 3, pp. 1650–51.
38   Stankevich, p. 122.
39   Woytinsky, pp. 355, 357.
40   Browder and Kerensky, vol. 3, pp. 1634–35.
41   Browder and Kerensky, vol. 3, pp. 1620–21.
42   Browder and Kerensky, vol. 3, pp. 1634–35.
43   Golder, p. 547.
44   Chamberlin, vol. 1, pp. 278–79.
45   Radkey, *The Agrarian Foes of Bolshevism*, pp. 429–30.
46   Trotsky, *History of the Russian Revolution*, pp. 783–84.
47   Sukhanov, p. 523.

CHAPTER 17: STATE AND REVOLUTION

1   Lenin, *Collected Works*, vol. 35, p. 286.
2   Lenin, *Collected Works*, vol. 36, p. 454.
3   Lenin, *Collected Works*, vol. 25, p. 385.
4   Marx and Engels, *Selected Correspondence*, London 1941, p. 57.
5   In A. Neuberg, *Armed Insurrection*, London 1970, p. 31.
6   K. Kautsky, *The Labour Revolution*, London 1925, pp. 53–54.
7   In Neuberg, p. 32.
8   In Neuberg, pp. 37–38.
9   Lenin, *Collected Works*, vol. 25, p. 386.
10   Lenin, *Collected Works*, vol. 25, p. 387.
11   Lenin, *Collected Works*, vol. 28, p. 243.
12   Lenin, *Collected Works*, vol. 28, p. 325.
13   Lenin, *Collected Works*, vol. 25, p. 388.
14   Lenin, *Collected Works*, vol. 25, p. 406.
15   Lenin, *Collected Works*, vol. 25, p. 404.
16   Lenin, *Collected Works*, vol. 25, p. 412.
17   Lenin, *Collected Works*, vol. 25, pp. 418–19.
18   Lenin, *Collected Works*, vol. 25, pp. 419–20.
19   Lenin, *Collected Works*, vol. 25, p. 423.
20   Lenin, *Collected Works*, vol. 25, pp. 425–26.
21   Lenin, *Collected Works*, vol. 25, p. 463.
22   Lenin, *Collected Works*, vol. 25, p. 462.
23   Lenin, *Collected Works*, vol. 25, p. 464.
24   Lenin, *Collected Works*, vol. 25, p. 465.
25   Lenin, *Collected Works*, vol. 25, pp. 465–66.

26 Lenin, *Collected Works*, vol. 25, p. 467.
27 Lenin, *Collected Works*, vol. 25, pp. 467–68.
28 T. Cliff, *State Capitalism in Russia*, London 1974, pp. 132–33.
29 Lenin, *Collected Works*, vol. 25, p. 492.
30 Lenin, *Collected Works*, vol. 10, pp. 253–54.
31 Lenin, *Collected Works*, vol. 10, p. 259.

CHAPTER 18: THE PROLETARIAT CAN WIELD STATE POWER

1   Lenin, *Collected Works*, vol. 26, p. 101.
2   Lenin, *Collected Works*, vol. 26, pp. 107–09.
3   Lenin, *Collected Works*, vol. 26, pp. 111–13.
4   Lenin, *Collected Works*, vol. 26, pp. 114–15.
5   Lenin, *Collected Works*, vol. 26, pp. 118–20.
6   Reed, p. 12.
7   Lenin, *Collected Works*, vol. 26, p. 109.
8   M. Gorky, *Untimely Thoughts: Essays on Revolution, Culture, and the Bolsheviks 1917–1918*, New York 1968, p. 7.
9   Gorky, pp. 32–33.
10 Gorky, p. 72.
11 Gorky, p. 75.
12 Gorky, p. 83.

CHAPTER 19: LENIN CALLS UP THE INSURRECTION

1   See p. 356ff. for Nevsky's report on behalf of the Military Organization at the meeting of the Petersburg Committee on October 15, Kudelli, pp. 310–12; or Krylenko's Report to the Central Committee on October 16, *Minutes of the Central Committee*, p. 98.
2   V.I. Nevsky, "In October: Brief notes from memory," *Katorga i ssylka*, nos. 11–12 (96–97), 1932, p. 36.
3   Lenin, *Collected Works*, vol. 26, p. 19.
4   Lenin, *Collected Works*, vol. 26, p. 20.
5   Lenin, *Collected Works*, vol. 26, p. 24.
6   Lenin, *Collected Works*, vol. 26, pp. 22–23.
7   Lenin, *Collected Works*, vol. 26, p. 27.
8   I.V. Stalin, *Sochineniia*, vol. 4, Moscow 1947, pp. 317–18.
9   N. Bukharin, "From the speech of Comrade Bukharin in a commemorative evening in 1921," *Proletarskaia revoliutsiia*, no. 10, 1922.
10 *Minutes of the Central Committee*, p. 58.
11 *Minutes of the Central Committee*, p. 58.

12 Lenin, *Collected Works,* vol. 26, pp. 46–48, 50.
13 *Minutes of the Central Committee,* p. 67.
14 Lenin, *Collected Works,* vol. 26, p. 54.
15 See Cliff, *Lenin: Building the Party,* pp. 281–85.
16 Lenin, *Collected Works,* vol. 26, p. 55.
17 Lenin, *Collected Works,* vol. 26, pp. 56–57.
18 Lenin, *Collected Works,* vol. 26, p. 57.
19 Lenin, *Collected Works,* vol. 26, p. 58.
20 *Minutes of the Central Committee,* p. 78.
21 Browder and Kerensky, vol. 3, p. 1729.
22 Sukhanov, p. 541.
23 Lenin, *Collected Works,* vol. 26, p. 69.
24 Lenin, *Collected Works,* vol. 26, p. 70.
25 Lenin, *Collected Works,* vol. 26, p. 72.
26 Lenin, *Collected Works,* vol. 26, pp. 82–83.
27 Lenin, *Collected Works,* vol. 26, p. 83.
28 Lenin, *Collected Works,* vol. 26, p. 84.
29 Lenin, *Collected Works,* vol. 26, p. 141.
30 Lenin, *Collected Works,* vol. 26, pp. 143–44.
31 Lenin, *Collected Works,* vol. 26, p. 146.
32 Lenin, *Collected Works,* vol. 26, p. 180.
33 Lenin, *Collected Works,* vol. 26, pp. 180–81.
34 Trotsky, *History of the Russian Revolution,* pp. 987–88.
35 Sukhanov, p. 556.
36 *Minutes of the Central Committee,* p. 86.
37 *Minutes of the Central Committee,* pp. 86–87.
38 *Minutes of the Central Committee,* p. 88.
39 *Minutes of the Central Committee,* pp. 90–95.
40 Lenin, *Collected Works,* vol. 36, p. 196.
41 Lenin, *Collected Works,* vol. 36, pp. 199–200.
42 Lenin, *Collected Works,* vol. 36, pp. 202–03.
43 Lenin, *Collected Works,* vol. 36, p. 203.
44 Lenin, *Collected Works,* vol. 36, p. 209.
45 Lenin, *Collected Works,* vol. 36, p. 212.
46 Lenin, *Collected Works,* vol. 36, p. 210.
47 Lenin, *Collected Works,* vol. 36, pp. 212–13.
48 Lenin, *Collected Works,* vol. 36, p. 207.
49 Kudelli, pp. 310–16; J. Bunyan and H.H. Fisher, *The Bolshevik Revolution, 1917–1918: Documents and Materials,* Stanford 1924, pp. 69–74.
50 N.I. Podvoisky, *Krasnaia gvardiia v Oktiabrskie dni,* Moscow-Leningrad 1927, pp. 16–17; R.V. Daniels, *Russia,* New Jersey 1964, pp. 107–08.
51 *Minutes of the Central Committee,* pp. 95–109.

52 *Minutes of the Central Committee,* pp. 121–22.
53 Lenin, *Collected Works,* vol. 26, p. 223.
54 Lenin, *Collected Works,* vol. 26, pp. 226–27.
55 *Minutes of the Central Committee,* p. 112.
56 *Minutes of the Central Committee,* p. 112.
57 Lenin, *Collected Works,* vol. 26, pp. 234–35.
58 G.S. lgnatev, *Oktiabr 1917 goda v Moskve,* Moscow 1964, p. 4.
59 P.V. Volubuev, *Proletariat i burzhuaziia Rossii V 1917 godu,* Moscow 1964, pp. 25–26.
60 See Volubuev, p. 28.
61 Trotsky, *History of the Russian Revolution,* p. 1130.
62 Woytinsky, pp. 366–68.
63 Browder and Kerensky, vol. 3, pp. 1728–30.
64 Reed, p. 36.
65 Browder and Kerensky, vol. 3, p. 1770.
66 Daniels, pp. 121–22.
67 Trotsky, *History of the Russian Revolution,* pp. 1054–55.
68 Trotsky, *Lessons of October,* New York 1937, p. 83.
69 Sukhanov, pp. 620–21.
70 Sukhanov, p. 47.
71 M. Libman, *The Russian Revolution,* London 1970, pp. 285–86.
72 V. Serge, *Year One of the Russian Revolution,* London 1972, pp. 68–69.
73 Lenin, *Sochineniia,* 1st edition, vol. 14, p. 482.
74 Sukhanov, p. 578.
75 Cliff, *Lenin: Building the Party,* p. 350.
76 Cliff, *Lenin: Building the Party,* chap. 9.
77 Cliff, *Lenin: Building the Party,* p. 234.
78 Reed, pp. 104–05.

INDEX

A

Alekseev, General M.V., 79–81, 100, 187, 193, 196, 286, 296
Alexinsky, G.A., 33
Armand, I., 25, 28, 160
Axelrod, P., 26, 55, 346

B

Badaev, A.Y., 40
Baevsky, D.A., 33
Bagdatev, S.Ia., 133–35, 172
Balabanoff, A., 21
Bauer, O., 56, 60, 140
Bebel, A., 16–17, 100
Bolsheviks, and Lenin and the revolution, 7–10, 361–64; leaders vacillate on attitude to war, 31–33; antiwar propaganda, 34–42; mass arrest of, at beginning of war, 35; members of Duma deported, 33, 40–41; state of organization during war, 40–42; infiltration by okhrana, 39–45; Vyborg District in the van, 41, 44, 46; and flight of intellectuals from them, 45; financial penury, 45; increasing mass influence, 46–51; and War Industry Committees, 47–50; and the national question, 53–55; Petrograd

fails to lead in February Revolution, 89–90; supporting Provisional Government, 103–104, 107–113; Vyborg Distsrict Committee on far left, 105–107; Kamenev and Stalin support Provisional Government and war and for unity with Mensheviks, 109–113; swift expansion of membership (April–July 1917), 150–51; administrative weakness of Party center, 151–56; social composition of, 159–60; intelligentsia keeps away from Bolsheviks, 160; youth of Party members, 160; steeled in struggle, 161; central role of Party press, 160; discipline through struggle, 163–64; school of strategy and tactics, 164–67 in June demonstration, 197–200; influence in armed forces spreads swiftly, 197–200; overwhelming influence on factory committees, 224–26, 236–38; in July Petrograd leadership and Army Organization impatient, to "left" of Lenin, 251–54; breaking discipline, 255–56; during the month of extreme slander of Lenin, 265–78; leading the resistance to

F

February Revolution, strikes in January and early February, 84; Putilov works lockout, 84; food riots, 84; insurrection joined almost by whole garrison, 87–88; International Women's Day, 90; Petrograd Soviet established, 93; spontaneous revolution, 94

Fedorov, G.F., 109, 135, 178

G

Ganetsky, J.S., 116, 271; see Hanecki

German Social Democratic Party, attitude to war, 12–13; prominent place in international labor movement, 15–16; and militarism, 15–18; and parliamentarism, 19

Goldenberg, I.P., 33, 125

Golytsin, N.D., prime minister, 75

Goremykin, I.L., prime minister, 37–38, 73–75

Gorky, M., 184, 271, 297, 322–323

Grimm, R., 21

Guchkov, A.I., minister of war, 47, 80–81, 83, 189, 192

H

Hanecki, J.S., Lenin letter to, 116; see Ganetsky

I

Ioffe, A.A., 42, 139

International Women's Conference (1915), 25

International Youth Conference (915), 25

Intelligentsia, scarcity of cadres in Bolshevik Party, 45, 159–60

K

Kaiurov, V., 90–91

Kaledin, General A.M., 281–82

Kalinin, M.I., 105, 133, 256, 345

Kamenev, L.B., 139, 182, 271, 305, 361; vacillates in attitude to war, 32–33; takes control of Pravda, 109–10; supports war and Provisional Government, 109–12; polemicizes with Lenin, 122, 129–30; opposes Lenin's April thesis, 134–36; opposes June demonstration, 178, 180; opposes insurrection, 329, 332, 339–41; slammed by Lenin, 341–44; open defiance of Central Committee decision regarding insurrection, 352

Kautsky, K., great authority in international labor movement, 16; Lenin's illusions in, 16, 19–20; and ultra–imperialism, 18; and parliamentary cretinism, 19; R. Luxemburg on, 20; and mechanistic conception of history, 140; distorts Marxist theory of the state, 307–309

Kerensky, A.F., 81, 331; detests Order No. 1, 190; decrees "Declaration of Soldiers' Rights", 193–94; launches military offensive in June 1917, 177; at General Headquarters, 80–81; restores military death penalty, 193-94; suppresses agrarian disorders, 208; caricature Bonaparte, 278–79; at Moscow State Conference, 280, 283; relations with Kornilov, 286–89; tries to reimpose iron discipline on armed forces, 300; on eve of October insurrection, 356–59
Khabalov, General S.S., 88
Kidron, M., 68
Kienthal Conference, (1916), 23–24
Klembovskii, General V.N., 194, 288
Kollontai, A.M., 305
Kornilov, General L.G., suppresses agrarian disorders, 208; restores death penalty to the front, 266-67; at Moscow State Conference attacks anarchy in the army, 281; failed coup, 285–94
Krasnov, General P.N., 288
Krivoshein, A.V., 73, 74, 80
Krzhizhanovsky, G.M., 33
Kronstadt, ferment in navy (1916), 40–41; Soviet of naval arsenal breaks relation with Provisional Government (May 1917), 145–47; workers and sailors impatient to overthrow Provisional Government in April, 172; impatient with Lenin during July days, 252, 256–57
Krupskaya, N.K., 337; on Lenin's arrest in Galicia, 11; at International Women's Conference, 25; on international activities of Lenin during war, 26; on financial difficulties of Bolsheviks during war, 26–27; on penury of Lenin and Krupskaya, 27–28; on Lenin's nervousness and convalescence after Zimmerwald Conference, 28; on Lenin's effort to return from Switzerland to Russia, 119–20; on difficulties to act as fireman restraining hotheaded Bolsheviks during July days, 169
Krylenko, N.V., 348-51

L

Latsis, M.Ia., 180–81, 254, 259, 274, 345, 350
Lenin, V.I., the party and the revolution, 7-10, 361–64; arrest in Galicia, 11; release and move to Switzerland, 11; at Stuttgart Conference (1907) 12; shocked by German Socialist leaders' support of war, 11–13; preaches revolutionary defeatism, 28–29; against pacifism, 14–15; for a new international, 15, 20; illusions in Kautsky, 15, 19–20; attacks Kautsky, 20; at Zimmerwald Conference, 20–23; at Kienthal Conference, 23–24; organizes international tendencies, 25–26; complete isolation from Russia, 27–28; financial penury, 27–28; "bending the stick" in his revolutionary defeatist position, 19; meets resistance in Bolshevik leadership to his revolutionary defeatist position, 31–33; condemns behavior of Bolshevik leaders at Tsarist Court, 32–33; Bolshevik Party organization in Russia not ready to adopt Lenin's revolutionary defeatist position, 34; on international-

ism of vanguard section of Russian proletariat, 47, 50; polemicizes
with Austro-Marxists on national question, 45–49; polemicizes with
Rosa Luxemburg on national question, 57–62; polemicizes with
Bukharin, Piatakov and Radek on national question, 60–63; on
tremendous revolutionary potential of national liberation
movements, 62–63; on theory of imperialism, 65–69; defines imperialism, 65-66; on relation between imperialism and opportunism, 66–
67; condemnation of Kautsky's theory of ultraimperialism, 66–67;
borrowed from Bukharin, Hilferding, and Hobson, 67–69; his theory
of imperialism as a weapon of action, 69; defines the preconditions
for a revolutionary situation, 71; wrong evaluation of role of Liberal
coup in February Revolution, 83; on nature of Dual Power, 101–102;
"Letters from Afar", 116–19; Petrograd leaders disagree with Letters
and do not publish majority of them, 116; on dictatorship of proletariat, 117–18, 305–11; peace policy, 114–15, 141–42; attempts to
leave Switzerland, 118–19; arrives at Finland Station, 122–23; addresses a speech on world revolution, 123; isolated among Bolshevik
leaders, 123–24, 127–33; April Theses, 125–26; Captures the Petrograd City Conference, 134–35; wins the national April Conference,
135; attacks "old Bolshevism", 137–40; wins the Party, 137–39; on
the need to win majority of proletariat, 141–42; tempering revolutionary impatience of Party members, 144–45; on Bolshevik
discipline forged in struggle, 163; on perspectives for victory of revolution, 164–67; restrains hotheads during April days, 169–74; and
the June demonstration, 178, 180–82, 181–82; on elections of officers by soldiers, 196–97; for fraternization with German soldiers,
196–97; for peasant revolution, 211–17; steals SR agrarian program,
215–17; on workers' control, 224, 232–36, 238; comes to the conclusion that factory committees can serve instead of soviets as instruments of workers' power, 237; supports rebellious nationalities,
247–49; restraining role during July days, 252–57; teaches how to
retreat, 258–59; wrong estimate of decline of Soviets after July days,
262–63; month of slander against Lenin as German agent, 265–78;
going into hiding, 271–72; on Kerensky's Bonapartism, 278–79,
282–83; during Kornilov coup, 289–91; argues immediately after
defeat of Kornilov, possibility of peaceful road to proletarian power)
294–96; on Marxist theory of the state, 305–11; on transition from
capitalism to communism, 311–14; on fantastic potentialities of the
masses, 320–22; on timing of uprising, 325–26, 354; meets resistance
of Central Committee to his summons to insurrection, 328–29;
against participation in pre-parliament, 331–32; spurring on for insurrection, 332–37; at last convinces Central Committee (October
10) 337–39; sharp polemics with Zinoviev and Kamenev, 339–44;
calls for expulsion of Zinoviev and Kamenev, 352–53; differs with
Trotsky regarding technicalities of insurrection, and proved wrong,
354–60
Liebknecht, K., 16–17

N

O

P

Smilga, I.T., 135, 154, 180, 332–33
Socialist Revolutionary Party, its petty bourgeois nature, 98–99; granting power to Provisional Government, 98–99; and "pure democracy, 100–01; with Mensheviks in leadership of Petrograd Soviet, (February 1917), 103–04; entering coalition government, 176; support military offensive, (June 1917), 177; denounce Kerensky's declaration of soldiers' rights, 191; condemn restoration of death penalty at the front, 194; losing soldiers' support meant losing peasantry, 197; call on peasants to wait patiently until Constituent Assembly met to solve land question, 206–07; split between Right and Left, 210–11; agrarian program "stolen" by Lenin, 215–17; for conciliation between classes, 229; no support to Finnish people asking for autonomy, 241–42; no support for Ukrainian people, 244–45; slander Lenin as German agent, 267–68; decline of influence in Petrograd after July days, 276–77
Sokolnikov, G.Y., 350, 352
Soldiers, unrest in army (1915), 38, 40; Bolshevik Petersburg Committee active propaganda among them, 44; fraternize with workers on mass strike (January 1916), 46; fraternize with workers striking and demonstrating (February 1917), 87; join the revolution, (February 1917), 88–89; thrown into suicidal offensive by Provisional Government, (June 1917), 177; number

killed and maimed during the war, 185, connection between soldiers' mutinies and peasant unrest, 185, 197; rebellion officers imposed discipline, 186–88; and Order No. 1, 188–89; and Order No. 2, 190; "Declaration of Soldiers' Rights", 190–91; army disintegrates, 191–93, 281–83; generals try unsuccessfully to restore discipline, 193–95, 281–83; Lenin calls on soldiers to elect officers, 196–197; Lenin calls on soldiers to fraternize with German brethren, 196–97; mass desertion of soldiers, 197; spread of Bolshevik influence among soldiers, 197–200; impatient during July days, 252–53, 255–56; ordered by Kornilov to act against Petrograd, 285–87; refused to obey, 288–89, 299; quixotic efforts to re-establish discipline after Kornilov coup, 297–300; swing to Bolsheviks after failure of Kornilov coup, 302–03; Kerensky's plot to evacuate troops from Petrograd failed, 356–57, 359; role in October insurrection, 360
Soviets, Petrograd Soviet established, 93; soviet has the real power but formal power given to Provisional Government, 93–94, 95–98; marriage of convenience with Provisional Government, 98; dual power with Provisional Government, 99–101; under-representation of workers as against soldiers in the soviet, 98; Bolshevik leaders moderate line in the soviet, 103–04; Vyborg District Committee of Bolsheviks for power to the soviets, 105–106;

on arriving in Russia, 124; on
political nature of Kamenev,
131; on Stalin, 132; on enemies
of Bolshevism's glee at rift between Lenin and Bolshevik
leaders over April Theses, 132;
explains how Lenin managed
to win Bolshevik Party in April,
138; describing June demonstration, 183; on Order No.
1, 189; on peasants' mistrust of
Kerensky, 201; on Lenin's
speech to Congress of Peasants'
Soviets, 217; disdain towards
peasants, 217–18; criticizes
Lenin's decision to go into hiding after July days, 272; on execution of October
insurrection, 360–61
Sukhomlinov, V.A., minister of
war, 75
Sverdlov, Ia.M., 135, 151–53,
157, 180, 329

T

Tereschenko, M.I., foreign minister of Provisional Government,
195, 245
Tomsky, M.P., 182
Trotsky, L.D., 31, 55, 176, 271;
his History of the Russian Revolution, 7–9; on Lenin's decisive role in revolution, 9;
shocked by German Social Democratic leaders support of
war; in Zimmerwald Conference, 21–23; and "revolutionary defeatism", 22, 23–24; on
patriotic moods of masses, 35;
and Mezhraiontsy, 139; on
spontaneity of February revolution, 89–91; On permanent
revolution, 130; on decisive
role of Lenin in rearming the
Bolshevik Party in April, 137;
joining Bolsheviks, 137–38;

cold-shouldered by Old Bolsheviks, 137–38; on Sverdlov as
organizer, 151–52; on Order
No. 1, 189; on workers' control 237–38; thinks Lenin
made mistake in going into
hiding after July days, 272; on
slander campaign against Lenin
after July days, 293–94; leads
the struggle against Kornilov,
291–94; differs on technicalities of insurrection with Lenin,
and is right, 354–61; organizer
of October insurrection, 354–
61; Stalin on Trotsky as organizer of October, 361;
Sukhanov
on Trotsky as organizer of
October, 361–62
Tsar, 71–84, 92–93
Tsarina, 76–79
Tsereteli, I.G., minister of interior
in Provisional Government,
196, 289, 331; moves Menshevik-SR coalition to the Right,
114; challenges Bolshevism in
June demonstration, 182; votes
for reintroduction of death
penalty at the front, 194; takes
measures for suppressing re-
belling peasants, 266, 270; tar-
get for Cadet
counterrevolutionary propaganda, 268

U

Ulyanov, Anna, 49, 63
Ulyanov, Maria, 27

V

Volodarsky, V., 181, 272, 349–50

W

Workers, rising storm of political
strikes on eve of war, 35; col-

ABOUT HAYMARKET BOOKS

We believe that activists need to take ideas, history and politics into the many struggles for social justice today. Learning the lessons of past victories as well as defeats can arm a new generation of fighters for a better world. As Karl Marx said, "The philosophers have merely interpreted the world; the point however is to change it."

We take inspiration and courage from our namesakes, the Haymarket Martyrs, who gave their lives fighting for a better world. Their struggle for the eight hour day in 1886, which gave us May Day, the international workers' holiday, reminds workers around the world that ordinary people can organize and struggle for their own liberation. These struggles continue today around the globe—struggles against oppression, exploitation, hunger and poverty.

It was August Spies, one of the Martyrs who was targeted for being an immigrant and an anarchist, who predicted the battles being fought to this day. "If you think that by hanging us you can stamp out the labor movement," Spies told the judge, "then hang us. Here you will tread upon a spark, but here, and there, and behind you, and in front of you, and everywhere, the flames will blaze up. It is a subterranean fire. You cannot put it out. The ground is on fire upon which you stand."

Visit our online bookstore at www.haymarketbooks.org.

Also from Haymarket Books:

BUILDING THE PARTY: LENIN 1893–1914
By Tony Cliff   ISBN 1931859019   2002   360 pages

The Russian Revolution of 1917 was one of the pivotal events in world history, and the Russian Bolshevik Party played a central role in that revolution. This book by Tony Cliff traces the building of that party and, in particular, the work of its main architect, Lenin. First of three volumes.

TROTSKY'S MARXISM AND OTHER ESSAYS
By Duncan Hallas   ISBN 1931859035   2003   208 pages

No serious attempt to understand the tragedy of the Russian Revolution—and its relevance to the building of socialism today—can ignore the unique contribution made by Leon Trotsky.

THE BOLSHEVIKS COME TO POWER
by Alexander Rabinowitch   ISBN 1931859000   2004   256 pages
"...a brilliant, convincing, and exciting book."
—Stanley Plastrik, *Dissent*
"Essential reading...with a narrative skill which all too few historians could match."   —Robert M. Slusser, *Baltimore Sun*